200 Easy Homemade Cheese recipes

D1118409

200 Easy Homemade Cheese
recipes

Debra Amrein-Boyes

Robert
ROSE

200 Easy Homemade Cheese Recipes
Text copyright © 2009 Debra Amrein-Boyes
Photographs and illustrations copyright © 2009 Robert Rose Inc.
Cover and text design copyright © 2009 Robert Rose Inc.

No part of this publication may be reproduced, stored in a retrieval system or transmitted, in any form or by any means, without the prior written consent of the publisher or a licence from the Canadian Copyright Licensing Agency (Access Copyright). For an Access Copyright licence, visit www.accesscopyright.ca or call toll-free: 1-800-893-5777.

For complete cataloguing information, see page 365.

Disclaimer
The recipes in this book have been carefully tested by our kitchen and our tasters. To the best of our knowledge, they are safe and nutritious for ordinary use and users. For those people with food or other allergies, or who have special food requirements or health issues, please read the suggested contents of each recipe carefully and determine whether or not they may create a problem for you. All recipes are used at the risk of the consumer.

We cannot be responsible for any hazards, loss or damage that may occur as a result of any recipe use.

For those with special needs, allergies, requirements or health problems, in the event of any doubt, please contact your medical adviser prior to the use of any recipe.

Editor: Carol Sherman
Copy Editor: Christina Anson Mine
Recipe Editor: Jennifer MacKenzie
Indexer: Gillian Watts

Design and Production: Daniella Zanchetta/PageWave Graphics Inc.
Illustrations: Kveta (Three in a Box)
Photography: Colin Erricson
Food Styling: Kathryn Robertson
Prop Styling: Charlene Erricson

Cover image: *(clockwise from left)* Port Salut (page 156), Goat's Milk Cheddar (page 266), Castle Blue (page 128) and Camembert (page 100).

We acknowledge the financial support of the Government of Canada through the Book Publishing Industry Development Program (BPIDP) for our publishing activities.

Published by Robert Rose Inc.
120 Eglinton Avenue East, Suite 800, Toronto, Ontario, Canada M4P 1E2
Tel: (416) 322-6552 Fax: (416) 322-6936

Printed and bound in Canada.

2 3 4 5 6 7 8 9 TCP 17 16 15 14 13 12 11 10

To my parents, Gordon and Inez Dewar,
who taught me to live with integrity
and to love learning, and that
life is about relationships.

Contents

Acknowledgments

THANK YOU TO Margaret Morris of Glengarry Cheesemaking for sharing her knowledge and experience and for her generous help and guidance over the years. I could not have come this far without it!

Thank you to my husband, George, who never complains even though he must be tired of take-out food. You are the best.

A very special thank you to my editor, Carol Sherman, who has earned many halos for her patience and long-suffering with this inexperienced writer; to Tina Anson Mine and Jennifer MacKenzie for their dedication and excellent work on this book; and to Daniella Zanchetta at PageWave Graphics for a beautifully designed book and guiding the fine photography and illustrations. What a great team!

And finally, a huge thank you to publisher Bob Dees for his faith in the project and for his support throughout.

Introduction

"A BOOK OF VERSES underneath the Bough, a Jug of Wine, a Loaf of Bread — and Thou…." This well-known quote comes from one of the most famous romantics of all time, but what is missing from this picnic in paradise? The cheese, of course! While not mentioned in the poem, it is quite possible that cheese was on the menu that day. When Omar Khayyám penned these words more than 800 years ago, cheese was already a staple food.

Though the origin of cheese, like that of so many things in human history, is shrouded in mystery, it is safe to say that people of many cultures and traditions found ways early on to preserve the bounty and goodness of fresh milk, whether from cow, sheep, goat or camel, in this form. However it came to be, cheese is a valuable food, packed with important nutrients and a vital staple in the diets of most cultures.

In traditional agriculture, cheese making was a way of preserving the summer's milk surplus for consumption in the leaner winter season, when the animals were awaiting the arrival of their young in the spring. Domesticated milk-producing animals have a period during which they are "dry," or not lactating, while their bodies store energy for the birth of their young. Since this phase can last from a few weeks up to several months, depending on the breed of animal, it was important to be prepared for that interval of no milk production. In the summer months, the farmer's wife would often become a cheese maker, filling the cellar with enough cheese for the family's own needs and producing a bit extra to sell at the market to supplement the farm income in the winter.

The making of cheese on the farm was, and to some extent still is, an important part of many Old World cultures, but it was not continued to the same degree in the New World. However, things are changing. In the last 20 years or so, there has been a rediscovery of farmstead, or artisanal, cheese making, thanks to consumers who are actively seeking a more local, natural diet as an alternative to an increasingly industrialized and globalized food industry.

> In Greek mythology, Aristaeus, son of Apollo and Cyrene, was sent to the Greeks as a gift from the gods. He was to teach them the art of cheese making, an ability that would become known as "a gift of everlasting value."

My personal story of cheese making began in 1978 with a trip to the Swiss Alps. I was attending a wedding, and the bride's parents invited me to spend several days with them at their holiday chalet in the mountains. While there, we visited a *Senn*, or Alpine herdsman, who was in charge of the farmers' cows on the summer pasture. I remember the copper cauldron hanging over the wood fire in a low-ceilinged hut and the fresh cheeses draining on the boards along the walls. Right on the other side of the stone wall were the cows, back in their stalls for the evening milking after a day of grazing the Alpine meadows. After I returned to Canada, I tried my hand at cheese making, but my information was sketchy and I failed dismally. The long-suffering barn cats finished off what was left of my inedible cheese, and I shelved the idea. But destiny had other plans for me: several years later I returned to the Swiss Alps to live and raise a family, and there began again to learn the satisfying art of cheese making.

> Cheese was once used as a currency in medieval Europe. Cheese and other agricultural products were regularly used to pay church taxes. Some "tithe barns," ancient buildings where the portion owed to the state, landowner or church was collected, still exist.

The History of Cheese

WHEN DID PEOPLE first begin to make cheese? The most-repeated story is that it was discovered by nomadic peoples, who found that the milk they transported in skin bags (often made of animal stomachs) had solidified at the end of a long day of jostling along on the back of a camel or horse. In fact, it doesn't take a camel trip to cause milk to curdle — leaving a bowl of milk sitting out in any hut or tent for a couple of days will do the job. Separate the curds from the whey and voilà — cheese!

Certainly cheese making has been documented since ancient Greek and Roman times, when it was already an important foodstuff. Later, the monasteries of medieval Europe became the keepers of cheese-making tradition, maintaining a thriving small industry using the milk produced on church-owned land. Monasteries used local labor and ingredients, which made them the hubs of local economies. Peasant farmers and herders also made cheese from the milk of their sheep, goats and cows to feed their families in the season when no milk was available. Isolated valleys throughout Europe were home to local societies with traditions and foods that were unique to their small worlds, many of which still exist and have influenced the wonderful variety of European cheeses we know today.

As society grew and became less localized and more mobile, cheese making was gradually taken over by industrial concerns that could produce huge amounts of cheap cheese for distribution over ever-larger distances.

This book will help you discover a bit of this cheese-making heritage for yourself, at home in your own kitchen. Some of the recipes are time-tested ones that your great-grandmother could very likely have made in her farm kitchen, while others have been collected from around the world. There are also some new ideas to try, with unusual ingredients. We will cover everything from simple fresh cheeses and related dairy products (such as butter, crème fraîche and ricotta) to traditional hard cheeses (such as Cheddar, Gruyère and Parmesan) to special ethnic cheeses.

I hope you enjoy the process, but most of all the result. There's nothing like a fresh pizza on which even the mozzarella is made from scratch. Be sure to take some along on that perfect picnic!

A note on *Appellation d'origine contrôlée* (AOC) and *Denominazione di origine controllata* (DOC) cheeses: like fine wines, many cheeses are traditional to certain areas of the world and are made according to clearly outlined specifications to maintain their authenticity. In this book, we will be speaking of cheeses made in the style of many of these specialty cheeses.

Because industrial production was capable of feeding more people at lower cost, it almost wiped out the market for small producers and cheese makers. The advent of centralized industry and regulatory bodies, which enforce sanitation and production standards, made it less and less profitable for artisans to continue. One exception is France, which, because it started with a very large artisan community, was able to maintain a presence in the field. However, the European Union is gradually instituting policies that are difficult for some farmstead producers to comply with, leading them to give up their craft.

As with most developments in society, there are positive and negative sides to industrialization, and now consumers are wondering if something valuable has been lost in the process. The desire for transparency in food production is growing, with consumers wanting to know exactly what they are eating. Also, the awareness that the long distances required for transportation carry a high cost to the environment is causing more and more people to choose locally grown and artisan-produced food over imported and industrially produced foods.

The interest in artisanal cheeses is also growing, and though every year sees an increase in artisanal cheese consumption, the number of small-scale cheese makers is still quite small. With this book, you now

> The terms *big wheel* and *big cheese* originally referred to those who were wealthy enough to purchase a whole wheel of cheese.

can experience the taste of fresh handmade cheeses and discover the joy of creating a wonderful food from a simple ingredient: fresh milk.

How to Use This Book

THIS BOOK IS DESIGNED to help you create cheeses that approximate the flavor and texture of many cheeses from around the world. As you gain insight and expertise, you'll be able to create your own unique cheeses.

There are literally thousands of known and documented cheeses, and the variations are endless. Because milk is a natural ingredient produced by a living animal, its quality and nutrient content are directly influenced by what the animal eats, the local climate and season, and the breed. All these factors contribute greatly to the flavor and quality of the cheese made from the milk. Cheeses made with the same recipe in different parts of the world under different conditions will not be identical. For instance, a Gruyère made in your kitchen with store-bought homogenized milk can only ever approximate the flavor of a Gruyère made from the raw milk of cows grazed on Alpine pastures abundant with wildflowers. However, your cheese will still be very good, and the experience a satisfying exercise in self-sufficiency.

You will find recipes for everything from fresh unripened cheeses to aged ones with complex rinds. Hard cheese recipes usually call for a larger amount of milk — 8 to 16 quarts (8 to 16 L). These cheeses usually require several months to ripen to

perfection, so the effort might as well be worth it. Recipes for fresh and mold-ripened cheeses require a smaller amount of milk, as they can either be produced easily and quickly, or have a shorter shelf life. For cheeses that spoil quickly, the recipes are designed to make smaller batches so you can consume the cheese before it begins to deteriorate.

Please read the recipe all the way through before beginning. It is important to be aware of the many steps involved so you can make sure you have enough time to finish the job. Note the techniques and refer to the equipment section (page 33) if necessary. Always adhere to the rules of sanitation (see page 40), beginning by sterilizing equipment and surfaces. Wash your hands with soap and water and dry with a clean cloth whenever leaving or returning to your cheese-making tasks. Sanitation in cheese making is absolutely key to success.

Please read the section on equipment, tools and accessories carefully. Much of the equipment used in cheese making is specialized for that purpose only, so source and purchase the necessary tools, including molds and presses, in advance. You don't want to find yourself with a perfect batch of Cheddar ready for pressing but no way to press it.

Included in the book are recipes designed to show off your cheeses to their fullest. These recipes are listed in italics at the beginning of each chapter.

> One of the essential amino acids in cheese — tryptophan — has been shown to reduce stress and induce sleep.

I have tried to keep the language simple, but there are some terms that apply to cheese making that cannot be substituted. See the Glossary (page 366) for an explanation of these special terms.

What if things don't turn out as expected? Each chapter has a trouble-shooting section for its particular cheeses. A lot of problems can be avoided by following the recipes exactly and sanitizing all equipment as directed. It is also important to oversee the conditions of the ripening area carefully, since many cheeses spend a long time in that environment. This is the area where your cheese can blossom into a treat fit for a king or wither into a mess fit for the compost heap. After all that hard work, you want it to end up on the table to the oohs and aahs of your family and guests!

What Is Cheese?

THOUGH COMMON IN so many societies, cheese is still a bit of a mystery food. We know it is made of milk, but how exactly?

Most cheese begins when milk meets lactic bacteria. These organisms are naturally present in milk and in the environment, and the warm, sweet, protein-rich liquid is the perfect growth medium for them. If a bowl of unpasteurized milk or cream is left out for a few days, it will "go sour" and become thick. This happens because lactic bacteria have populated the milk and multiplied exponentially, feeding on the lactose, or milk sugar, and turning it into lactic acid.

The acidic environment created by this bacterial action is favored by the coagulant, which, when added to milk, causes it to curdle and thicken. The

traditional coagulant used in cheese making is rennet, an enzyme found in the stomach of a calf or kid, which curdles the milk the young animal drinks, making it digestible. This natural animal rennet is used to make many cheeses, especially firmer types. Vegetable rennet can be made from various plants, usually of the thistle family, though they are not as widely available commercially. Microbial rennet is a good choice if you prefer not to use animal rennet, though it does not perform as well as animal rennet when making hard aged cheeses. Microbial, or fungal, rennet is derived from the fermentation of the mold *Rhizomucor miehei* or *Cryphonectria parasitica*. The mold is grown in vats where the enzyme responsible for coagulation is produced, which is then extracted and purified. Also available is genetically engineered rennet, which is created by taking the gene for the chymosin enzyme from the cow and growing it in a host microorganism, such as a mold, yeast or bacterium.

> The original Cheddar cheese was matured in the caves of Cheddar Gorge in southwest England, and to be considered authentic it had to be made within 30 miles of Wells Cathedral. Today, Cheddar is too widely produced to have protected status and is made in Britain, as well as countries that were historically tied to it, including Canada, Australia, New Zealand and the United States.

Families of Cheese

Fresh Lactic Cheese

This family includes most soft spreadable cheeses. Cream cheese, fromage frais, fromage blanc, chèvre and quark belong to this category. They are made by adding lactic bacteria to milk, which is then left to "ripen," or set, for up to 24 hours. The activity of the bacteria causes the milk to become more acidic and tart, and forms a soft curd, called coagulum, that is similar to yogurt. Sometimes the addition of a small amount of rennet helps firm up the curd to maximize the final yield. The curd is then drained in a draining bag or cloth-lined colander. When the desired consistency has been reached, usually a spreadable paste, the cheese is mixed with a bit of salt and refrigerated. It can be blended with herbs, fruit or other flavorings and used as a spread, or used plain for cooking and baking. Fresh lactic cheeses have a short shelf life, usually 1 to 2 weeks, and must be kept refrigerated.

Sweet Curd Cheese

These cheeses are made mainly from milk inoculated with rennet or another coagulant, without the addition of lactic bacteria. A firm curd forms fairly quickly and is usually drained and pressed to form a brick shape. Sweet curd cheeses are characterized by a mild, even bland, flavor and a supple, rubbery paste (see Glossary, page 366). They are often used in cooked dishes and can even be fried, as they soften but do not melt when heated. Queso blanco (white cheese) from Mexico, paneer from India and halloumi from Cyprus are examples of this type of cheese.

Mold-Ripened Cheese

In this family we find some of the most famous cheeses, such as Camembert and Brie, and some of the blue cheeses. They are uncooked and unpressed, usually drained for 1 to 2 days in a bottomless form, or mold. The forms are flipped several times during draining. Traditionally, a solution of mold is sprayed on the surface of the cheese, but a safer and easier method is to inoculate the milk with the mold at the same time that the culture is added. After draining, the cheese is salted and left to develop a fuzzy white mold crust. It is then wrapped in a special type of paper that causes the mold to ripen the cheese from the outside in. These cheeses usually become soft, even runny, and are ready to eat at 3 to 4 weeks. They have a shelf life of 8 to 12 weeks, depending on cheese size and storage conditions.

Washed-Rind Cheese

Port Salut, St-Paulin, Oka, Limburger, raclette and Morbier are cheeses whose flavor is greatly influenced by the addition of ripening bacteria to the rind, usually a strain of *Brevibacterium linens*. The rind is then washed regularly with a brine-soaked cloth to encourage growth of a reddish-orange "smear." These cheeses are usually cooked-curd cheeses, meaning the curds are heated to a higher temperature during the process, and may or may not be lightly pressed. They are typically salted by immersing them for several hours in a saturated brine solution (see page 19 for instructions for making brine solutions). Most cheeses in this family are ready for consumption 4 to 8 weeks after production and can be kept for several months if properly wrapped and stored.

Washed-Curd Cheese

Gouda, Edam, Havarti and Colby fall into this category, as do most washed-rind cheeses. The curd in this type of cheese is "cooked" by removing some of the whey after cutting and replacing it with hot water to bring up the temperature. This reduces the acidity of the whey, resulting in a cheese that has a smoother, more flexible texture than other cooked pressed cheeses. Most washed-curd cheeses are ready to eat after 6 to 8 weeks of curing and, though they will age very nicely, are usually not aged for more than 2 years.

Cooked Pressed Cheese

Here you will find the traditional, immensely popular British and Alpine cheeses, such as Cheddar, Caerphilly, Gruyère and Emmental, and hard cheeses such as Parmesan and Asiago. The curd is cooked to a high temperature using external heat, which makes it drier with a sharper flavor. Cooked pressed cheeses require long, firm pressing to ensure that the curd knits together and seals the rind. They are usually ripened at cooler temperatures and are often not at their peak before one year. They will continue to ripen and improve their flavor after that point, sometimes for many years.

Stretched-Curd (Pasta Filata) Cheese

Great melting cheeses such as mozzarella, scamorza, provolone and bocconcini are included in the stretched-curd category. At a certain point in production, the cheese mass is dipped into very hot water until it softens, then it is literally stretched and pulled into long strands before folding and twisting it into balls

or braids. *Pasta filata* means "spun curd." These cheeses can be stored in a bit of brine in the refrigerator for a few weeks but are best consumed relatively fresh.

Ethnic Cheese

Though this is not a real category in the cheese world, there are many cheeses produced in various societies that do not exactly belong to any of the above families. One of these is feta, a "pickled" cheese that is made using a unique process and which is stored for many months in a heavy brine solution. For fun, we will look at some really unusual cheeses in this chapter.

Basic Cheese-Making Steps and Techniques

1. Warm the milk to cheese-making temperature.

For some cheeses, it is sufficient to warm the pot of milk in a sinkful of hot water, but most require some type of heating on the stovetop. Use a large stainless-steel pot, such as a soup or spaghetti pot, that is large enough to contain the milk and leave at least 2 inches (5 cm) of space at the top. For small batches (1 to 8 quarts or liters) of milk, you can heat directly on the burner over medium-low heat. Otherwise, use a hot water bath to heat the milk indirectly: place the cheese pot inside a stainless-steel pot a size larger than itself or in a large canner. Fill the cheese pot with the milk, then fill the outer pot with enough water so that it comes to just below the level of the milk in the inner pot.

Warming the milk — directly over burner

Warming the milk — in a hot water bath

2. Inoculate the milk with lactic bacteria, ripening bacteria and/or mold.

Sprinkle the powdered culture over the surface of the milk and let it rehydrate for a few minutes before stirring it into the milk. Use a large perforated skimmer for best results. Holding the skimmer flat just under the surface, stir the milk using a slow up-and-down motion. This will draw the culture down into the milk without splashing or incorporating too

Inoculating the milk

4. Add the coagulant to the milk and allow it to set until it forms a solid curd.

To ascertain whether the curd is ready for the next step, check for a "clean break": insert the long flat blade of a spatula or knife into the curd at a 30-degree angle and slowly lift the blade toward the surface of the curd. If the curd splits into a long clean break or crack, it is ready to cut. If the cut is wobbly or uneven, let the curd set for a few more minutes before trying again.

Checking for a clean break

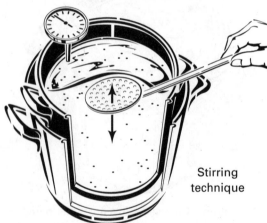

Stirring technique

much air, which hinders the growth of the bacteria. Use the same stirring technique to incorporate the rennet and other ingredients. Be sure the culture is thoroughly incorporated into the milk, making at least 10 to 20 strokes.

3. Ripen the milk.

The milk is "ripened," or set aside, to allow the bacteria to acidify it. The length of time depends on the type of cheese you're making.

5. Once the milk has become curd, either drain through a cloth for fresh cheese or cut into pieces and process further.

To cut curds: Holding a long-bladed stainless-steel knife straight up and down, draw knife through the curd, cutting it into strips. Proceed across the pot until you have reached the other side. Turn the pot and cut across the first strips to create squares. Using a skimmer, cut horizontally from side to side just under the surface of the curd to create cubes. Gradually move skimmer down through curd to cut layers

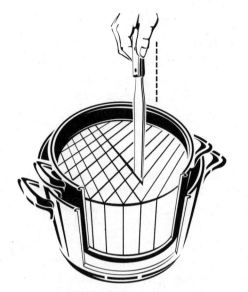

Cutting the curd into strips

as little as possible in order to maximize the final yield. Hang the draining bag or the gathered ends of the cloth from a wooden spoon set across the top of a large pot or sink so that it hangs freely. If your situation allows, you can place a hook in the ceiling and hang the bag from that with a cord or cable, catching the whey in a pot below.

For soft cheeses like Camembert, ladle the delicate curds carefully into the molds, filling them as directed in the recipe. To make a draining container, see page 37.

Cutting the curd horizontally
with the skimmer

Draining the curd in a bag

of cubes. Using the skimmer, gently stir curd cubes. Using a knife, cut any pieces that have been missed or are too large. For small-cut curds, you can use a large whisk for cutting.

6. **For fresh or soft-ripened cheeses, drain the cut curds, either through a cloth or in a mold.**

If draining through a bag or cloth-lined colander, ladle the curd carefully, breaking

Draining the curd in a colander

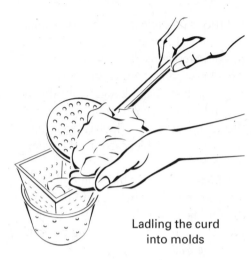

Ladling the curd
into molds

7. For cooked-curd cheeses, heat the curds.

The cut curd is "cooked" or "scalded" by heating it very gradually until it reaches the final cooking temperature specified in the recipe. Begin heating the outer pot very gently, stirring continuously, so the curd mass warms only a degree or two every several minutes. The curds will shrink in size and become firmer to the touch. It is very important not to heat the curds too quickly in this step. If cooked too high too fast, the curd will lose moisture too quickly, and resulting cheese could be dry and brittle, and not press well.

To pace the heating properly, divide the number of degrees by the amount of time allowed for cooking. For instance, for Cheddar cheese, warm the milk about 2°F (1°C) approximately every 7 minutes to raise the temperature from 88° to 100°F (31° to 38°C) in 45 to 50 minutes. During this time, the curd shrinks and acidifies, resulting in a firm but springy curd that will press into a firm cheese.

Make sure to stir continually as the curd cooks. This prevents any curds from matting or settling. Inadequately cooked curds can result in pockets of moisture, which can

negatively affect the final cheese.

Monitor this heating process very carefully. During cooking, it may be necessary to adjust the heat on the stove or even turn it off for a few minutes to keep the heating pace gradual.

8. Press the cheese.

Line the mold with cheese cloth and fill, piling the curd higher in the centre. Pull the cheese cloth up neatly around the curd, fold the excess across the top of the cheese and put on the lid. Press the cheese in a cheese press (see Sources, page 370) or by weighting it with a sufficiently heavy object. For most semisoft cheeses, a few clean bricks or a large container filled

Piling the curd in a mold
lined with cheese cloth

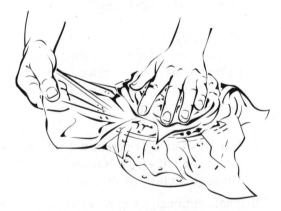

Pulling the cheese cloth up around
the curd and folding over

with water can be sufficient for pressing (see Cheese press, page 37).

9. Salt the cheese.

The curd has now become cheese and is salted either by immersing it in a saturated brine (as in the case of Gouda) or by dry-salting the surface (as in the case of Brie). Some cheeses, such as Cheddar, are salted before pressing.

To make an 18 to 22% saturated brine: Mix 1 part salt to 5 parts water. It may be necessary to warm the water to successfully dissolve the salt. If so, let the brine cool before immersing the cheese. The best temperature for brining cheese is 55°F (13°C). The brine can be used over and over again for several batches of cheese (refrigerate between uses). Replenish the salt after several uses and remove any floating bits of cheese with a strainer.

To make a 10% brine solution: Mix 1 part salt to 10 parts water. Then follow the instructions for saturated brine above.

When dry-salting cheese, distribute the salt equally over the surface to ensure that the surface ripens evenly. See page 32 for types of salt to use.

10. Age the cheese.

The cheese is now removed to a ripening area, where humidity and temperature are carefully controlled. Here, it is further tended until ready for consumption.

11. Care for the rind of washed-rind cheeses.

Many washed-rind cheeses have *Brevibacterium linens* in the cheese or in a brine made for washing the rind. This ripening bacteria creates an orange or red-brown smear on the rind, which lends a

distinctive taste and aroma to the cheese. To facilitate the growth of the bacteria and help create a firm rind, the cheese is "washed" in the following way:

1. Always use a fresh solution of brine.

2. Dip a clean cloth or small sponge into a small amount of brine and squeeze it out until just damp.

3. Rub the cheese over the whole surface with the damp cloth or sponge to just dampen it. Do not leave wet spots on the rind.

4. Discard used brine.

Washing the rind

Ripening and Aging

CHEESE IS AGED for flavor development and for future use. This process takes varying lengths of time for different varieties, sometimes years, before the cheese reaches its peak of development.

For optimal aging, most cheeses require an environment of relatively high humidity and a temperature range of 50° to 55°F (10° to 13°C). In a home environment, it is difficult to create a place for the purpose of ripening cheese. If you

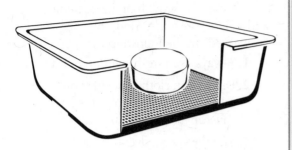

Ripening container

Cheese continues to ripen even when in cold storage. Hard cheeses will generally keep for several months, even years, and softer cheeses will keep for between 1 and 3 weeks after opening, depending on the cheese's age and whether it has been protected from the air.

have a natural cellar, you are one of the lucky ones. If you own land, you can dig your own cellar into the side of a hill and fit it out for a cheese cave, but not all of us are so fortunate. A cool basement, cellar or cold room, an old-fashioned "dairy" or an insulated garage could work, though close attention must be paid to fluctuating temperatures.

However, cheese can be aged successfully in a refrigerator. If you have the space and resources, it is a good idea to purchase a small apartment-size refrigerator that you can use specifically for cheese ripening. Make sure that you can set the temperature as high as 60°F (16°C). You may need to have a refrigeration specialist change the thermostat to accommodate your purpose. Special thermostats are also available

from some cheese-making supply houses. You cannot use your regular refrigerator unless it is no longer being used in the household. Home refrigerators should be set at 40°F (4°C) to keep food safe from harmful bacteria. Because the temperatures for ripening cheese are typically higher than 40°F (4°C), the cheese requires its own refrigerator specific to its needs.

Refrigerators tend to be dry, so you will need to increase the humidity around your cheese. This can easily be done by ripening the cheese in a plastic storage container and adjusting the lid as required to control the amount of dry air that enters and humidity that leaves. Using this method, you can ripen several kinds of cheese at once without too much concern for cross-contamination of bacteria. You can

Guide to Equivalents when Cooking with Cheese

Amount Ungrated Cheese	Resulting Grated Cheese
1 ounce (30 g)	¼ cup (50 mL)
2 ounces (60 g)	½ cup (125 mL)
4 ounces (125 g)	1 cup (250 mL)
8 ounces (250 g)	2 cups (500 mL)
1 pound (500 g)	4 cups (1 L)

measure the humidity with a hygrometer, available at restaurant, kitchen and cheese-making supply stores. If you are aging hard waxed cheeses, place them on boards on the shelves of the refrigerator and turn weekly to ensure even ripening.

Waxing

MANY TYPES OF hard cheese can be waxed for successful long-term aging. You must use special cheese wax for this purpose; do not use paraffin wax, as it is not acceptable.

There are many colors of wax available from cheese-making supply houses. Melt the wax over low to medium heat in an old pot or disposable flat-bottomed foil roaster (putting two together to double the bottom thickness is a good idea). An old hotplate can be handy and prevents a mess on the kitchen stove or cooktop. Hold the cheese on the top and bottom with your fingertips and dip the sides in the wax, rolling it around to coat. Let drip for a few seconds over the pot, then set down on parchment

Dipping the cheese in wax

paper to dry. Repeat. When the sides are dry, dip the top and bottom of the cheese, alternating top and bottom and allowing to dry between each coat. Apply two or three coats of wax in this manner. If properly waxed, a cheese can be aged indefinitely and will not be negatively affected by drying or unwelcome molds and bacteria. Waxing is a good solution if you are not able to control the humidity of your ripening area or want to simplify the aging process.

Serving Cheese

CHEESE IS ONE of the world's favorite foods, with many households serving cheese several times a week. It is perhaps the most versatile food served on its own as a snack, appetizer or dessert, or as an ingredient in dishes served from morning through night in many cuisines. To maximize the benefits and pleasure of eating cheese, here are some tips and pointers.

- Ripened cheeses are best served at room temperature because it allows the flavors and aromas to be fully appreciated. Remove these cheeses from the refrigerator about 1 hour, no longer, before serving. If they sit too long before serving, the rinds of some cheeses can collapse, some cheeses can "sweat" or become discolored, and others can become too soft. Fresh cheeses should be kept refrigerated until you're ready to use or serve them.

- If you're serving a cheese course between the main course and dessert, be sensitive to the menu. One special cheese is usually adequate if served with fruit. A large selection of rich cheeses is usually too much after a heavy meal.

- When creating a cheese platter or board, restrict the number of cheeses offered to five or fewer. Select one cheese from each of the main cheese families — mold-ripened (such as Brie), washed-rind (such as Muenster), blue-veined (such as Stilton) and hard pressed (such as Cheddar) — and one other, perhaps a fresh spreadable cheese, a delicate goat cheese or a spiced cheese.

- To calculate the amount of cheese required, consider the following:

  1. For a wine and cheese event, you will need approximately 4 oz (125 g) of cheese per person, divided up between the types of cheese chosen.

  2. For a buffet where other foods and appetizers will be offered, you will need 2 to 3 oz (60 to 90 g) per person, depending on the amount and variety of foods served.

  3. The time of day will dictate how much cheese you will need to provide. People are usually hungriest at noon and 5 p.m., so you will need a larger amount than you would at 9 or 10 p.m.

- To serve and display the cheese to greatest effect and to preserve the best flavor, choose a serving platter made of wood, ceramic or stone. Glass and metal are not as appealing because they appear cold and don't show off the warm rustic nature of cheese as well. Allow the cheese lots of space on the platter, and don't crowd it with too many additions like fruit, bread and crackers. A sprinkling of nuts and a few pieces of fruit can be a complement, but more can become messy, detracting from the cheese. Serve bread and crackers on a separate plate or in a basket.

- For eye appeal, cut or select cheeses of differing shapes. A wedge of Brie, a block of Cheddar, a small round of Muenster, a pyramid of Valençay and a half-moon of Fourme d'Ambert look spectacular together.

- Provide individual knives or cutting tools for each cheese so your guests will not have smears of soft cheese on pieces of hard cheese.

- Make the first cut on each cheese to guide your guests. For instance, remove a slice from the side of a wedge of Brie to communicate to your guests that it is not acceptable to cut off the point of the wedge.

Wine and Cheese

WITH SO MANY KINDS of cheese and so many different wines to choose from, here are some basic guidelines to follow.

- If possible, choose a wine that is from the same area as the cheese. Try an Alsatian white wine with Muenster or a hard cider with a ripe Camembert.

- The wine should never be stronger in flavor than the cheese served with it, and the cheese should never overwhelm the wine. Seek a balance of flavors and aromas.

> Aged cheeses contain almost no lactose, and ripened cheeses such as Cheddar and Swiss naturally contain very little. In fact, Cheddar has just 5% of the lactose found in whole milk.

All About Milk

Kinds of Milk and Milk Components

Cheese can be made from the milk of cows, goats and sheep, or other animals, such as water buffaloes, camels, mares, yaks or even reindeer. We will be concentrating on cow's, goat's and sheep's milk, as they are the types usually available. Though similar in many ways, there are some distinct differences. Below is a table of comparisons. However, please keep in mind that these are averages and are to be used as a guideline only. Each individual animal, herd or flock will have slightly different numbers, depending on the breed, the type of feed and the time of year. For instance, milk from a Jersey cow can have a milk-fat content of 5.5%, while that from a Holstein cow can be as low as 3.2%. This difference can really affect your cheese yield and consistency.

Timing can also affect the quality and nutritional content of milk. Usually milking animals produce larger quantities of milk and less fat during the summer, and lower volumes of milk with higher fat content in the winter. Another consideration when judging milk quality is the stage of lactation. Lactation is the period of time that the animal is producing milk, and it is divided into early, mid- and late stage. More milk is produced in the mid-stage than the late stage, and the milk is usually of higher quality than during either early- or late-stage lactation.

The diet of the animal also makes a difference in the milk's flavor and its fat and protein content. As the feed changes throughout the year (for instance, from dry winter fodder to fresh grass in the spring), the flavor of the milk will change and be especially obvious for a short period of time until the animal's body adjusts to the new regime.

If you are buying milk from a store or processor, it will already be "standardized," which means it has been processed to create a standard product, with a given fat, protein and solids content, so you will not need to consider the variations mentioned above. If you're purchasing privately or producing your own milk, you can have it analyzed in a lab to quantify the different components, though when making artisanal cheese, it is not really a necessary step in producing tasty cheese. You will learn to be sensitive to any differences in the milk, such as increased fat content.

Animal	pH	Fat	Protein	Lactose	Total solids	Expected cheese yield: %		
						Fresh	*Soft*	*Hard*
Cow	6.7	3.8	3.8	4.6	12.5	20–22	12–15	10–12
Goat	6.4	4.0	3.5	4.5	12.4	22–25	12–15	10–12
Sheep	6.7	7.0	5.6	4.9	19.0	40–50	25–30	18–20

About Yields

The yield percentage is the amount of solids in the form of cheese that you can expect to have from the milk. One quart (1 liter) of milk weighs 2 pounds (1 kg), so a 10% yield would be 3.2 oz (100 g).

Throughout the recipes there is a yield percentage noted. This percentage depends on several factors:

1. The type of milk used. Because the solids are in the fat, the lower the fat content of the milk, the lower the yield. For a hard cheese made with 10 quarts (10 L) whole milk, you can expect a 10 to 11% yield, or 2 to 2.2 lbs (1 to 1.1 kg) of cheese. The same cheese made with skim milk would yield about 8%, or 1.6 lbs (800 g) of cheese.

2. Use of calcium chloride. Milk that has been homogenized or pasteurized loses some stability in its calcium makeup. The addition of calcium chloride offers a free source of calcium ions, which can improve the yield. If you do not use calcium chloride, the yield can drop 2 to 3 percentage points.

3. Cheese maker's ability. It is important to gently handle the milk while stirring and the curd when ladling, cutting, stirring and cooking. The more roughly the fragile curd is handled, the more it can break down, and valuable solids will be lost in the whey. Temperature control is also important: if a cheese is cooked too high, it can become hard and brittle, and the yield will decrease.

Substituting Milk in Recipes

Most of the recipes in this book do not specify which kind of milk to use or whether the milk is raw or pasteurized. However, some cheeses are made specifically from one kind of milk; in that case, the recipe will clearly state which kind of milk to use. If a recipe calls for just "whole milk," you may use your milk of choice, applying the adjustments stated below. The default milk, when not otherwise stated, is always whole cow's milk. See pages 25 and 26 for recommendations regarding raw and pasteurized milk.

You can easily substitute one kind of milk for another, keeping the following in mind.

- Goat's milk has a lower pH; that is, it is more acidic than cow's milk. You will need to reduce the amount of rennet, a milk-coagulating enzyme that favors an acidic environment in order to coagulate the milk, by 15 to 25%. For instance, if a recipe calls for $^3/_4$ tsp (3.75 mL) rennet, use just slightly more than $^1/_2$ tsp (2.5 mL). Conversely, use 15 to 25% more rennet in a recipe calling for goat's milk in which you wish to substitute cow's milk.

- Goat's milk has finer fat particles than cow's milk, which means the fat remains more or less suspended in the milk rather than rising to the top as in cow's milk. This finer fat is also responsible for the smooth, delicate texture of goat's milk cheeses.

- Sheep's milk has a higher milk solids content than either cow's or goat's milk; reduce the rennet as you would for goat's milk. You will also need to recalculate the number of molds you use, as your yield will be higher from the same amount of milk.

Nutritional Benefits of Milk and Cheese

MILK IS AN EXCELLENT source of calcium, riboflavin, potassium, protein, carbohydrates, and vitamins A, B_6, B_{12} and D. Milk, however, is highly perishable and cannot be stored without refrigeration, making it inconvenient as a long-term food sources. The nutritional benefits of cheese equal those of milk but with the added advantage that many cheeses can be stored for long periods of time under less-exacting conditions.

Many people who are lactose intolerant can enjoy cheese, especially hard aged cheeses, because the lactose in the milk has been changed into lactic acid through the action of the lactic bacteria. Another alternative is goat cheese, as the finer fat particles in goat's milk make it more digestible than cow's milk for some people. Goat's milk cheese tends, therefore, to have a more delicate curd, requiring careful handling to avoid loss in the final cheese yield. The addition of calcium chloride to goat cheese helps stabilize the curd and increase the final yield.

Remember, the fresher the milk, the better the final product, as bacteria — including unwelcome bacteria — will already be growing in the milk, changing lactose to lactic acid and souring it. If you are using raw milk, be sure to make cheese no later than five days after milking. If you're purchasing pasteurized milk, check the best-before date for the freshest possible product.

Raw Milk

RAW MILK IS fresh milk that has been neither homogenized nor pasteurized (see Pasteurized Milk, page 26, for information on both processes). The interest in raw milk consumption is increasing, and it definitely offers some health benefits. But because of the potential risks, most countries have regulations governing the sale and purchase of it. Please check with your local governing body to learn about the law in your area (see Sources, page 372).

If you are able to purchase raw milk or produce it yourself, cleanliness in all areas of production and animal health are absolutely key. Milk is a perfect medium for bacterial growth, which is why it makes great cheese. However, the characteristics that favor cheese making also create the perfect environment for unwanted bacteria to flourish. Because raw milk has not undergone pasteurization, it contains all the bacteria and enzymes of a natural product, and, because of its source, can also contain spoilage bacteria and pathogenic bacteria such as *E. coli*, *Staphylococcus aureus* and *Listeria monocytogenes*. These can cause serious foodborne illness in humans, sometimes with dire consequences.

Things to consider are the general health and condition of the animals, the cleanliness of the animal housing and milking areas, and the handling of the milk during and after milking. Some animal health conditions can so adversely affect milk quality that your cheese may not turn out well. Some examples are:

- **Mastitis:** This inflammation of the udder releases large amounts of bacteria into the milk. This raises the pH of the milk, making it necessary to increase the amount of lactic bacteria used to adequately acidify the milk; inhibits

coagulation; increases the risk of pathogens being present in the milk; and decreases yield.

- **Stage of lactation:** During late-stage lactation, milk tends to be higher in bacteria. This is determined by somatic cell count, a measurement of the white blood cells that fight bacteria. An increased number of these cells indicates increased presence of bacteria, which, in turn, indicates disease or infection.

Using raw milk can be especially risky if you are not familiar with the source. See Sources (page 372) for more information. When using raw milk, process as soon as possible after milking. Otherwise, cool the milk to less than 40°F (4°C) within 30 minutes of milking and store at this temperature for no longer than 5 days before using.

It is recommended that raw-milk cheeses be aged for at least 60 days before consuming and that fresh cheeses and cultured products destined to be consumed before 60 days of ripening be pasteurized for safety and increased shelf life.

Pasteurized Milk

PASTEURIZATION KILLS pathogenic bacteria, rendering milk safe for consumption. There are certain beneficial enzymes and bacteria that are killed during the process, but, for the most part, pasteurized milk retains all the health benefits and flavor of raw milk without the danger of harmful bacteria.

To pasteurize raw milk, heat it slowly over medium heat in a stainless-steel pot or double boiler to 145°F (63°C), stirring slowly. When the temperature is reached, cover the pot and reduce the heat to the lowest setting and maintain the temperature

for 30 minutes. This holding period is the actual pasteurization. Cool the milk quickly to cheese-making temperature. Since milk has high thermal qualities (due to the fat and solids it contains), it can be difficult to cool quickly. Immerse the pot in a sinkful of ice water and stir until it cools to the required cheese-making temperature, refreshing water as necessary to keep it cold. The rule is: Heat up slowly, cool quickly. If you cannot process the milk right away, refrigerate it until you can. But remember, the fresher the milk, the better the cheese.

Types of Pasteurized Milk

- Homogenized milk is milk that has been extruded through a very small opening in order to shatter the fat into tiny particles so it remains in suspension. It is available with milk fat contents of 1%, 2%, and 3% to 4% (whole milk). If using homogenized milk for cheese making, choose the milk with the highest percentage of fat, as it will offer more flavor.

- Non-homogenized milk, also known as cream line or standard milk, is pasteurized milk that has not been homogenized. Check with local dairies and creameries to see if they offer this type of milk (see Sources, page 372). It is always preferable over homogenized milk for cheese making because the milk structure has not been changed. Therefore, the milk coagulates better, and the final yield of cheese will be higher.

- UHT milk (ultra heat treated) has been sterilized for increased shelf life. It can be kept at room temperature for very long periods of time and is often used in areas of the world where refrigeration is not available. It is NOT suitable for cheese making.

- Skim milk powder can be reconstituted and used for cheese making, though its low fat content gives it limited flavor. You can approximate whole milk by adding 1 cup (250 mL) whipping (35%) cream to every 2 quarts (2 L) reconstituted skim milk.

Ingredients

Lactic Bacterial Starters

If you set a bowl of fresh raw milk out on the table for a couple of days, it will curdle and sour, the solids eventually separating from the liquid, or whey. This process is caused by lactic bacteria present in both the milk and the air, which have populated the milk. Because they love the warm, sweet environment of the milk, they have grown exponentially, finally souring the whole bowl. At this point, you can use the curds and the whey, either processing them further or eating them as is and enjoying their healthful nutrients. This is a simple illustration of how cheese making begins. (Using store-bought homogenized milk, however, will not give you the same result, as homogenization shatters the fat particles, causing them to go rancid rather than sour when exposed to air.)

In our recipes, rather than leave the bacteria selection up to chance, we introduce our choice of bacteria and control the amount. Cheese-making bacteria are lactic (or milk) bacteria that acidify and flavor the milk by feeding on the lactose, or milk sugar, and creating lactic acid. Another word for lactic bacteria is *starter*, as it starts the acidification of the milk for cheese making.

Choosing Lactic Bacterial Starters

There are seven different strains of lactic bacteria used in cheese making, producing lactic acid, carbon dioxide gas or diacetyl (an aroma compound that adds a creamy, buttery flavor). These are divided into two main types: mesophilic, which performs best at low to medium temperatures, and thermophilic, which performs well at higher temperatures.

Lactic bacterial starter cultures are made up of one or more strains of bacteria, which create a variety of characteristics in cheese. There are several companies that produce lactic bacterial cultures for cheese making, and most suppliers sell only one brand. Your supplier will be able to help you select the best culture for your application and advise on inoculation rates of cultures should they vary from the amount called for in the recipe. The following information will help you when buying cultures.

Mesophilic bacteria strains:

- *Lactococcus lactis* ssp. *lactis* and *Lactococcus lactis* ssp. *cremoris* are the two main mesophilic strains, both of which produce lactic acid optimally at temperatures ranging from 77° to 86°F (25° to 30°C). They are used alone or in a blend for most cheeses ripened at the above temperatures, such as Cheddar, feta, Colby, Brie and cottage cheese.

- *Lactococcus lactis* ssp. *diacetylactis* and *Leuconostoc mesenteroides* ssp. *cremoris* ferment at a fast rate, producing large amounts of carbon dioxide gas and diacetyl during the process. They are used in conjunction with basic mesophilic strains in cheeses where an open texture in the paste is desired, such as Havarti or blue cheese.

Mesophilic culture called for in the recipes in this book refers to a lactic starter made of *Lactococcus lactis* ssp. *lactis* or *Lactococcus lactis* ssp. *cremoris*, or a blend of both.

Aroma mesophilic culture called for in some recipes refers to a lactic starter made with one or both of the above strains plus *Lactococcus lactis* ssp. *diacetylactis* or *Leuconostoc mesenteroides* ssp. *cremoris*. This is a nice choice for butter, crème fraîche, fromage frais and chèvre, as it provides a pleasant creamy aroma.

Rapid acidifying mesophilic cultures have the addition of a thermophilic strain and a gas-producing strain. This blend produces both aroma and CO_2 and acidifies the milk more quickly than the regular mesophilic culture called for in the recipes. Rapid acidifying cultures can be substituted for the mesophilic culture called for in a recipe; however, you must reduce the inoculation rate, using two-thirds to one-half the amount called for.

Thermophilic strains:
- *Streptococcus thermophilus, Lactobacillus delbrueckii* ssp. *bulgaricus* and *Lactobacillus helveticus* are the main strains of thermophilic bacteria. All of them produce lactic acid optimally at temperatures ranging from 95° to 105°F (35° to 41°C) and survive up to 140°F (60°C). They are used in cheeses such as Parmesan, Gruyère, Romano and Emmental.

Thermophilic culture called for in the recipes refers to a lactic starter made of *Streptococcus thermophilus*, usually with the addition of either *Lactobacillus delbrueckii* or *Lactobacillus helveticus*, or both.

The preferred method for home cheese makers and small producers is to "direct-set" the milk with freeze-dried cultures in powdered form. These are available in small foil packets and can be kept successfully for long periods of time in the freezer. Partially used packets should be closed and sealed in a resealable plastic bag before storing in the freezer. Packets are labeled with a production date and a best-before date, but, when kept frozen, the bacteria are viable for up to 1 year after expiration. All of the recipes in this book use direct-set cultures.

In large commercial cheese plants, the starter is usually a so-called "mother culture." Milk is sterilized and inoculated with lactic bacteria, then set aside to thicken, like yogurt. It is then used to inoculate the milk for cheese making. The process of making and using a mother culture is time-consuming and requires very strict attention to sanitation and storage. Since the culture cannot be kept for more than a few days and deteriorates when frozen, this method is not recommended for home and small-scale cheese makers. If you would prefer to use a mother culture, the method of preparation is as follows.

Mother Culture

- 1 quart (1 L) sealable glass jar
- Cooking pot large enough to completely immerse the jar
- Tongs

Yields 1 quart (1 L)

Skim milk (can be made with reconstituted skim milk powder)

Powdered mesophilic or thermophilic lactic bacterial mother culture starter*

*(Note: Not every culture is suited to re-culturing as a mother culture; consult with your supplier.)

1. Sterilize jar and lid by boiling in a large pot of water for 5 minutes. The jar must be completely immersed to be thoroughly sterilized. Remove jar from water with tongs. Allow jar to cool slightly and fill with skim milk, leaving about 1 inch (2.5 cm) headspace at the top to allow for expansion of the milk during heating.

2. Tighten lid on jar and return to pot of hot water, ensuring that the jar is completely covered by the water. Bring water to a boil. Reduce heat and simmer for 25 minutes.

3. Remove jar from water and let cool. For a mesophilic mother culture, let milk cool to 72° to 75°F (22°C to 24°C). For a thermophilic mother culture, let milk cool to 110°F (43°C). Remove lid of jar and sprinkle mother culture starter (either the contents of the packet if you have purchased it in a pre-measured amount or about 1/4 tsp/1.25 mL dry powder) over milk.

4. Quickly replace lid and let stand for about 5 minutes for the culture to rehydrate. Gently agitate the jar (do not shake) to blend culture into milk, then let ripen at room temperature for approximately 18 hours or until thickened like yogurt. If the room is cool, cover with a towel or tea cozy to keep warm.

5. Refrigerate immediately after incubation and use as soon as possible. If you cannot use it right away, the mother culture can be kept in the refrigerator for up to 2 weeks before using, if the jar has remained unopened. However, once you have opened the jar to use some culture, the whole batch must be used within 3 days.

6. You can freeze your bulk starter in small portions (for instance in an ice cube tray) for future use. Be sure to sterilize the tray well before using, and wrap and seal before freezing. The frozen culture is good for a maximum of 3 months.

7. You can use the frozen cubes of starter to make a new batch of mother culture. After three or four batches made with frozen culture, make a new batch of mother culture with dry powder, as the strength diminishes with continued use.

8. To use mother culture, substitute 1 oz (30 mL) or 2 tbsp (30 mL) mother culture for 1/4 tsp (1.25 mL) mesophilic culture in the recipe.

Troubleshooting

THE MAIN DIFFICULTY with making a mother culture (see page 29) is effective sanitation. Most problems are due to some sort of contamination.

The culture is bubbly, stringy or slimy.
It has been infected with yeasts or unwanted bacteria. You must discard it and begin again. Sterilize rigorously.

The milk did not coagulate at all.
The culture was no longer live. Start again with fresh culture. The culture could have been killed by detergent or bleach residue in the equipment. Rinse thoroughly. If you are re-culturing using an earlier batch of your own, the culture may be too old. Begin again with new dry powdered culture.

As mentioned earlier, it is difficult to make a starter culture and maintain it at highest quality. If you have any doubts about the quality, do not use it. Many cheeses take months to ripen, and you do not want to find that the cheese you waited so long to taste is bad. Dry powdered culture is always of good quality and easy to use.

> Most cheeses can be frozen, but there will be some change in texture when thawed. If you must freeze cheese, cut it into small pieces and wrap tightly, ensuring that the package is airtight. Freeze for up to 2 months. Thaw in the refrigerator and serve within a few days.

Ripening Cultures

IN ADDITION TO lactic starters, other bacteria and molds can be added to the milk to create different effects. These include:

Molds

Penicillium candidum are white fuzzy molds that grow on the surfaces of cheeses such as Brie and Camembert. There are many strains of this mold with differing characteristics, such as the length of "hair" the mold grows, color, rate of growth and flavor.

Penicillium roquefortii is the blue mold associated with Roquefort and other blue-veined cheeses. It is available in either powder or liquid form, though in this book we use the powder form for versatility. There are different strains, which result in slightly different-colored molds, either a dark or a light blue-green. Very small amounts of mold are necessary to inoculate the milk, as it grows very quickly and spreads easily.

Geotrichum candidum is most often used in French-style goat cheeses and tommes, often in conjunction with P. candidum to create an especially flavorful crust. It grows rapidly and therefore helps prevent unwanted mold growth on very moist cheeses.

Cylindrocarpon mold creates lovely natural rinds on tommes and other mixed-rind cheeses. The surface will show a blend of white, gray-brown and yellow coloring, with a velvety texture.

Yeasts

Certain strains of yeast can be added to milk to create strong-flavored cheeses, especially in the washed-rind family. If you appreciate these kinds of cheeses, consult with your supplier to find one that is suitable.

Ripening Bacteria

The most common are the *Brevibacterium linens* group. These bacteria are usually added to the milk when making washed-rind cheeses, such as Limburger. They are also diluted in the brine that is used to rub on the surface of the cheese to create the smelly yellow-orange smear associated with these cheeses.

Propionic Bacteria

These bacteria, which are added to the milk during processing, are responsible for the sweet, nutty flavor and holes in Swiss-style cheeses, especially Emmental. As these bacteria grow, they produce gases that form bubbles that displace the cheese, causing the whole cheese to puff up and holes to form in the interior.

Coagulants and Other Ingredients

Rennet

The most commonly used coagulant is rennet, which is composed of enzymes found in the stomachs of calves and kids, and is extracted at the time of slaughter. Rennet is usually used in liquid form but is also available in tablets.

Vegetable rennet can be made from various plants, usually of the thistle family, though they are not as widely available commercially. Microbial rennet is a good choice if you prefer not to use animal rennet, though it does not perform as well as animal rennet when making hard aged cheeses. Microbial, or fungal, rennet is derived from the fermentation of the mold *Rhizomucor miehei* or *Cryphonectria parasitica*. The mold is grown in vats, where the enzyme responsible for coagulation is produced and is then extracted and purified. Also available are genetically engineered

rennets, which are created by taking the gene for the chymosin enzyme from the cow and growing it in a host microorganism, such as a mold, yeast or bacterium. The recipes in this book all call for natural calf rennet in liquid form because it is the most effective and readily available. In addition to performing better in aged cheeses, it is also easier to make exact measurements with liquid than with crushed tablets.

When substituting rennet tablets for liquid rennet, substitute half a tablet, crushed and dissolved in 1/4 cup (50 mL) cool water, for 1/4 tsp (1 mL) liquid rennet.

Natural calf rennet comes in different strengths; in this book the standard is liquid rennet of 300 IMCU (international milk clotting units). Rennet should always be diluted at a ratio of 1:20 with cool water before incorporating into the milk. If you are not sure of the strength of your rennet, consult your supplier, who can recommend the amount necessary for the cheese recipe in question. Rennet can be kept for up to a year in the refrigerator and can be frozen successfully.

Make sure the water used to dilute the rennet has no residual chlorine, as chlorine kills the enzyme. To be sure, boil the water and let it cool before using. Any equipment that has been sanitized with bleach must be thoroughly rinsed and dried.

Calcium Chloride

During homogenization and pasteurization, the calcium in milk decreases and becomes slightly destabilized. Adding calcium chloride boosts the number of calcium ions in the milk and helps firm up the curd and increase the yield. This step is always recommended when making goat's milk cheeses, because the fine fat particles in goats' milk stay in suspension instead of separating out, as in the case of cow's milk. As a result of this "natural homogenization,"

the resulting curd is often soft and weak. Add calcium chloride to the milk before the rennet and stir in thoroughly. Calcium chloride is available from cheese-making supply houses and keeps indefinitely in the refrigerator.

Lipase

Lipase is an enzyme often added to cow's milk cheeses to impart a stronger flavor. Add to the milk before the rennet. Keep sealed and frozen for up to one year. Lipase is available through cheese-making supply houses.

Annatto

This natural coloring is derived from the seeds of the South American achiote shrub. It imparts an orange color and is often used in Cheddar cheese to approximate the deep yellow of creamy milk.

Salt

All cheese must be salted, either by brining, dry-salting or mixing salt into the curd. The salt should not have any additives, such as fluoride, anti-clumping agents or iodine, which can hinder bacterial growth or even kill lactic bacteria. Pickling salt is suitable, as is kosher flake salt, though it is more expensive.

Water

The water used to dilute the ingredients should be completely free of chlorine. If your tap water is chlorinated, boil it and let it cool before using. Filtered tap water is fine. If you're using well water, or untreated or untested water, boil to kill any bacteria.

Ash

Many delicate cheeses, especially goat cheeses, are sprinkled with a light coating of vegetable ash. This is a very finely ground charcoal, usually French in origin from the maritime pine tree. You can buy ash from a cheese-making supply house.

Ash protects the exterior of the cheese from bacteria and can firm up the surface of shaped cheeses. In days gone by, when cheese was made under simple circumstances on the farm, the day's yield of milk was often not enough to make an entire batch of cheese. Because raw milk could not be adequately stored until the next day, the cheese was begun even though it did not completely fill the molds, then a layer of ash was added to protect the surface from bacteria and pests. The next morning, more cheese was made to fill up the mold. Thus, a cheese with a line of charcoal through the middle was created, a tradition that continues in modern-day cheeses such as Morbier.

Today there are several French goat cheeses that are ripened with an ash coating, including Selles-sur-Cher and the pyramid-shaped Valençay. These moist cheeses benefit from the ash coating, which firms up the surface and protects them from unwanted mold growth as they ripen.

Spices and Additives

ANY SPICES THAT are added to cheeses should be free of contaminants, such as pesticides, herbicides, bacteria and insects. Any residues of these can contaminate and ruin the cheese as it ages. If you are not sure of your source, it is always a good idea to boil spices for 10 minutes, then cool them before adding to the curd. The cooking liquid can also be added to enhance the flavor. Examples of spices include dried chiles, cumin seeds and peppercorns. You can also microwave the spices on High for 1 minute. If you are using your own garden herbs, wash thoroughly and dry in the oven or food dehydrator.

For herbs and spices used in cheeses that are to be consumed fresh, it is not necessary to take such elaborate precautions; just make sure they are washed and clean.

Equipment and Tools

THE ACID PRODUCED during cheese making can react with some metals, so it is necessary to use stainless-steel, glass and food-grade plastic equipment. Some of the tools and equipment you will need are available in hardware stores, others in specialized cheese-making supply houses.

For home cheese making, you will need:

Stainless-steel pot, such as a soup or spaghetti pot, that is large enough to accommodate the milk in the recipe plus enough space for stirring, about 2 inches (5 cm) above the level of the milk. Restaurant supply houses have pots larger than the usual spaghetti pot size; just be sure to purchase stainless steel.

An even larger pot that will accommodate the cheese pot and create a hot water bath. A stainless-steel pot a size larger than the cheese pot is ideal — the handles of the inner pot should sit very nicely on the edge of the outer pot, holding it just up off the bottom of the outer pot. A less-expensive option is a canner (just never heat the milk in this type of pot, because the quality of the enameling is usually inferior and the exposed metal could negatively affect the cheese). Canners have ridges on the bottom, which prevent the inner pot from sitting directly on the bottom. Or you can use the wire insert on the bottom of the canner to keep the inner pot up off the bottom.

Stainless-steel measuring cups that include $1/4$ cup (50 mL), $1/3$ cup (75 mL), $1/2$ cup (125 mL) and 1 cup (250 mL) sizes.

Stainless-steel measuring spoons that include an $1/8$ tsp (0.65 mL) size.

Large pot

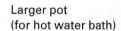
Larger pot
(for hot water bath)

Long-handled stainless-steel skimmer
with small holes or a slotted spoon.
Available at restaurant supply houses.

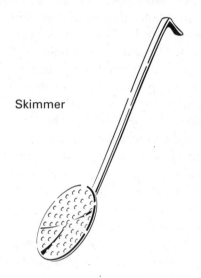

Skimmer

Long-handled stainless-steel whisk.
This whisk is often used in certain recipes
to cut the curd into very small pieces.
Available at kitchen or restaurant supply
houses.

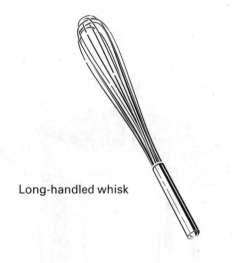

Long-handled whisk

**Stainless-steel or food-grade plastic
colander.** Do not use metal mesh strainers.

Draining bag or cloth made of quality
woven fabric that can be washed and
bleached. A linen kitchen towel can
work. Ready-made bags are available from
cheese-making supply houses (to make a
fresh cheese draining bag, see page 47).

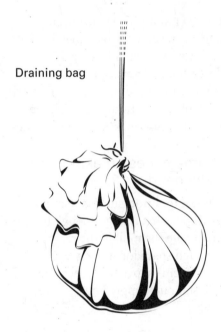

Draining bag

**Long-bladed curd knife with a
rounded tip.** The knife should be long
enough to reach the bottom of the pot
without immersing the handle. It will be
used for checking the curd for a clean break
and cutting the curd. The rounded tip makes
it look rather like a cake-decorating knife.

Dairy thermometer. Do not use a glass
candy-making thermometer. A dairy
thermometer has a flat dial on the top
and a long stainless-steel stem. Many have
a clip on the side to attach to the cheese
pot. Be sure to check the accuracy of the
thermometer before starting. Instructions

Long-bladed knife

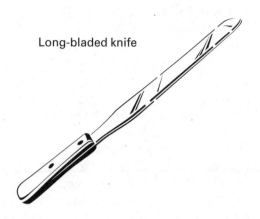

- 4-inch (10 cm) Camembert molds
- 8-inch (20 cm) half-Brie mold (Brie can also be made very successfully with a tomme mold)
- Crottin molds (one size)
- St-Marcellin molds (one size)
- 8-inch (20 cm) tomme mold for 4-lb (2 kg) cheeses
- Pyramid-shaped molds for Valençay (one size)
- 10-lb (4.5 kg) mold for Emmental
- Brousse molds (one size)
- Fresh goat cheese molds (cup shape) (one size)
- Ste-Maure molds (one size)
- Rectangular brick-shaped mold (one size)

for calibrating come with the thermometer. Otherwise, make a slush of crushed ice and a little water and immerse the thermometer to check that the setting is at 32°F (0°C). Adjust the dial if necessary.

Cheese molds. These come in many sizes and shapes. Feel free to experiment with heart-shaped Brie or baby Goudas. The following molds are used in the recipes in this book.

Drying rack for pressed cheeses. A stainless-steel cake rack will do if outfitted with a piece of cheese matting and set over a baking sheet to catch any drips.

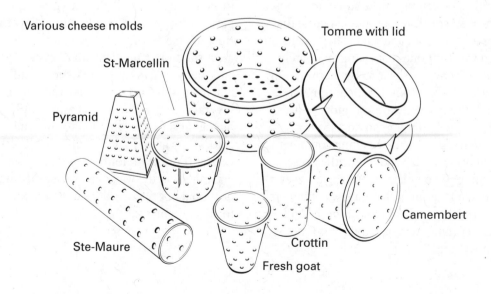

Various cheese molds

St-Marcellin

Tomme with lid

Pyramid

Ste-Maure

Crottin

Fresh goat

Camembert

Cheese cloth. This is not the "cheesecloth" for sale in grocery stores, but rather muslin or plastic cheese bandage netting made for lining molds and wrapping cheeses for pressing. This cheese cloth can be washed and reused. It is available from cheese-making supply houses.

Cheese matting. These stiff plastic mesh mats are used for draining and ripening cheeses. They are available from cheese-making supply houses and can be used indefinitely if they are washed and sanitized between uses.

Draining and ripening containers. Many cheeses are drained in molds, which form the final shape of the cheese. Some molds have no bottoms and must sit on a draining mat on a flat, firm surface. The container underneath catches the whey as it drains out of the developing cheese. It's easy to make one at home (see right for instructions on assembling a container for draining).

These plastic bins or containers are used for draining your cheeses and for ripening them. There are many containers on the market, but make sure you choose one made of clear food-grade plastic that has a flat bottom and a lid. The dimensions can vary, but one that is approximately 14 by 20 by 6 inches (35 by 50 by 15 cm) is a good size. Look for them in most department, hardware and grocery stores. The same container can be used for draining, then as the ripening container: simply clean, dry and line with cheese matting. If you plan on making cheese often, it is useful to have a few containers, as ripening can take many months and one container will be required for the whole time.

To make a draining container:
You will need a large clear-plastic 30-quart (30 L) food storage container (not the colored kind) with a lid. Place a large stainless-steel cake rack inside the container and top the rack with a large white plastic cutting board. On top of the cutting board, place a piece of cheese matting. Bamboo sushi mats are often used instead, but be careful to sanitize them well before and after using.

The draining cheeses sit on the matting on the board on the rack in the container, which catches the whey. The container is emptied from time to time as the whey builds up. The flat surface of the cutting board is essential for soft ripened cheeses such as Camembert, which are made in bottomless molds. Without the board, the curd would escape from under the mold. When draining cheeses in molds with bottoms (such as Crottin, St-Marcellin and tomme), the cheese matting helps raise the mold off the board so the whey drains off easily.

Cheese wax. This is used to coat hard cheeses to protect them from bacteria and from drying out during the long aging period. If your situation does not allow for ripening natural-rind cheeses, waxing is a great solution. Cheddar, Gouda, Caerphilly and many others ripen very successfully when waxed. Cheese wax is available in several colors at cheese-making supply houses and can be blended for unique colors. Use an old pot or a disposable foil roaster (double up for better stability) for waxing. Heat the wax over low to medium heat on a hot plate or burner. Be prepared to clean up messes!

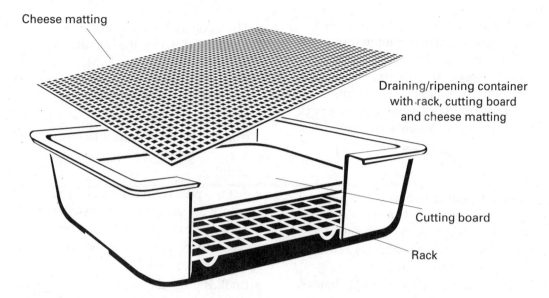

Cheese matting

Draining/ripening container
with rack, cutting board
and cheese matting

Cutting board

Rack

Cheese press. For the home cheese maker, there are several cheese presses available on the market. These usually consist of a board set on a draining tray, an outer sleeve that accommodates the cheese wrapped in cheesecloth, a "follower," or lid, that fits down onto the cheese, and a screw mechanism to tighten down the press. Check with your cheese-making supply house to find out what models of presses are available. Often the press will include a mold. Make sure the size suits your recipe.

You can also create your own press, or improvise. When choosing the method of pressing, keep these facts in mind:

> Light pressure = 5 to 10 psi
> Medium pressure = 10 to 20 psi
> Firm pressure = 20 to 45 psi, or higher

Psi means pounds per square inch, so the weight is divided up among the inches of surface area. For a large cheese requiring firm pressure, this means a very heavy weight indeed to exert 40 lbs (20 kg) on each inch. Hard cheeses really need a proper press, or a weight of at least 50 lbs

(25 kg) for even a small cheese as in our recipes, to press adequately.

Light to medium pressure can be achieved by weighting the cheese with something like a brick; small ones weigh from 4 to 5 lbs (2 to 2.5 kg) and heavier cement building blocks can weigh approximately 10 to 20 lbs (5 to 10 kg).

Remember, the size of the cheese will dictate the weight required to press it. A bucket filled with water can also work; you can fill the bucket to get the weight you need. 1 quart (1 L) water weighs about 2 lbs (1 kg), so a 5-gallon (20 L) pail of water would give you a weight of 40 lbs (20 kg) for medium to firm pressure, depending on the size of the cheese. For a tomme mold with a cheese requiring medium pressure, this method would be adequate to press. Place a cutting board or other board on the mold, then the weight, remembering that the pressure must distribute itself over the surface, so it is diminished by a large board. If pressing two cheeses under one weight, you must double the weight for it to have the same effect as it would when pressing one cheese.

If you plan to make mainly pressed hard cheeses, you may want to invest in a cheese press to facilitate the process. See Sources (page 370) for suppliers.

Plans for building your own press are also available from various sources. Check your local library for books that specialize in homesteading, or the Internet for resources.

Cheese ripening paper. This is a special layered paper designed for ripening soft cheeses, such as Brie and Camembert. It allows for an exchange of gases as the cheese ripens and keeps it moist. It is available at cheese-making supply houses.

Parchment or waxed paper can be used to wrap and store finished cheeses in the refrigerator, but they are not acceptable substitutes for cheese-ripening paper.

Wrapping and Storing Cheeses

ONCE YOUR CHEESE is ripened to your liking, it can be stored for a longer period in several ways. Of course, if you have a natural cheese cave or cellar, you can store your cheese just like Swiss farmers do: simply leave it on the shelf, unwrapped and open to the air. However, for most of us, wrapping whole or cut cheese well and storing it in the refrigerator is the obvious choice.

Some points to remember:

- Cheese is a living, breathing food. It continues to ripen or develop even when in cold storage, though at a slower rate. Once a whole cheese is cut, ripening will be affected but will still continue.

- The lactic bacteria in the cheese continue to change the chemistry of the milk, creating gases, which, if not allowed to escape, can affect the taste and consistency of the paste and rind.

- The humidity and temperature of the storage area are important factors in keeping cheese for a longer period of time.

- Salt is a preservative. If you wish to reduce the salt content in any of your homemade cheeses because of dietary concerns, remember that they could spoil more quickly.

- Cooked pressed cheeses, such as Cheddar and Gruyère, will keep for a long time, due to the relative lack of moisture in the paste. If properly wrapped and monitored, they can keep for 1 to 6 months in cold storage, depending on the dryness of the cheese when stored. Hard grating cheeses, such as Parmesan, Sbrinz or Kefalotyri, have an even lower moisture content and will keep even longer than a Gruyère.

- Surface-ripened cheeses, such as Brie or Reblochon, have a shorter shelf life due to their higher moisture content and the aggressive ripening action of the bacteria and molds in the cheese. With proper storage, they can keep for 1 to 2 months after they reach peak ripeness. Delicate surface-ripened cheeses made from goat's milk tend to suffer the most from airtight wrapping, and many of them actually improve in flavor and intensity if allowed to dry. The rinds of washed-rind cheeses can often become sticky and wet underneath the wrap.

- Unripened or fresh lactic cheeses, such as fromage frais, quark or chèvre, have a relatively short shelf life, even when kept refrigerated. If packaged in airtight containers and refrigerated at 40°F (4°C) immediately after processing, they can keep for up to 4 weeks, though 2 weeks is recommended for maximum freshness.

- Each time you unwrap and cut a cheese, replace the wrap. Milk residues on the wrap can promote spoilage.

There is much discussion about the best way to wrap and store cheese. Some options include:

1. **Plastic wrap** — This keeps the moisture in the cheese but can also smother it, preventing the natural ripening gases from escaping. Plastic can also lend an unpleasant taste to a piece of cut cheese. Try placing a layer of parchment or waxed paper against the cut surface before wrapping the whole piece in plastic wrap.

2. **Waxed paper** — While it is less likely to add an unwelcome taste to the cheese, waxed paper is difficult to fold into an airtight package. Moisture can still escape from the cheese allowing it to dry out. If using waxed paper, try placing the wrapped piece of cheese inside a loosely covered container for added moisture retention.

3. **Parchment paper** — This is especially good for delicate cheeses and those that, due to a moist rind, could stick to the wrap.

4. **Aluminum foil** — A good choice for many cheeses, foil keeps moisture in. On the other hand, like plastic wrap, it can prevent the cheese from breathing.

5. **Cheese storage containers** — These special containers are designed to allow the cheese to breathe but still retain moisture. Some have a ribbed surface to allow air to move around the cheese and a loose-fitting lid, which allows some air movement.

6. **Cheesecloth or muslin dampened with water** — This can be a useful choice for wrapping large pieces of hard cheese, though the cheese must still be wrapped in foil or placed in a covered container to keep it from drying out.

7. **Butcher paper** — With its greaseproof coating, this paper often performs well for cheese storage.

Cheese making, especially of hard pressed cheeses in the Cheddar style, is an old tradition in Scotland. In the region of Caithness in northern Scotland, one can still see cheese presses built right into the walls of old stone cottages.

Sanitation

THE IMPORTANCE OF cleanliness in cheese making cannot be overemphasized. Remember that milk is perfect for growing bacteria, good or bad. If your tools are not scrupulously clean, unwanted bacteria can ruin the cheese.

Don't be tempted to make the most of your time in the kitchen by baking bread or other yeasted products while you make cheese. Yeast in the air can infect the cheese and seriously sabotage your efforts. Keep the dog and cat out, close the windows and schedule visitors for another day.

All of your equipment, including pots, stirring spoons, measuring cups and spoons, and any work surfaces that you will set your utensils down upon, must be washed with hot soapy water, rinsed, then rinsed again with a bleach solution — 2 tbsp (30 mL) household bleach per 4 quarts (4 L) water. Air-dry on clean cloth or paper towels or wipe dry with clean paper towels.

If you prefer not to use bleach, you can partially fill the cheese pot with water, bring to a boil, immerse all of your tools in it and boil for 5 more minutes.

Wash your hands with warm soapy water and rinse thoroughly. Wash hands again if you touch anything other than your sterilized equipment.

Set out all tools and utensils on a clean cloth or paper towel on the counter until you're ready to use them.

Choosing Your First Cheeses

As you try the various recipes in this book, you will gain insight into and a feel for the craft of cheese making. To ease your way in and reward yourself with delicious cheese right from the start, I would suggest beginning with some of the simplest cheeses. Fresh cheeses such as Fromage Frais (page 43), Chèvre (page 55) and Quark (page 42) are easy to make, versatile and delicious. Once you have mastered them, move on to some of the ethnic cheeses such as Queso Blanco (page 296), Paneer (page 294) and Feta (page 292). If you just cannot wait to fill your cellar with ripening cheese, start by trying your hand at Gouda (page 186), Edam (page 182) or Gruyère (page 232). Choosing cheeses that are waxed can simplify the ripening process. As you gain expertise, move on to explore more complicated cheeses, such as Cheddar (page 213), Mozzarella (page 74) and blue-veined or other natural-rind cheeses. Brie (page 96) and Camembert (page 100) are not difficult to make if you have a suitable environment for developing the rind. Soon your biggest problem will be keeping friends and neighbors away from your cheese cellar!

Fresh Cheeses

Some of the most delicious and satisfying cheeses are the simplest to make. This chapter includes a large array of favorites that can get you off to a good start with home cheese making. The equipment required for most of these cheeses is simple: a large cooking pot, a skimmer, and a draining bag or cloth-lined colander, and you are on your way.

Quark

Makes about
3½ lbs (1.75 kg),
20 to 25% yield

Quark is a light, fresh unripened cheese that is versatile and hugely popular, especially in German cooking.

Tip: If you are using homogenized cow's milk, it is strongly recommended that you add calcium chloride (see page 31) for best results. The addition of calcium chloride will stabilize the curd, hasten setting and increase yield. Use the same amount of calcium chloride as rennet called for in the recipe, dilute it with at least 10 times the amount of water and stir into the milk before adding the rennet.

Serving suggestion: For a light supper or lunch, use 1 cup (250 mL) quark as a dip for boiled new potatoes. Serve with a side salad and some crusty bread.

- Draining bag or cloth-lined colander

4 quarts	partly skimmed (1 or 2%) milk	4 L
4 quarts	whole milk	4 L
¼ tsp	aroma or mesophilic culture	1.25 mL
⅛ tsp	liquid rennet	0.65 mL
1 tbsp	pickling (canning) or kosher salt, or to taste	15 mL

1. Sterilize all equipment (see page 40). In a large stainless-steel pot over medium heat, combine skim and whole milks. Warm milk to 77°F (25°C), stirring gently to prevent scorching. Remove from heat.

2. Sprinkle culture over surface of milk and let stand for about 5 minutes to rehydrate. Using skimmer and an up-and-down motion, gently draw culture down into milk without breaking surface of milk.

3. Dilute rennet in ¼ cup (50 mL) cool water. Add to milk and, using the same up-and-down motion, draw rennet down into milk until well blended. Cover and let set at room temperature in a draft-free location for 24 hours.

4. Tip pot slightly to drain off any surface whey. Using a long-bladed knife, cut curd into vertical strips about 2 inches (5 cm) wide. Let stand for 5 minutes. Whey will collect on the surface. Tip pot again to pour off the collected whey.

5. Using skimmer, ladle curd into a draining bag or cloth-lined colander and let drain for 4 hours.

6. Remove cheese from bag and place in a bowl. Blend in salt. Store in the refrigerator for up to 2 weeks (see Tips, page 45).

Fromage Frais

Makes 2 lbs (1 kg)

25% yield

This fresh, creamy cheese is so delicious you will want to eat it with everything!

Tips: Unless otherwise specified, all the recipes use cow's milk.

The longer the cheese is drained, the firmer it will become. Check at intervals to decide when you think it is firm enough for your preference. Feel the bottom of the bag with your hand; it should be quite damp but not still freely dripping. You can remove some cheese from the bag to check the consistency, then return it to the bag to continue draining with no harm done. Remember, as the cheese stands in the refrigerator, it will firm up a bit more.

- Draining bag or cloth-lined colander

4 quarts	whole milk	4 L
¼ tsp	aroma or mesophilic culture	1.25 mL
2	drops liquid rennet	2
	Pickling (canning) or kosher salt	

1. Sterilize all equipment (see page 40). In a large stainless-steel pot over medium heat, warm milk to 77°F (25°C), stirring gently to prevent scorching. Remove from heat.

2. Sprinkle culture over surface of milk and let stand for about 5 minutes to rehydrate. Using skimmer and an up-and-down motion, gently draw culture down into milk without breaking surface of milk.

3. Dilute rennet in 1 tbsp (15 mL) cool water. Add to milk and, using the same up-and-down motion, draw rennet down into milk until well blended. Cover and let set at room temperature in a draft-free location for 12 hours.

4. Using skimmer, ladle curd into a draining bag or cloth-lined colander and let drain. The draining can take several hours; the time depends on how firm you want your final product to be (see Tip, left).

5. Remove cheese from bag and place in a bowl. Weigh cheese, then add 1% of the weight in salt. Store in the refrigerator for up to 2 weeks (see Tips, page 45).

Fromage Blanc

| **Makes 1 quart (1 L)** |
| *30% yield* |

A fresh milky cheese, fromage blanc is delicious for breakfast or a snack blended with a little fruit and topped with a drizzle of honey.

Tips: To make the diluted rennet solution required for this cheese, add 1 drop liquid rennet to 2 tbsp (30 mL) cool water. Use 1 tbsp (15 mL) as directed, discarding remaining solution.

If you are using homogenized cow's milk, it is strongly recommended that you add calcium chloride (see page 31) for best results. The addition of calcium chloride will stabilize the curd, hasten setting and increase yield. Use the same amount of calcium chloride as rennet called for in the recipe, dilute it with at least 10 times the amount of water and stir into the milk before adding the rennet.

- Draining bag or cloth-lined colander

3 quarts	whole or partly skimmed (1 or 2%) milk	3 L
⅛ tsp	aroma or mesophilic culture	0.65 mL
1 tbsp	diluted rennet solution (see Tip, left)	15 mL
2 tsp	pickling (canning) or kosher salt	10 mL

1. Sterilize all equipment (see page 40). In a large stainless-steel pot over medium heat, warm milk to 72°F (22°C), stirring gently to prevent scorching. Remove from heat.

2. Sprinkle culture over surface of milk and let stand for about 5 minutes to rehydrate. Using skimmer and an up-and-down motion, gently draw culture down into milk without breaking surface of milk.

3. Add diluted rennet solution to milk, stirring gently to blend. Cover and let set at room temperature in a draft-free location for 12 hours.

4. Using skimmer, ladle curd into a draining bag or cloth-lined colander and let drain for 4 hours or for up to 6 hours if you prefer a thicker cheese.

5. Remove cheese from bag and place in a bowl. Blend in salt. Beat with a whisk or mixer for a light, smooth texture. Store in the refrigerator for up to 2 weeks (see Tips, page 45).

Cream Cheese

Makes 1 lb (500 g)

25% yield

The typical supermarket variety just cannot compare.

Tips: This cheese is quite stiff, so you can't easily blend in the salt with a spoon. You'll have to knead it in with your hands to evenly distribute it through the cheese.

Fresh cheeses are highly perishable. Store them in the coldest part of the refrigerator for up to 2 weeks.

• Draining bag or cloth-lined colander

1 quart	whole milk	1 L
1 quart	whipping (35%) cream	1 L
¼ tsp	aroma or mesophilic culture	1.25 mL
2	drops liquid rennet	2
1 tsp	pickling (canning) or kosher salt	5 mL

1. Sterilize all equipment (see page 40). In a large stainless-steel pot over medium heat, combine milk and cream. Warm milk mixture to 72°F (22°C), stirring gently to prevent scorching. Remove from heat.

2. Sprinkle culture over surface of milk and let stand for about 5 minutes to rehydrate. Using skimmer and an up-and-down motion, gently draw culture down into milk without breaking surface of milk.

3. Dilute rennet in 2 tbsp (30 mL) cool water. Add to milk and, using the same up-and-down motion, draw rennet down into milk until well blended. Cover and let set at room temperature in a draft-free location for 12 to 16 hours or until a firm curd has formed.

4. Using skimmer, ladle curd into a draining bag or cloth-lined colander and let drain for about 6 hours or until cheese is thick.

5. Remove cheese from bag and place in a bowl. Knead salt into cheese (see Tips, left). Store in the refrigerator.

French Cream Cheese

Makes about 1¾ lbs (800 g)

20% yield

Called fromage à la *crème in France, this unripened cheese is soft and rich.*

Tip: Non-homogenized milk, also known as cream line or standard milk, is always the best choice for successful cheese making. Non-homogenized milk is pasteurized milk that hasn't been homogenized and shouldn't be confused with raw milk. See Sources, page 372, for more information.

- Cloth-lined colander
- 4 small molds, such as St-Marcellin, or 1 square basket mold

3 quarts	whole milk	3 L
1 quart	whipping (35%) cream	1 L
⅛ tsp	mesophilic culture	0.65 mL
2	drops liquid rennet	2
	Pickling (canning) or kosher salt	

1. Sterilize all equipment (see page 40). In a large stainless-steel pot over medium heat, combine milk and cream. Warm milk mixture to 70°F (21°C), stirring gently to prevent scorching. Remove from heat.

2. Sprinkle culture over surface of milk and let stand for about 5 minutes to rehydrate. Using skimmer and an up-and-down motion, gently draw culture down into milk without breaking surface of milk.

3. Dilute rennet in 1 tbsp (15 mL) cool water. Add to milk and, using the same up-and-down motion, draw rennet down into milk until well blended. Cover and let set at room temperature in a draft-free location for 24 hours or until a firm curd forms with whey on the surface of the curd.

4. Tip pot slightly to drain off whey. Using a long-bladed knife, cut curd into vertical strips about 2 inches (5 cm) wide. Let stand for 5 minutes. Whey will collect on the surface. Tip pot again to pour off the collected whey.

5. Using skimmer, ladle curd into a cloth-lined colander and let drain for about 30 minutes. Gather the four corners of the cloth together and tie to create a bag. Hang the bag and let drain over a bowl or the sink for 12 hours or until a fairly firm curd has formed.

Tips: If you are using homogenized cow's milk, it is strongly recommended that you add calcium chloride (see page 31) for best results. The addition of calcium chloride will stabilize the curd, hasten setting and increase yield. Use the same amount of calcium chloride as rennet called for in the recipe, dilute it with at least 10 times the amount of water and stir into the milk before adding the rennet.

Traditionally, this cheese was drained in wicker baskets. If you would like to try this, substitute the molds in Step 7 with one or more wicker baskets that have been washed, rinsed and dried, then lined with cheese cloth. Press the salted curd into the basket and drain as directed.

6. Remove cheese from bag and place in a bowl. It will be quite stiff and a bit lumpy. Knead with a spoon or your hands to create a smooth homogeneous paste, adding more cream, if required. Weigh cheese, then add 1% of the weight in salt.

7. Pack cheese into molds and let drain on a rack for 6 to 7 hours at room temperature or until the cheese has firmed up.

8. Remove from molds and wrap in foil or plastic wrap. Store in the refrigerator for up to 10 days.

To Make a Fresh Cheese Draining Bag

This makes a bag that will drain about 10 quarts (10 L) of fresh cheese.

You will need a 12- by 30-inch (30 by 75 cm) piece of nylon muslin or other light but sturdy cloth that will allow moisture to drain through. Choose a fabric that will withstand frequent washing and bleaching.

Fold the cloth in half, right sides together, to create a 12- by 15-inch (30 by 37.5 cm) rectangle, with the fold at the bottom. Stitch both sides using a ½-inch (1.25 cm) seam allowance. Turn the bag right side out and stitch both sides, ½ inch (1.25 cm) in from each edge to make a sturdy double seam.

Fold over ½ inch (1.25 cm) of fabric around the top, then fold it over again to enclose the raw edge; sew with 2 rows of stitching — one close to the edge, then one more row ¼ inch (0.5 cm) from the first. When you use the bag to drain cheese, all of the seams should be on the outside of the bag.

After removing the drained cheese, immediately rinse the bag well under warm water, then wash with hot water and regular laundry detergent. Rinse twice, adding bleach to the final rinse. Hang or tumble dry. With proper care, your draining bag should last for years.

Easy Cheesecake Pie

Makes 8 servings

This is a perfect dessert to show off your homemade cream cheese without going to a lot of work. It is easy but absolutely delicious.

Variation: Use 1 tsp (5 mL) grated lemon zest and 1 tbsp (15 mL) freshly squeezed lemon juice in place of the vanilla.

- Preheat oven to 350°F (180°C)
- 1 prebaked 9-inch (23 cm) pie crust

1 lb	Cream Cheese (page 45) or Fromage Frais (page 43)	500 g
1 cup	crème fraîche	250 mL
½ cup	granulated sugar	125 mL
1	egg	1
1 tsp	vanilla extract	5 mL
	Fresh or thawed frozen berries	

1. In a bowl, using an electric mixer, mix together cream cheese, crème fraîche, sugar, egg and vanilla until well blended and smooth. Pour into the prepared pie crust and bake in preheated oven for 35 minutes or until set.

2. Let cool for 1 hour on a rack, then chill for 6 hours or until cold. Serve topped with berries.

Greek Island Mizithra

**Makes about
1¼ lbs (600 g)**

20% yield

*Mizithra is a traditional
Greek cheese made in
kitchens around the
country. It is essential to
many authentic Greek
dishes. There are several
variations of this cheese;
choose the one that gives
you the taste you are
looking for.*

Tip: Non-homogenized
milk, also known as
cream line or standard
milk, is always the best
choice for successful
cheese making.
Non-homogenized
milk is pasteurized
milk that hasn't been
homogenized and
shouldn't be confused
with raw milk. See
Sources, page 372,
for more information.

- Cloth-lined colander

3 quarts	whole milk	3 L
1 tbsp	pickling (canning) or kosher salt	15 mL
½ tsp	liquid rennet	2.5 mL

1. Sterilize all equipment (see page 40). In a large
   stainless-steel pot over medium heat, warm milk to
   90°F (32°C), stirring gently to prevent scorching.
   Remove from heat and stir in salt.

2. Dilute rennet in ¼ cup (50 mL) cool water. Add to milk
   and, using an up-and-down motion, draw rennet down
   into milk until well blended. Cover and set aside at
   room temperature for 30 minutes to 1 hour or until
   a firm curd has formed.

3. Using a whisk, gently break up curd, stirring until curd
   pieces are approximately ½ inch (1.25 cm) in size. Let
   stand for 2 to 3 minutes. Using skimmer, stir gently for
   5 minutes.

4. Gently pour curd into a cloth-lined colander and let
   drain for 1 hour. Scrape cheese into center of cloth.
   Gather the four corners of the cloth together and tie
   to create a bag. Hang the bag and let drain over a bowl
   or the sink for another 5 hours at room temperature.
   Place a colander in a bowl; place bag in colander and
   let drain in the refrigerator for another 12 hours. Twist
   the cloth tighter from time to time to aid draining.

5. Remove cheese from cloth and place in a bowl. Store
   in the refrigerator for up to 2 weeks (see Tips, page 45).

Vangelis' Sour Mizithra

<table>
<tr><td colspan="2">Makes about
1¼ lbs (600 g)
20% yield</td></tr>
</table>

While on a trip to the island of Paros in Greece, I visited the local cheese plant, a cooperative of area farmers, and was given a tour by the dairy technician. This is his mizithra recipe.

Tip: Always use the freshest possible milk for your cheeses. If you are purchasing packaged milk, look for the latest best-before date. If using your own milk, plan your cheese making for as soon after milking as possible. The older the milk, the more bacteria there are in it to compete with the lactic bacterial starter.

- Draining bag or cloth-lined colander

3 quarts	whole milk	3 L
¼ tsp	mesophilic culture	1.25 mL
2	drops liquid rennet	2
1 tsp	pickling (canning) or kosher salt, or to taste	5 mL

1. Sterilize all equipment (see page 40). In a large stainless-steel pot over medium heat, warm milk to 90°F (32°C), stirring gently to prevent scorching. Remove from heat.

2. Sprinkle culture over surface of milk and let stand for about 5 minutes to rehydrate. Using skimmer and an up-and-down motion, gently draw culture down into milk without breaking surface of milk. Cover and let ripen at room temperature for 1 hour.

3. Dilute rennet in 2 tbsp (30 mL) cool water. Add to milk and, using the same up-and-down motion, draw rennet down into milk until well blended. Cover and let set at room temperature in a draft-free location for 24 hours.

4. Using skimmer, ladle curd into a draining bag or cloth-lined colander and let drain for 12 hours.

5. Remove cheese from bag and place in a bowl. Blend in salt. Store in the refrigerator for up to 2 weeks (see Tips, page 45).

Shepherd's Mizithra

<table>
<tr><td colspan="3">Makes 1 lb (500 g)
10% yield</td></tr>
</table>

This is the simplest fresh cheese, made for hundreds of years in primitive conditions by the shepherds who tend the flocks in the hills of Greece. For an authentic taste, reserve the whey (see Tip, below) when you make Feta (page 292) and mix it with fresh goat's or sheep's milk.

Tip: When using leftover whey for cheese making, be sure to use it within 3 to 6 hours. The whey is full of lactic bacteria and acidifies further as it sits. If left too long, unhealthy bacteria will begin to grow and make the whey unusable.

Variation: Use sheep's milk in place of the goat's milk. The yield will increase to approximately 25%, and the cheese will be richer due to the higher fat content of the sheep's milk.

- Cloth-lined colander

4 quarts	fresh whey	4 L
2 quarts	goat's milk	2 L
	Juice of 1 lemon	
1 tsp	pickling (canning) or kosher salt	5 mL

1. Sterilize all equipment (see page 40). In a large stainless-steel pot over low heat, combine whey and milk. Warm whey mixture to 90°F (32°C), stirring gently to prevent scorching. Remove from heat.

2. Using skimmer, stir in lemon juice and salt.

3. Cover pot and let ripen at room temperature for 2 or 3 days or until milk is thick and curdled.

4. Pour curd into a cloth-lined colander and let drain at room temperature for 6 hours for a soft cheese. If you want a hard cheese that can be grated over pasta, gather up the corners of the cloth and twist cloth around cheese to make a ball, squeezing out as much moisture as possible. Let drain for up to 48 hours more or until cheese is firm and dry.

5. Remove cheese from cloth and place in a bowl. Store soft cheese in the refrigerator for up to 2 weeks, and hard cheese for up to 1 month.

Alpine Ziger

Makes 5 oz (150 g)

3% yield

This cheese is a favorite
in the Alpine regions
of Switzerland. It is
made from the whey
left after the production
of Emmental or other
Alpine-style cheeses and
has a fresh, sweet taste.

Tip: To increase the
yield, catch the drained
whey in a bowl placed
under the colander and
boil again for a minute
or two. Pour it once
more through the cloth
to collect any leftover
solids.

- Draining bag or cloth-lined colander

½ cup	water	125 mL
	Juice of 1 lemon	
1 to 2 tsp	pickling (canning) or kosher salt, or to taste	5 to 10 mL
4 to 5 quarts	fresh whey (see Tip, left and page 51)	4 to 5 L

1. Sterilize all equipment (see page 40). In a bowl, combine water, lemon juice and salt and set aside.

2. In a large stainless-steel pot over medium heat, bring whey just to the boiling point. Stir in lemon juice mixture. Remove from heat and let stand for 5 minutes. The curds will rise to the top of the pot. Tip the pot slightly to drain off any surface whey.

3. Using a skimmer, ladle solids into a draining bag or cloth-lined colander and let drain for 1 hour for a soft cheese, or for 6 to 7 hours for a firm cheese.

4. Remove cheese from cloth and place in a bowl. Store in the refrigerator for up to 2 weeks (see Tips, page 45).

Traditional Ricotta

**Makes 6 to 8 oz
(175 to 250 g)**

2 to 3% yield

Making ricotta is a great way to use the whey left over from hard cheese making. It is absolutely necessary to process it within a few hours though, so have your equipment ready as you drain your hard cheese curd. Try your fresh ricotta in lasagna for incredibly creamy results.

- Cloth-lined colander

8 quarts	fresh whey	8 L
½ cup	white vinegar	125 mL
	Pickling (canning) or kosher salt	

1. Sterilize all equipment (see page 40). In a large stainless-steel pot over medium heat, warm whey to 195°F (90.5°C), stirring gently to prevent scorching.

2. Just before whey begins to boil, remove from heat and add vinegar. The whey will curdle and any curds will rise to the top of the pot.

3. Using skimmer, ladle solids into a cloth-lined colander. Let drain for 1 hour for a soft cheese, or for 6 to 7 hours for a firm cheese.

4. Blend in salt to taste. Remove cheese from cloth and place in a bowl. Store in the refrigerator for up to 1 week.

Sweet Ricotta

**Makes about
13 oz (400 g)**

10% yield

*Ricotta, which means
"re-cooked" in Italian,
is traditionally made
from the whey left over
from cheese making,
especially sheep's milk
cheese, but this delicious
ricotta is made from
whole cow's milk.*

Tip: Sweet ricotta
is made without salt,
which means it is highly
perishable. Use within a
few hours of production.

Variation: For a richer
cheese, mix in a small
amount of whipping
(35%) cream to the
finished cheese.

- Cloth-lined colander

1 tsp	citric acid powder	5 mL
4 quarts	whole milk	4 L

1. Sterilize all equipment (see page 40). Dissolve citric acid powder in $1/4$ cup (50 mL) cool water.

2. In a large stainless-steel pot, combine milk and citric acid mixture. Warm milk mixture to 190°F (88°C), or almost boiling, stirring gently to prevent scorching.

3. When mixture begins to curdle, remove from heat. Let stand for 10 minutes or until the curds rise to the top. Using skimmer, ladle curds carefully into a cloth-lined colander. Let drain until desired consistency is reached, about 1 hour for a soft cheese. Use immediately.

Chèvre

Makes 2 lbs (1 kg)

25% yield

Chèvre is the common name for fresh spreadable goat cheese. It is just as versatile as any other spreadable cheese and can be blended with herbs, spices or fruit for variety.

Tip: Fresh cheeses are highly perishable. Store them in the coldest part of the refrigerator for up to 2 weeks.

- Draining bag or cloth-lined colander

4 quarts	goat's milk	4 L
1/4 tsp	mesophilic culture	1.25 mL
1	drop liquid rennet	1
	Pickling (canning) or kosher salt	

1. Sterilize all equipment (see page 40). In a large stainless-steel pot over medium heat, warm milk to 77°F (25°C), stirring gently to prevent scorching. Remove from heat.

2. Sprinkle culture over surface of milk and let stand for about 5 minutes to rehydrate. Using skimmer and an up-and-down motion, gently draw culture down into milk without breaking surface of milk.

3. Dilute rennet in 1 tbsp (15 mL) cool water. Add to milk and, using the same up-and-down motion, draw rennet down into milk until well blended. Cover and let set at room temperature in a draft-free location for 24 hours.

4. Tip pot slightly to drain off collected whey. Using skimmer, ladle curd into a draining bag or cloth-lined colander. Let drain for 6 to 7 hours or until desired thickness is reached. Keep in mind that the cheese will firm up further once refrigerated.

5. Remove cheese from bag and place in a bowl. Weigh cheese, then add 1% of the weight in salt. Store in the refrigerator for up to 2 weeks (see Tip, left).

Traditional Provençal Chèvre

Makes 5 cheeses,
each 4 oz (125 g),
or 6 cheeses, each
3½ oz (100 g)
15% yield

These cheeses are eaten while still fresh and creamy and are often accompanied by a sprig of fresh savory — a very good reason to have this herb in your garden.

- Cloth-lined colander
- Draining container
- Cheese matting
- 5 or 6 St-Marcellin molds
- Ripening container

4 quarts	goat's milk	4 L
⅛ tsp	liquid rennet	0.65 mL
	Pickling (canning) or kosher salt	
	Sprigs of fresh savory	

1. Sterilize all equipment (see page 40). In a large stainless-steel pot over low heat, warm milk to 95°F (35°C), stirring gently to prevent scorching. Remove from heat.

2. Dilute rennet in ¼ cup (50 mL) cool water. Add to milk and, using skimmer and an up-and-down motion, gently draw rennet down into milk without breaking surface of milk until well blended. Cover and let set at room temperature for 8 to 9 hours or until a firm curd has formed.

3. Using a long-bladed knife and skimmer, cut curd into vertical strips about ¾ inch (2 cm) wide. Using skimmer, cut through curd horizontally until you have cut it all into ¾-inch (2 cm) cubes. Stir gently for 5 minutes. Let stand for 10 minutes.

4. Ladle curd into a cloth-lined colander and let drain for 45 minutes.

5. Prepare a draining container by placing a rack inside. Then place a cutting board on top, followed by a cheese mat, then the molds. Using skimmer, fill molds with curd. Cover container and let drain for 3 hours at room temperature. Flip cheeses over in the molds and let drain at room temperature for another 10 hours. Keep container covered to maintain warmth around the cheeses.

Tip: Remember, any time you use raw milk, you must be very sure of your source. It is recommended that you use raw milk only for cheeses that are to be aged for at least 60 days. Aging them for less than 60 days doesn't allow enough time for the good lactic bacteria in the milk to destroy any pathogens present in the milk. When using raw milk, remember that the milk from the morning milking will set more quickly than that from the evening milking, as it contains more solids.

6. Unmold cheeses onto a clean cheese mat and replace on the rack in the draining container. Sprinkle top of each cheese with 1/4 tsp (1.25 mL) salt. Cover container and let drain at room temperature for 6 hours. Turn cheeses and salt the other side. Cover container and let drain at room temperature for another 6 hours.

7. Transfer cheeses to a clean cheese mat (traditionally a straw mat) in a ripening container. Let dry for 4 or 5 days at cool room temperature. Remove any collected whey from the container and flip the cheeses daily.

8. Place a sprig of fresh savory on the cheeses and consume immediately.

Why is goat's milk white and cow's milk yellow?

Beta-carotene, a fat-soluble pigment found in grass and hay, is deposited in the fat of cow's milk, giving it a creamy yellow color. Goats and sheep convert beta-carotene into pure vitamin A, which is colorless, so the milk from these animals is white.

Chèvre Cheesecake

People who do not eat cow's milk products are often faced with a limited selection of baking and desserts. Now you can make this New York–style cheesecake from your homemade chèvre. The fresh lemon is brilliant with the goat's milk cheese.

- Preheat oven to 325°F (160°C)
- 6-inch (15 cm) cheesecake pan with removable bottom, or springform pan, lined with parchment paper

Crust

¼ cup	graham wafer crumbs	50 mL
¼ cup	ground hazelnuts	50 mL
2 tbsp	butter, melted	30 mL

Filling

1½ lbs	Chèvre (page 55)	750 g
1 cup	granulated sugar	250 mL
1 tbsp	cornstarch	15 mL
3	eggs	3
	Grated zest and juice of 1 lemon	
	Fresh berry coulis or chocolate sauce, optional	

1. *Crust:* In a bowl, combine graham wafer crumbs, hazelnuts and butter to form a crumbly mass. Press mixture into bottom of prepared cheesecake pan. Set aside.

2. *Filling:* In a bowl, using a spoon or electric mixer on low, beat chèvre for 1 minute to soften. Add sugar and cornstarch and beat just until blended. Do not overbeat the cheese at any stage or it will become greasy. Add eggs, one at a time, beating well after each addition, scraping down the side of the bowl often. Blend in lemon zest and juice.

3. Pour cheese mixture over crust. Bake in preheated oven for 1½ hours or until slightly puffed around the edge but still moist in the center. Let cool in pan on a wire rack. Cover and refrigerate for several hours or overnight until well chilled.

4. Unmold cheesecake, remove parchment and serve with fresh berry coulis or chocolate sauce, if desired.

Chèvre Panna Cotta

Makes 12 servings

For a small taste of heaven, try this gorgeous variation on the traditional Italian dessert panna cotta, which means "cooked cream." Serve it with fresh berries or a sauce of your choice.

- 12 ramekins or custard cups

1	package (¼ oz/7 g) unflavored gelatin powder	1
1 cup	milk	250 mL
½ cup	granulated sugar	125 mL
1	vanilla bean	1
3 cups	whipping (35%) cream	750 mL
1 cup	Chèvre (page 55), at room temperature	250 mL

1. In a small bowl, sprinkle gelatin over ¼ cup (50 mL) water. Set aside to soften for 5 minutes.

2. In a large saucepan, combine milk and sugar. Slit vanilla bean lengthwise. Using a small pointed knife, scrape out the seeds and add to milk. (Discard pod or use to flavor sugar or custard, or infuse in vodka to create your own vanilla extract.)

3. Heat milk mixture over medium heat until simmering. Stir in the softened gelatin. Remove from heat and whisk until the gelatin is completely dissolved.

4. In a bowl, using an electric mixer, beat cream and chèvre until very smooth. Pour in the warm milk mixture and whisk until the mixture is thoroughly blended.

5. Pour into ramekins and chill for 6 to 7 hours or until set, or overnight.

6. To serve, dip cups into warm water and unmold panna cotta onto plates.

Brousse

Makes 4 cheeses,
each 1²/₃ oz (50 g)

20% yield

This rare cheese is made by a few farmers in the South of France using fresh milk from a local rustic breed of goat. The goats of Rove are not a milking breed but rather a meat-producing one, so their milk has a higher solids content than that of milk goats. Traditionally, the fresh Brousse was placed into a horn-shaped mold and drained for a few hours. The farmers would take baskets filled with these little cones of cheese into the nearby city of Marseille and sell them on the streets. Nowadays, finger-shaped plastic molds are available from some cheese-making supply houses. The cheese has a fresh, slightly acidic taste and should be eaten right away.

Serving suggestion:
To eat, unmold onto a plate. Enjoy it plain, sprinkle with herbs or drizzle with honey.

- Cloth-lined colander
- 4 Brousse molds

1 quart	goat's milk	1 L
¼ cup	white vinegar	50 mL

1. Sterilize all equipment (see page 40). In a stainless-steel pot over medium heat, bring milk just to the boiling point, stirring gently to prevent scorching. Remove from heat.

2. Dilute vinegar in ¾ cup (175 mL) cool water and add to milk, stirring quickly with skimmer. Continue to stir milk vigorously with skimmer or a whisk until it curdles and small flakes of cheese rise to the top of the pot.

3. Using skimmer, ladle curds into a cloth-lined colander. Let drain over a bowl for 2 to 3 minutes. Using your hands or a spoon, fill Brousse molds, packing curd down. Pour remaining milk through a cloth to strain out any remaining solids and add these to the molds. Tap molds slightly to ensure they are completely filled to the bottom.

4. Place molds in a basket or bowl so they stand upright. Let drain for about 6 hours. Place in the refrigerator and unmold cheeses as you use them. Brousse must be eaten fresh, preferably the day it is made or within 24 hours.

Savory Brousse Omelet

Makes 1 serving

This is a nice way to enjoy your fresh Brousse.

3	eggs	3
	Salt and pepper	
3 or 4	fresh mint leaves, chopped	3 or 4
1	portion (mold) Brousse (page 60)	1
	Butter or oil for frying	

1. In a bowl, beat eggs lightly. Add salt and pepper to taste.

2. In another bowl, combine mint leaves and Brousse.

3. In a skillet over medium heat, melt butter. Add egg mixture and cook just until set.

4. Spoon Brousse mixture into center and fold half of omelet over cheese. Slide from pan onto plate.

Sheep's Milk Brousse

Makes 6 cheeses,
each 2¾ oz (83 g),
or 8 cheeses,
each 2 oz (60 g)
25% yield

This recipe is different than the goat's milk Brousse on page 60: the milk is coagulated and ladled rather than acidified. Because it is not ripened with lactic bacteria, salted or dried, it must be kept cold and eaten fresh. Try it sweetened with jam or preserves, or drizzle a little liqueur over top for a quick dairy treat.

- Draining container
- 6 to 8 Crottin or St-Marcellin molds

| 2 quarts | sheep's milk | 2 L |
| ⅛ tsp | liquid rennet | 0.65 mL |

1. Sterilize all equipment (see page 40). In a large stainless-steel pot over medium heat, warm milk to 175°F (79°C), stirring gently to prevent scorching. Reduce heat to lowest setting and let stand for 2 to 3 minutes. Immerse the pot in a sinkful of ice water and let milk cool to 100°F (38°C), stirring constantly.

2. Dilute rennet in 2 tbsp (30 mL) cool water. Add to milk and, using skimmer and an up-and-down motion, gently draw rennet down into milk without breaking surface of milk until well blended. Cover and let set for 15 minutes or until a soft curd has formed.

3. Using skimmer, carefully ladle slivers of curd into the molds, giving each one time to drain down before adding the next sliver of curd. Finish with a nice slice of curd, mounding it above the top of the mold so that it will make a flat surface when finished draining.

4. Place the molds in a draining container. Cover container and refrigerate for about 12 hours or until cheeses are firm enough to maintain their shape when removed from the molds.

5. Unmold the cheeses just before using and consume immediately. Store cheeses in molds in the refrigerator and use within 2 days of production.

Cottage Cheese

<table>
<tr><td colspan="2">Makes about
2 cups (500 mL)
12% yield</td></tr>
</table>

A simple old-fashioned favorite, cottage cheese was made in many variations in households around the world. You can leave it as a dry-curd cheese or add cream for a richer, creamier version.

Tip: To keep cottage cheese fresher longer, simply turn the sealed container over and store upside down.

Variation: For creamed cottage cheese, add ½ cup (125 mL) whipping (35%) cream to the curds after salting.

• Draining bag or cloth-lined colander

4 quarts	whole or partly skimmed (1 or 2%) milk	4 L
¼ tsp	mesophilic culture	1.25 mL
¼ tsp	calcium chloride	1.25 mL
¼ tsp	liquid rennet	1.25 mL
	Pickling (canning) or kosher salt	

1. Sterilize all equipment (see page 40). In a large stainless-steel pot over medium heat, warm milk to 70°F (21°C), stirring gently to prevent scorching. Remove from heat.

2. Sprinkle culture over surface of milk and let stand for about 5 minutes to rehydrate. Using skimmer and an up-and-down motion, gently draw culture down into milk without breaking surface of milk.

3. Dilute calcium chloride in ¼ cup (50 mL) cool water. Add to milk using the same up-and-down motion.

4. Dilute rennet in ¼ cup (50 mL) cool water. Add to milk and, using the same up-and-down motion, draw rennet down into milk until well blended. Cover and let set at room temperature in a draft-free location for 2 hours or until a firm curd has formed.

5. Using a long-bladed knife, cut curd into vertical strips about ½ inch (1.25 cm) wide. Using skimmer, cut through curd horizontally until you have cut it all into ½-inch (1.25 cm) cubes. Let stand for 5 minutes. Stir curd for 2 to 3 minutes.

6. Warm curd over low heat to 115°F (46°C) over 1 hour, stirring gently the whole time. Do not raise the temperature too quickly; it should increase by only 2°F (1°C) every 3 or 4 minutes, so you may need to adjust the heat periodically.

7. Once you have reached the final temperature, the curds should be the size of navy beans, and firm but not hard. Using skimmer, ladle curds into a draining bag or cloth-lined colander. Rinse with cold tap water until all traces of whey are removed. Place curds in a bowl and add salt to taste. Store in the refrigerator for up to 1 week.

English Farmhouse Cheese

> **Makes 2 cheeses, each 1½ lbs (750 g), or 4 cheeses, each 12 oz (375 g)**
> ___
> *15% yield*

Also known as English-style Coulommiers, this cheese is made in a similar fashion to French Coulommiers but is not mold-ripened. A simple cheese to make, it conjures up images of old-fashioned farmhouse kitchens. It is very versatile: try a slice with a muffin for breakfast, or drizzle with olive oil and sprinkle with herbs and a few capers for an easy gourmet appetizer.

- Two 8-inch (20 cm) half-Brie molds or four 4-inch (10 cm) Camembert molds
- Cheese matting
- Draining container

10 quarts	whole or partly skimmed (1 or 2%) milk	10 L
¼ tsp	mesophilic culture	1.25 mL
¼ tsp	calcium chloride	1.25 mL
¼ tsp	liquid rennet	1.25 mL
4 tsp	pickling (canning) or kosher salt	20 mL

1. Sterilize all equipment (see page 40). In a large stainless-steel pot set in a hot water bath, warm milk over medium heat to 90°F (32°C), stirring gently. Sprinkle culture over surface of milk and let stand for about 5 minutes to rehydrate. Using skimmer and an up-and-down motion, gently draw culture down into milk without breaking surface of milk.

2. Dilute calcium chloride in ¼ cup (50 mL) cool water. Add to milk using the same up-and-down motion.

3. Dilute rennet in ¼ cup (50 mL) cool water. Add to milk and, using the same up-and-down motion, draw rennet down into milk until well blended. Cover and let set for 1¼ hours, maintaining the temperature at 90°F (32°C).

4. Check for a clean break (see Tips, right). If necessary, let set for another 15 minutes.

5. Prepare a draining container by placing a rack inside. Then place a cutting board on top, followed by a cheese mat, then the molds. Using skimmer, ladle thin slices of curd into molds. Refill several times until all curd is used, always layering thin slices of curd into the molds. You may have to wait for the curd to drain down before continuing to fill.

Tips: To ascertain whether the curd is ready for cutting, check for what's called a "clean break." Insert the long flat blade of a cheese knife into the curd at a 30-degree angle and slowly lift the blade toward the surface of the curd. If the curd splits into a long clean break or crack, it is ready to cut. If the break is wobbly or uneven, let the curd set for a few more minutes before trying again.

If you are using homogenized cow's milk, it is strongly recommended that you add calcium chloride (see page 31) for best results. The addition of calcium chloride will stabilize the curd, hasten setting and increase yield. Use the same amount of calcium chloride as rennet called for in the recipe, dilute it with at least 10 times the amount of water and stir into the milk before adding the rennet.

6. Cover draining container and let cheese drain at room temperature for 12 hours or overnight. The next morning, flip the cheeses over in the molds and let drain for another 12 hours. If the cheese sticks to the mats, use a sharp knife to slice carefully underneath and loosen. Cheeses should be fairly firm when fully drained and slightly higher around the edges. Sprinkle 1 tsp (5 mL) salt over each side of the larger cheeses or 1/2 tsp (2 mL) over each side of the smaller cheeses. Place on clean cheese mats in a clean container and refrigerate for 6 to 7 hours or until cold. Wipe up any collected whey in the bottom of the container with a paper towel. Wrap cheeses individually and store in the refrigerator for up to 10 days.

Fresh Goat Cheeses

	Makes 6 cheeses, each 5 oz (150 g)
	25% yield

These are delightfully fresh and tasty. Try the flavored variations at the end of the recipe, or use your imagination to create new ones.

Tips: The yield percentage is the amount of solids in the form of cheese that you can expect to have from the milk. For this recipe, 4 quarts (4 L) of milk weighs 8 lbs (4 kg), so a 25% yield would be 2 lbs (1 kg).

Don't worry if your fresh goat cheeses become a little misshapen once they have been removed from the molds; simply reshape gently by hand and return to the refrigerator.

- Draining container
- 6 goat cheese molds

4 quarts	goat's milk	4 L
¼ tsp	mesophilic culture	1.25 mL
1	drop liquid rennet	1
1½ tsp	pickling (canning) or kosher salt	7 mL

1. Sterilize all equipment (see page 40). In a large stainless-steel pot over medium heat, warm milk to 77°F (25°C), stirring gently to prevent scorching. Remove from heat.

2. Sprinkle culture over surface of milk and let stand for about 5 minutes to rehydrate. Using skimmer and an up-and-down motion, gently draw culture down into milk without breaking surface of milk.

3. Dilute rennet in 1 tbsp (15 mL) cool water. Add to milk and, using the same up-and-down motion, draw rennet down into milk until well blended. Cover and let set at room temperature in a draft-free location for 24 hours.

4. Prepare a draining container and molds (see page 36).

5. Tip pot slightly to drain off any surface whey. Carefully dip each mold into the curd, filling it as full as possible. Let drain for 30 minutes. Using a slotted spoon or skimmer, refill molds. Continue to drain and refill molds until all the curd is used up.

6. Set molds in draining container. Cover container and let drain at room temperature for 24 hours. If you have used straight-sided molds, you can flip them at this time. If not, let them drain for another 24 hours.

7. Sprinkle ¼ tsp (1.25 mL) salt over each cheese, dividing it evenly between both sides. If you have used molds that cannot be flipped, just salt the exposed end. Refrigerate for 24 hours to firm up. Unmold the cheese (see Tips, left). Wrap and store in the refrigerator for up to 10 days.

Serving suggestion:
Pizza doesn't always need mozzarella. Try this delicious version with your fresh goat cheese: Spread a 12-inch (30 cm) prebaked pizza crust with ¼ cup (50 mL) tomato sauce. Slice 2 fresh goat cheeses into rounds and distribute over the sauce. Sprinkle 1 tbsp (15 mL) drained capers then ¼ cup (50 mL) roughly chopped fresh basil leaves over the surface. Drizzle with 3 tbsp (45 mL) olive oil and season with freshly ground pepper. Bake in preheated 400°F (200°C) oven for 10 minutes or until the edges are browned and the cheese is slightly toasted.

Variations: These cheeses are highly versatile. Try a dressing of different herbs and condiments to complement them. Some examples:

Rosemary and Olive Oil: Infuse a fresh sprig of rosemary in olive oil for 1 to 2 hours at room temperature. Chop some fresh rosemary and roll the sides of the cheese in the herb. Top with fresh sprig and drizzle with olive oil.

Rose Petal and Hazelnut: Wash and chop fresh scented rose petals. Mix with roasted chopped hazelnuts. Press top of cheese into rose-petal mixture and top with a whole rose petal. Use only pesticide-free rose petals from a reliable source.

Lavender and Honey: Warm some liquid honey and add 1 or 2 sprigs of lavender. Allow to infuse for 2 hours at room temperature. Drizzle goat cheese with lavender-scented honey and top with a fresh sprig of lavender. Be sure to use pesticide-free, food-grade lavender.

Garden Herbs: Chop equal amounts of fresh parsley and chives. Press top of cheese into the mixture. Add a chive blossom for color.

Maple Walnut: Boil some walnut halves in pure maple syrup until syrup is reduced and nuts are caramelized. Let cool. Drizzle goat cheeses with fresh maple syrup and top with caramelized walnuts.

Mascarpone

<table>
<tr><td>

**Makes 2 cups
(500 mL)**

50% yield

</td></tr>
</table>

Mascarpone is a thick
sweet cream "cheese"
made by acidifying
cream and draining it
until thick — decadent
and delicious! Try it in
tiramisu or mound in
a bowl and serve with
fresh seasonal berries.
It's a dream.

Tip: Traditionally,
mascarpone is kept in
a square of muslin in a
small pot or jar, which
allows any residual
whey to drain away
from the cheese.

- Double boiler
- Draining bag or cloth-lined colander

| 4 cups | whipping (35%) cream | 1 L |
| ¼ tsp | tartaric acid | 1.25 mL |

1. Sterilize all equipment (see page 40). Place cream in inner pan of a double boiler. Add cold water to outer pan. Place double boiler over medium heat and warm cream to 195°F (90.5°C), stirring gently with a stainless-steel spoon.

2. When cream reaches temperature, remove entire double boiler from heat. Add tartaric acid to milk, stirring well for about 30 seconds.

3. Remove inner pan from outer pan and stir cream for 2 to 3 minutes more or until cream is thick and curdled.

4. Pour into a draining bag or cloth-lined colander set over a large bowl. Cover and let stand in a cool place or in the refrigerator for 12 hours or until desired thickness is reached.

5. Spoon into a container or place in a bowl. Cover and store in the refrigerator for up to 3 days.

Coeur à la Crème

Makes 4 servings

A special ceramic heart-shaped mold is used to make this dessert. You can buy small individual-size molds or one large one to serve several people. Line the molds with a piece of moistened cheese cloth.

- 4 coeur à la crème molds, lined with enough cheese cloth to leave a 2-inch (5 cm) overhang

1 cup	Cream Cheese (page 45) or Mascarpone (page 68)	250 mL
1	piece (1 inch/2.5 cm long) vanilla bean, split	1
1 cup	whipping (35%) cream	250 mL
¼ cup	confectioner's (icing) sugar	50 mL
	Fresh seasonal berries	

1. In a bowl, using an electric mixer, beat cream cheese until light. Scrape the seeds from vanilla bean into cream cheese and beat again to blend evenly. Set aside.

2. In another bowl, whip cream with sugar until soft peaks form.

3. Fold into cheese. Spread in coeur à la crème molds. Fold the cheese cloth overhang over the top of the filling.

4. Place molds on a plate or in a baking dish to catch any drips. Refrigerate overnight.

5. To serve, turn out onto a serving dish and remove cheese cloth. Garnish with berries.

Cow's Milk Faisselle

Makes 6 cheeses, each 3 to 4 oz (90 to 125 g)

54 to 75% yield

A fresh unripened cheese, faisselle is actually the name of the strainer used to drain it. In French markets, the cheese comes in its own little strainer, which is lifted out of an outer container and placed in a plastic bag to carry home. The outer container holds the whey around the cheese and keeps it moist and fresh until you're ready to use it. It's so easy to make that you'll want to have it in the house all the time for a quick, healthy breakfast.

Tip: Once you have made a batch of faisselle, you can save 1 to 2 tbsp (15 to 30 mL) to inoculate your next batch instead of using the mesophilic culture (as you would when making yogurt). After three or four inoculations, you will need to use fresh mesophilic culture again, as the strength of the curd will diminish with time.

- 6 goat cheese molds
- Flat-bottomed baking dish

1 quart	whole or partly skimmed (2%) cow's milk	1 L
Pinch	mesophilic culture	Pinch
3	drops liquid rennet	3

1. Sterilize all equipment (see page 40). In a large stainless-steel pot over medium heat, warm milk to 86°F (30°C), stirring gently to prevent scorching. Remove from heat.

2. Sprinkle culture over surface of milk and let stand for about 5 minutes to rehydrate. Using skimmer and an up-and-down motion, gently draw culture down into milk without breaking surface of milk.

3. Dilute rennet in 1 tbsp (15 mL) cool water. Add to milk and, using the same up-and-down motion, draw rennet down into milk until well blended. Cover and let set at room temperature in a draft-free location for 12 hours.

4. Place molds in a flat-bottomed baking dish. Using skimmer, gently ladle curd into molds, taking care not to break up the curd. The whey will begin draining out of the holes in the molds right away and will collect in the dish.

5. As soon as the curd has drained down below the tops of the molds, cover the dish and place in the refrigerator. The faisselle is ready to use as soon as it has drained to your desired texture. The longer it drains, the firmer it will become (because the molds are sitting in the whey, it will stay fairly moist). Store in the refrigerator for up to 4 days. To serve, unmold onto a plate.

Goat's Milk Faisselle

**Makes 6 cheeses,
each 3 to 4 oz
(90 to 125 g)**
54 to 75% yield

The fresh taste of goat's
milk makes a perfect
faisselle. It's a tangier
alternative to the cow's
milk version (page 70).

Serving suggestion:
Serve faisselle as a
dessert with a fruit
compote, or drizzle with
honey and sprinkle with
chopped pistachios. Try
it as a salad accompanied
with fresh ripe tomatoes,
capers, herbs and a bit
of olive oil.

- 6 goat cheese molds
- Flat-bottomed baking dish

1 quart	goat's milk	1 L
Pinch	mesophilic culture	Pinch
2	drops liquid rennet	2

1. Sterilize all equipment (see page 40). In a large stainless-steel pot over medium heat, warm milk to 86°F (30°C), stirring gently to prevent scorching. Remove from heat.

2. Sprinkle culture over surface of milk and let stand for about 5 minutes to rehydrate. Using skimmer and an up-and-down motion, gently draw culture down into milk without breaking surface of milk.

3. Dilute rennet in 1 tbsp (15 mL) cool water. Add to milk and, using the same up-and-down motion, draw rennet down into milk until well blended. Cover and let set at room temperature in a draft-free location for 12 hours.

4. Place molds in a flat-bottomed baking dish. Using skimmer, gently ladle curd into molds, taking care not to break up the curd. The whey will begin draining out of the holes in the molds right away and will collect in the dish.

5. As soon as the curd has drained down below the tops of the molds, cover the dish and place in the refrigerator. The faisselle is ready to use as soon as it has drained to your desired texture. The longer it drains, the firmer it will become (because the molds are sitting in the whey, it will stay fairly moist). Store in the refrigerator for up to 4 days. To serve, unmold onto a plate.

Troubleshooting

Curd is very firm.
Too much rennet was added; reduce rennet. Or the cheese is too acidic; ripen for less time or add less culture.

Curd is too soft.
Not enough rennet was added; add a drop more rennet. Or curd is not acidic enough; ripen longer or add a bit more culture.

Milk did not coagulate at all.
Milk is of low quality; be sure there are no antibiotics in the milk and that the cows it came from do not suffer from mastitis. Or the lactic bacteria were inactive; keep dry cultures frozen until use. Cultures can remain viable for up to 18 months after the expiry date; if using one that's past its best-before date, double the amount.

Fresh-curd cheese is gritty.
Milk was overheated; use a thermometer and stir gently when heating.

Cheese begins to smell fermented after a few days.
Not enough salt or inadequate refrigeration; increase salt and keep cold.

Stretched-Curd (Pasta Filata) Cheeses

Stretched-curd cheese, also known as plastic curd cheese, undergoes a special phase during production. Once the curd is made and shaped, it is heated in very hot water, whey or brine and stretched by hand into long strands. This action textures the cheese and is responsible for its soft but chewy consistency when melted. Famous as *the* cheeses for pizza, fresh pasta filata cheeses are a delight in salads and appetizers, and bear almost no resemblance to the rubbery packaged equivalent in supermarkets. To make these cheeses, you will need extra equipment: a pair of heat-resistant rubber gloves, a bowl or pot of ice water and, in some cases, a long-handled wooden spoon.

Mozzarella

<table>
<tr><td>Makes 1 lb (500 g)
10 to 12% yield</td></tr>
</table>

Mozzarella is, without a doubt, the best-known cheese of the pasta filata family. It is great fun to make your own pizza with fresh homemade mozzarella.

Mozzarella is a popular and simple fresh cheese but can be tricky to make. As well as using non-homogenized milk, be sure to watch the times carefully and begin testing the curd for "stretchability" after about 2 hours during the holding period in Step 7.

Tip: Non-homogenized milk, also known as cream line or standard milk, is always the best choice for successful cheese making. Non-homogenized milk is pasteurized milk that hasn't been homogenized and shouldn't be confused with raw milk. See Sources, page 372, for more information.

- Cloth-lined colander
- Heat-resistant rubber gloves

4 quarts	non-homogenized whole milk (see Sources, page 372)	4 L
1/4 tsp	thermophilic culture	1.25 mL
1/4 tsp	calcium chloride	1.25 mL
1/4 tsp	liquid rennet	1.25 mL
	Bowl of ice water	
	Cool 18% saturated brine (see Tip, page 83)	

1. Sterilize all equipment (see page 40). In a large stainless-steel pot set in a hot water bath over low heat, warm milk to 90°F (32°C), stirring gently. Turn off heat.

2. Sprinkle culture over surface of milk and let stand for about 5 minutes to rehydrate. Using skimmer and an up-and-down motion, gently draw culture down into milk without breaking surface of milk. Cover and let ripen for 45 minutes.

3. Dilute calcium chloride in 1/4 cup (50 mL) cool water. Add to milk using the same up-and-down motion.

4. Dilute rennet in 1/4 cup (50 mL) cool water. Add to milk and, using the same up-and-down motion, draw rennet down into milk until well blended. Cover and let set for about 1 hour. Check for a clean break (see Tips, opposite). If the curd is still too fragile, cover and let set for another 15 minutes or until a clean break is achieved.

5. Using a long-bladed knife and skimmer, cut curd into 1/2-inch (1.25 cm) cubes (see Tips, opposite). Let stand for 5 minutes to firm up the curds.

6. Return heat to low and slowly warm curds to 102°F (39°C), stirring gently and continuously, adjusting the heat as necessary to make sure it takes 30 minutes to do so, stirring gently the whole time. Do not heat too quickly. Turn off heat and stir gently for 15 minutes to prevent curds from matting. Let settle.

Tips: To ascertain whether the curd is ready for cutting, check for what's called a "clean break." Insert the long flat blade of a cheese knife into the curd at a 30-degree angle and slowly lift the blade toward the surface of the curd. If the curd splits into a long clean break or crack, it is ready to cut. If the break is wobbly or uneven, let the curd set for a few more minutes before trying again.

To cut curds: Holding a long-bladed stainless-steel knife straight up and down, draw knife through the curd, cutting it into strips. Proceed across the pot until you have reached the other side. Turn the pot and cut across the first strips to create squares. Using a skimmer, cut horizontally from side to side just under the surface of the curd to create cubes. Gradually move skimmer down through curd to cut layers of cubes. Using skimmer, gently stir curd cubes. Using a knife, cut any pieces that have been missed or are too large. For small-cut curds, you can use a large whisk for cutting.

7. Drain off whey through a cloth-lined colander and return curds to the empty cheese pot. Place pot in a hot water bath at 102°F (39°C) and cover. Hold temperature for 3 hours, testing for readiness after 2 hours (see Tip, page 76). Adjust heat under the pot as necessary to maintain temperature, turning the curd slab over a few times, and draining off any collected whey. This will knit the curd together and acidify it.

8. Remove curd from pot. Place on a cutting board and, with a knife, cut into 1-inch (2.5 cm) cubes. Place cubes in a large stainless-steel bowl.

9. Meanwhile, clean the cheese pot. Add 4 quarts (4 L) fresh water to the pot. Heat to 168°F (76°C) and pour over the cubes in the bowl.

10. Wearing heat-resistant rubber gloves, work pieces of curds into one large ball, kneading and shaping it under the water. Once it has formed a firm ball, lift it from the water and pull and stretch it into a long rope (see Tip, page 76). Loop rope back on itself, then pull it out again. Repeat pulling and looping until the curd is shiny and smooth. You must work quickly or the curd will cool and become brittle. If necessary, dip the curd under the hot water again to warm it.

11. Shape the cheese into a ball, tucking the edges under. You can also work the rope into a braid or twist. Once formed into the desired shape, place in a bowl of ice water to chill and firm up.

12. Place the chilled cheese in brine solution for 2 to 3 hours, turning over a few times as it soaks. Remove from brine and use immediately, or store in a covered container in the refrigerator for up to 1 week. Fresh mozzarella can be kept longer if enough brine is placed in the container with the cheese to almost cover it.

Mozzarella II

Makes
1¼ lbs (600 g)
10% yield

This mozzarella is acidified by citric acid rather than lactic bacteria, which is used in the Mozzarella recipe (page 74).

Tip: One of the most important steps in making stretched-curd cheeses is determining the right moment to do the stretching. The acidity of the curd must be just right. To test whether your pasta filata cheese is ready for stretching, pinch off a small piece of curd and immerse it in a bowl of 175°F (79°C) water. Work the ball of cheese with your fingertips to soften, then try to stretch it into a long strand. If it breaks or will not stretch, it is not yet ready. Wait for a while longer before trying again.

- Cloth-lined colander
- Heat-resistant rubber gloves

1½ tsp	citric acid powder	7.5 mL
6 quarts	non-homogenized whole milk (see Sources, page 372)	6 L
¼ tsp	calcium chloride	1.25 mL
¼ tsp	liquid rennet	1.25 mL
6 tbsp	pickling (canning) or kosher salt	90 mL
	Bowl of ice water	

1. Sterilize all equipment (see page 40). In a small glass bowl or measuring cup, dissolve citric acid powder in ¼ cup (50 mL) lukewarm water, stirring with a stainless-steel spoon.

2. In a large stainless-steel pot, combine milk and dissolved citric acid, stirring to blend well with an up-and-down motion.

3. Place pot over medium heat and warm milk mixture to 88°F (31°C), stirring gently to prevent scorching. Remove from heat.

4. Dilute calcium chloride in ¼ cup (50 mL) cool water. Add to milk using the same up-and-down motion.

5. Dilute rennet in ¼ cup (50 mL) cool water. Add to milk and, using the same up-and-down motion, draw rennet down into milk until well blended. Cover and let set for 30 minutes. Check for a clean break (see Tip, page 75). If the curd is still too fragile, cover and let set for another 15 minutes or until a clean break is achieved.

6. Using a long-bladed knife and skimmer, cut curd into ½-inch (1.25 cm) cubes (see Tip, page 75). Let stand for 5 minutes to firm up the curds.

7. Place pot over low heat and slowly warm curds to 106°F (41°C), stirring gently and continuously, adjusting the heat as necessary to make sure it takes 20 minutes to do so. Turn off heat and continue to stir for 20 more minutes. Let stand for 5 minutes.

Tip: The yield percentage is the amount of solids in the form of cheese that you can expect to have from the milk. One quart (1 L) of milk weighs 2 lbs (1 kg), so a 10% yield would be 3.2 oz (100 g).

8. Meanwhile, in another pot, bring 4 quarts (4 L) fresh water to a boil. Add salt and stir until dissolved. Turn off heat.

9. Drain off whey through a cloth-lined colander. Let drain for 15 minutes.

10. Place curd mass on a clean cutting board and cut into 1-inch (2.5 cm) strips. Place in a large bowl. Pour salt water over strips.

11. Wearing heat-resistant rubber gloves or using a long-handled wooden spoon, work strips under the hot water (the cheese will become very soft), pushing and pulling and stretching them (see Tip, page 76). The curd will begin to stretch. Pull cheese out into a long rope, folding it back on itself and stretching again until it is smooth and shiny. Use your hands to shape the cheese into a single ball or pinch off pieces for small bocconcini-size cheeses.

12. Place cheese in a bowl of ice water for 5 minutes. Remove and drain on paper towel. Use immediately or wrap and refrigerate.

Mozzarella di Bufala

<table>
<tr><td colspan="3">Makes about
2¾ lbs (1.4 kg)
about 18% yield</td></tr>
</table>

Originally, mozzarella was made with the milk from water buffaloes, whose introduction to Italy is still shrouded in mystery. If you can get water buffalo milk, you can make mozzarella that is like no other. The milk is so much richer than cow's milk, giving this mozzarella a uniquely creamy texture and taste. Traditionally, the milk is ripened by adding whey from the previous day's cheese making.

- Cloth-lined colander
- Heat-resistant rubber gloves

8 quarts	water buffalo milk	8 L
⅛ tsp	mesophilic culture	0.65 mL
⅛ tsp	thermophilic culture	0.65 mL
½ tsp	calcium chloride	2.5 mL
½ tsp	liquid rennet	2.5 mL
	Bowl of ice water	
	Cool 18% saturated brine (see Tip, page 83)	

1. Sterilize all equipment (see page 40). In a large stainless-steel pot over medium heat, warm milk to 86°F (30°C), stirring gently to prevent scorching. Turn off heat.

2. Sprinkle mesophilic and thermophilic cultures over surface of milk and let stand for about 5 minutes to rehydrate. Using skimmer and an up-and-down motion, gently draw cultures down into milk without breaking surface of milk. Cover and let ripen for 1 hour.

3. Dilute calcium chloride in ¼ cup (50 mL) cool water. Add to milk using the same up-and-down motion.

4. Dilute rennet in ¼ cup (50 mL) cool water. Add to milk and, using the same up-and-down motion, draw rennet down into milk until well blended. Cover and let set for 30 minutes or until a firm curd forms. Check for a clean break (see Tip, page 75). If the curd is still too fragile, cover and let set for another 15 minutes or until a clean break is achieved.

5. Using a long-bladed knife and skimmer (see Tip, page 75), cut curd into ⅓-inch (0.8 cm) pieces. Let stand for 5 minutes to firm up the curds.

6. Place heat on low and slowly warm curds to 102°F (39°C), stirring gently to prevent curds from matting, adjusting the heat as necessary to make sure it takes 45 minutes to do so. Do not heat too quickly. Let curds settle and hold temperature for 30 minutes.

Variation:

Bocconcini: Bocconcini simply means "small mouthfuls." When cutting the rope of curd for Mozzarella di Bufala, snip small bite-size pieces. Float in brine for 1 hour in Step 11.

7. Place a cloth-lined colander in a bowl to catch whey; strain curds in colander. Return whey to the cheese pot. Let curds drain in colander for 15 minutes or until they have matted together and formed a solid mass.

8. Place curd mass on a cutting board and cut into 4 equal pieces. Return to pot of whey. Let cheese stand in the whey at room temperature for 4 hours.

9. Wearing heat-resistant rubber gloves, pinch off a piece of cheese and immerse in a bowl of 160°F (71°C) water. Knead cheese under water with your fingers and stretch it into a long string. If the cheese does not stretch, let ripen in the whey a bit longer. Repeat the stretching test.

10. Once curd is ready to stretch, fill a large bowl with 160°F (71°C) water and immerse curd. Knead curd, wearing rubber gloves, if necessary. Stretch and pull curd into long strands until it is shiny and smooth. Form a thick rope of cheese, then cut into 4-inch (10 cm) pieces. Drop into a bowl of ice water to firm up. Let stand for about 15 minutes.

11. Place cheese in brine solution for 2 to 3 hours. Use immediately or place in container with a bit of brine and store in the refrigerator.

Marinated Bocconcini

<table>
<tr><td>¼ cup</td><td>chopped fresh herbs, such as oregano, thyme, basil or parsley</td><td>50 mL</td></tr>
<tr><td>1 tbsp</td><td>freshly squeezed lemon juice</td><td>15 mL</td></tr>
<tr><td>¼ tsp</td><td>salt</td><td>1.25 mL</td></tr>
<tr><td>½ cup</td><td>olive oil</td><td>125 mL</td></tr>
<tr><td>1 cup</td><td>drained Bocconcini (see variation, page 79)</td><td>250 mL</td></tr>
</table>

Makes 1¼ cups (300 mL)

Keep a jar of these handy for a ready appetizer or a great addition to a salad.

1. In a small bowl, combine herbs, lemon juice and salt. Add olive oil and stir to combine.

2. Place bocconcini in a jar with a lid and pour herb-oil mixture over top. Cover and tilt to distribute around cheese. Let marinate for 4 hours at room temperature. Serve immediately or store in the refrigerator for up to 10 days. The olive oil will become cloudy when cold but will clear again when at room temperature. Remove from the refrigerator 1 hour before serving.

About Water Buffalo Milk

Water buffaloes are milked in countries as diverse as Canada, Italy, India and Venezuela. About 5% of the dairy milk produced in the world is water buffalo milk.

Like goat's milk, water buffalo milk is white, because it lacks the beta-carotene that is present in cow's milk. It has high solids (16%) and fat (8%) contents, which give it a high energy value with good digestibility and, in cheese making, larger yields. It is well suited for soft cheeses and is best known for traditional mozzarella di bufala. Because of the quality and amount of fat it contains, water buffalo milk is less desirable for making hard cheeses.

Mozzarella di Bufala Salad

Makes 4 servings

Nothing is simpler or tastier for a summer lunch.

4	Roma tomatoes	4
2	pieces Mozzarella di Bufala (page 78)	2
4	fresh basil leaves	4
4 tsp	drained capers	20 mL
	Olive oil	
	Balsamic vinegar	
	Freshly ground black pepper	

1. Slice tomatoes and cheese into rounds. Divide equally between 4 plates, alternating and overlapping slices of cheese and tomatoes.

2. Chop basil and sprinkle over cheese and tomatoes.

3. Sprinkle 1 tsp (5 mL) capers on each plate. Drizzle with olive oil and balsamic vinegar and season with freshly ground black pepper to taste.

Provolone

<table>
<tr><td rowspan="3" style="text-align:center;">Makes
3¼ lbs (1.6 kg)
10% yield</td></tr>
</table>

Makes
3¼ lbs (1.6 kg)
10% yield

A semifirm Italian cheese, provolone can be made from cow's milk or buffalo milk, or a blend of the two. It has a smooth, flexible paste, a shiny golden rind and a mellow, creamy flavor. It comes in different sizes and is often twisted and formed into various shapes, most commonly a pear shape.

- Cloth-lined colander
- Heat-resistant rubber gloves
- Cheese matting
- Ripening container

16 quarts	non-homogenized whole milk (see Sources, page 372)	16 L
¼ tsp	mesophilic culture	1.25 mL
¼ tsp	thermophilic culture	1.25 mL
¾ tsp	calcium chloride	3.75 mL
¾ tsp	liquid rennet	3.75 mL
	Bowl of ice water	
	Cool 18% saturated brine (see Tip, opposite)	
	Olive oil	

1. Sterilize all equipment (see page 40). In a large stainless-steel pot set in a hot water bath over low heat, warm milk to 96°F (35.5°C), stirring gently with a skimmer. Turn off heat.

2. Sprinkle mesophilic and thermophilic cultures over surface of milk and let stand for about 5 minutes to rehydrate. Using skimmer and an up-and-down motion, gently draw cultures down into milk without breaking surface of milk. Cover and let ripen for 45 minutes.

3. Dilute calcium chloride in ¼ cup (50 mL) cool water. Add to milk using the same up-and-down motion.

4. Dilute rennet in ¼ cup (50 mL) cool water. Add to milk and, using the same up-and-down motion, draw rennet down into milk until well blended. Cover and let set for about 1 hour. Check for a clean break (see Tip, page 75). If the curd is still too fragile, cover and let set for another 15 minutes or until a clean break is achieved.

5. Using a long-bladed knife and skimmer, cut curd into ½-inch (1.25 cm) cubes (see Tip, page 75). Let stand for 5 minutes to firm up the curds.

6. Return heat to low and slowly warm curds to 115°F (46°C), stirring gently and continuously, adjusting the heat as necessary to make sure it takes 30 minutes to

Tip: To make an 18% saturated brine: Mix 1 part salt to 5 parts water. It may be necessary to warm the water to successfully dissolve the salt. If so, let the brine cool before immersing the cheese. The brine can be used over and over again for several batches of cheese (refrigerate between uses). The best temperature for brining cheese is 55°F (13°C). Replenish the salt after several uses and remove any floating bits of cheese with a strainer.

do so. Do not heat too quickly. Turn off heat and stir gently for 15 minutes to prevent curds from matting. Let settle.

7. Drain off whey through a cloth-lined colander. Let curds drain for 15 to 20 minutes or until they have matted together and formed a solid mass. Place curd mass on a cutting board and, with a knife, cut into 1-inch (2.5 cm) cubes. Return cubes to the cheese pot or place in a large stainless-steel bowl. Cover with 145°F (63°C) water. Let stand until temperature drops to 130°F (54°C). This will take 1 to 2 hours.

8. Wearing heat-resistant rubber gloves, pick up cubes and work them into one large ball, kneading and shaping it under the water. Once it has formed a firm ball, lift it from the water and pull and stretch into a long rope. Loop rope back on itself, then pull it out again. Repeat pulling and looping until curd is shiny and smooth. You must work quickly or the curd will cool and become brittle. If necessary, dip the curd under the hot water again to warm it. A wooden spoon can be useful in this step to stretch the curd (see Tips, page 90). The cheese will become very soft. Press down with the spoon then lift it up above the level of the water. Shape into desired shape and place in a bowl of ice water to chill and firm up.

9. Place the chilled cheese in brine solution; let stand at room temperature for 12 hours, turning once after 6 hours. Remove from brine. Place on a rack and let dry at room temperature, turning periodically to dry each side equally, for 1 to 2 days.

10. Place cheese on a cheese mat in a ripening container. Cure at 62° to 65°F (17° to 18°C) and 80 to 85% humidity. Turn cheese daily for the first 2 weeks, then twice weekly thereafter. If any mold appears, wipe it away with a vinegar-and-salt solution (1 tsp/5 mL salt to 1/4 cup/50 mL vinegar).

11. After 1 month of curing, rub rind with olive oil. Repeat once a month, if necessary, to help create a nice rind. Cure for 2 to 4 months for table cheese, or for 6 to 12 months for hard grating cheese.

Caciocavallo

Makes
2½ to 3¼ lbs
(1.28 to 1.6 kg)

8 to 10% yield

This is the Italian version of a pasta filata cheese that is made with slight variations in many cultures. Called katschkawalj in Serbia, kaşar in Turkey, kashkaval in Bulgaria and caşcaval in Romania, they are all stretched-curd cheeses made with either ewe's or cow's milk. The name is a shortened form of "cacio a cavallo," which means "cheese on horseback," reflecting the fact that the cheeses are traditionally tied in pairs and hung over a beam to cure, as if over a saddle.

- Cloth-lined colander
- Heat-resistant rubber gloves
- Natural twine, optional
- Cheese matting, optional
- Ripening container, optional

16 quarts	non-homogenized whole milk (see Sources, page 372)	16 L
¼ tsp	mesophilic culture	1.25 mL
¼ tsp	thermophilic culture	1.25 mL
¾ tsp	calcium chloride	3.75 mL
¾ tsp	liquid rennet	3.75 mL
	Bowl of ice water	
	Cool 18% saturated brine (see Tip, page 89)	
	Olive oil	

1. Sterilize all equipment (see page 40). In a large stainless-steel pot set in a hot water bath over low heat, warm milk to 96°F (35.5°C), stirring gently with a skimmer. Turn off heat.

2. Sprinkle mesophilic and thermophilic cultures over surface of milk and let stand for about 5 minutes to rehydrate. Using skimmer and an up-and-down motion, gently draw cultures down into milk without breaking surface of milk. Cover and let ripen for 45 minutes.

3. Dilute calcium chloride in ¼ cup (50 mL) cool water. Add to milk using the same up-and-down motion.

4. Dilute rennet in ¼ cup (50 mL) cool water. Add to milk and, using the same up-and-down motion, draw rennet down into milk until well blended. Cover and let set for about 1 hour. Check for a clean break (see Tip, page 75). If the curd is still too fragile, cover and let set for another 15 minutes or until a clean break is achieved.

5. Using a long-bladed knife and skimmer, cut curd into ½-inch (1.25 cm) cubes (see Tip, page 75). Let stand for 5 minutes to firm up the curds.

6. Return heat to low and slowly warm curds to 104°F (40°C), stirring gently and continuously, adjusting the heat as necessary to make sure it takes 30 minutes to do so. Do not heat too quickly. Turn off heat and stir gently for 15 minutes to prevent curds from matting. Let settle.

Tips: Most cheeses can be frozen, but there will be some change in texture when thawed. If you must freeze cheese, cut it into small pieces and wrap well, ensuring airtightness, and freeze for up to 2 months. Thaw in the refrigerator and serve within a few days.

Instead of working and stretching the cheese in the hot water while wearing heat-resistant gloves, you can try using two wooden spoons. Use one spoon to hold the ball of curd down and the other to push and lift the cheese as it softens.

7. Drain off whey through a cloth-lined colander. Let curds drain for 15 to 20 minutes or until they have matted together and formed a solid mass. Place curd mass on a cutting board and, with a knife, cut into 1-inch (2.5 cm) cubes. Return cubes to the cheese pot or place in a large stainless-steel bowl. Cover with 145°F (63°C) water. Let stand until temperature drops to 130°F (54°C). This will take 1 to 2 hours.

8. Wearing heat-resistant rubber gloves, pick up cubes and work them into one large ball, kneading and shaping it under the water. Once ball is firm, lift it from the water and pull and stretch into a long rope. Loop rope back on itself, then pull it out again. Repeat pulling and looping until curd is shiny and smooth. You must work quickly or the curd will cool and become brittle. If necessary, dip the curd under the hot water again to warm it. A wooden spoon can be useful in this step to stretch the curd (see Tip, left). The cheese will become very soft. Press down with the spoon then lift it up above the level of the water.

9. Shape into traditional cheese by forming a fat roll and twisting a small ball shape at one end of the cheese (this is where the twine will be tied to hang the cheese). Place in a bowl of ice water to chill and firm up, about 15 minutes.

10. Place the chilled cheese in brine solution; let stand for 12 hours for one large cheese, or 6 hours for smaller cheeses, turning halfway through brining period. Remove from brine. Place on a rack and let dry at room temperature, turning periodically to dry each side equally, for 1 to 2 days.

11. Tie with twine, if using or place on a cheese mat in a ripening container. If using twine, hang the cheeses in pairs over a beam or pole. Cure at 62° to 65°F (17° to 18°C) and 80 to 85% humidity. If curing in a container, turn daily for the first 2 weeks, then twice weekly thereafter. For either method, wipe away any mold with a vinegar-and-salt solution (1 tsp/5 mL salt to 1/4 cup/50 mL vinegar).

12. After 1 month of curing, rub rind with olive oil. Cure for 2 to 4 months for table cheese, or for 6 to 12 months for hard grating cheese.

Scamorza

Makes
2½ to 3¼ lbs
(1.28 to 1.6 kg)
8 to 10% yield

Scamorza is an Italian pasta filata cheese that is eaten fresh rather than cured, as in the case of caciocavallo. It is a cheese to have fun with, as the warm curd can be braided or twisted into unique shapes.

Tip: Non-homogenized milk, also known as cream line or standard milk, is always the best choice for successful cheese making. Non-homogenized milk is pasteurized milk that hasn't been homogenized and shouldn't be confused with raw milk. See Sources, page 372, for more information.

- Cloth-lined colander
- Heat-resistant rubber gloves

16 quarts	non-homogenized whole milk (see Sources, page 372)	16 L
¼ tsp	mesophilic culture	1.25 mL
¼ tsp	thermophilic culture	1.25 mL
⅛ tsp	annatto coloring	0.65 mL
¾ tsp	calcium chloride	3.75 mL
¾ tsp	liquid rennet	3.75 mL
	Bowl of ice water	
	Cool 18% saturated brine (see Tip, page 89)	

1. Sterilize all equipment (see page 40). In a large stainless-steel pot set in a hot water bath over low heat, warm milk to 96°F (35.5°C), stirring gently. Turn off heat.

2. Using a measuring cup, remove ¼ cup (50 mL) warm milk for dissolving the annatto. Set aside.

3. Sprinkle mesophilic and thermophilic cultures over surface of milk and let stand for about 5 minutes to rehydrate. Using skimmer and an up-and-down motion, gently draw cultures down into milk without breaking surface of milk. Cover and let ripen for 45 minutes.

4. Meanwhile, dilute annatto in reserved milk. Stir into pot.

5. Dilute calcium chloride in ¼ cup (50 mL) cool water. Add to milk using the same up-and-down motion.

6. Dilute rennet in ¼ cup (50 mL) cool water. Add to milk and, using the same up-and-down motion, draw rennet down into milk until well blended. Cover and let set for about 1 hour. Check for a clean break (see Tip, page 75). If the curd is still too fragile, cover and let set for another 15 minutes or until a clean break is achieved.

Variation: Scamorza is often smoked for an added flavor experience (see Smoked Cheese, page 208).

7. Using a long-bladed knife and skimmer, cut curd into $1/2$-inch (1.25 cm) cubes (see Tip, page 75). Let stand for 5 minutes to firm up the curds.

8. Return heat to low and slowly warm curds to 104°F (40°C), stirring gently and continuously, adjusting the heat as necessary to make sure it takes 30 minutes to do so. Do not heat too quickly.

9. When curd has reached temperature, hold temperature steady for another 15 minutes, stirring gently to prevent curds from matting. Let settle.

10. Pour curds into a cloth-lined colander and let drain for 15 to 20 minutes or until they have matted together and formed a solid mass. Place curd mass on a cutting board and, with a knife, cut into 1-inch (2.5 cm) cubes. Return cubes to the cheese pot or place in a large stainless-steel bowl. Cover with 145°F (63°C) water. Let stand until temperature drops to 130°F (54°C). This will take 1 to 2 hours.

11. Wearing heat-resistant rubber gloves, pick up cubes and work them into one large ball, kneading and shaping it under the water. Once ball is firm, lift it from the water and pull and stretch into a long rope. Cut the rope into pieces the size of a lemon. Pull and stretch out each piece of the cheese, dipping back into the hot water as necessary to warm, until shiny and smooth. Form it into the desired shape, such as a ball or braid. Place in a bowl of ice water to chill and firm up.

12. Place the chilled cheese in brine solution; let stand at room temperature for 12 hours for one large cheese, or for 1 to 2 hours for a dozen small cheeses.

13. Air-dry cheeses on a rack at room temperature for 1 to 2 days. When dry, wrap and store in the refrigerator for up to 2 weeks.

Asadero

Makes about
2 lbs (1 kg)
about 12% yield

Also called Oaxaca,
this is a Mexican
cheese made of whole
milk. Asadero means
"roastable," so named
for its great melting
qualities.

Tip: To remove 30%
of the whey, measure
down the side of the
pot and remove the
top one-third, basically
until you see the surface
of the settled curd. The
amount you remove can
be crucial, because the
same amount of water
must be added, and this
will affect the character
of the finished cheese
(see Troubleshooting,
page 94).

- Cloth-lined colander
- Heat-resistant rubber gloves

8 quarts	non-homogenized whole milk (see Sources, page 372)	8 L
¼ tsp	thermophilic culture	1.25 mL
¼ tsp	calcium chloride	1.25 mL
¼ tsp	liquid rennet	1.25 mL
	Bowl of ice water	
	Cool 18% saturated brine (see Tip, opposite)	

1. Sterilize all equipment (see page 40). In a large stainless-steel pot over medium heat, warm milk to 99°F (37°C), stirring gently to prevent scorching. Remove from heat.

2. Sprinkle culture over surface of milk and let stand for about 5 minutes to rehydrate. Using skimmer and an up-and-down motion, gently draw culture down into milk without breaking surface of milk. Cover and let ripen for 45 minutes.

3. Dilute calcium chloride in ¼ cup (50 mL) cool water. Add to milk using the same up-and-down motion.

4. Dilute rennet in ¼ cup (50 mL) cool water. Add to milk and, using the same up-and-down motion, draw rennet down into milk until well blended. Cover and let set for 45 minutes. Check for a clean break (see Tip, page 75). If the curd is still too fragile, cover and let set for another 15 minutes or until a clean break is achieved.

5. Using a long-bladed knife and skimmer, cut curds into ¾-inch (2 cm) cubes (see Tip, page 75). Let stand for 5 minutes to firm up the curds. Stir curds in the pot for 30 minutes. Let settle.

6. Using a measuring cup, remove 30% of the whey (see Tip, left) and replace with hot water to bring the temperature to 108°F (42°C), adjusting with more hot or cool water as necessary but not exceeding the original amount of whey. Stir the mixture continuously for 30 minutes. Let curds settle and hold, maintaining temperature for 1 hour.

Tip: To make an 18% saturated brine: Mix 1 part salt to 5 parts water. It may be necessary to warm the water to successfully dissolve the salt. If so, let the brine cool before immersing the cheese. The brine can be used over and over again for several batches of cheese (refrigerate between uses). The best temperature for brining cheese is 55°F (13°C). Replenish the salt after several uses and remove any floating bits of cheese with a strainer.

7. Meanwhile, heat 5 quarts (5 L) water to 185°F (85°C).

8. Pour curds into a cloth-lined colander and let drain until they have matted together. Place mass on a cutting board and, with a knife, cut into 2-inch (5 cm) cubes. Place cubes in a large wide bowl and pour 185°F (85°C) water over them to soften. Wearing heat-resistant rubber gloves, knead and pull cheese under the water until it is all melted together.

9. Return cheese to cutting board and knead it further until shiny and smooth. Shape into a smooth ball. Place cheese in a bowl of ice water for 15 minutes to chill and firm up. Immerse the chilled cheese in brine solution for 30 minutes. Use immediately or wrap tightly and store in the refrigerator for up to 2 weeks.

Kasseri

**Makes about
2¾ lbs (1.4 kg)**
18% yield

This Greek cheese is aged longer than is usual for cheeses of the pasta filata family. For a traditional taste of Greece, try it flambéed in Saganaki (page 93).

Tips: Instead of working and stretching the cheese in the hot water while wearing heat-resistant gloves, you can try using two wooden spoons. Use one spoon to hold the ball of curd down and the other to push and lift the cheese as it softens.

To ascertain whether the curd is ready for cutting, check for what's called a "clean break." Insert the long flat blade of a cheese knife into the curd at a 30-degree angle and slowly lift the blade toward the surface of the curd. If the curd splits into a long clean break or crack, it is ready to cut. If the break is wobbly or uneven, let the curd set for a few more minutes before trying again.

- Cloth-lined colander
- Heat-resistant rubber gloves
- 1 tomme mold or square block mold
- Draining container
- Cheese matting
- Ripening container

6 quarts	sheep's milk	6 L
2 quarts	goat's milk	2 L
¼ tsp	thermophilic culture	1.25 mL
¼ tsp	calcium chloride	1.25 mL
¼ tsp	liquid rennet	1.25 mL
	Pickling (canning) or kosher salt	

1. Sterilize all equipment (see page 40). In a large stainless-steel pot set in a hot water bath over medium heat, combine sheep's and goat's milks. Warm milk mixture to 97°F (36°C), stirring gently. Turn off heat.

2. Sprinkle culture over surface of milk and let stand for about 5 minutes to rehydrate. Using skimmer and an up-and-down motion, gently draw culture down into milk without breaking surface of milk. Cover and let ripen for 30 minutes.

3. Dilute calcium chloride in ¼ cup (50 mL) cool water. Add to milk using the same up-and-down motion.

4. Dilute rennet in ¼ cup (50 mL) cool water. Add to milk and, using the same up-and-down motion, draw rennet down into milk until well blended. Cover and let set for 35 minutes or until a firm curd forms. Check for a clean break (see Tips, left). If the curd is still too fragile, cover and let set for another 5 to 10 minutes or until a clean break is achieved.

5. Using a long-bladed knife and skimmer, cut curd into small pieces the size of navy beans. You may use a long whisk to aid in cutting, but be gentle to avoid losing the fat from the milk. Let stand for 5 minutes to firm up the curds.

Tip: The process of releasing whey from the curd while cooking and stirring the cheese is called "syneresis." It is important that this take place at a slow, even pace to ensure a smooth-textured paste in the finished cheese. Stirring gently and constantly while cooking the curd ensures that none of the curds settle and mat in the bottom of the pot, and all are equally exposed to the heat and movement.

6. Return heat to low and slowly warm curds to 104°F (40°C), adjusting the heat as necessary to make sure it takes 30 minutes to do so (this means 1 to 2°F/0.5° to 1°C every 7 minutes), stirring gently and continuously to distribute the heat and ensure all curds are cooked evenly. Let settle for 10 minutes.

7. Drain curds in a cloth-lined colander. Mix curds with your hands to loosen them up and aid in draining. When curds seem well drained, gather them up in the cloth and form a tight, flat package. Place on a plate and cover with another plate. Place a weight of approximately 4 lbs (2 kg) on the upper plate to press the curd. Leave curd to press and drain at room temperature for 7 to 8 hours. Alternatively, place in the refrigerator for up to 24 hours.

8. Check to see if curd is ready (i.e, acidic enough) by slicing off a small piece and, wearing heat-resistant rubber gloves, dipping it into a bowl of 175°F (79°C) water. Press and knead between your fingers. If ready, the curd will stretch into a long string.

9. When ready, cut slab of curd into 1-inch (2.5 cm) slices and place in a bowl. Pour 175°F (79°C) water over slices. Wearing heat-resistant rubber gloves, knead and stretch slices until they are smooth and elastic. Form curds into one large smooth ball and place in mold, pressing to fit if necessary.

10. Place mold on a rack in a draining container and let drain at room temperature for 2 hours, flipping cheese in mold several times to aid in draining. Cover container to keep warm and let drain overnight.

11. Remove cheese from mold and place on a cheese mat in a clean draining container. Rub 1 tsp (5 mL) salt onto top of cheese and let dissolve for 2 hours at room temperature. Turn cheese and salt the other side in the same manner. Leave the cheese for 24 hours, then repeat the salting routine. Leave for another 24 hours and repeat salting again.

continued on next page…

Kasseri continued...

12. After three saltings, wash cheese with warm water. Dry and place on a cheese mat in a ripening container. Let ripen at 65°F (18°C) and 85% humidity for 4 to 10 months, depending on your taste. Turn cheese daily for the first week, then twice weekly, for even ripening. If mold appears on cheese, wipe away with a cloth dipped in vinegar. A firm yellowish-brown rind will form. When ready, wrap in foil and store in the refrigerator for up to 2 months.

Cheese Making is Part Science, Part Art

At various stages of the process, you can test the pH to measure the acidity of the milk or curd in order to determine what to do next, and when. However, perhaps even more important, with time you will develop a sense of what is happening with your curd. The final quality of your cheese is usually determined by the action you take when the curds are cooking or holding in the pot. Develop this intuition by performing the texture test and comparing with the pH measurement. Make detailed notes that you can consult later, and look for characteristics in your finished cheese, such as texture, moisture and length of time required for ripening.

Saganaki

Makes 1 serving

A great appetizer or light meal, saganaki is fried cheese with a twist. Serve with lemon wedges and fresh bread.

- Flameproof dish

5 oz	Kasseri (page 90)	150 g
1/2 cup	all-purpose flour	125 mL
1	egg	1
1 tbsp	milk	15 mL
	Olive oil for frying	
1 tbsp	brandy or ouzo	15 mL
	Lemon wedges	
	Bread	

1. Cut kasseri into 1/4-inch (0.5 cm) slices.

2. Place flour on a small plate. In a small bowl, beat together egg and milk.

3. Dip slices of cheese into egg mixture, then into flour, coating both sides well. Shake off any excess flour.

4. Pour oil into sauté pan until it is 1/2 inch (1.25 cm) deep; heat over medium heat. Fry cheese slices, in batches if necessary, until golden brown, about 3 minutes per side. Remove from oil and place in a small flameproof dish.

5. Warm brandy in a small saucepan and pour over cheese. Using a long match, light the brandy. When the flames have died down, squeeze a little fresh lemon juice over top. Serve with bread.

Troubleshooting

Mozzarella will not stretch.

The acidity is incorrect; use a pH test strip to determine when the pH is at 5.0 to 5.2. If the acidity is too low, ripen the curd longer. If the acidity is too high, next time shorten the ripening time of the curd slab.

The texture of the finished cheese is rubbery.

Too much rennet in the curd; reduce rennet. Or lactic bacteria is too weak, because washed-curd cheese was too diluted during washing; remove less whey when washing curd or add less water after whey removal.

Mold-Ripened Cheeses

This family includes some of the most renowned cheeses, such as Brie, Camembert, Chaource and Ste-Maure, all of which originated in France and are copied all over the world.

In traditional farmstead production, the mold that covers the surface of the cheese is naturally present in the ripening rooms, so the milk does not need to be inoculated with powdered mold spores, as it is here. Once the cheese is completely covered in white fuzzy mold, it is wrapped in a special double-layer paper and ripened for another 2 to 4 weeks. During this time, the mold ripens the cheese from the outside in, causing the paste to become soft and supple under a crust redolent of mushrooms or truffles. When overripe, these cheeses can exude a strong ammonia smell, which is delightful to some but rather too pungent for others.

This chapter also includes French-style goat cheeses. France has a bounty of beautiful cheeses made from goat's milk. Each area, or department, is rightly proud of its local cheeses, traditionally made on the farm from raw milk. These cheeses are called *fermier*, or made-on-the-farm, cheeses and often come with the *Appellation d'origine contrôlée (AOC)* label.

Brie

**Makes 2 cheeses,
each 1¼ to 1½ lbs
(600 to 750 g)**

15 to 18% yield

*Brie is definitely one
of the world's favorite
cheeses, even boasting a
royal title: it was crowned
roi des fromages (king of
cheeses) in 1815 by 30
European ambassadors
at the Congress of Vienna.
From then on, Brie was
also known as fromage
des rois (cheese of kings)
for its titled connoisseurs.
You can make beautiful
Brie at home, but you
will need to watch the
ripening humidity and
temperature carefully.*

Tip: Non-homogenized
milk, also known as
cream line or standard
milk, is always the best
choice for successful
cheese making.
Non-homogenized
milk is pasteurized
milk that hasn't been
homogenized and
shouldn't be confused
with raw milk. See
Sources, page 372,
for more information.

- Draining container
- Cheese matting
- Two 8-inch (20 cm) half-Brie molds
- Ripening container

8 quarts	whole milk	8 L
¼ tsp	mesophilic culture	1.25 mL
⅛ tsp	*Penicillium candidum* mold powder	0.65 mL
¼ tsp	calcium chloride	1.25 mL
¼ tsp	liquid rennet	1.25 mL
4 tsp	pickling (canning) or kosher salt	20 mL

1. Sterilize all equipment (see page 40). Prepare a draining container by placing a rack inside. Then place a cutting board on top, followed by a cheese mat, then the molds.

2. In a large stainless-steel pot set in a hot water bath over medium heat, warm milk to 88°F (31°C), stirring gently. Turn off heat.

3. Sprinkle culture and mold powder over surface of milk and let stand for about 5 minutes to rehydrate. Using skimmer and an up-and-down motion, gently draw culture and mold down into milk without breaking surface of milk.

4. Dilute calcium chloride in ¼ cup (50 mL) cool water. Add to milk using the same up-and-down motion.

5. Dilute rennet in ¼ cup (50 mL) cool water. Add to milk and, using the same up-and-down motion, draw rennet down into milk until well blended. Cover pot and let set for 1½ hours, maintaining the temperature at 88°F (31°C).

6. Check for a clean break (see Tip, page 103). If curd is still too fragile, cover and let set for another 10 minutes or until a clean break is achieved. Using a long-bladed knife and skimmer, cut curd into 1-inch (2.5 cm) cubes (see Tip, page 113). Let stand for 5 minutes to firm up the curds.

Variation:

Double-Cream Brie:
Use 6 quarts (6 L) whole milk and 2 quarts (2 L) whipping (35%) cream in place of whole milk.

7. Using a skimmer, stir curd very gently, lifting from bottom all around perimeter of pot for 5 to 10 minutes or until pieces of curd start to shrink slightly in size and edges become rounded. (This is more lifting and moving the curd rather than actually stirring it around.) Let curds settle.

8. Using a measuring cup, dip off whey until you see the surface of the curd.

9. Using a skimmer, carefully ladle curd into prepared molds. Ladle a spoonful of curds into one mold, then the other, and repeat. It will take time for the curds to drain down, but all the curd will fit into the molds. Don't be tempted to add another mold. Let curds drain for 2 hours. Carefully lift cheese and mold together and flip over. Repeat in 2 hours, then again. Cover container and leave to drain at room temperature overnight.

10. Flip cheeses in the morning and leave for another 2 hours. By this time, they should have had almost 24 hours of draining. Remove the molds and prepare a cheese mat in a ripening container.

11. Sprinkle top of each cheese with 1 tsp (5 mL) salt. Turn salted side down on mat in clean container and salt other side. Cover with lid.

12. Let cheese ripen at 50° to 55°F (10° to 13°C) and 90% humidity. Flip cheeses daily and remove any whey that has collected, wiping bottom of container with paper towel. Keep covered and make sure the cheeses don't become dry.

13. After about 1 week, a fine fuzzy white mold will begin to grow on cheese. Continue to turn cheese daily. When it is fully covered in white mold, after about 12 days, wrap it in cheese-ripening paper and return to ripening area. Within 1 week or so, the cheese will begin to soften. It will be ready to eat at 4 to 5 weeks after production. After 4 weeks, remove from ripening area and store in the refrigerator for up to 6 weeks, depending on how ripe you like it. The cheese will continue to ripen, though more slowly due to the colder temperature.

Cranberry Almond Baked Brie

**Makes 10 to
12 servings**

*Brie makes a wonderful
appetizer, and this recipe
makes it even more
spectacular. If using
a smaller Brie, adjust
ingredients accordingly.
Serve immediately with
baguette or crackers.
A glass of sparkling
wine goes perfectly
with this dish.*

- Preheat oven to 350°F (180°C)
- 10-inch (25 cm) pie plate or similar-size baking dish, buttered

½ cup	packed brown sugar	125 mL
1 cup	almonds, roughly chopped	250 mL
1 cup	dried cranberries, roughly chopped	250 mL
1	8-inch (20 cm) round Brie (page 96)	1
1 to 2 tsp	butter, softened	5 to 10 mL

1. In a small saucepan over medium heat, combine brown sugar and ½ cup (125 mL) water and bring to a boil. Reduce heat to low and cook, stirring continuously, until sugar is dissolved. Add almonds and stir until well coated. Cook, stirring, for 1 minute, taking care not to scorch the sugar. Remove from heat and place saucepan in a sinkful of cold water to stop the cooking process.

2. When nut mixture is cool enough to touch, stir in cranberries until evenly blended.

3. Place Brie in prepared pie plate. Using a pastry brush, butter top of Brie. Spread cranberry-almond mixture over top of Brie. Bake in preheated oven for 15 minutes or until centre is soft when pressed with the back of a spoon.

Pasta with Broccoli and Brie

Makes 4 servings

The creamy Brie contrasts nicely with the bright green freshness of the broccoli.

6 oz	Brie (page 96)	175 g
½ cup	whipping (35%) cream	125 mL
10 oz	dried pasta, any type	300 g
1 tbsp	butter	15 mL
¼ cup	slivered almonds	50 mL
2 cups	broccoli florets	500 mL
	Freshly ground pepper	

1. Cut Brie into ½-inch (1.25 cm) pieces. Pour cream over cheese and set aside.

2. In a large pot of boiling salted water, cook pasta according to package directions or until tender but still firm to the bite (al dente).

3. Meanwhile, in a small saucepan over medium heat, melt butter. Add almonds and cook, stirring, until just barely beginning to brown. Remove from heat and set aside.

4. Meanwhile, boil or steam broccoli florets until tender but still slightly crunchy. Drain and set aside.

5. Fill a large bowl with hot water and let stand until warm. Drain and dry. Drain pasta and immediately pour into the heated bowl. Add broccoli, almonds and cheese mixture and toss well to mix. Season with pepper to taste. Serve immediately.

Brie vs. Camembert

Brie and Camembert are similar in many ways and people often confuse them, but there are certain differences, beginning with the process by which they're made. The milk for Brie is warmed to 88°F (31°C) before inoculating; for Camembert, to 84°F (29°C). Brie cheeses are usually 12 to 14 inches (30 to 35 cm) across and 1 inch (2.5 cm) thick, while Camembert cheeses are 4 inches (10 cm) in diameter and slightly thicker. The final size of the cheese, determined by the mold the cheese is shaped in, does affect the ripening process. Since mold-ripened cheeses ripen from the outside in, the larger surface area of the mold crust on a Brie results in a runnier and stronger-flavored cheese than the more petite Camembert. The smaller the cheese, the more quickly it reaches its peak ripeness. Camembert is usually ripe after 4 weeks of curing, whereas Brie takes a week or so longer. Both cheeses, however, become more pungent and softer with continued aging.

Camembert

Makes 4 cheeses, each 10 oz (300 g)		
15% yield		

Camembert is an AOC cheese from the region of Normandy in northwestern France that is known and loved the world over. Using whole milk guarantees a traditional, rich, creamy cheese.

Tip: To cut curds: Holding a long-bladed stainless-steel knife straight up and down, draw knife through the curd, cutting it into strips. Proceed across the pot until you have reached the other side. Turn the pot and cut across the first strips to create squares. Using a skimmer, cut horizontally from side to side just under the surface of the curd to create cubes. Gradually move skimmer down through curd to cut layers of cubes. Using skimmer, gently stir curd cubes. Using a knife, cut any pieces that have been missed or are too large. For small-cut curds, you can use a large whisk for cutting.

- Draining container
- Cheese matting
- Four 4-inch (10 cm) bottomless Camembert molds
- Ripening container

8 quarts	whole milk	8 L
¼ tsp	mesophilic culture	1.25 mL
⅛ tsp	*Penicillium candidum* mold powder	0.65 mL
¼ tsp	calcium chloride	1.25 mL
¼ tsp	liquid rennet	1.25 mL
4 tsp	pickling (canning) or kosher salt	20 mL

1. Sterilize all equipment (see page 40). Prepare a draining container by placing a rack inside. Then place a cutting board on top, followed by a cheese mat, then the molds.

2. In a large stainless-steel pot set in a hot water bath over medium heat, warm milk to 85°F (29°C), stirring gently. Turn off heat.

3. Sprinkle culture and mold powder over surface of milk and let stand for about 5 minutes to rehydrate. Using skimmer and an up-and-down motion, gently draw culture and mold down into milk without breaking surface of milk.

4. Dilute calcium chloride in ¼ cup (50 mL) cool water. Add to milk using the same up-and-down motion.

5. Dilute rennet in ¼ cup (50 mL) cool water. Add to milk and, using the same up-and-down motion, draw rennet down into milk until well blended. Cover pot and let set for 1½ hours, maintaining the temperature at 85°F (29°C).

6. Check for a clean break (see Tip, page 103). If curd is still too fragile, cover and let set for another 15 minutes or until a clean break is achieved. Using a long-bladed knife and skimmer, cut curd into 1-inch (2.5 cm) cubes (see Tip, left). Let stand for 5 minutes to firm up the curds.

Tip: To bring mold-ripened cheese, such as Brie and Camembert, to its full flavor before serving, remove it from the ripening area or refrigerator, wrap in parchment paper and let it sit at cool room temperature for 24 to 36 hours. This will allow the cheese to develop flavor and aroma more quickly than it would in colder storage. Check its readiness by opening the paper and giving the cheese a good sniff. If it meets your approval, rewrap and refrigerate. Remove from the refrigerator 1 hour before serving.

Variation:
Double-Cream Camembert: For an extra-rich treat, replace 2 cups (500 mL) of the milk with whipping (35%) cream.

Serving suggestion:
Camembert presents itself beautifully when accompanied by chutneys and preserves. Try a mango and cranberry chutney, or a rose petal and white wine jelly.

7. Using a skimmer, stir curds very gently, lifting from bottom all around perimeter of pot for 5 to 10 minutes or until pieces of curd start to shrink slightly in size and edges become rounded. (This is more lifting and moving the curd rather than actually stirring it around.) Let curds settle.

8. Using a measuring cup, dip off whey until you see the surface of the curd.

9. Using a skimmer, carefully ladle curd into prepared molds. Ladle a spoonful of curds into one mold, then the others, and repeat. It will take time for the curds to drain down, but all the curd will fit into the molds. Don't be tempted to add another mold. Let curds drain for 2 hours. Carefully lift cheese and mold together and flip over. Repeat in 2 hours, then again. Cover container and let drain at room temperature overnight.

10. Flip the cheeses in the morning and leave for another 2 hours. By this time, they should have had almost 24 hours of draining. Remove the molds and prepare a clean cheese mat in a ripening container.

11. Sprinkle top of each cheese with $\frac{1}{2}$ tsp (2.5 mL) salt. Turn salted side down on mat in ripening container and salt other side. Cover with lid.

12. Let cheese ripen at 50° to 55°F (10° to 13°C) and 90% humidity. Flip cheeses daily and remove any whey that has collected, wiping bottom of container with paper towel. Keep covered and make sure the cheeses don't become dry.

13. After about 1 week, a fine fuzzy mold will begin to grow on cheese. Continue to turn cheese daily. When it is fully covered in white mold, after about 12 days, wrap it in cheese-ripening paper and return to ripening area. Within 1 week or so, the cheese will begin to soften. It will be ready to eat at 3 to 4 weeks after production. After 4 weeks, remove from ripening area and store in the refrigerator for up to 6 weeks, depending on how ripe you like it. The cheese will continue to ripen, though more slowly due to the colder temperature.

Camembert with Calvados

Makes 12 cheeses,
each 3½ oz (100 g)

about 15% yield

Calvados is an apple
brandy made in
Normandy, France, an
area known for its apples
and its Camembert. This
recipe combines the two
delicacies brilliantly!
Serve on a cheese board
with fresh apple slices
and some walnuts.

- Draining container
- Cheese matting
- 12 St-Marcellin molds
- Ripening container

8 quarts	whole milk	8 L
¼ tsp	mesophilic culture	1.25 mL
⅛ tsp	*Penicillium candidum* mold powder	0.65 mL
¼ tsp	calcium chloride	1.25 mL
¼ tsp	liquid rennet	1.25 mL
2 tbsp	pickling (canning) or kosher salt	30 mL
2 cups	Calvados or other apple brandy	500 mL
	Fine bread crumbs	
12	walnut halves	12

1. Sterilize all equipment (see page 40). Prepare a draining container by placing a rack inside. Then place a cutting board on top, followed by a cheese mat, then the molds.

2. In a large stainless-steel pot set in a hot water bath over medium heat, warm milk to 85°F (29°C), stirring gently. Turn off heat.

3. Sprinkle culture and mold powder over surface of milk and let stand for about 5 minutes to rehydrate. Using skimmer and an up-and-down motion, gently draw culture and mold down into milk without breaking surface of milk.

4. Dilute calcium chloride in ¼ cup (50 mL) cool water. Add to milk using the same up-and-down motion.

5. Dilute rennet in ¼ cup (50 mL) cool water. Add to milk and, using the same up-and-down motion, draw rennet down into milk until well blended. Cover pot and let set for 1½ hours, maintaining the temperature at 85°F (29°C).

Tip: To ascertain whether the curd is ready for the next step, check for a clean break: insert the long flat blade of a knife into the curd at a 30-degree angle and slowly lift the blade toward the surface of the curd. If the curd splits into a long clean break or crack, it is ready to cut. If the cut is wobbly or uneven, let the curd set for a few more minutes before trying again.

6. Check for a clean break (see Tip, left). If curd is still too fragile, cover and let set for another 5 to 10 minutes or until a clean break is achieved. Using a long-bladed knife and skimmer, cut curd into 1-inch (2.5 cm) cubes (see Tip, page 100). Let stand for 5 minutes to firm up the curds.

7. Using a skimmer, stir curds very gently, lifting from bottom all around perimeter of pot for 5 to 10 minutes or until pieces of curd start to shrink slightly in size and edges become rounded. (This is more lifting and moving the curd rather than actually stirring it around.) Let curds settle.

8. Using a measuring cup, dip off whey until you see the surface of the curd.

9. Using a skimmer, carefully fill the prepared molds to the top, then continue to top off until all the curd is used. It will take time for the curds to drain down, but all the curd will fit into the molds. Do not be tempted to add more molds. Let drain for 2 hours. Carefully unmold the cheese into your hand, flip it over and replace it in the mold. Let drain for 2 hours, then flip again. Cover the container and let drain at room temperature overnight.

10. Flip the cheeses in the morning and leave for another 2 hours. By this time, they should have had almost 24 hours of draining. Prepare a clean cheese mat in a ripening container.

11. Sprinkle top surface of each cheese with ¼ tsp (1.25 mL) salt. Turn salted side down on mat in prepared container and remove the mold. Salt the other side in same manner. Cover with lid.

12. Let cheese ripen at 50° to 55°F (10° to 13°C) and 90% humidity. Flip cheeses daily and remove any whey that has collected, wiping bottom of container with paper towel. Keep covered and make sure the cheeses don't become dry.

continued on next page…

Variation:

Double-Cream Camembert with Calvados: For an extra-rich treat, replace 2 cups (500 mL) of the milk with whipping (35%) cream.

13. After about 1 week, a fine fuzzy white mold will begin to grow on cheese. Continue to turn cheese daily. When it is fully covered in white mold, after 10 to 12 days, wrap it in cheese-ripening paper and return to ripening area. Within 1 week or so, the cheese will begin to soften. It will be ready to eat at 3 weeks after production.

14. Pour Calvados into a flat-bottomed glass dish. Unwrap cheeses and place in the Calvados. Cover with plastic wrap and let stand in a cool place (not the refrigerator) for 12 hours. Turn cheeses and let stand for another 12 hours.

15. After 24 hours, remove cheeses from brandy and roll in bread crumbs. Top each with one walnut half and serve.

Baked Red Peppers

Makes 6 servings

This is an elegant and delicious appetizer to prepare with your French-style goat cheeses.

Variation: Add a slice of fennel bulb to the onion and garlic mixture.

- Preheat oven to 250°F (120°C)
- Baking sheet or dish, oiled

3	red bell peppers	3
1	medium red onion, thinly sliced	1
3	cloves garlic, minced	3
	Sea salt and freshly ground pepper	
	Olive oil	
1 or 2	Crottin (page 122) or other goat cheeses, sliced	1 or 2

1. Halve peppers lengthwise and remove ribs and seeds.

2. Place peppers, skin side down, on prepared baking sheet.

3. In a small bowl, combine onion and garlic. Season with salt and pepper to taste and drizzle with olive oil. Toss to coat.

4. Fill pepper halves with onion mixture. Bake, uncovered, in preheated oven for 1 hour and 20 minutes.

5. Remove from oven and increase heat to 375°F (190°C). Place a slice of goat cheese in each pepper and bake for 5 minutes or until cheese is soft and just beginning to brown around the edges. Serve with a drizzle of olive oil.

Coulommiers

Makes
2 cheeses, each
1½ lbs (750 g)
15% yield

Some people prefer Coulommiers over Brie or Camembert because it tends to be consumed younger and is therefore milder in taste. This cheese is slightly thicker than Brie, which means it takes longer for the center to ripen.

- Draining container
- Cheese matting
- Two 8-inch (20 cm) half-Brie molds
- Ripening container

10 quarts	whole milk	10 L
¼ tsp	mesophilic culture	1.25 mL
Pinch	*Penicillium candidum* mold powder	Pinch
¼ tsp	calcium chloride	1.25 mL
¼ tsp	liquid rennet	1.25 mL
4 tsp	pickling (canning) or kosher salt	20 mL

1. Sterilize all equipment (see page 40). Prepare a draining container by placing a rack inside. Then place a cutting board on top, followed by a cheese mat, then the molds.

2. In a large stainless-steel pot set in a hot water bath over medium heat, warm milk to 90°F (32°C), stirring gently. Turn off heat.

3. Sprinkle culture and mold powder over surface of milk and let stand for about 5 minutes to rehydrate. Using skimmer and an up-and-down motion, gently draw culture and mold down into milk without breaking surface of milk.

4. Dilute calcium chloride in ¼ cup (50 mL) cool water. Add to milk using the same up-and-down motion.

5. Dilute rennet in ¼ cup (50 mL) cool water. Add to milk and, using the same up-and-down motion, draw rennet down into milk until well blended. Cover pot and let set for 1¼ hours, maintaining the temperature at 90°F (32°C).

6. Check for a clean break (see Tip, opposite). If curd is still too fragile, cover and let set for another 15 minutes or until a clean break is achieved.

7. Using a long-bladed knife and skimmer, cut curd into 1-inch (2.5 cm) cubes (see Tip, page 100). Let stand for 5 minutes to firm up the curds.

Tip: To ascertain whether the curd is ready for the next step, check for a clean break: insert the long flat blade of a knife into the curd at a 30-degree angle and slowly lift the blade toward the surface of the curd. If the curd splits into a long clean break or crack, it is ready to cut. If the cut is wobbly or uneven, let the curd set for a few more minutes before trying again.

8. Using a skimmer, carefully fill the prepared molds to the top, then continue to top off until all the curd is used. It will take time for the curds to drain down, but all the curd will fit into the molds. Do not be tempted to add more molds. Cover container and let drain for 4 to 5 hours.

9. Carefully lift cheeses and molds together and flip over. Let drain for another 8 to 12 hours or overnight. Flip again and let drain for another 3 hours. Remove from molds and prepare a clean cheese mat in a ripening container.

10. Sprinkle top surface of each cheese with 1 tsp (5 mL) salt. Turn and salt other side in same manner. The cheeses will be about 2 inches (5 cm) thick. Place on mat in prepared container. Cover with lid.

11. Let cheese ripen at 50° to 55°F (10° to 13°C) and 90% humidity. Flip cheeses daily and remove any whey that has collected, wiping bottom of container with paper towel. Keep covered and make sure the cheeses don't become dry.

12. After 10 to 12 days, a fine white fuzzy mold will cover the surface of the cheese. When all the cheese is evenly covered in mold, wrap it in cheese-ripening paper and return to the ripening area. Continue to ripen for another 2 weeks. The cheese will be creamy and soft around the edges and have a bit of chalky firmness in the center. It will be ready to eat at 3 to 4 weeks after production. Store in the refrigerator for up to 10 weeks for longer shelf life.

Chaource

> **Makes 8 cheeses,
> each 7 oz (210 g)**
> *20% yield*

This is one of those delectable French cheeses that you just want to eat more and more of! A satisfying cheese to make, Chaource is ready for the table in 2 weeks but can be aged longer for a more pronounced flavor. Try it with a croissant for breakfast or as an appetizer with a glass of champagne.

Tip: This is an authentic recipe usually made with raw or non-homogenized whole milk. If you are using homogenized cow's milk, it is strongly recommended that you add calcium chloride (see page 31) for best results. The addition of calcium chloride will stabilize the curd, hasten setting and increase yield. Use the same amount of calcium chloride as rennet called for in the recipe, dilute it with at least 10 times the amount of water and stir into the milk before adding the rennet.

- Draining container
- 8 Crottin molds
- Cheese matting
- Ripening container

8 quarts	whole milk	8 L
¼ tsp	aroma mesophilic culture	1.25 mL
Pinch	*Penicillium candidum* mold powder	Pinch
Pinch	*Geotrichum candidum* 15 mold powder	Pinch
2	drops liquid rennet	2
4 tsp	pickling (canning) or kosher salt	20 mL

1. Sterilize all equipment (see page 40). Prepare a draining container by placing a rack inside, then the molds.

2. In a large stainless-steel pot over low heat, warm milk to 77°F (25°C), stirring gently to prevent scorching. Remove from heat.

3. Sprinkle culture and both mold powders over surface of milk and let stand for about 5 minutes to rehydrate. Using skimmer and an up-and-down motion, gently draw culture and molds down into milk without breaking surface of milk.

4. Dilute rennet in 1 tbsp (15 mL) cool water. Add to milk and, using the same up-and-down motion, draw rennet down into milk until well blended. Cover pot and let set for 12 hours, maintaining the temperature at 77°F (25°C).

5. Remove any whey that has collected on surface of curd, without disturbing the curd. Using a skimmer, carefully fill the prepared molds to the top, then continue to top off until all the curd is used. It will take time for the curds to drain down, but all the curd will fit into the molds. Do not be tempted to add more molds.

Tip: Chaource is a beautiful cheese to eat after only 2 weeks of ripening, but when ripened for a longer time, it develops a delicious fruity-earthy sharpness. To ripen, leave the cheese for another 4 weeks in the ripening container with the lid slightly ajar to allow for air movement. Continue to turn the cheese daily. The cheese will show a slight reddish mottling on the crust and have a layer of softened paste just under the rind.

6. Place molds in prepared draining container. Cover and let drain overnight at room temperature.

7. Carefully lift cheeses and molds together and flip over. Drain any collected whey from the container. If cheese is too delicate to flip, wait another 6 to 7 hours before attempting again. Continue draining molds in container for another day.

8. Prepare a clean cheese mat in a ripening container. Unmold cheeses and place them on mat. Sprinkle top surface of each cheese with $1/4$ tsp (1.25 mL) salt and let dissolve for a few minutes. Turn cheese over and salt other side in same manner. Cover container.

9. Let cheese ripen at 50° to 55°F (10° to 13°C) and 95% humidity. Flip cheeses daily and drain any whey that has collected, wiping bottom of container with paper towel. Keep covered and make sure the cheeses don't become dry. After about 1 week, a fine white fuzzy mold will begin to cover cheeses. As soon as the mold completely covers the surface, remove from the box and wrap in foil or plastic wrap. The cheeses are now ready to eat. You may continue to ripen them if you prefer a stronger flavor (see Tip, left); however, this cheese will not soften in the same way that other mold-ripened cheeses do.

French Neufchâtel

<table>
<tr><td>Makes 2 cheeses,
each 10 oz (300 g)
15% yield</td></tr>
</table>

Neufchâtel can be eaten
fresh when it resembles
cream cheese or cured
for several days until it is
covered with a fine white
mold. Either way, it is
meant to be consumed
young and is a creamy
delight. It is fun to shape
it in the traditional
heart-shaped mold.

- Draining bag or cloth-lined colander
- Draining container
- 2 heart-shaped molds or other small molds
- Ripening containers
- Cheese matting

4 quarts	whole milk	4 L
¼ tsp	mesophilic culture	1.25 mL
Pinch	*Penicillium candidum* mold powder	Pinch
3	drops liquid rennet	3
½ tsp	pickling (canning) or kosher salt, approx.	2.5 mL

1. Sterilize all equipment (see page 40). In a large
   stainless-steel pot over medium heat, warm milk to
   79°F (26°C), stirring gently to prevent scorching.
   Remove from heat.

2. Sprinkle culture and mold powder over surface of milk
   and let stand for about 5 minutes to rehydrate. Using
   skimmer and an up-and-down motion, gently draw
   culture and mold down into milk without breaking
   surface of milk.

3. Dilute rennet in ¼ cup (50 mL) cool water. Add to milk
   and, using the same up-and-down motion, draw rennet
   down into milk until well blended. Cover pot and let
   set at room temperature for 24 hours.

4. Remove any whey that has collected on surface of curd
   without disturbing the curd. You can tip the pot slightly
   or skim whey off the top with a measuring cup. Carefully
   ladle curd into a draining bag or cloth-lined colander.
   Hang bag or gather up corners of cloth and tie to form
   a bag and hang. Let drain for 12 hours.

5. Fold bag with the curd still in it and place in a draining
   container. Place a cutting board on top of the bag of
   curd and weigh down with a brick or 1- to 2-lb (500 g
   to 1 kg) weight. Cover container and refrigerate
   overnight.

Tip: Timing is an important factor when making cheese: the longer the milk ripens, the more acidic it becomes; the more acidic the milk, the quicker the action of the rennet to set the milk. When making fresh cheeses that ripen for a long time at a relatively low temperature, you can be more flexible with the timing. But remember that the longer the milk is allowed to ripen, the sharper the finished cheese will be.

6. Remove cheese from bag and place in a bowl. Knead in salt to taste. Press curds into molds and place in ripening container. Cover and return to refrigerator.

7. Let drain for 1 day, removing any collected whey from container, wiping it with paper towel. When cheeses are firm, remove from molds and place on a cheese mat in clean ripening container. Cover and return to refrigerator for 6 to 7 days, flipping cheeses daily. After about 1 week, a fine fuzzy white mold will cover the cheeses and they will be ready to eat. You can wrap them in foil and continue ripening for another 2 to 3 weeks for a soft-ripened cheese, if preferred. Once ripened to taste, store in the refrigerator.

St-Marcellin

Makes 8 cheeses,
each 4 oz (125 g)
about 15% yield

This delicate little disk of mold-ripened cow's milk cheese often has some spots of light blue mold on the surface.

Tip: In France, St-Marcellin is sold in little round glazed terra-cotta dishes, which just fit the cheese. If you wish to do the same, look for food-grade crocks or pottery dishes just over 3 inches (7.5 cm) in diameter with flat bottoms and straight 1-inch (2.5 cm) high sides. (Perhaps a local potter can custom-make some for you.) Ripen the cheese until it has a good covering of white mold. Transfer to a clean dish and cover with plastic wrap or waxed paper and store in the refrigerator. The pottery seems to even out the moisture of the cheese, allowing it to keep at optimum condition a bit longer.

- 8 St-Marcellin molds
- Draining container
- Cheese matting
- Ripening container

6 quarts	whole milk	6 L
¼ tsp	mesophilic culture	1.25 mL
⅛ tsp	*Penicillium candidum* mold powder	0.65 mL
Pinch	*Geotrichum candidum* 15 mold powder	Pinch
⅛ tsp	liquid rennet	0.65 mL
4 tsp	pickling (canning) or kosher salt	20 mL

1. Sterilize all equipment (see page 40). In a large stainless-steel pot over low heat, warm milk to 75°F (24°C), stirring gently to prevent scorching. Remove from heat.

2. Sprinkle culture and both mold powders over surface of milk and let stand for about 5 minutes to rehydrate. Using skimmer and an up-and-down motion, gently draw culture and molds down into milk without breaking surface of milk.

3. Dilute rennet in ¼ cup (50 mL) cool water. Add to milk and, using the same up-and-down motion, draw rennet down into milk until well blended. Cover pot and let set at room temperature for 12 hours.

4. Using a long-bladed knife and skimmer, cut curd into 1-inch (2.5 cm) cubes (see Tip, opposite), stirring gently. Let stand for 5 minutes to firm up the curds.

5. Place molds on a rack in a draining container. Using skimmer, carefully fill the prepared molds to the top, then continue to top off until all the curd is used. It will take time for the curds to drain down, but all the curd will fit into the molds. Do not be tempted to add more molds. Let drain for 6 hours. Flip the cheeses in the molds.

Tip: To cut curds: Holding a long-bladed stainless-steel knife straight up and down, draw knife through the curd, cutting it into strips. Proceed across the pot until you have reached the other side. Turn the pot and cut across the first strips to create squares. Using a skimmer, cut horizontally from side to side just under the surface of the curd to create cubes. Gradually move skimmer down through curd to cut layers of cubes. Using skimmer, gently stir curd cubes. Using a knife, cut any pieces that have been missed or are too large. For small-cut curds, you can use a large whisk for cutting.

6. Sprinkle top surface of each cheese with ¼ tsp (1.25 mL) salt. Let drain for another 6 hours.

7. Flip cheeses in molds and salt other side in same manner. Let drain for another 6 hours.

8. Prepare a clean cheese mat in a ripening container. Unmold the cheeses onto the mat. Cover and let drain for another 48 hours. Flip cheeses daily and remove any whey that has collected, wiping bottom of container with paper towel.

9. Let cheese ripen at 60°F (16°C) and 80% humidity for another 2 weeks. Flip cheeses daily and remove any collected whey. The cheeses should be covered with a light fuzzy white mold. Wrap in parchment paper and store in the refrigerator for 6 weeks.

Valençay

Perhaps the most distinctive of the French goat's milk cheeses, Valençay is shaped like a pyramid with the point cut off. It is dusted with fine ash to firm up the exterior and aid in ripening. Valençay has a fruity, complex flavor and is a beautiful cheese at any stage of ripeness. When fresh, slice and serve with fruit and crackers; if dry and hard, grate it over a salad or an omelet for sensational flavor.

- Draining container
- 8 pyramid-shaped molds
- Cheese matting
- Ripening container

8 quarts	goat's milk	8 L
½ tsp	mesophilic culture	2.5 mL
Pinch	*Geotrichum candidum* 15 mold powder	Pinch
Pinch	*Penicillium candidum* mold powder	Pinch
¼ tsp	calcium chloride	1.25 mL
¼ tsp	liquid rennet	1.25 mL
2 tbsp	pickling (canning) or kosher salt	30 mL
	Ash (see Tip, opposite)	

1. Sterilize all equipment (see page 40). Prepare a draining container by placing a rack inside, then the molds. For stability, it is helpful to set each pyramid-shaped mold in a Camembert mold.

2. In a large stainless-steel pot over medium heat, warm milk to 72°F (22°C), stirring gently to prevent scorching. Remove from heat.

3. Sprinkle culture and both molds over surface of milk and let stand for about 5 minutes to rehydrate. Using skimmer and an up-and-down motion, gently draw culture and molds down into milk without breaking surface of milk.

4. Dilute calcium chloride in ¼ cup (50 mL) cool water. Add to milk using the same up-and-down motion.

5. Dilute rennet in ¼ cup (50 mL) cool water. Add to milk and, using the same up-and-down motion, draw rennet down into milk until well blended. Cover pot and let set at room temperature for 18 hours or until a firm curd forms with a bit of whey on top. Remove excess whey. To remove whey, you can tip the pot slightly or skim whey off the top with a measuring cup.

Tip: Ash is very finely ground charcoal, usually French in origin, from the maritime pine tree. You can find it at cheese-making supply houses (see Sources, page 370).

6. Using skimmer, carefully take thin slices of curd and ladle into molds without breaking up the curd. Continue from mold to mold, placing thin layer upon layer until all the curd is used up. You may have to wait for some time between fillings to allow the curd to drain down. Don't be tempted to add more molds or your resulting cheeses will be too small. Once all the curd is used up, cover the container and let drain at room temperature for 48 hours, draining out the collected whey at regular intervals.

7. Clean the draining container and wipe it dry. Line with paper towel. Remove cheeses from molds and sprinkle ¾ tsp (3.75 mL) salt over all sides of each. Set on paper towel after salting.

8. Using a small sieve or tea strainer, dust cheeses with ash, moving the strainer over them and tapping with your finger so the ash drifts down onto the cheeses. You do not want a thick coating, but there should not be too much white showing. A light dusting on all surfaces is best. The paper towel will protect the container from developing black ash stains, which are really difficult to remove. Cover container and let cheeses stand for 24 hours at room temperature.

9. Prepare a clean cheese mat in a ripening container. Place cheeses carefully on the mat, discarding the paper towel. Let ripen at 50°F (10°C) and 85% humidity for 2 weeks. Adjust the lid of the container to control the humidity. If there is too much moisture, cheeses can develop spots of blue mold. Too little moisture can dry out the cheese.

10. Wrap or place in a small covered container and store in the refrigerator for up to 10 weeks. If wrapped loosely or placed in a loosely covered container, the cheese will dry as it ages.

Ste-Maure

Makes 4 cheeses,
each 10 oz (300 g)
15% yield

The log shape of this
cheese makes it difficult
to mold and drain but
a delight to use — slice
crosswise for perfect
rounds. The special
feature of French AOC
Ste-Maure de Touraine
is a piece of natural
rye straw that runs
lengthwise through the
center of the cheese. Its
original purpose was to
help stabilize the tender
paste, but now it serves
more as an identifying
mark. Slice into rounds
and serve with fruit and
crackers, or on a salad
plate.

- Draining container
- Cheese matting
- 4 Ste-Maure molds
- Ripening container

8 quarts	goat's milk	8 L
½ tsp	mesophilic culture	2.5 mL
Pinch	*Geotrichum candidum* 15 mold powder	Pinch
Pinch	*Penicillium candidum* mold powder	Pinch
¼ tsp	calcium chloride	1.25 mL
¼ tsp	liquid rennet	1.25 mL
2 to 3 tsp	pickling (canning) or kosher salt	10 to 15 mL
	Ash (see Tip, opposite)	

1. Sterilize all equipment (see page 40). Prepare a draining container by placing a rack inside. Then place a cutting board on top, followed by a cheese mat, then the molds, standing on end. For stability, it is helpful to set each Ste-Maure mold in a Camembert mold.

2. In a large stainless-steel pot over medium heat, warm milk to 72°F (22°C), stirring gently to prevent scorching. Remove from heat.

3. Sprinkle culture and both molds over surface of milk and let stand for about 5 minutes to rehydrate. Using skimmer and an up-and-down motion, gently draw culture and molds down into milk without breaking surface of milk.

4. Dilute calcium chloride in ¼ cup (50 mL) cool water. Add to milk using the same up-and-down motion.

5. Dilute rennet in ¼ cup (50 mL) cool water. Add to milk and, using the same up-and-down motion, draw rennet down into milk until well blended. Cover pot and let set at room temperature for 18 hours or until a firm curd forms with a bit of whey on top. Remove excess whey. To remove whey, you can tip the pot slightly or skim whey off the top with a measuring cup.

Tip: Many delicate cheeses, especially goat cheeses, are sprinkled with a light coating of vegetable ash. This is very finely ground charcoal, usually French in origin, from the maritime pine tree (see Sources, page 370).

6. Using skimmer, carefully take thin slices of curd and ladle into molds without breaking up the curd. Continue from mold to mold, placing thin layer upon layer until all the curd is used up. You may have to wait for some time between fillings to allow the curd to drain down. Don't be tempted to add more molds or your resulting cheeses will be too small. Once all the curd is used up, cover the container and let drain at room temperature for 24 hours, turning the molds once or twice (the molds are standing upright) and draining out the collected whey at regular intervals.

7. Clean the draining container and wipe it dry. Line with paper towel. Remove cheeses from molds and sprinkle each with 1/2 to 3/4 tsp (2.5 to 3.75 mL) salt. Set each on paper towel after salting.

8. Using a small sieve or tea strainer, dust cheeses with ash, moving the strainer over them and tapping with your finger so the ash drifts down onto the cheeses. Turn the cheeses to coat all around. You do not want a thick coating, but there should not be too much white showing. A light dusting on all surfaces is best. The paper towel will protect the container from developing black ash stains, which are really difficult to remove. Cover container and let cheeses stand for 24 hours at room temperature.

9. Prepare a clean cheese mat in a ripening container. Place cheeses carefully on the mat, discarding the paper towel. Let ripen at 50°F (10°C) and 85% humidity for 2 weeks. Turn the cheeses a quarter-turn daily to maintain the log shape and facilitate even draining. Remove any collected moisture from the container, wiping the bottom with paper towel. Adjust the lid of the container to control the humidity. If there is too much moisture, cheeses can develop spots of blue mold. Too little moisture can dry out the cheese.

10. After about 10 days, a fine fuzzy white mold will begin to cover the cheeses. Once cheese is no longer losing moisture and mold covers the entire surface of the cheeses, about 2 weeks, wrap or place in a small covered container and store in the refrigerator for up to 10 weeks.

Selles-sur-Cher

<table>
<tr><td rowspan="2">

Makes 8 cheeses, each 5 oz (150 g)

15% yield
</td></tr>
</table>

Originally created for consumption by the farm family who made them, these small round cheeses are now renowned for their fine white paste and floral notes. The name comes from the town in the center of the area where these AOC cheeses are produced.

- Draining container
- Cheese matting
- Eight 3-inch (7.5 cm) St-Marcellin molds
- Ripening container

8 quarts	goat's milk	8 L
½ tsp	mesophilic culture	2.5 mL
Pinch	*Geotrichum candidum* 15 mold powder	Pinch
Pinch	*Penicillium candidum* mold powder	Pinch
¼ tsp	calcium chloride	1.25 mL
¼ tsp	liquid rennet	1.25 mL
	Pickling (canning) or kosher salt	
	Ash (see Tip, page 117)	

1. Sterilize all equipment (see page 40). Prepare a draining container by placing a rack inside. Then place a cutting board on top, followed by a cheese mat, then the molds.

2. In a large stainless-steel pot over medium heat, warm milk to 72°F (22°C), stirring gently to prevent scorching. Remove from heat.

3. Sprinkle culture and both molds over surface of milk and let stand for about 5 minutes to rehydrate. Using skimmer and an up-and-down motion, gently draw culture and molds down into milk without breaking surface of milk.

4. Dilute calcium chloride in ¼ cup (50 mL) cool water. Add to milk using the same up-and-down motion.

5. Dilute rennet in ¼ cup (50 mL) cool water. Add to milk and, using the same up-and-down motion, draw rennet down into milk until well blended. Cover pot and let set at room temperature for 18 hours or until a firm curd forms with a bit of whey on top. Remove excess whey. To remove whey, you can tip the pot slightly or skim whey off the top with a measuring cup.

Tip: Don't worry if your fresh goat cheeses become a little misshapen once they have been removed from the molds; simply reshape gently by hand and return to the refrigerator.

6. Using skimmer, carefully take thin slices of curd and ladle into molds without breaking up the curd. Continue from mold to mold, placing thin layer upon layer until all the curd is used up. You may have to wait for some time between fillings to allow the curd to drain down. Don't be tempted to add more molds or your resulting cheeses will be too small. Once all the curd is used up, cover the container and let drain at room temperature for 24 hours. Remove the collected whey. Carefully lift the cheeses and molds together and flip over. Continue draining for another 24 hours.

7. Clean the draining container and wipe it dry. Line with paper towel. Remove cheeses from molds and sprinkle each side with $\frac{1}{4}$ tsp (1.25 mL) salt. Set each on paper towel after salting.

8. Using a small sieve or tea strainer, dust the cheeses with ash, moving the strainer over them and tapping with your finger so the ash drifts down onto the cheeses. You do not want a thick coating, but there should not be too much white showing. A light dusting on all surfaces is best. The paper towel will protect the container from developing black ash stains, which are really difficult to remove. Turn cheeses and dust the other side.

9. Prepare a clean cheese mat in a ripening container. Place cheeses carefully on the mat, discarding the paper towel. Let ripen at 50°F (10°C) and 85% humidity for 2 weeks. Adjust the lid of the container to control the humidity. If there is too much moisture, cheeses can develop spots of blue mold. Too little moisture can dry out the cheese.

10. Wrap or place in a small covered container and store in the refrigerator for up to 1 month. Cheese is best eaten between 10 days and 3 weeks after production.

Pouligny-St-Pierre

<table>
<tr><td rowspan="3">Makes 8 cheeses,
each 5 oz (150 g)
15% yield</td></tr>
</table>

**Makes 8 cheeses,
each 5 oz (150 g)**
15% yield

This is another
pyramid-shaped goat
cheese like Valençay,
but it is not ash-ripened.
With a beautiful
melting paste and
a faint fruity goatiness,
Pouligny-St-Pierre is a
fine French AOC cheese
traditionally made from
raw goat's milk.

- Draining container
- Cheese matting
- 8 pyramid-shaped molds
- Ripening container

8 quarts	goat's milk	8 L
½ tsp	mesophilic culture	2.5 mL
Pinch	*Geotrichum candidum* 15 mold powder	Pinch
Pinch	*Penicillium candidum* mold powder	Pinch
¼ tsp	calcium chloride	1.25 mL
¼ tsp	liquid rennet	1.25 mL
	Pickling (canning) or kosher salt	

1. Sterilize all equipment (see page 40). Prepare a draining container by placing a rack inside. Then place a cutting board on top, followed by a cheese mat, then the molds. For stability, it is helpful to set each pyramid-shaped mold in a Camembert mold.

2. In a large stainless-steel pot over medium heat, warm milk to 72°F (22°C), stirring gently to prevent scorching. Remove from heat.

3. Sprinkle culture and both molds over surface of milk and let stand for about 5 minutes to rehydrate. Using skimmer and an up-and-down motion, gently draw culture and molds down into milk without breaking surface of milk.

4. Dilute calcium chloride in ¼ cup (50 mL) cool water. Add to milk using the same up-and-down motion.

5. Dilute rennet in ¼ cup (50 mL) cool water. Add to milk and, using the same up-and-down motion, draw rennet down into milk until well blended. Cover pot and let set at room temperature for 18 to 20 hours or until a firm curd forms with a bit of whey on top. Remove excess whey. To remove whey, you can tip the pot slightly or skim whey off the top with a measuring cup.

Tip: Timing is an important factor when making cheese: the longer the milk ripens, the more acidic it becomes; the more acidic the milk, the quicker the action of the rennet to set the milk. When making fresh cheeses that ripen for a long time at a relatively low temperature, you can be more flexible with the timing. But remember that the longer the milk is allowed to ripen, the sharper the finished cheese will be.

6. Using skimmer, carefully take thin slices of curd and ladle into molds without breaking up the curd. Continue from mold to mold, placing thin layer upon layer until all the curd is used up. You may have to wait for some time between fillings to allow the curd to drain down. Don't be tempted to add more molds or your resulting cheeses will be too small. Once all the curd is used up, cover the container and let drain at room temperature for 48 hours, draining out the collected whey at regular intervals.

7. Clean the draining container and wipe it dry. Line with paper towel. Remove cheeses from molds and sprinkle sides with a total of ¾ tsp (3.75 mL) salt. Set on paper towel after salting. Cover container and let cheeses stand at room temperature for 24 hours.

8. Prepare a clean cheese mat in a ripening container. Place cheeses carefully on the mat, discarding the paper towel. Let ripen at 50°F (10°C) and 85% humidity for 2 weeks. Adjust the lid of the container to control the humidity. If there is too much moisture, cheeses can develop spots of blue mold. Too little moisture can dry out the cheese.

9. Wrap or place in a small covered container and store in the refrigerator for up to 6 weeks. This cheese is best consumed at 10 days to 3 weeks after production.

Crottin

<table>
<tr><td rowspan="3">**Makes 10 cheeses, each 2 oz (60 g)**
15% yield</td></tr>
</table>

Makes 10 cheeses,
each 2 oz (60 g)
15% yield

This is a small drum of goat's milk cheese with a fine mold crust. Enjoy it after a meal with a glass of cool sweet white wine.

- Draining container
- Cheese matting
- 10 Crottin molds
- Ripening container

4 quarts	goat's milk	4 L
¼ tsp	mesophilic culture	1.25 mL
Pinch	*Geotrichum candidum* 15 mold powder	Pinch
Pinch	*Penicillium candidum* mold powder	Pinch
⅛ tsp	calcium chloride	0.65 mL
⅛ tsp	liquid rennet	0.65 mL
5 tsp	pickling (canning) or kosher salt	25 mL

1. Sterilize all equipment (see page 40). Prepare a draining container by placing a rack inside. Then place a cutting board on top, followed by a cheese mat, then the molds.

2. In a large stainless-steel pot over medium heat, warm milk to 72°F (22°C), stirring gently to prevent scorching. Remove from heat.

3. Sprinkle culture and both molds over surface of milk and let stand for about 5 minutes to rehydrate. Using skimmer and an up-and-down motion, gently draw culture and molds down into milk without breaking surface of milk.

4. Dilute calcium chloride in ¼ cup (50 mL) cool water. Add to milk using the same up-and-down motion.

5. Dilute rennet in ¼ cup (50 mL) cool water. Add to milk and, using the same up-and-down motion, draw rennet down into milk until well blended. Cover pot and let set at room temperature for 18 to 20 hours or until a firm curd forms with a bit of whey on top. Remove excess whey. To remove whey, you can tip the pot slightly or skim whey off the top with a measuring cup.

6. Using skimmer, carefully take thin slices of curd and ladle into molds without breaking up the curd. Continue from mold to mold, placing thin layer upon layer until all the curd is used up. You may have to wait for some time between fillings to allow the curd to drain down. Don't be tempted to add more molds or your resulting cheeses will be too small. Once all the curd is used up, cover the container and let drain at room temperature for 48 hours, draining out the collected whey at regular intervals. Flip the cheeses in the molds after 24 hours of draining.

7. Remove cheeses from molds and sprinkle top and bottom with ¼ tsp (1.25 mL) salt each. Return to container. Cover and let cheeses stand at room temperature for 24 hours. Remove any collected whey from the container, drying bottom of container with paper towel.

8. Place on cheese mat in a ripening container and let ripen at 50°F (10°C) and 90% humidity for 2 weeks. Adjust the lid of the container to control the humidity. If there is too much moisture, cheeses can develop spots of blue mold. Too little moisture can dry out the cheese.

9. Wrap or place in a small covered container and store in the refrigerator for up to 6 weeks. This cheese is best consumed at 10 days to 3 weeks after production.

Goat Brie

**Makes 6 cheeses,
each 7 oz (210 g)**
15% yield

*Goat's milk Brie is more
delicate than cow's milk
Brie, and the paste is
usually softer. Ripening
it at a cooler temperature
can slow down the
process and help firm
up the paste — though
runny is not a bad thing!*

Tip: To ascertain
whether the curd is
ready for the next step,
check for a clean break:
insert the long flat blade
of a knife into the curd
at a 30-degree angle
and slowly lift the blade
toward the surface of
the curd. If the curd
splits into a long clean
break or crack, it is
ready to cut. If the cut
is wobbly or uneven,
let the curd set for a
few more minutes
before trying again.

- Draining container
- Cheese matting
- Six 4-inch (10 cm) bottomless Camembert molds
- Ripening container

8 quarts	goat's milk	8 L
¼ tsp	mesophilic culture	1.25 mL
Pinch	*Penicillium candidum* mold powder	Pinch
¼ tsp	calcium chloride	1.25 mL
¼ tsp	liquid rennet	1.25 mL
2 tbsp	pickling (canning) or kosher salt	30 mL

1. Sterilize all equipment (see page 40). Prepare a draining container by placing a rack inside. Then place a cutting board on top, followed by a cheese mat, then the molds.

2. In a large stainless-steel pot set in a hot water bath over medium heat, warm milk to 88°F (31°C), stirring gently. Turn off heat.

3. Sprinkle culture and mold powder over surface of milk and let stand for about 5 minutes to rehydrate. Using skimmer and an up-and-down motion, gently draw culture and mold down into milk without breaking surface of milk.

4. Dilute calcium chloride in ¼ cup (50 mL) cool water. Add to milk using the same up-and-down motion.

5. Dilute rennet in ¼ cup (50 mL) cool water. Add to milk and, using the same up-and-down motion, draw rennet down into milk until well blended. Cover pot and let set for 1 hour, maintaining the temperature at 88°F (31°C).

6. Check for a clean break (see Tip, left). If curd is still too fragile, cover and let set for another 5 to 10 minutes or until a clean break is achieved. Using a long-bladed knife and skimmer, cut curd into 1-inch (2.5 cm) cubes (see Tip, opposite). Let stand for 10 minutes to firm up the curds.

Tip: To cut curds: Holding a long-bladed stainless-steel knife straight up and down, draw knife through the curd, cutting it into strips. Proceed across the pot until you have reached the other side. Turn the pot and cut across the first strips to create squares. Using a skimmer, cut horizontally from side to side just under the surface of the curd to create cubes. Gradually move skimmer down through curd to cut layers of cubes. Using skimmer, gently stir curd cubes. Using a knife, cut any pieces that have been missed or are too large. For small-cut curds, you can use a large whisk for cutting.

7. Using skimmer, stir curd very gently by lifting and moving it from the bottom all around perimeter of the pot for 5 to 10 minutes or until pieces of curd start to shrink slightly in size and edges become rounded. (This is more lifting and moving the curd rather than actually stirring it around.) Let curds settle.

8. Using a measuring cup, dip off whey until you see the surface of the curd.

9. Using a skimmer, carefully ladle curd into prepared molds. Ladle a spoonful of curds into one mold, then the others, and repeat. It will take time for the curds to drain down, but all the curd will fit into the molds. Don't be tempted to add another mold. Let drain for 2 to 3 hours. Carefully lift cheeses and molds together and flip over. Remove any collected whey from the container. Continue draining for a total of 20 to 24 hours, flipping once or twice during this time and removing any whey.

10. Prepare a clean cheese mat in ripening container. Remove molds and place cheeses on mat. Sprinkle top and bottom of each cheese with a scant ½ tsp (2.5 mL) salt each. Cover with lid.

11. Let cheese ripen at 50° to 55°F (10° to 13°C) and 90% humidity. Flip cheeses daily and remove any whey that has collected, wiping bottom of container with paper towel.

12. After about 8 days, a fine white fuzzy mold will begin to grow. Continue to turn cheese daily. Once cheese is completely covered with mold, after 12 days, wrap it and return to ripening area. The cheese should be softened and ready to eat at about 4 weeks after production. Store in the refrigerator for up to 4 weeks.

Troubleshooting

Pink color appears on the surface of mold-ripened cheese during aging.
Moisture is too high in ripening area; decrease humidity. Be sure to drain and dry the container for the first few days after production, when the fresh cheeses are still losing whey. It is still safe to eat if pink appears.

Black or brown mold appears on the surface of the cheese.
Too much moisture in the ripening area; decrease humidity. Airborne bacteria in the ripening area; clean all surfaces and environment with bleach solution (2 tbsp/30 mL bleach to 4 quarts/4 L water). To combat the mold, rub cheese rind with a mixture of salt and vinegar (1 tsp/5 mL salt and 1/4 cup/50 mL vinegar).

The crust on mold-ripened cheese is thick and gritty.
Too much development of mold; reduce amount of mold powder used to inoculate the milk and wrap the cheese as soon as white mold has completely covered it.

Mold-ripened cheese ripens too quickly and tastes of ammonia.
Cheese is overripe; slow down ripening by reducing the temperature of the ripening area. Too much moisture in the cheese; stir curd slightly longer to reduce the amount of moisture in it when ladled.

Mold-ripened cheese is very runny.
Too much moisture in the curd; stir longer before ladling.

Mold-ripened cheese is too firm and will not soften when ripened.
Curd was stirred too long before ladling, expelling too much moisture; stir gently and for a shorter time. Handle curd gently during ladling.

Mold takes a long time to develop on mold-ripened cheese (mold should completely cover the cheese within 12 to 14 days).
The temperature of the milk was too low at inoculation; watch thermometer carefully and reheat milk if necessary. The ripening temperature is too low; raise temperature. Ripening area is too dry; increase humidity. The cheese has been salted too heavily; measure salt carefully.

Blue-Veined Cheeses

Some of the world's greatest cheeses are those of the blue family. Blue-veined cheeses have been inoculated with mold, usually a strain of *Penicillium roquefortii*, which creates a blue-green marbled effect in the curd and a bluish-gray crust. The flavor tends to be sharp and acidic but is often offset by a rich, creamy paste, as in the case of Italian Gorgonzola and French Roquefort. Though not as creamy, semifirm and hard cheeses also make excellent blues.

Traditionally, the blue mold is grown on bread made from rye flour, which is set aside to "go moldy." The blue mold is then harvested from the bread and used for cheese making. The mold spores are introduced into the milk during production. When the cheeses have firmed up enough, usually 1 to 2 weeks after they're formed, they are pierced with a sharp tool (in the recipes here, a sterilized knitting needle or skewer) to open up the cheese to the air, allowing the mold to grow into the interior of the cheese.

Blue cheeses often make the perfect finish to a fine meal, especially when paired with fresh fruit and sweet or full-bodied wines.

Castle Blue

**Makes 3 cheeses,
each 12½ oz (375 g)**

15% yield

- Draining container
- Cheese matting
- Three 4-inch (10 cm) Camembert molds
- Ripening container
- Thin knitting needle or metal skewer

*The added cream makes
this a wonderful dessert
cheese, especially when
served with fresh fruit
and a sip of icewine or
a berry port.*

Tip: To cut curds:
Holding a long-bladed
stainless-steel knife
straight up and down,
draw knife through
the curd, cutting it into
strips. Proceed across
the pot until you have
reached the other side.
Turn the pot and cut
across the first strips
to create squares.
Using a skimmer, cut
horizontally from side
to side just under the
surface of the curd to
create cubes. Gradually
move skimmer down
through curd to cut
layers of cubes. Using
skimmer, gently stir
curd cubes. Using a
knife, cut any pieces
that have been missed
or are too large. For
small-cut curds, you
can use a large whisk
for cutting.

6½ quarts	whole milk	6.5 L
2 cups	whipping (35%) cream	500 mL
¼ tsp	mesophilic culture	1.25 mL
⅛ tsp	*Penicillium roquefortii* mold powder	0.65 mL
¼ tsp	calcium chloride	1.25 mL
¼ tsp	rennet	1.25 mL
	Pickling (canning) or kosher salt	

1. Sterilize all equipment (see page 40). Prepare a draining container by placing a rack inside. Then place a cutting board on top, followed by a cheese mat, then the molds.

2. In a large stainless-steel pot set in a hot water bath over medium heat, warm milk and cream to 90°F (32°C), stirring gently. Turn off heat.

3. Sprinkle culture and *Penicillium roquefortii* mold powder over surface of milk mixture and let stand for about 5 minutes to rehydrate. Using skimmer and an up-and-down motion, gently draw culture and mold down into milk without breaking surface of milk. Cover and let ripen for 1½ hours, maintaining the temperature at 90°F (32°C).

4. Dilute calcium chloride in ¼ cup (50 mL) cool water. Add to milk using the same up-and-down motion.

5. Dilute rennet in ¼ cup (50 mL) cool water. Add to milk and, using the same up-and-down motion, draw rennet down into milk until well blended. Cover pot and let set at room temperature for 1 hour.

6. Check for a clean break (see Tip, page 131). Using a long-bladed knife and skimmer, cut curd into 1-inch (2.5 cm) cubes (see Tip, left). Let stand for 10 minutes.

continued on page 129…

Fromage Frais (page 43)

Fresh Goat Cheeses
(Variations: Rose Petal and Hazelnut,
Rosemary and Olive Oil and Maple Walnut (page 67)

Bocconcini (Variation, page 79)

Camembert (page 100)

Valençay (page 114)

Castle Blue (page 128)

Port Salut (page 156)

Hot Chile Gouda and Herbed Gouda (Variations, page 188)

Tips: Always use the freshest possible milk for your cheeses. If you are purchasing packaged milk, look for the latest best-before date. If using your own milk, plan your cheese making for as soon after milking as possible. The older the milk, the more bacteria there are in it to compete with the lactic bacterial starter.

Non-homogenized milk, also known as cream line or standard milk, is always the best choice for successful cheese making. Non-homogenized milk is pasteurized milk that hasn't been homogenized and shouldn't be confused with raw milk. See Sources, page 372, for more information.

7. Stir curds gently with skimmer constantly for 30 minutes, or until curd pieces shrink in size and begin to mat (the curds will begin to stick together in clumps and will heap up on the skimmer). Let settle.

8. Using a measuring cup, dip off whey until you see the surface of the curds. Ladle curds into prepared molds, refilling until all the curd is used up. Let drain for 2 hours, then flip cheeses and molds together. Continue draining for several hours or overnight.

9. In the morning, flip cheeses again and let drain for another 2 hours. Remove from molds and salt tops of cheeses with ¾ tsp (3.75 mL) salt. Place salted side down on a clean cheese mat in a ripening container and salt remaining side.

10. Cover container and place in the ripening area. Let cheeses ripen at 50°F (10°C) and 90% humidity. Turn cheeses daily for the first week, removing any collected whey from the bottom of the container and wiping with a paper towel.

11. One week after production, pierce cheeses 8 to 12 times with knitting needle or skewer, through from top to bottom and side to side. Return to container and continue to ripen.

12. After approximately 10 days of ripening, blue mold should be visible on the outside of the cheese.

13. Pierce cheese again in the same manner at 2 weeks. Continue to ripen for another 4 weeks, turning cheeses weekly. The rind will develop blue-gray mold, and cheese will soften slightly. Wrap in parchment paper and store in the refrigerator for up to 1 month.

Cambozola

Makes 6 cheeses,
each 7 to 8 oz
(210 to 250 g),
or 2 cheeses, each
1¼ to 1½ lbs
(600 to 750 g)

15 to 18% yield

This delicious blend
of Camembert and
Gorgonzola-style cheese
was developed by a
German cheese maker.
The addition of cream
imparts a richness that
tempers the acidity of
the blue flavor. Try it
with a platter of sliced
pears and apples.

- Draining container
- Cheese matting
- Six 4-inch (10 cm) Camembert molds or two 8-inch (20 cm) half-Brie molds
- Cloth-lined colander
- Ripening container
- Thin knitting needle or metal skewer

4 quarts	whole milk	4 L
4 quarts	whipping (35%) cream	4 L
¼ tsp	mesophilic culture	1.25 mL
⅛ tsp	*Penicillium candidum* mold powder	0.65 mL
¼ tsp	calcium chloride	1.25 mL
¼ tsp	liquid rennet	1.25 mL
⅛ tsp	*Penicillium roquefortii* mold powder	0.65 mL
	Pickling (canning) or kosher salt	

1. Sterilize all equipment (see page 40). Prepare a draining container by placing a rack inside. Then place a cutting board on top, followed by a cheese mat, then the molds.

2. In a large stainless-steel pot set in a hot water bath over medium heat, warm milk and cream to 86°F (30°C), stirring gently. Remove from heat.

3. Sprinkle culture and *Penicillium candidum* mold powder over surface of milk mixture and let stand for about 5 minutes to rehydrate. Using skimmer and an up-and-down motion, gently draw culture and mold down into milk without breaking surface of milk. Cover and let ripen for 15 minutes.

4. Dilute calcium chloride in ¼ cup (50 mL) cool water. Add to milk using the same up-and-down motion.

5. Dilute rennet in ¼ cup (50 mL) cool water. Add to milk and, using the same up-and-down motion, draw rennet down into milk until well blended. Cover pot and let set at room temperature for 1 hour.

Tip: To ascertain whether the curd is ready for the next step, check for a clean break: insert the long flat blade of a knife into the curd at a 30-degree angle and slowly lift the blade toward the surface of the curd. If the curd splits into a long clean break or crack, it is ready to cut. If the cut is wobbly or uneven, let the curd set for a few more minutes before trying again.

6. Check for a clean break (see Tip, left). If the curd is still too fragile, cover and let set for another 15 minutes or until a clean break is achieved.

7. Using a long-bladed knife and skimmer, cut curd into ½-inch (1.25 cm) cubes (see Tip, page 128). Let stand for 5 minutes to firm up the curds.

8. Using skimmer, stir curd by very gently lifting and moving it from the bottom all around the perimeter of the pot for 10 minutes or until pieces of curd start to shrink in size and edges become rounded. Cut any large pieces of curd with a knife. Let settle.

9. Using a measuring cup, dip off whey until you see the surface of the curds. Carefully ladle curds into cloth-lined colander. Let drain for 8 to 10 minutes.

10. Fill cheese molds half-full of drained curds. Let stand for 15 minutes, covering colander with pot lid to keep remaining curds warm.

11. After 15 minutes, sprinkle the top of the curds in the molds with *Penicillium roquefortii* mold powder. Continue ladling remaining curds into the molds on top of the mold powder, waiting 15 minutes between additions, until all of the curd is used up and the molds are full. Cover and let drain for about 6 hours at room temperature. Flip cheeses over and let drain overnight.

12. Remove molds and sprinkle top surface of each cheese with ½ tsp (2.5 mL) salt. Flip cheeses over and salt other side in same manner. Prepare a clean cheese mat in a ripening container. Place cheeses on mat. Cover and place container in ripening area.

continued on next page…

Cambozola continued...

13. Let cheeses ripen at 50° to 55°F (10° to 13°C) and 85 to 90% humidity. Turn cheeses daily, removing any collected whey from the container and wiping with a paper towel. Once the cheeses are fairly dry, after about 4 days, pierce cheeses all the way through in several places, horizontally and vertically, with knitting needle or skewer. Return to container to continue ripening.

14. After 10 to 12 days, white fuzzy mold should completely cover the cheeses. At this point, wrap the cheeses in cheese-ripening paper and return to the ripening area. The cheese should be ready for consumption at 4 weeks after production. Once ripened to your liking, store wrapped cheeses in the refrigerator.

Piercing Blue Cheeses

Blue cheeses are usually pierced with a special tool that has many long needles. When making small amounts of cheese, a sterilized knitting needle or skewer can do the job just as effectively. Boil the metal needles or skewer for 10 minutes and let cool. Do not use bleach to sterilize the needle. The idea of piercing is to encourage mold growth on the inside of the cheese, and too much bleach will kill any bacteria and mold. To pierce the cheese, hold it in your hand or set it on a flat surface and place your hand on top. Slowly push the needle right through the cheese, being careful not to break it. Press down on the cheese lightly while withdrawing the needle to prevent breaking or tearing. Repeat at intervals all over the top and sides of the cheese.

Gorgonzola

Makes
5³⁄₄ lbs (2.88 kg)
18% yield

Gorgonzola is the most famous blue-veined cheese of Italy. It is rich and aromatic, with interior blue veining. Traditionally, it was made by processing the milk from the evening milking, then processing the next morning's milk and blending both batches into the mold. We will follow that tradition, somewhat modified, in our recipe.

- Draining bag
- 1 tomme mold, lined with cheese cloth
- Cheese press
- Cheese matting
- Ripening container
- Thin knitting needle or metal skewer

16 quarts	whole milk, divided	16 L
½ tsp	mesophilic culture, divided	2.5 mL
½ tsp	calcium chloride, divided	2.5 mL
½ tsp	liquid rennet, divided	2.5 mL
⅛ tsp	*Penicillium roquefortii* mold powder	0.65 mL
	Pickling (canning) or kosher salt	

1. Sterilize all equipment (see page 40). In a large stainless-steel pot set in a hot water bath over medium heat, warm 8 quarts (8 L) of the milk to 90°F (32°C), stirring gently. Turn off heat.

2. Sprinkle ¼ tsp (1.25 mL) of the culture over surface of milk and let stand for about 5 minutes to rehydrate. Using skimmer and an up-and-down motion, gently draw culture down into milk without breaking surface of milk.

3. Dilute ¼ tsp (1.25 mL) of the calcium chloride in ¼ cup (50 mL) cool water. Add to milk using the same up-and-down motion.

4. Dilute ¼ tsp (1.25 mL) of the rennet in ¼ cup (50 mL) cool water. Add to milk and, using the same up-and-down motion, draw rennet down into milk until well blended. Cover pot and let set for 20 minutes.

5. Check for a clean break (see Tip, page 131). If the curd is still too fragile, cover and let set for another 15 minutes or until a clean break is achieved. Using a long-bladed knife and skimmer, cut curd into ³⁄₄-inch (2 cm) cubes (see Tip, page 128). Let stand for 5 minutes to firm up the curds.

continued on next two pages…

Gorgonzola continued...

Tip: Always use the freshest possible milk for your cheeses. If you are purchasing packaged milk, look for the latest best-before date. If using your own milk, plan your cheese making for as soon after milking as possible. The older the milk, the more bacteria there are in it to compete with the lactic bacterial starter.

6. Using a skimmer, gently stir curd constantly for 20 minutes or until the curd size is reduced to about $\frac{1}{2}$ inch (1.25 cm). Let settle.

7. Using a measuring cup, dip off whey until you see the surface of the curds. Ladle curds into a draining bag and let drain overnight at 60°F (16°C).

8. The next morning, make another batch of cheese exactly the same as the one from the previous day, draining it for 6 to 7 hours but not cooling it.

9. Keeping the two batches of curds separate, break up or cut the curds into 1- to 2-inch (2.5 to 5 cm) chunks or slices.

10. Fill mold with cheese chunks, placing warm curds that were just made on the bottom and sides and the cool firmer evening curds in the center. Reserve some warm curds for the top. As you fill, sprinkle pinches of *Penicillium roquefortii* mold powder on cool curds. Finish with warm curds. Pull cloth up around curds and fold excess neatly over the top, with as few wrinkles as possible. Put on the lid.

11. Place mold in cheese press or place a weight on top. Press cheese at light pressure for 2 hours, then re-dress (see Tip, opposite). Continue pressing at light pressure for 2 hours. Repeat three more times at 2-hour intervals.

12. Prepare a clean cheese mat in a ripening container. Remove cheese from press. Unwrap and place on mat. Sprinkle top surface with 1 tsp (5 mL) salt and place the upturned mold over the cheese to help keep its shape as it drains. After 6 to 7 hours, turn cheese over and salt other side in same manner. Replace the upturned mold over top. Remove any collected whey from the container, wiping with paper towel.

13. Repeat this process once daily for 3 more days, each time sprinkling each side with $\frac{1}{4}$ tsp (1.25 mL) salt.

Tip: To re-dress the cheese, remove the mold from the press. Remove the cheese from the mold and unwrap. Place the cloth back in the mold; turn the cheese over and put back in the mold, then rewrap. Return mold to the press.

14. Remove mold, replace cover on ripening container and place cheese in ripening area. Let cheese ripen at 50°F (10°C) and 75% humidity. Turn cheese daily for another 2 weeks, maintaining the humidity by adjusting the lid of the container.

15. Once cheese has ceased to lose whey, pierce it all the way through in several places, horizontally and vertically, with knitting needle or skewer.

16. Increase ripening area humidity to 90% and decrease temperature to 48°F (9°C). Pierce cheese again in same manner. Wipe or scrape the surface of the cheese daily. Scrape slime off with a knife or wipe it off with a cloth.

17. After 2 months, increase ripening area humidity to 95% and decrease temperature to 45°F (7°C). Let cheese ripen for another 30 days. At the end of this time, the cheese should be ready to eat, though it can be ripened further, for up to 1 year.

Fourme d'Ambert

Makes 4 lbs (2 kg)

12% yield

This delectable blue cheese is a specialty of south central France, loved the world over for its creamy and moist but firm paste and rich blue flavor. Traditionally, this cheese is made into a cylinder 4 to 5 inches (10 to 12.5 cm) wide and 8 inches (20 cm) high. You can buy a specific mold to make this shape but you can just as easily use a tomme mold. Unlike Stilton, Fourme d'Ambert is a pressed cheese.

Tip: To re-dress the cheese, remove the mold from the press. Remove the cheese from the mold and unwrap. Place the cloth back in the mold; turn the cheese over and put back in the mold, then rewrap. Return mold to the press.

- 1 tomme mold, lined with cheese cloth
- Cheese press
- Thin knitting needle or metal skewer
- Cheese matting
- Ripening container

16 quarts	whole milk	16 L
½ tsp	mesophilic culture	2.5 mL
⅛ tsp	*Penicillium roquefortii* mold powder	0.65 mL
½ tsp	calcium chloride	2.5 mL
½ tsp	liquid rennet	2.5 mL
	Cool 18% saturated brine (see Tip, opposite)	

1. Sterilize all equipment (see page 40). In a large stainless-steel pot set in a hot water bath over medium heat, warm milk to 90°F (32°C), stirring gently. Turn off heat.

2. Sprinkle culture and mold powder over surface of milk and let stand for about 5 minutes to rehydrate. Using skimmer and an up-and-down motion, gently draw culture down into milk without breaking surface of milk.

3. Dilute calcium chloride in ¼ cup (50 mL) cool water. Add to milk using the same up-and-down motion.

4. Dilute rennet in ¼ cup (50 mL) cool water. Add to milk and, using the same up-and-down motion, draw rennet down into milk until well blended. Cover pot and let set for 1½ hours, maintaining the temperature at 90°F (32°C).

5. Check for a clean break (see Tip, page 131). If the curd is still too fragile, cover and let set for another 5 minutes or until a clean break is achieved. Using a long-bladed knife and skimmer, cut curd into ½-inch (1.25 cm) cubes (see Tip, page 128). Let stand for 5 minutes to firm up the curds.

Tip: To make an 18% saturated brine: Mix 1 part salt to 5 parts water. It may be necessary to warm the water to successfully dissolve the salt. If so, let the brine cool before immersing the cheese. The brine can be used over and over again for several batches of cheese (refrigerate between uses). The best temperature for brining cheese is 55°F (13°C). Replenish the salt after several uses and remove any floating bits of cheese with a strainer.

6. Using a skimmer, gently stir curds constantly for 1 hour, maintaining the temperature, until curd grains are small and firm. Let settle.

7. Using a measuring cup, dip off whey until you see the surface of the curds. Ladle curds into prepared mold. Pull cloth up around curds and fold excess neatly over the top, with as few wrinkles as possible. Put on the lid.

8. Place mold in cheese press. Press cheese at light pressure for 1 hour, then re-dress (see Tip, far left) and continue pressing at light pressure for 6 to 7 hours.

9. Remove cheese from press. Unwrap and place in brine solution for 12 hours, turning over after 6 hours.

10. Dry cheese on a rack for 2 days at room temperature. Pierce cheese all the way through in several places, horizontally and vertically, with knitting needle or skewer. Prepare a clean cheese mat in a ripening container.

11. Place cheese on mat. Cover container and place in ripening area. Let cheese ripen at 50°F (10°C) and 90% humidity. Turn cheese daily, removing any collected whey from the container and wiping with a paper towel. A blue-gray moldy crust will begin to form after about 2 weeks. Continue to ripen for 1 month, at which time the cheese is ready to consume. Wrap in foil and store in the refrigerator for 2 to 3 months.

Roquefort

**Makes 4 cheeses,
each 13 oz (390 g)**
18 to 20% yield

*Roquefort is the
blue-veined cheese
against which most
other blue cheeses are
measured. Originating
in south central France,
Roquefort is a sheep's
milk cheese naturally
aged in caves that offer
perfect conditions for
ripening: constant
temperature and
humidity with natural
air movement, favorable
to the growth of the
blue mold.*

- Draining container
- Cheese matting
- Four 4-inch (10 cm) Camembert molds
- Cloth-lined colander
- Ripening container
- Thin knitting needle or metal skewer

8 quarts	sheep's milk	8 L
¼ tsp	mesophilic culture	1.25 mL
¼ tsp	calcium chloride	1.25 mL
¼ tsp	liquid rennet	1.25 mL
⅛ tsp	*Penicillium roquefortii* mold powder	0.65 mL
	Pickling (canning) or kosher salt	

1. Sterilize all equipment (see page 40). Prepare a draining container by placing a rack inside. Then place a cutting board on top, followed by a cheese mat, then the molds.

2. In a large stainless-steel pot set in a hot water bath over medium heat, warm milk to 90°F (32°C), stirring gently. Turn off heat.

3. Sprinkle culture over surface of milk and let stand for about 5 minutes to rehydrate. Using skimmer and an up-and-down motion, gently draw culture down into milk without breaking surface of milk.

4. Dilute calcium chloride in ¼ cup (50 mL) cool water. Add to milk using the same up-and-down motion.

5. Dilute rennet in ¼ cup (50 mL) cool water. Add to milk and, using the same up-and-down motion, draw rennet down into milk until well blended. Cover pot and let set for 1½ hours, maintaining the temperature at 90°F (32°C).

6. Check for a clean break (see Tip, page 131). Using a long-bladed knife and skimmer, cut curd into 1-inch (2.5 cm) cubes (see Tip, opposite). Let stand for 10 minutes to firm up the curds.

Tip: To cut curds: Holding a long-bladed stainless-steel knife straight up and down, draw knife through the curd, cutting it into strips. Proceed across the pot until you have reached the other side. Turn the pot and cut across the first strips to create squares. Using a skimmer, cut horizontally from side to side just under the surface of the curd to create cubes. Gradually move skimmer down through curd to cut layers of cubes. Using skimmer, gently stir curd cubes. Using a knife, cut any pieces that have been missed or are too large. For small-cut curds, you can use a large whisk for cutting.

7. Using a measuring cup, dip off whey until you see the surface of the curd.

8. Using a skimmer, carefully ladle curds into a cloth-lined colander and let drain for 30 minutes, lifting gently from time to time to facilitate draining.

9. Ladle 1 scoop of curds into each mold and let drain for 10 minutes. Sprinkle a pinch of *Penicillium roquefortii* mold powder over curds in each mold, then add another layer of curd. Add more mold powder, then another layer of curd. Continue in this manner until all the curd and mold powder are used.

10. Cover container and let cheeses drain at room temperature for 2 days, flipping every few hours to aid draining. After 2 days, remove cheeses from molds. Sprinkle ¾ tsp (3.75 mL) salt over each side of each cheese. Prepare a clean cheese mat in a ripening container.

11. Place cheeses on mat. Cover and place in the ripening area. Let cheeses ripen at 50° to 55°F (10° to 13°C) and 85 to 90% humidity. Leave the lid slightly ajar to allow for air movement and to aid in drying. Turn cheeses daily, removing any collected whey from the bottom of the container and wiping with a paper towel.

12. One week after production, pierce cheeses all the way through, horizontally and vertically, 12 or so times with knitting needle or skewer. This will allow air to penetrate to the center of the cheese, aiding mold growth. Continue to ripen and turn cheeses daily.

13. Approximately 10 days after production, blue mold should be visible on the outside of the cheese.

continued on next page…

14. Pierce cheeses again in same manner at 2 weeks. Continue to ripen until a bluish-gray rind forms. You must watch the humidity carefully with this cheese. Too much moisture will cause the cheese to become soft, and the rind will develop too quickly. Too little moisture will cause the cheese to dry out, and the rind will not develop properly. Keep the humidity at 85 to 90%; adjusting the lid of the container can help.

15. Ripen cheese for 2 to 5 months, according to your preference. When ready, wrap in foil and store in the refrigerator for 2 to 3 months.

Roquefort Caves

The village of Roquefort on the high plateau of south central France is home to natural limestone caves that, over the years, have been transformed into functional cheese cellars, each one said to contribute its own unique character to the cheese ripened within. The temperature in the caves remains constant, and there is always just the right gentle air movement to maintain the perfect ripening conditions.

Roquefort and Mushroom Salad

Makes 4 servings

Blue cheese is a favorite salad dressing ingredient. This salad takes the taste experience one step further, combining a generous amount of aromatic Roquefort cheese with fresh button mushrooms.

2 oz	Roquefort (page 138)	60 g
½ cup	crème fraîche	125 mL
	Juice of 1 lemon	
	Salt and freshly ground pepper	
2 tsp	chopped fresh chives	10 mL
2 tsp	chopped fresh chervil	10 mL
4 oz	button mushrooms, sliced	125 g
2	lettuce hearts, cut into ribbons	2

1. In a salad bowl, using a fork, mash Roquefort.

2. Gradually incorporate crème fraîche, then lemon juice. Season with salt and pepper to taste.

3. Add chives and chervil.

4. Add mushrooms and lettuce to Roquefort mixture and toss well. Serve immediately or refrigerate until ready to serve.

Stilton

Makes 4 lbs (2 kg)
12% yield

Stilton is one of the finest of the traditional English cheeses. It has a semifirm paste that is rich and mellow with a slight acidity from the blue veining. Traditionally, the curd was not pierced but rather processed so that it had an open, flaky texture ideal for the promotion of blue mold growth.

- Cloth-lined colander, placed in a large bowl
- Draining container
- 1 tomme mold
- Cheese matting
- Ripening container
- Thin knitting needle or metal skewer

15 quarts	whole milk	15 L
4 cups	whipping (35%) cream	1 L
½ tsp	mesophilic culture	2.5 mL
⅛ tsp	*Penicillium roquefortii* mold powder	0.65 mL
½ tsp	calcium chloride	2.5 mL
½ tsp	liquid rennet	2.5 mL
4 tbsp	pickling (canning) or kosher salt	60 mL

1. Sterilize all equipment (see page 40). In a large stainless-steel pot set in a hot water bath over medium heat, warm milk and cream to 86°F (30°C), stirring gently. Turn off heat.

2. Sprinkle culture and mold powder over surface of milk and let stand for about 5 minutes to rehydrate. Using skimmer and an up-and-down motion, gently draw culture and mold down into milk without breaking surface of milk. Cover and let ripen for 1 hour.

3. Dilute calcium chloride in ¼ cup (50 mL) cool water. Add to milk using the same up-and-down motion.

4. Dilute rennet in ¼ cup (50 mL) cool water. Add to milk and, using the same up-and-down motion, draw rennet down into milk until well blended. Cover and let set for 1½ hours.

5. Check for a clean break (see Tip, page 147). When a clean break is achieved, using skimmer, ladle thin slices of curd into prepared colander. As they drain, the curds will be sitting in the whey that has collected in the bowl below. Cover colander with pot lid to help maintain the temperature during the draining time. Let drain for 1½ hours.

Tip: Always use the freshest possible milk for your cheeses. If you are purchasing packaged milk, look for the latest best-before date. If using your own milk, plan your cheese making for as soon after milking as possible. The older the milk, the more bacteria there are in it to compete with the lactic bacterial starter.

6. As the curd drains, lift and turn it with skimmer to help break it up into smaller pieces, which facilitates acidification and firming.

7. Lift the cloth out of the whey and tie the corners to create a draining bag. Suspend bag and let drain for another 30 to 40 minutes or until dripping stops.

8. Place bag with curds on a cutting board in a draining container and place another cutting board on top of it. Weigh down the upper board with a large bowl or jug filled with water, a few bricks or anything that weighs 8 to 10 pounds (4 to 5 kg). Press overnight at room temperature.

9. Remove curd from bag and break up into coarse pieces. Toss gently with salt. Fill cheese mold with curd. Put the lid on the mold and place on a rack in a clean draining container. Turn cheese every 2 or 3 hours for 1 day, then once a day for 4 more days, removing any collected whey from the container.

10. Remove cheese from mold. If it is still too soft to maintain its shape, replace in the mold and let drain for another day. Prepare a clean cheese mat in a ripening container. Place cheese on mat. Cover and place container in ripening area.

11. Let cheese ripen at 53°F (12°C) and 85% humidity. Turn cheese daily for 1 week, draining off any collected whey and wiping the container dry with paper towel. Wipe the rind daily with a cloth soaked in salted water for the first week.

12. After 2 weeks, the cheese should have developed a moldy coating, and the blue mold should be growing inside the cheese. To be sure it is, pierce the cheese all the way through in several places, horizontally and vertically, with knitting needle or skewer. Turn at regular intervals, once or twice a week, for 4 more months. Wrap in foil and store in the refrigerator for 2 to 3 months.

White Stilton

Makes 4 lbs (2 kg)

12% yield

White Stilton is made in the same manner as traditional blue Stilton (page 142) but without the blue mold. It is a creamy, rich-tasting cheese with fresh, tangy undertones and is really lovely with the addition of dried fruits (see Variation, opposite).

- Cloth-lined colander, placed in a large bowl
- Draining container
- 1 tomme mold
- Cheese matting
- Ripening container

15 quarts	whole milk	15 L
4 cups	whipping (35%) cream	1 L
½ tsp	mesophilic culture	2.5 mL
½ tsp	calcium chloride	2.5 mL
½ tsp	liquid rennet	2.5 mL
4 tbsp	pickling (canning) or kosher salt	60 mL

1. Sterilize all equipment (see page 40). In a large stainless-steel pot set in a hot water bath over medium heat, warm milk and cream to 86°F (30°C), stirring gently. Turn off heat.

2. Sprinkle culture over surface of milk and let stand for about 5 minutes to rehydrate. Using skimmer and an up-and-down motion, gently draw culture and mold down into milk without breaking surface of milk. Cover and let ripen for 1 hour.

3. Dilute calcium chloride in ¼ cup (50 mL) cool water. Add to milk using the same up-and-down motion.

4. Dilute rennet in ¼ cup (50 mL) cool water. Add to milk and, using the same up-and-down motion, draw rennet down into milk until well blended. Cover and let set for 1½ hours.

5. Check for a clean break (see Tip, page 147). When a clean break is achieved, using skimmer, ladle thin slices of curd into prepared colander. As they drain, the curds will be sitting in the whey that has collected in the bowl below. Cover colander with pot lid to help maintain the temperature during the draining time. Let drain for 1½ hours.

Variation: *White Stilton with Dried Fruit:* Steam approximately ½ cup (125 mL) dried cranberries, dried blueberries, crystallized ginger, candied pineapple or candied orange peel for 10 minutes to plump up and sterilize. Add to the curd just before filling the mold. Remember, dried fruits will rehydrate a bit more in the cheese and cause the paste to be slightly drier.

6. As the curd drains, lift and turn it with skimmer to help break it up into smaller pieces, which facilitates acidification and firming.

7. Lift the cloth out of the whey and tie the corners to create a draining bag. Suspend bag and let drain for another 30 to 40 minutes or until dripping stops.

8. Place bag with curds on a cutting board in a draining container and place another cutting board on top of it. Weigh down the upper board with a large bowl or jug filled with water, a few bricks or anything that weighs 8 to 10 pounds (4 to 5 kg). Press overnight at room temperature.

9. Remove curd from bag and break up into coarse pieces. Toss curds gently with salt. Fill cheese mold with curd. Put the lid on the mold and place on a rack in a clean draining container. Turn cheese every 2 or 3 hours for 1 day, then once a day for 4 more days, removing any collected whey from the container.

10. Remove cheese from mold. If it is still too soft to maintain its shape, replace in the mold and let drain for another day. Prepare a clean cheese mat in a ripening container. Place cheese on mat. Cover and place container in the ripening area.

11. Let cheese ripen at 53°F (12°C) and 85% humidity. Turn cheese daily for 1 week, draining off any collected whey and wiping the container dry with paper towel. Wipe the rind daily with a cloth soaked in salted water for the first week.

12. After the first week, turn twice a week for the next 4 months, wiping cheese with a cloth soaked in salted water to keep the rind clean. Wrap in foil and store in the refrigerator for 2 to 3 months.

Blue Pyrenees

<table>
<tr><td colspan="2">

Makes
2³/₄ lbs (1.4 kg)

18% yield

</td></tr>
</table>

This is a rich sheep's milk cheese with lovely blue marbling throughout, which creates a balance of creaminess and acidity. Enjoy with fresh fruit and a sturdy white wine.

- Cloth-lined colander
- 1 tomme mold, lined with cheese cloth
- Cheese press
- Cheese matting
- Ripening container
- Thin knitting needle or metal skewer

8 quarts	sheep's milk	8 L
Generous ¼ tsp	mesophilic culture	Generous 1.25 mL
Pinch	*Penicillium roquefortii* mold powder	Pinch
Generous ¼ tsp	calcium chloride	Generous 1.25 mL
Generous ¼ tsp	liquid rennet	Generous 1.25 mL
3 tbsp	pickling (canning) or kosher salt	45 mL

1. Sterilize all equipment (see page 40). In a large stainless-steel pot set in a hot water bath over medium heat, warm milk to 90°F (32°C), stirring gently. Turn off heat.

2. Sprinkle culture and mold powder over surface of milk and let stand for about 5 minutes to rehydrate. Using skimmer and an up-and-down motion, gently draw culture and mold down into milk without breaking surface of milk. Cover and let ripen for 45 minutes.

3. Dilute calcium chloride in ¼ cup (50 mL) cool water. Add to milk using the same up-and-down motion.

4. Dilute rennet in ¼ cup (50 mL) cool water. Add to milk and, using the same up-and-down motion, draw rennet down into milk until well blended. Cover and let set for 30 to 40 minutes, maintaining the temperature at 90°F (32°C).

5. Check for a clean break (see Tips, opposite). Using a long-bladed knife and skimmer, cut curd into ½-inch (1.25 cm) cubes (see Tip, page 149). Let stand for 5 minutes to firm up the curds.

6. Warm curds over low heat to 100°F (38°C), adjusting the heat as necessary to make sure it takes 30 minutes to do so, stirring gently the whole time. Do not heat too quickly. Cover and hold for 10 minutes.

Tips: To ascertain whether the curd is ready for the next step, check for a clean break: insert the long flat blade of a knife into the curd at a 30-degree angle and slowly lift the blade toward the surface of the curd. If the curd splits into a long clean break or crack, it is ready to cut. If the cut is wobbly or uneven, let the curd set for a few more minutes before trying again.

To re-dress the cheese, remove the mold from the press. Remove the cheese from the mold and unwrap. Place the cloth back in the mold; turn the cheese over and put back in the mold, then rewrap. Return mold to the press.

7. Pour curds and whey into a cloth-lined colander. Cover colander with the pot lid to keep curd warm. Let drain for 1 hour. Break up the curds once or twice during this time to aid in draining, but do not squeeze them.

8. Place drained curds in a large bowl and break up with your hands, creating pieces about ¾ inch (2 cm) in size. Sprinkle salt evenly over curds and mix in well. Do not squeeze curds; handle them lightly.

9. Fill prepared mold with curds, pressing firmly to pack down. Pull cloth up around curds and fold excess neatly over the top, with as few wrinkles as possible. Put on the lid.

10. Place mold in cheese press. Press cheese at light to medium pressure for 15 minutes. Increase to medium pressure and press for another 15 minutes. This should knit the curds together well enough that you can re-dress the cheese. Re-dress (see Tip, left) and continue pressing at firm pressure for 6 to 7 hours or overnight.

11. Remove cheese from press and unwrap. Dry cheese on a rack for 2 days at room temperature, turning once or twice. Prepare a clean cheese mat in a ripening container. When rind is sufficiently dry, place on mat. Cover and place container in ripening area.

12. Let cheese ripen at 55°F (13°C) and 85% humidity. Turn cheese daily for the first week, removing any collected whey from the container and wiping with paper towel. After 10 days, pierce the cheese all the way through in several places, horizontally and vertically, with knitting needle or skewer. Continue ripening, turning twice weekly. After 3 weeks, pierce again in same manner.

13. Continue ripening cheese for another 3 months, turning weekly. The cheese will develop a gray-blue rind. If the mold is too intense, rub it down with your hands or a fine brush. When cheese is sufficiently ripe for your tastes, wrap in foil and store in the refrigerator for up to 3 months.

Bleu du Queyras

Makes 3 cheeses,
each about
15 oz (425 g)

15% yield

Queyras is an Alpine area in eastern France near the Italian border. This blue-veined cheese is made of cow's milk, originally by small fruitières, or village cheese makers, who processed the milk from local small dairy farms.

Tip: This is an authentic recipe usually made with raw or non-homogenized whole milk. If you are using homogenized cow's milk, it is strongly recommended that you add calcium chloride (see page 31) for best results. The addition of calcium chloride will stabilize the curd, hasten setting and increase yield. Use the same amount of calcium chloride as rennet called for in the recipe, dilute it with at least 10 times the amount of water and stir into the milk before adding the rennet.

- Draining container
- Cheese matting
- Three 4-inch (10 cm) Camembert molds
- Cloth-lined colander
- Ripening container
- Thin knitting needle or metal skewer

8 quarts	whole or partly skimmed (2%) milk	8 L
1/4 tsp	mesophilic culture	1.25 mL
1/4 tsp	liquid rennet	1.25 mL
	Pickling (canning) or kosher salt	
Pinch	*Penicillium roquefortii* mold powder	Pinch

1. Sterilize all equipment (see page 40). Prepare a draining container by placing a rack inside. Then place a cutting board on top, followed by a cheese mat, then the molds.

2. In a large stainless-steel pot over medium heat, warm milk to 86°F (30°C), stirring gently to prevent scorching. Remove from heat.

3. Sprinkle culture over surface of milk and let stand for about 5 minutes to rehydrate. Using skimmer and an up-and-down motion, gently draw culture down into milk without breaking surface of milk. Cover and let ripen for 30 minutes.

4. Dilute rennet in 1/4 cup (50 mL) cool water. Add to milk and, using the same up-and-down motion, draw rennet down into milk until well blended. Cover and let set for 45 minutes at room temperature. If the room is cool, keep pot warm by wrapping with a towel or setting it in a sinkful of warm water.

5. Check for a clean break (see Tip, page 147). Using a long-bladed knife and skimmer, cut curd into 3/4-inch (2 cm) cubes (see Tip, opposite). Let stand for 15 minutes to firm up the curds.

Tip: To cut curds: Holding a long-bladed stainless-steel knife straight up and down, draw knife through the curd, cutting it into strips. Proceed across the pot until you have reached the other side. Turn the pot and cut across the first strips to create squares. Using a skimmer, cut horizontally from side to side just under the surface of the curd to create cubes. Gradually move skimmer down through curd to cut layers of cubes. Using skimmer, gently stir curd cubes. Using a knife, cut any pieces that have been missed or are too large. For small-cut curds, you can use a large whisk for cutting.

6. Using a measuring cup, dip off excess whey. Carefully ladle curds into a cloth-lined colander. Let drain for 4 hours, flipping after 2 hours.

7. Using your hands, break up and mix the curds. Let drain for another 10 minutes, then break up again.

8. Using your hands, gently mix in 2 tsp (10 mL) salt and mold powder. Fill cheese molds to top with curd, letting drain and refilling until all the curd is used up. Do not press down. Place on a rack in draining contatiner.

9. Cover container and let cheeses drain for 1 week at cool room temperature (65°F/18°C), removing any collected whey daily. Flip the cheeses 6 to 7 times daily, leaving them in the molds.

10. One week after production, remove cheeses from molds and sprinkle each side of each cheese with ½ tsp (2.5 mL) salt. Prepare a clean cheese mat in a ripening container. Place cheese on mat. Dry, uncovered, for 1 week at 65°F (18°C), turning the cheeses daily.

11. Pierce the cheeses all the way through in several places, horizontally and vertically, with knitting needle or skewer.

12. Replace in the container. Cover and place in the ripening area. Let cheeses ripen at 42° to 44°F (6° to 7°C) and 85% humidity for 1 month, turning twice a week. After 1 week, pierce the cheeses again in same manner. After 1 month, wrap cheeses in foil and refrigerate.

Flan au Bleu du Queyras

**Makes 4 to
6 servings**

*For a classy luncheon
with friends, serve this
flan with a green salad
and a glass of chilled
white wine.*

Tip: Use a flan pan
that does not have a
removable bottom. It
may also be called a
quiche dish, or you can
use a glass pie plate.

- Preheat oven to 325°F (160°C)
- Baking pan large enough to hold 10-inch (25 cm) flan pan
- 10-inch (25 cm) flan pan (see Tip, left), buttered

5	eggs	5
Pinch	salt	Pinch
10 oz	Bleu du Queyras (page 148), crumbled into small pieces	300 g
1½ tbsp	cornstarch	22.5 mL
1 tbsp	crème fraîche	15 mL
2 tbsp	cognac or Armagnac	30 mL

1. Prepare a water bath by filling baking pan with 1 inch (2.5 cm) hot water.

2. In a bowl, using an electric mixer, beat eggs and salt until foamy and light.

3. Add cheese, a few pieces at a time, beating well to blend.

4. Beat in cornstarch and crème fraîche until smooth. Beat in cognac.

5. Pour mixture into prepared flan pan and place in the water bath. Bake in preheated oven for about 50 minutes or until a knife inserted into the center comes out clean. Remove from water bath and let cool in flan pan on a wire rack. Serve warm or cold.

Septmoncel

<table>
<tr><td>

Makes
3¼ lbs (1.6 kg)

10% yield

</td></tr>
</table>

This hard blue cheese is made in eastern France in the Jura region. The addition of goat's milk gives it a stronger flavor.

- Cloth-lined colander
- 1 tomme mold, lined with cheese cloth
- Cheese press
- Cheese matting
- Ripening container
- Thin knitting needle or metal skewer

14 quarts	partly skimmed (2%) cow's milk	14 L
2 quarts	goat's milk	2 L
½ tsp	mesophilic culture	2.5 mL
⅛ tsp	*Penicillium roquefortii* mold powder	0.65 mL
¾ tsp	calcium chloride	3.75 mL
¾ tsp	liquid rennet	3.75 mL
4 tsp	pickling (canning) or kosher salt	20 mL

1. Sterilize all equipment (see page 40). In a large stainless-steel pot set in a hot water bath over medium heat, warm cow's and goat's milk to 85°F (29°C), stirring gently. Turn off heat.

2. Sprinkle culture and mold powder over surface of milk and let stand for about 5 minutes to rehydrate. Using skimmer and an up-and-down motion, gently draw culture and mold down into milk without breaking surface of milk.

3. Dilute calcium chloride in ¼ cup (50 mL) cool water. Add to milk using the same up-and-down motion.

4. Dilute rennet in ¼ cup (50 mL) cool water. Add to milk and, using the same up-and-down motion, draw rennet down into milk until well blended. Cover and let set for 1½ hours, maintaining the temperature at 85°F (29°C), or until a firm curd forms.

5. Check for a clean break (see Tip, page 147). Using a long-bladed knife and skimmer, cut curd into ½-inch (1.25 cm) cubes (see Tip, page 149). Let stand for 5 minutes to firm up the curds. The curds will settle. Stir for 10 minutes. Let settle again.

continued on next page…

Septmoncel continued...

Tip: To re-dress the cheese, remove the mold from the press. Remove the cheese from the mold and unwrap. Place the cloth back in the mold; turn the cheese over and put back in the mold, then rewrap. Return mold to the press.

6. Using a measuring cup, dip off whey until you can see the surface of the curds. Stir the curds for another 10 minutes. Let settle again.

7. Drain off whey down to the level of the curds. Stir the curds for another 10 minutes. Let settle again. The curds should be firm and ready to mat, or cling together. If not, stir for another 5 to 10 minutes.

8. Pour curds and whey into a cloth-lined colander. Let curds drain for 10 minutes.

9. Fill prepared mold with curds. Pull cloth up around curds and fold excess neatly over the top, with as few wrinkles as possible. Put on the lid.

10. Place mold in cheese press or place a weight on top. Press cheese at medium pressure for 12 hours. Re-dress (see Tip, left) and press at medium pressure for another 12 hours.

11. Prepare a clean cheese mat in a ripening container. Remove cheese from press and unwrap. Place on mat. Sprinkle top surface of cheese with 1 tsp (5 mL) salt and rub in. Wait 2 hours, then turn cheese and salt other side in same manner. Let stand overnight at room temperature. Repeat salting both sides in same manner.

12. Remove any collected whey from container, wiping with a paper towel. Let cheese ripen at 50°F (10°C) and 90% humidity for 3 to 4 weeks. Turn cheese daily. A blue mold will begin to grow on the surface of the cheese. After 2 weeks, pierce the cheese all the way through in several places, horizontally and vertically, with knitting needle or skewer.

13. After 4 weeks, reduce humidity to 80% and ripen for another 3 to 4 weeks. Wrap in foil and store in the refrigerator for up to 4 months.

Bite-Size Cheese Canapés

Cheese and entertaining are perfect partners. However, balancing a wineglass and a plate of appetizers can be a challenge while socializing. Try some of these bite-size canapés at your next wine-and-cheese party.

1. Cut ¾-inch (2 cm) cubes of firm blue cheese. Top with a sweet green grape or wedge of kiwifruit and spear with a toothpick.

2. Slice small fresh figs in half and top with a piece of Roquefort or other semisoft blue cheese.

3. Sandwich one ¼-inch (0.5 cm) thick slice of blue cheese between two ¼-inch (0.5 cm) thick slices of Havarti, Gouda or Cheddar, then cut into ¾-inch (2 cm) cubes. Spear each with a toothpick.

4. Using canapé cutters, cut out ¾-inch (2 cm) thick shapes from a firm blue-veined cheese. Top each with a maraschino cherry and spear with a toothpick.

5. Wash and core a fresh apple, then cut into wedges. Place one ¼-inch (0.5 cm) thick piece of St-Paulin or other washed-rind cheese on top of the apple wedge and spear with a toothpick.

6. Roll up thin, narrow slices of prosciutto. Place on top of ¾-inch (2 cm) cubes of smoked Gouda or similar cheeses and spear with a toothpick.

7. Cut Jarlsberg, Emmental or Leerdammer into ¾-inch (2 cm) cubes and top each with a walnut half.

8. Spear an olive to a cube of feta using a toothpick. Set the cubes on a plate and drizzle with olive oil.

9. Cut cherry tomatoes in half, scoop out the seeds and top with a bocconcini. Sprinkle with a pinch of herbes de Provence (a blend of thyme, oregano, rosemary and lavender) and drizzle with olive oil.

10. Break up Parmesan or Sbrinz into bite-size pieces and spear with toothpicks. Set on a plate scattered with small wedges of fresh pears.

11. Using canapé cutters, cut ¼-inch (0.5 cm) thick shapes from a firm cheese, such as Gruyère or Cheddar. Top each shape with a piped rosette of cream cheese that has been softened then blended with sweet paprika.

12. Pour ¼ inch (0.5 cm) of red wine onto a plate or into a shallow flat-bottomed dish. Cut ¾-inch (2 cm) cubes of firm goat or sheep cheese, pierce each with a toothpick and place in the wine.

Troubleshooting

Pink color appears on the surface of cheese during aging.
Moisture is too high in ripening area; decrease humidity. Be sure to
drain and dry the container for the first few days after production,
when the fresh cheese is still losing whey. The cheese is still safe to
eat if pink appears.

Black or brown mold appears on the surface of the cheese.
Too much moisture in the ripening area; reduce humidity. Airborne
bacteria in the ripening area; clean all surfaces and environment
with bleach water (2 tbsp/30 mL bleach to 4 quarts/4 L water).
To combat mold, rub cheese rind with a blend of salt and vinegar
(1 tsp/5 mL salt to $1/4$ cup/50 mL vinegar).

Blue mold has not developed in the interior of the cheese.
The cheese is too dense, and there are no pockets of air to
encourage mold growth; pierce the cheese several times at
different intervals, depending on the recipe. The cheese is too
moist to allow the holes to remain open; reduce moisture in the
curd by stirring or cooking it longer before ripening.

The cheese becomes very strong before the ripening time is up.
Humidity in ripening area is too high; reduce humidity.

Blue mold takes a very long time to develop on the rind.
Humidity is too low; increase humidity in ripening area. The
cheese is too dry; cook or stir less next time to maintain higher
moisture level in the curd.

Washed-Rind Cheeses

Washing the rinds of these cheeses with a cloth soaked in brine, to which a ripening bacteria (usually a strain of *Brevibacterium linens*) may be added, gives them their characteristic reddish-yellow color and pungent aroma. Often the smell of the cheese is stronger than the actual taste of the supple straw-colored paste, though these cheeses do become more intensely flavored with age. Some, like Muenster, become quite soft with ripening, while others maintain their semifirm state for many months.

Washed-rind cheeses are sometimes called "Trappist" cheeses because they were often the type of cheese produced by monasteries in Medieval Europe. This chapter contains recipes for cheeses traditionally made by monks in France, Germany, Denmark and Romania.

Port Salut

<table>
<tr><td>Makes about
2¾ lbs (1.44 kg)
12% yield</td></tr>
</table>

Originally made by monks in a French monastery, Port Salut has many cousins, such as St-Paulin and Oka. If you like your cheese smelly, don't be afraid to ripen it longer.

Tips: For a flavorful variation on a washed rind, wash cheeses with a solution of beer, apple cider or white wine and 3% salt. Remember to discard any used solution.

Non-homogenized milk, also known as cream line or standard milk, is always the best choice for successful cheese making. Non-homogenized milk is pasteurized milk that hasn't been homogenized and shouldn't be confused with raw milk. See Sources, page 372, for more information.

- 1 tomme mold, lined with cheese cloth
- Cheese press
- Cheese matting
- Ripening container

12 quarts	whole milk	12 L
½ tsp	mesophilic culture	2.5 mL
⅛ tsp	*Brevibacterium linens* ripening bacteria	0.65 mL
¾ tsp	calcium chloride	3.75 mL
¾ tsp	liquid rennet	3.75 mL
	Cool 18% saturated brine (see Tip, page 169)	
	Bacterial brine solution for washing rind	

1. Sterilize all equipment (see page 40). In a large stainless-steel pot set in a hot water bath over medium heat, warm milk to 90°F (32°C), stirring gently. Turn off heat.

2. Sprinkle culture and *B. linens* over surface of milk and let stand for about 5 minutes to rehydrate. Using skimmer and an up-and-down motion, gently draw culture down into milk without breaking surface of milk. Cover and let ripen for 1 hour, maintaining the temperature at 90°F (32°C).

3. Dilute calcium chloride in ¼ cup (50 mL) cool water. Add to milk using the same up-and-down motion.

4. Dilute rennet in ¼ cup (50 mL) cool water. Add to milk and, using the same up-and-down motion, draw rennet down into milk until well blended. Cover pot and let set for 30 minutes.

5. Check for a clean break (see Tip, page 162). If necessary, let set for another 10 minutes or until you achieve a clean break.

6. Using a long-bladed knife and skimmer, cut curd into ½-inch (1.25 cm) cubes (see Tip, page 167). Let stand for 5 minutes. Stir gently for 5 minutes. Let curds settle.

Tips: To remove 30% of the whey, measure down the side of the pot and remove the top one-third, basically until you see the surface of the settled curd. The amount you remove can be crucial, because the same amount of water must be added, and this will affect the character of the finished cheese (see Troubleshooting, page 178).

To re-dress the cheese, remove the mold from the press. Remove the cheese from the mold and unwrap. Place the cloth back in the mold; turn the cheese over and put back in the mold, then rewrap. Return mold to the press.

7. Using a measuring cup, remove one-third of the whey from top of curd (see Tips, left) and, while stirring gently, replace with an equal amount of 140°F (60C°) water to bring the temperature up to 92°F (33°C). Stir gently for 10 minutes. Let curds settle.

8. Again remove one-third of the whey and, while stirring gently, replace with an equal amount of warm water to bring the temperature this time to 98°F (37°C) (see Tips, page 187). Stir gently for 10 minutes. Let settle, allowing curds to begin to mat on bottom of pot.

9. Remove as much whey as possible. Place curd in prepared mold, pulling cheese cloth up neatly around curd and folding excess snugly across top. Put on lid. Place mold in cheese press. Press at light pressure for 30 minutes.

10. Remove cheese from press and re-dress (see Tips, left). Continue pressing at medium pressure for 8 to 12 hours or overnight.

11. Remove from press. Unwrap and place in 18% saturated brine solution for 8 hours, turning over after 4 hours.

12. Remove cheese from brine and dry on a rack at room temperature for 12 hours.

13. Place cheese on a cheese mat in a ripening container. Cover and move to ripening area. Let ripen at 50° to 55°F (10°C to 13°C) and 90% to 95% humidity. Turn daily for 1 week. Begin washing rind after 1 week of ripening.

14. Make the bacterial brine solution for washing rind as follows: Boil ½ cup (125 mL) water. Let cool. Add 1 tsp (5 mL) salt and tiny pinch (just the tip of a knife) *B. linens* ripening bacteria. Cover and set aside for 12 hours at room temperature to allow bacteria to rehydrate. Dip a small clean cloth or natural sponge into the bacterial brine, squeeze out excess and wash cheese all over. Return cheese to the ripening area. This will encourage the bacterial smear growth on the rind.

continued on next page…

15. Discard any leftover brine solution. Repeat this process again in 2 days, turning cheese over on the mat each time. After two washings, you may wash the cheese with a brine solution made with salt only, leaving out the bacteria. In about 2 weeks, a light orange-yellow color will develop on the rind, which will darken to a deeper orange-red with time. Continue to wash and ripen for 6 weeks to 2 months. When ripe, the cheese should bulge slightly around the side and feel semisoft in the center. The rind should be moist but not sticky.

Port Salut Potatoes

Makes 4 servings

This is a wonderful way to serve potatoes and enjoy the great flavor of Port Salut or another washed-rind cheese. This recipe serves four as a side dish or as a light lunch with a salad.

- Preheat oven to 350°F (180°C)
- 8-cup (2 L) baking dish, buttered

4	medium potatoes, peeled or skin-on, cooked and cooled	4
2	pears	2
1 tbsp	butter	15 mL
8 oz	Port Salut (page 156) or other washed-rind cheese, thinly sliced	250 g
½ cup	whipping (35%) cream	125 mL
	Paprika	
	Salt and freshly ground pepper	

1. Cut potatoes and pears into ¼-inch (0.5 cm) thick slices.

2. Layer potatoes and pears in prepared baking dish. Dot with butter. Layer cheese over top.

3. Pour in cream. Season with paprika, salt and pepper to taste.

4. Bake in preheated oven for 20 minutes or until cheese is bubbly and pears are tender.

Reblochon

Makes 2 cheeses, each 1 1/2 lbs (750 g)
15% yield

Reblochon is a soft washed-rind cheese made in the mountainous eastern region of France. It is a rich, creamy cheese, almost like Brie in consistency.

- Draining container
- 2 tomme molds
- 5-lb (2.5 kg) weight (see Tip, page 168)
- Cheese matting
- Ripening container

8 quarts	whole milk	8 L
1/4 tsp	mesophilic culture	1.25 mL
1/8 tsp	*Brevibacterium linens* ripening bacteria	0.65 mL
1/4 tsp	calcium chloride	1.25 mL
1/4 tsp	liquid rennet	1.25 mL
	Pickling (canning) or kosher salt	
	Brine solution for washing rind (see Tip, page 160)	

1. Sterilize all equipment (see page 40). Prepare a draining container by placing a rack inside, then the molds.

2. In a large stainless-steel pot set in a hot water bath over medium heat, warm milk to 85°F (29°C), stirring gently. Turn off heat.

3. Sprinkle culture and *B. linens* over surface of milk and let stand for about 5 minutes to rehydrate. Using skimmer and an up-and-down motion, gently draw culture down into milk without breaking surface of milk. Cover and let ripen for 15 minutes.

4. Dilute calcium chloride in 1/4 cup (50 mL) cool water. Add to milk using the same up-and-down motion.

5. Dilute rennet in 1/4 cup (50 mL) cool water. Add to milk and, using the same up-and-down motion, draw rennet down into milk until well blended. Cover pot and let set for 30 minutes, maintaining the temperature at 85°F (29°C).

6. Check for a clean break (see Tip, page 162). If necessary, let set for another 5 to 10 minutes or until you achieve a clean break.

7. Using a long-handled whisk, cut curd into pea-size pieces. Using skimmer, lift and move curd to ensure all pieces are cut. Let stand for 5 minutes.

continued on next page…

Reblochon continued...

Tip: To make a brine solution for washing rind: Boil ½ cup (125 mL) water. Let cool and then mix with 1 tsp (5 mL) salt.

The brine solution may be kept and used for several days, as long as you have not dipped your cloth into it. Remove a small amount to another container for washing, or make a new batch each time.

8. Return heat to low and slowly warm curds to 95°F (35°C), adjusting the heat as necessary to make sure it takes 35 minutes to do so. Do not heat too quickly. Let curds settle.

9. Using a measuring cup, dip off whey until you can see top of curds. Using skimmer, ladle curds into molds. Put lids on molds and let drain for 30 minutes.

10. Flip cheeses in molds and replace lids. Repeat for another 2 hours, flipping every 30 minutes.

11. After 2 hours of draining and flipping, place a 5-lb (2.5 kg) weight on top of each lid and press in this gentle way for 12 hours or overnight.

12. Remove cheeses from molds. They should be about 1 to 2 inches (2.5 to 5 cm) thick. Sprinkle 1 tsp (5 mL) salt on each side of each cheese. Place cheeses on a cheese mat in a ripening container. Let ripen at 60°F (16°C) and 90% humidity.

13. Turn cheeses every second day and wipe with a cloth soaked in brine solution to encourage the bacterial smear growth (see Tip, left). Remove any initial moisture from the bottom of the container, wiping bottom with paper towel.

14. Continue to wash and turn cheeses every second day for 4 to 5 weeks. The cheese will develop an aromatic orange smear on the rind and will be soft when pressed in the center. The paste is creamy, though not runny, when ripe.

15. Wrap finished cheeses in parchment or waxed paper, then in plastic wrap, and store in the refrigerator.

Reblochon and Apple Sandwich

Makes 1 serving

This sandwich is simply delicious. It's a wonderful way to enjoy the classic combination of cheese and apples.

1 tsp	chopped walnuts	5 mL
1 tsp	mayonnaise	5 mL
½ tsp	Dijon mustard	2.5 mL
2	slices light rye bread, lightly toasted	2
	Few leaves fresh spinach	
1	apple, cut into ⅛-inch (0.25 cm) thick slices	1
2 oz	Reblochon (page 159), cut into ⅛-inch (0.25 cm) thick slices	60 g

1. In a small bowl, mix together walnuts, mayonnaise and mustard.

2. Spread one side of each slice of bread with mayonnaise mixture. Layer spinach, sliced apples and sliced cheese on bread and sandwich together.

Limburger

**Makes about
2 lbs (1 kg)**

*12 to 15% yield (see
Variation, opposite)*

The "stinky cheese"
of fact and fiction,
Limburger is a
washed-rind cheese
with a punch. This
cheese is traditionally
made in a square or
rectangular mold, so
you can use that if
you have one.

Tip: To ascertain
whether the curd is
ready for the next step,
check for a clean break:
insert the long flat blade
of a knife into the curd
at a 30-degree angle
and slowly lift the blade
toward the surface of
the curd. If the curd
splits into a long clean
break or crack, it is
ready to cut. If the cut
is wobbly or uneven,
let the curd set for a
few more minutes
before trying again.

- Draining container
- 1 tomme mold
- Cloth-lined colander
- Cheese matting
- Ripening container

8 quarts	whole milk	8 L
¼ tsp	mesophilic culture	1.25 mL
⅛ tsp	*Brevibacterium linens* ripening bacteria	0.65 mL
½ tsp	calcium chloride	2.5 mL
½ tsp	liquid rennet	2.5 mL
	Pickling (canning) or kosher salt	
	Brine solution for washing rind (see Tip, page 160)	

1. Sterilize all equipment (see page 40). Prepare a draining container by placing a rack inside, then the mold.

2. In a large stainless-steel pot set in a hot water bath over medium heat, warm milk to 91°F (33°C), stirring gently. Turn off heat.

3. Sprinkle culture and *B. linens* over surface of milk and let stand for about 5 minutes to rehydrate. Using skimmer and an up-and-down motion, gently draw culture down into milk without breaking surface of milk.

4. Dilute calcium chloride in ¼ cup (50 mL) cool water. Add to milk using the same up-and-down motion.

5. Dilute rennet in ¼ cup (50 mL) cool water. Add to milk and, using the same up-and-down motion, draw rennet down into milk until well blended. Cover pot and let set for 30 minutes, maintaining the temperature at 91°F (33°C).

6. Check for a clean break (see Tip, left). Using a long-handled knife and skimmer, cut curd into ½-inch (1.25 cm) pieces (see Tip, page 167). Stir gently for 10 minutes. Let curds settle. Let stand for 5 more minutes.

Variation: *Individual Limburgers:* You can use 5 St-Marcellin molds to make individual cheeses (each 7 oz/ 210 g). Follow method but, in Step 8, sprinkle each cheese with ¼ tsp (1.25 mL) salt per side.

7. Carefully pour the contents of the pot into a cloth-lined colander. Let drain for 30 minutes, lifting the corners of the cloth periodically to ensure maximum drainage.

8. Carefully ladle semidrained curds into mold. Place lid on mold and draining container. Drain for 8 hours, flipping cheese in mold once or twice. Remove any collected whey from bottom of container. Remove cheese from mold.

9. Sprinkle cheese with 1 tsp (5 mL) salt on one side. Place cheese, salt side down, on a cheese mat in a ripening container and salt other side in same manner. Cover container and ripen at 50° to 55°F (10° to 13°C). Turn cheese daily and remove any moisture from bottom of container, wiping with paper towel.

10. After 1 week of ripening, begin to wipe cheese once daily with a cloth soaked in a brine solution (see Tip, page 173). Continue to turn cheese daily.

11. After approximately 12 days, an orange-yellow bacterial growth will appear on the surface of the cheese. Continue to turn cheese twice weekly and wash twice weekly with brine. The smear will continue to spread and become darker. Ripen for at least 1 month, or longer for more intense flavor and aroma. The rind should be moist to the touch, and with aging, it can become very strong-smelling and gritty.

12. Once the cheese has a developed rind, wrap and store in an airtight container in the refrigerator to maintain the level of rind development.

Muenster

Makes 2 cheeses,
each 1 lb (500 g),
or 12 cheeses,
each 3 oz (90 g)

12% yield

It seems that monks
specialized in
washed-rind cheeses.
They are ripened in
damp cellars, so perhaps
there was abundance
of them in medieval
monasteries! Muenster
(from the Latin word
for "monastery") is
a delightfully smelly
soft cheese from the
Alsace-Lorraine region
of France. Serve it like
the locals, with potatoes
boiled in their skins
and a side salad.

- Draining container
- Cloth-lined colander
- 2 tomme molds or 12 St-Marcellin molds
- Cheese matting
- Ripening container

8 quarts	whole milk	8 L
¼ tsp	mesophilic culture	1.25 mL
⅛ tsp	*Brevibacterium linens* ripening bacteria	0.65 mL
½ tsp	calcium chloride	2.5 mL
½ tsp	liquid rennet	2.5 mL
	Pickling (canning) or kosher salt	
	Brine solution for washing rind	

1. Sterilize all equipment (see page 40). Prepare a draining container by placing a rack inside. In a large stainless-steel pot set in a hot water bath over medium heat, warm milk to 90°F (32°C), stirring gently. Turn off heat.

2. Sprinkle culture and B. linens over surface of milk and let stand for about 5 minutes to rehydrate. Using skimmer and an up-and-down motion, gently draw culture down into milk without breaking surface of milk.

3. Dilute calcium chloride in ¼ cup (50 mL) cool water. Add to milk using the same up-and-down motion.

4. Dilute rennet in ¼ cup (50 mL) cool water. Add to milk and, using the same up-and-down motion, draw rennet down into milk until well blended. Cover pot and let set for 40 minutes, maintaining the temperature at 90°F (32°C).

5. Check for a clean break (see Tip, page 162). If necessary, let set for another 10 minutes until you achieve a clean break. Using a long-bladed knife and skimmer, cut curd into ½-inch (1.25 cm) cubes (see Tip, page 167). Let curds settle. Cover and hold for 30 minutes, maintaining temperature.

Variations: *Spiced Muenster:* In small saucepan, combine 1 cup (250 mL) water and 2 tsp (10 mL) cumin seeds; boil for 10 minutes. Let cool. Follow method but, in Step 6, drain the curds for 5 minutes, then pour cooled cumin seeds and water over curds. Mix gently with clean hands to distribute evenly. Let drain for another 5 minutes. Continue with recipe.

Wine-Washed Muenster: For a special cheese that reflects the agricultural products of the Alsace region of France, where Muenster is made, wash the ripening cheese with a mix of 1 tsp (5 mL) salt and ½ cup (125 mL) Alsatian white wine, such as Gewürztraminer, instead of the usual brine.

6. Carefully pour the contents of the pot into a cloth-lined colander. Let drain for 10 minutes. Carefully ladle soft curds into molds.

7. Cover and let drain at room temperature for 24 hours, removing any collected whey and flipping cheeses in their molds several times during this period. Keep container covered to avoid drafts. If cheeses are still too soft to handle after 24 hours, let drain for another 6 to 7 hours.

8. Remove cheeses from molds. Sprinkle each side with 1 tsp (5 mL) salt for larger cheeses or ¼ tsp (1.25 mL) salt for smaller cheeses. Place on a cheese mat in a ripening container. Ripen at 55°F (13°C) and 85% humidity.

9. Turn cheeses daily, removing any collected whey from container, until no more whey is released, about 3 days.

10. Wash cheeses every second day with a cloth dipped in brine solution — 1 cup (250 mL) water and 2 tsp (10 mL) salt — to aid the rind to form. After 10 to 12 days, an orange smear will develop on the surface. Continue to wash and turn the cheeses every second day for at least 2 weeks for the small cheeses, or 3 weeks for the large cheeses. Longer ripening will intensify the smell of the rind. Ripen for up to 3 months for authentic Muenster (though it can still be eaten at this point).

11. The cheese rind should be fairly soft and moist to the touch but not sticky. Once the rind has developed, wrap in parchment paper and store in the refrigerator for longer shelf life.

Morbier

Makes
3½ lbs (1.75 kg)
11% yield

This cheese originated in the mountain valleys of the Jura mountain range of eastern France, where the main cheese produced is the very large Comté. In the winter, isolated farmers could not deliver enough milk in one milking to make a whole Comté, so they made smaller cheeses at home on the farm. The morning milk was transformed into cheese, then the soot collected from the bottom of the copper cheese cauldron, which was heated over a wood fire, was rubbed over the surface of the cheese to protect it until the evening milk was available. Then the evening milk was made into cheese and placed in the mold over the morning cheese. It went into the press overnight, and voilà! Cheese with a black center stripe.

- 2 cloth-lined colanders
- 1 tomme mold, lined with cheese cloth
- Cheese press
- Cheese matting
- Ripening container

16 quarts	whole milk	16 L
½ tsp	mesophilic culture	2.5 mL
¾ tsp	calcium chloride	3.75 mL
¾ tsp	liquid rennet	3.75 mL
	Charcoal ash	
	Cool 18% saturated brine (see Tip, page 169)	
	Bacterial brine for washing rind	

1. Sterilize all equipment (see page 40). In a large stainless-steel pot set in a hot water bath over medium heat, warm milk to 90°F (32°C), stirring gently. Turn off heat.

2. Sprinkle culture over surface of milk and let stand for about 5 minutes to rehydrate. Using skimmer and an up-and-down motion, gently draw culture down into milk without breaking surface of milk. Cover and let ripen for 1 hour, maintaining the temperature at 90°F (32°C).

3. Dilute calcium chloride in ¼ cup (50 mL) cool water. Add to milk using the same up-and-down motion.

4. Dilute rennet in ¼ cup (50 mL) cool water. Add to milk and, using the same up-and-down motion, draw rennet down into milk until well blended. Cover pot and let set for 40 minutes, maintaining the temperature at 90°F (32°C).

5. Check for a clean break (see Tip, page 162). If necessary, let set for another 5 to 10 minutes or until you achieve a clean break. Using a long-bladed knife and skimmer, cut curd into ½-inch (1.25 cm) cubes (see Tip, opposite). Let stand for 5 minutes.

6. Return heat to low and slowly cook curds to 100°F (38°C), adjusting the heat as necessary to make sure it takes 20 minutes to do so. Let curds settle.

Tip: To cut curds: Holding a long-bladed stainless-steel knife straight up and down, draw knife through the curd, cutting it into strips. Proceed across the pot until you have reached the other side. Turn the pot and cut across the first strips to create squares. Using a skimmer, cut horizontally from side to side just under the surface of the curd to create cubes. Gradually move skimmer down through curd to cut layers of cubes. Using skimmer, gently stir curd cubes. Using a knife, cut any pieces that have been missed or are too large. For small-cut curds, you can use a large whisk for cutting.

7. Using a measuring cup, remove half of the whey and, while stirring gently, replace with an equal amount of 100°F (38°C) water. Stir gently for 10 minutes. Let curds settle.

8. Divide curds evenly between 2 cloth-lined colanders and let drain. Let curds mat in colander for 10 minutes, shaping each piece of cheese during this time into one relatively flat round.

9. Place one piece of curd in prepared mold. Sprinkle liberally with ash. Place the second piece of curd on top. Pull cheese cloth up neatly around curd, folding excess snugly across top. Place lid on mold. Place in a cheese press and press at light to medium pressure for 1 hour.

10. Remove cheese from press and re-dress (see Tip, page 157). Continue pressing at light to medium pressure for 8 to 12 hours or overnight.

11. Remove from press. Unwrap and place in 18% saturated brine solution for 8 hours, turning over after 4 hours.

12. Remove cheese from brine and dry on a rack at room temperature for 24 hours, turning once to aid drying. Place on a cheese mat in a ripening container. Ripen at 55°F (13°C) and 90% humidity for 1 week, turning daily. Remove any initial moisture from bottom of container wiping with a paper towel.

13. Make the bacterial brine solution for washing rind as follows: Boil ½ cup (125 mL) water. Let cool. Add 1 tsp (5 mL) salt and tiny pinch (just the tip of a knife) *B. linens* ripening bacteria. Cover and set aside for 12 hours at room temperature to allow bacteria to rehydrate. Dip a small clean cloth or natural sponge into the bacterial brine, squeeze out excess and wash cheese all over. Return cheese to the ripening area. This will encourage the bacterial smear growth on the rind.

14. Ripen for 2 months, turning and washing the cheese every second day with a cloth or small brush dipped in brine. The rind will gradually form, becoming a brownish-gray color.

Brick

**Makes about
2 lbs (1 kg)**

12% yield

This is a mild-flavored,
bacteria-ripened cheese
usually formed in a
loaf-shaped mold.
Alternatively, you may
use a square or round
mold with a lid, though
you will not have the
traditional shape. Line
mold with cheese cloth.

Tip: A brick is good to
use for the 5-lb (2.5 kg)
weight. Just clean it well
and wrap it in plastic
wrap for sanitation.

- Draining container
- Cheese matting
- Cloth-lined colander
- Rectangular (brick-shaped) mold
- 5-lb (2.5 kg) weight (see Tip, left)
- Ripening container

16 quarts	whole milk	16 L
½ tsp	thermophilic culture	2.5 mL
Pinch	*Brevibacterium linens* ripening bacteria	Pinch
¾ tsp	calcium chloride	3.75 mL
¾ tsp	liquid rennet	3.75 mL
	Cool 18% saturated brine (see Tips, opposite)	
	Brine solution for washing rind (see Tip, page 171)	

1. Sterilize all equipment (see page 40). Prepare a draining container by placing a rack inside. Then place a cutting board on top, followed by a cheese mat, then the molds.

2. In a large stainless-steel pot set in a hot water bath over medium heat, warm milk to 90°F (32°C), stirring gently. Turn off heat.

3. Sprinkle culture and *B. linens* over surface of milk and let stand for about 5 minutes to rehydrate. Using skimmer and an up-and-down motion, gently draw culture down into milk without breaking surface of milk. Cover and let ripen for 15 minutes.

4. Dilute calcium chloride in ¼ cup (50 mL) cool water. Add to milk using the same up-and-down motion.

5. Dilute rennet in ¼ cup (50 mL) cool water. Add to milk and, using the same up-and-down motion, draw rennet down into milk until well blended. Cover pot and let set for 30 to 40 minutes, maintaining the temperature at 90°F (32°C).

6. Check for a clean break (see Tip, page 162). Using a long-bladed knife and skimmer, cut curd into ⅜-inch (0.9 cm) pieces (see Tip, page 167). Let stand for 5 minutes.

Tips: Even hard cheeses need to be flipped regularly during the aging period. If left sitting on the same side for long periods, the cheese will tend to settle, becoming wider and denser on the bottom, creating an uneven texture.

To make an 18% saturated brine: Mix 1 part salt to 5 parts water. It may be necessary to warm the water to successfully dissolve the salt. If so, let the brine cool before immersing the cheese. The brine can be used over and over again for several batches of cheese (refrigerate between uses). The best temperature for brining cheese is 55°F (13°C). Replenish the salt after several uses and remove any floating bits of cheese with a strainer.

7. Return heat to low and slowly warm curds, stirring gently the whole time, to 104°F (40°C), adjusting heat as necessary to make sure it takes 40 minutes to do so. Do not heat too quickly. Cover and let stand for 5 minutes.

8. Using a measuring cup, dip off whey until only 1 inch (2.5 cm) remains above curds. While stirring gently, replace whey with an equal amount of 104°F (40°C) water. Stir gently for 10 minutes. Let curds settle and stand for 5 minutes.

9. Carefully pour contents of pot into cloth-lined colander. Using a ladle or clean hands, immediately fill prepared mold with warm curd, pulling cheese cloth up neatly around curds and folding excess snugly across top.

10. Cover container to keep cheese warm and let drain for 15 minutes. Turn mold over and continue to drain for another 20 minutes. Flip again.

11. Re-dress cheese (see Tip, page 157) and add the weight. Press for 6 hours, turning cheese every 2 hours.

12. Remove cheese from mold. Unwrap and place in 18% saturated brine solution for 8 hours, turning over after 4 hours.

13. Remove cheese from brine and place on a cheese mat on a rack in a ripening container. Let dry, uncovered, at room temperature for 24 hours.

14. Place cheese on a clean cheese mat in a clean ripening container and ripen at 60°F (16°C) and 90% humidity for 2 weeks. Turn cheese daily and wash rind with a cloth dipped in brine every second day (see Tip, page 173). A reddish smear will begin to appear on the surface of the cheese after 10 to 12 days.

15. Once rind has taken on a more solid red coloring, after about 2 weeks, clean surface of cheese with a clean damp cloth to remove some of the smear, then dry it thoroughly with a clean dry cloth or paper towel. You may wrap it in foil or wax it for longer storage at 45°F (7°C). Continue to turn the cheese once a week to even out the ripening (see Tip, left).

Taleggio

Makes about
2 lbs (1 kg)

12% yield

A semisoft washed-rind cheese from northern Italy, Taleggio has a long history. The traditional shape of Taleggio is a square, but if you don't have a square mold, you can use a tomme mold.

Tip: Most washed-rind cheeses have great melting qualities; the cheese becomes very soft and supple but does not run or release fat. Try cheeses such as St-Paulin, brick or taleggio for gratins, raclette and open-faced hot sandwiches.

- Draining container
- Cloth-lined colander
- One or two 7½-inch (19 cm) square by 6-inch (15 cm) deep molds or 1 tomme mold
- Cheese matting
- Ripening container

8 quarts	whole milk	8 L
¼ tsp	mesophilic culture	1.25 mL
Pinch	*Brevibacterium linens* ripening bacteria	Pinch
½ tsp	calcium chloride	2.5 mL
½ tsp	liquid rennet	2.5 mL
	Cool 18% saturated brine (see Tip, page 169)	
	Brine solution for washing rind (see Tip, opposite)	

1. Sterilize all equipment (see page 40). Prepare a draining container by placing a rack inside.

2. In a large stainless-steel pot set in a hot water bath over medium heat, warm milk to 90°F (32°C), stirring gently. Turn off heat.

3. Sprinkle culture and *B. linens* over surface of milk and let stand for about 5 minutes to rehydrate. Using skimmer and an up-and-down motion, gently draw culture down into milk without breaking surface of milk. Cover and let ripen for 1 hour, maintaining the temperature at 90°F (32°C).

4. Dilute calcium chloride in ¼ cup (50 mL) cool water. Add to milk using the same up-and-down motion.

5. Dilute rennet in ¼ cup (50 mL) cool water. Add to milk and, using the same up-and-down motion, draw rennet down into milk until well blended. Cover pot and let set for 20 to 30 minutes.

Tip: To make a brine solution for washing rind: Boil ½ cup (125 mL) water. Let cool and then mix with 1 tsp (5 mL) salt.

The brine solution may be kept and used for several days, as long as you have not dipped your cloth into it. Remove a small amount to another container for washing, or make a new batch each time.

6. Check for a clean break (see Tip, page 162). Using a long-bladed knife and skimmer, cut curd into ¾-inch (2 cm) cubes (see Tip, page 167). Let stand for 5 minutes. Stir gently for 30 minutes. Every 10 minutes, stop stirring and remove 2 cups (500 mL) whey.

7. After 30 minutes, let curds settle. Carefully pour contents of pot into cloth-lined colander. Fill mold(s) with the soft curds. Let drain for 12 hours, turning cheese over in the mold(s) 6 or 7 times. Keep container covered to keep the cheese warm.

8. Remove cheese from mold(s) and place in 18% saturated brine solution for 8 hours, turning over after 4 hours.

9. Removed cheese from brine and dry on rack at room temperature, turning once or twice, for 2 days.

10. Place cheese on a cheese mat in a ripening container. Ripen at 50°F (10°C) and 90% humidity for 4 to 5 weeks. Wash rind of cheese twice weekly with a cloth dipped in brine (see Tip, left and page 173) to control mold growth and help develop the reddish-orange color typical for this kind of rind. When ripe, the cheese should feel softer and bulge slightly around the side. It is ready to eat, though you may want to ripen it for another week or two for more developed flavor.

11. Wrap the finished cheese in foil or parchment paper and store in the refrigerator.

Monostorer

**Makes about
2½ lbs (1.25 kg)**

15% yield

This rare sheep's milk
cheese comes from the
Transylvania region of
Romania. The washed
rind gives an extra boost
of flavor to the rich,
creamy paste.

- Cloth-lined colander
- 1 tomme mold, lined with cheese cloth
- Cheese press
- Cheese matting
- Ripening container

8 quarts	sheep's milk	8 L
½ tsp	liquid rennet	2.5 mL
2 tsp	pickling (canning) or kosher salt	10 mL
	Cool 18% saturated brine (see Tip, page 169)	
	Brine solution for washing rind (see Tip, page 171)	

1. Sterilize all equipment (see page 40). In a large stainless-steel pot over low heat, warm milk to 88°F (31°C), stirring gently to prevent scorching. Remove from heat.

2. Dilute rennet in ¼ cup (50 mL) cool water. Add to milk and, using a skimmer and an up-and-down motion, draw rennet down into milk until well blended. Cover pot and let set for 1 to 2 hours or until a firm curd has formed.

3. Using a long-bladed knife and skimmer, cut curd into ½-inch (1.25 cm) cubes (see Tip, page 167). Let settle. Carefully pour contents of pot into a cloth-lined colander. Let drain for 10 minutes. Press the curd down by gathering the cloth and pressing the curd with your hands in the colander. When curd stops dripping, break it up with your hands into small pieces and blend in salt. Mix well with your hands while still in the cloth.

4. Sprinkle curd with ¼ cup (50 mL) warm water and mix again with your hands. Press down well again by twisting and pressing the cloth.

Tip: Wash cheese rind with a clean cloth, a small natural sponge or a soft surgical-type brush. Dip into a container of just enough solution for one washing and squeeze until just damp. Rub the whole surface of the cheese, removing any excess moisture, then turn it in the container and return to the ripening area. Repeat as indicated in the recipe, usually 2 to 3 times weekly for 1 to 2 months.

5. Once again, crumble the curd. Fill prepared mold with curd, pulling cloth up neatly around curd and folding excess snugly over top. Put on lid. Place mold in cheese press. Press at firm pressure for 8 to 10 hours.

6. Remove cheese from press. Unwrap and place in 18% saturated brine solution for 12 hours, turning over after 6 hours.

7. Remove cheese from brine and dry on a rack at room temperature for 2 days, turning after 1 day to aid drying.

8. Place cheese on a cheese mat in a ripening container. Let ripen at 55°F (13°C) and 90% humidity for 8 to 10 weeks. Every second day, turn cheese and wash with a cloth dipped in brine (see Tip, left). The rind will gradually become firmer and take on a pale yellow color, and the cheese will soften slightly.

9. Wrap the finished cheese in foil or parchment paper and store in the refrigerator.

Esrom

Makes 4 lbs (2 kg)

12% yield

Esrom is a Danish monastery cheese with a buttery, semisoft paste and a slightly open structure. It has a full flavor and aroma with a bit of milky sweetness and a dark golden rind.

Variation: Esrom is one cheese that lends itself well to the addition of herbs and spices. Try caraway seeds, a peppercorn blend or herbes de Provence. Be sure these seasonings are sterilized. Boil or microwave herbs or spices, then add them to the fresh curds before placing them in the mold for pressing.

- Cloth-lined colander
- 1 tomme mold, lined with cheese cloth
- Cheese press
- Cheese matting
- Ripening container

16 quarts	whole milk	16 L
½ tsp	mesophilic culture	2.5 mL
⅛ tsp	*Brevibacterium linens* ripening bacteria	0.65 mL
¾ tsp	calcium chloride	3.75 mL
¾ tsp	liquid rennet	3.75 mL
	Cool 18% saturated brine (see Tip, page 169)	
	Brine solution for washing rind (see Tip, page 171)	

1. Sterilize all equipment (see page 40). In a large stainless-steel pot set in a hot water bath over medium heat, warm milk to 90°F (32°C), stirring gently. Turn off heat.

2. Sprinkle culture and *B. linens* over surface of milk and let stand for about 5 minutes to rehydrate. Using skimmer and an up-and-down motion, gently draw culture down into milk without breaking surface of milk. Cover and let ripen for 30 minutes.

3. Dilute calcium chloride in ¼ cup (50 mL) cool water. Add to milk using the same up-and-down motion.

4. Dilute rennet in ¼ cup (50 mL) cool water. Add to milk and, using the same up-and-down motion, draw rennet down into milk until well blended. Cover and let set for 40 to 45 minutes, maintaining the temperature at 90°F (32°C).

5. Check for a clean break (see Tip, page 177). Using a long-bladed knife and skimmer, cut curd into ⅜-inch (0.9 cm) pieces (see Tip, opposite). Let stand for 5 minutes. Stir gently for 5 minutes. Let curds settle.

Tip: To cut curds: Holding a long-bladed stainless-steel knife straight up and down, draw knife through the curd, cutting it into strips. Proceed across the pot until you have reached the other side. Turn the pot and cut across the first strips to create squares. Using a skimmer, cut horizontally from side to side just under the surface of the curd to create cubes. Gradually move skimmer down through curd to cut layers of cubes. Using skimmer, gently stir curd cubes. Using a knife, cut any pieces that have been missed or are too large. For small-cut curds, you can use a large whisk for cutting.

6. Using a measuring cup, remove one-third of the whey from top of curd (see Tip, page 157) and, while stirring gently, replace with an equal amount of 90°F (32°C) water. Return heat to low and slowly warm the curd, stirring continuously, to 95°F (35°C), adjusting the heat as necessary to make sure it takes 20 minutes to do so. Do not heat too quickly. Turn off heat and continue stirring for another 15 minutes. Let curds settle.

7. Carefully pour contents of pot into a cloth-lined colander. Using a ladle or clean hands, fill the prepared mold with curds, pulling cheese cloth up neatly around curds and folding excess snugly across top. Put on the lid.

8. Place mold in cheese press or place weight on top. Press at medium pressure for 6 hours. Remove cheese from press and re-dress (see Tip, page 157). Continue pressing at medium pressure for 6 hours.

9. Remove from press. Unwrap and place in 18% saturated brine solution for 12 hours, turning over after 6 hours.

10. Remove cheese from brine and dry on a rack at room temperature for 24 hours, turning once.

11. Place cheese on a cheese mat in a ripening container. Ripen at 60°F (16°C) and 90% humidity for 6 weeks. Turn cheese daily for the first week, then begin washing it every second day with a cloth dipped in a brine solution (see Tip, page 173), turning the cheese each time. A reddish-orange rind will develop, and the cheese should feel semisoft when pressed with a finger in the center. Wrap the finished cheese and store in the refrigerator.

Tilsit

Makes 4 lbs (2 kg)
12% yield

Tilsit is a semifirm cheese with a pronounced piquancy similar to that of Limburger. It was developed in East Prussia by Dutch immigrants a century or so ago. It is also now made in Switzerland, where it enjoys great popularity.

Tip: There are several different strains of *Brevibacterium linens* and similar types of ripening bacteria. Depending on the strain used, the color that develops on the rind as the bacteria grow can range from pale ivory to orange-red to reddish brown. The humidity of the ripening area and the washing routine play a large role in the development of the smear.

- Draining container
- 1 tomme mold
- Cheese matting
- Ripening container

16 quarts	whole milk	16 L
½ tsp	thermophilic culture	2.5 mL
Pinch	*Brevibacterium linens* ripening bacteria	Pinch
¾ tsp	calcium chloride	3.75 mL
¾ tsp	liquid rennet	3.75 mL
	Cool 18% saturated brine (see Tip, page 169)	
	Brine solution for washing rind (see Tip, page 171)	

1. Sterilize all equipment (see page 40). Prepare a draining container by placing a rack inside.

2. In a large stainless-steel pot set in a hot water bath over medium heat, warm milk to 95°F (35°C), stirring gently. Turn off heat.

3. Sprinkle culture and *B. linens* over surface of milk and let stand for about 5 minutes to rehydrate. Using skimmer and an up-and-down motion, gently draw culture down into milk without breaking surface of milk. Cover and let ripen for 30 minutes.

4. Dilute calcium chloride in ¼ cup (50 mL) cool water. Add to milk using the same up-and-down motion.

5. Dilute rennet in ¼ cup (50 mL) cool water. Add to milk and, using the same up-and-down motion, draw rennet down into milk until well blended. Cover pot and let set for 40 minutes, maintaining the temperature at 95°F (35°C).

6. Check for a clean break (see Tip, opposite). Using a long-bladed knife and skimmer, cut curd into ½-inch (1.25 cm) cubes (see Tip, page 175). Let stand for 5 minutes.

Tip: To ascertain whether the curd is ready for cutting, check for what's called a "clean break." Insert the long flat blade of a cheese knife into the curd at a 30-degree angle and slowly lift the blade toward the surface of the curd. If the curd splits into a long clean break or crack, it is ready to cut. If the break is wobbly or uneven, let the curd set for a few more minutes before trying again.

7. Return heat to low and slowly warm curds, stirring gently, to 110°F (43°C), adjusting the heat as necessary to make sure it takes 40 minutes to do so. Do not heat too quickly. The curds will shrink to the size of peas. Turn off heat and let curds settle.

8. Using a measuring cup, dip off whey down to the level of the curd. Ladle warm curd into prepared mold right away. Place the lid on the mold. Place the lid on the draining container to keep the cheese warm. Flip cheese in the mold every 15 minutes for 1 hour, then every hour or two for the rest of the day. The cheese is not pressed.

9. When cheese is firm, remove from mold and place in 18% saturated brine solution for 12 hours, turning cheese over after 6 hours.

10. Remove cheese from brine and dry on a rack at room temperature for 24 hours, turning after 12 hours. Place cheese on a cheese mat in a clean ripening container. Ripen at 55°F (13°C) and 90% humidity.

11. After the first week of ripening, begin washing the rind of the cheese with a cloth dipped in brine (see Tip, page 173) twice weekly, turning the cheese each time. Continue to develop the rind in this way for up to 6 months, though the cheese is ready for consumption as a mild cheese after 2 months. The rind will develop a reddish-brown color and a distinct pungency. The longer you ripen it, the more intense the color and flavor will be.

Troubleshooting

The rind is sticky.
There is too much humidity in ripening area; wipe off excess stickiness with a damp cloth and reduce humidity.

Cheese is very soft but still has a few weeks of ripening before it's ready.
Excess humidity in the curd; stir curd longer and let stand longer before placing in the mold. Or too much humidity in ripening area; reduce humidity. Or not enough acidity in the curd; let milk ripen longer before adding rennet.

Cheese develops large holes and puffs up.
Excess moisture (whey) in the curd; stir curd longer before hooping, or filling molds, to increase moisture loss, and make sure all curd is cut equally. Or cheese was pressed too firmly too quickly, sealing the rind and trapping whey in the curd; begin pressing at low pressure, then increase slowly. Or animal fodder has legumes or silage present; remove silage and legumes from feed. Or there are yeasts or contaminants in the milk; use the highest-quality milk and maintain high standards of hygiene during all phases of processing. The cheese is still safe to eat. However, if cheese has a nasty off smell, it should be discarded.

Black or brown mold appears on the surface of the cheese.
Too much moisture in the ripening area; reduce humidity. Or airborne bacteria is present in the ripening area; clean all surfaces and environment with bleach water (2 tbsp/30 mL household bleach to 4 quarts/4 L water). To combat mold, rub cheese rind with a blend of salt and vinegar (1 tsp/5 mL salt to 1/4 cup/50 mL vinegar).

The texture of the finished cheese is rubbery.
Too much rennet in the curd; reduce rennet. Or lactic bacteria is too weak; use fresh culture next time. Or washed-curd cheese was too diluted during washing; remove less whey when washing curd or add less water after whey removal.

Washed-Curd and Semisoft Cheeses

Washed-curd cheeses have a mild flavor and a moist supple paste, created by diluting the whey with warm water during the cooking process. Though pressed and ripened like the harder cheeses, they don't usually require long-term aging to develop full aroma and flavor.

Colby

Makes 4 lbs (2 kg)

12% yield

Colby is an American
cheese with a flavor
similar to that of
Cheddar, only milder.
It is a great fresh-eating
cheese, a favorite with
kids, but it does not
age well.

Tip: To ascertain
whether the curd is
ready for the next step,
check for a clean break:
insert the long flat blade
of a knife into the curd
at a 30-degree angle
and slowly lift the blade
toward the surface of
the curd. If the curd splits
into a long clean break or
crack, it is ready to cut.
If the cut is wobbly or
uneven, let the curd set
for a few more minutes
before trying again.

- 1 tomme mold, lined with cheese cloth
- Cheese press
- Cheese matting

16 quarts	whole milk	16 L
½ tsp	mesophilic culture	2.5 mL
¾ tsp	calcium chloride	3.75 mL
¾ tsp	liquid rennet	3.75 mL
	Cool 18% saturated brine (see Tip, opposite)	
	Cheese wax	

1. Sterilize all equipment (see page 40). In a large
   stainless-steel pot set in a hot water bath over medium
   heat, warm milk to 86°F (30°C), stirring gently. Turn
   off heat.

2. Sprinkle culture over surface of milk and let stand for
   about 5 minutes to rehydrate. Using skimmer and an
   up-and-down motion, gently draw culture down into
   milk without breaking surface of milk. Cover and let
   ripen for 1 hour, maintaining the temperature at 86°F
   (30°C).

3. Dilute calcium chloride in ¼ cup (50 mL) cool water.
   Add to milk using the same up-and-down motion.

4. Dilute rennet in ¼ cup (50 mL) cool water. Add to milk
   and, using the same up-and-down motion, draw rennet
   down into milk until well blended. Cover pot and let
   set for 30 minutes, maintaining the temperature.

5. Check for a clean break (see Tip, left). If necessary, let
   set for another 5 to 10 minutes or until you achieve a
   clean break. Using a long-bladed knife and skimmer,
   cut curd into ½-inch (1.25 cm) cubes (see Tip, page
   191). Let stand for 5 minutes.

6. Return heat to low and slowly warm curds to 104°F
   (40°C), stirring slowly and gently, adjusting the heat
   as necessary to make sure it takes 45 minutes to do so.
   Do not heat too quickly. The curds should shrink to
   the size of navy beans. Allow curds to settle and stand
   for 10 to 15 minutes.

Tip: To make an 18% saturated brine: Mix 1 part salt to 5 parts water. It may be necessary to warm the water to successfully dissolve the salt. If so, let the brine cool before immersing the cheese. The brine can be used over and over again for several batches of cheese (refrigerate between uses). The best temperature for brining cheese is 55°F (13°C). Replenish the salt after several uses and remove any floating bits of cheese with a strainer.

7. Using a measuring cup, remove whey from pot until you see the surface of the curds. Replace with the same amount of 104°F (40°C) water and stir for 2 minutes. Cover and hold for another 10 to 15 minutes.

8. Drain off whey, pouring some through prepared mold to warm it. Fill mold with curds. Pull cloth up neatly around curds and fold snugly over the top. Put on the lid.

9. Place mold in cheese press. Press at medium pressure for 1 hour. Remove cheese from press and re-dress (see Tip, page 193). Continue pressing at firm pressure for 12 hours or overnight.

10. Remove cheese from press. Unwrap and place in brine solution for 12 hours, turning over after 6 hours. Remove from brine and let dry on a cheese mat placed on a rack at room temperature for 2 or 3 days or until the rind is almost dry to the touch.

11. Coat cheese with 2 or 3 layers of cheese wax (see page 21). Ripen at 50° to 54°F (10° to 12°C) and 85% humidity for 6 weeks to 2 months, turning the cheese weekly to ensure even ripening. By 2 months, the flavor will have increased, but the cheese will still be quite mild and not as sharp as Cheddar.

Edam

**Makes about
3¼ lbs (1.6 kg)**
10% yield

This cheese, originally
from the town in Holland
of the same name, can
be recognized by its ball
shape. It is a mild cheese,
great for sandwiches
and snacks. You can
use whole or partly
skimmed milk, though
with lower-fat milk,
you will have a smaller
yield and the cheese
will be harder.

Tip: Non-homogenized
milk, also known as
cream line or standard
milk, is always the best
choice for successful
cheese making.
Non-homogenized
milk is pasteurized
milk that hasn't been
homogenized and
shouldn't be confused
with raw milk. See
Sources, page 372,
for more information.

- 1 tomme mold, lined with cheese cloth
- Cheese press
- Cheese matting
- Ripening container, optional

16 quarts	whole or partly skimmed (1 or 2%) milk	16 L
½ tsp	mesophilic culture	2.5 mL
¾ tsp	calcium chloride	3.75 mL
¾ tsp	liquid rennet	3.75 mL
	Cool 18% saturated brine (see Tip, page 181)	
	Simple brine solution (see Tip, opposite)	
	Cheese wax, optional	

1. Sterilize all equipment (see page 40). In a large stainless-steel pot set in a hot water bath over medium heat, warm milk to 88°F (31°C), stirring gently. Turn off heat.

2. Sprinkle culture over surface of milk and let stand for about 5 minutes to rehydrate. Using skimmer and an up-and-down motion, gently draw culture down into milk without breaking surface of milk. Cover and let ripen for 30 minutes, maintaining the temperature at 88°F (31°C).

3. Dilute calcium chloride in ¼ cup (50 mL) cool water. Add to milk using the same up-and-down motion.

4. Dilute rennet in ¼ cup (50 mL) cool water. Add to milk and, using the same up-and-down motion, draw rennet down into milk until well blended. Cover pot and let set for 30 minutes, maintaining the temperature.

5. Check for a clean break (see Tip, page 180). If necessary, let set for another 5 to 10 minutes or until you achieve a clean break. Using a long-bladed knife and skimmer, cut curd into ½-inch (1.25 cm) cubes (see Tip, page 191). Let stand for 5 minutes.

6. Return heat to low and slowly warm curds to 92°F (33°C), stirring slowly and gently, adjusting heat as necessary to make sure it takes 15 to 20 minutes to do so. Do not heat too quickly. Let curds settle.

Tip: To make a simple brine solution for washing cheese rinds: Dissolve 1 tsp (5 mL) salt into ½ cup (125 mL) boiled water. Let cool. Do not reserve used brine for the next washing because there is danger of contamination from unwanted, even dangerous, bacteria.

7. Reserving whey in a large clean pot, drain off enough whey to expose surface of curds.

8. Replace the whey removed with an equal amount of warm water to bring the curds to 99°F (37°C) (see Tips, page 187). Stir continuously for 30 minutes, maintaining temperature. Turn on heat underneath water bath to help maintain the temperature.

9. Let curds settle and begin to mat together. Drain off whey, adding some to the reserved whey in the pot, and pouring some through prepared mold to warm it. Fill mold with curds. Pull cloth up neatly around curds and fold snugly over the top. Put on the lid.

10. Place mold in cheese press. Press at medium pressure for 30 minutes.

11. Meanwhile, warm reserved whey over medium heat to 122°F (50°C). Remove cheese from press. Unwrap and place in hot whey for 20 minutes. Turn cheese a few times to make sure all sides are equally exposed to whey.

12. Remove cheese from whey. Rewrap in cheese cloth and replace in mold. Put on the lid. Replace mold in press. Continue pressing at firm pressure for 6 to 7 hours. Remove from press and re-dress (see Tip, page 193). Continue pressing again for another 6 to 7 hours or overnight.

13. Remove cheese from press. Unwrap and place in 18% saturated brine solution for 12 hours, turning over after 6 hours.

14. Remove from brine and let dry on a cheese mat placed on a rack at room temperature for 2 to 3 days, turning cheese over once or twice per day to aid drying. You may wax (see page 21) the cheese once it is fairly dry to the touch, or you may age it unwaxed.

15. *For natural-rind cheese:* Place cheese on a clean cheese mat in a ripening container. Ripen at 50° to 54°F (10° to 12°C) and 85% humidity. Wash cheese every second day with a cloth soaked in simple brine solution, turning each time. Maintain humidity by adjusting the lid of the ripening container.

continued on next page…

Edam continued...

16. *For waxed cheese:* Coat cheese with 2 or 3 layers of cheese wax (see page 21). Ripen at 50° to 54°F (10° to 12°C) and 85% humidity, turning weekly to ensure even ripening.

17. Natural-rind or waxed cheese is ready to eat after 2 months, but you may age it longer for stronger flavor.

Cheese and Teeth

Dental studies have shown that a number of cheeses will actually help to prevent cavities. The cheeses studied include: Romano, Muenster, Gouda, Swiss, Edam, Monterey Jack, Tilsit, Port du Salut and Cheddar. Their high levels of phosphorus and calcium are especially beneficial. Eating cheese after a meal or sugary snack can help protect against tooth decay and even restore some of the minerals in our tooth enamel. The lactic bacteria in cheese fight against destructive bacteria, help neutralize and wash away the acid on teeth, and also prevent sugar on enamel from turning into tooth-damaging bacteria.

Baked Macaroni and Cheese

Makes 4 servings

When made from scratch with your own handmade cheese, this is comfort food with flair.

- Preheat oven to 350°F (180°C)
- 8-cup (2 L) casserole dish, buttered

10 oz	macaroni	300 g
2 tbsp	butter	30 mL
2 tbsp	all-purpose flour	30 mL
2 cups	milk	500 mL
	Salt and freshly ground pepper	
Pinch	freshly grated nutmeg	Pinch
4 oz	Colby (page 180), shredded	125 g

Topping

¼ cup	butter	50 mL
½ cup	fresh bread crumbs	125 mL

1. In a large pot of boiling salted water, cook macaroni until tender but not soft. Drain and place in large bowl.

2. Meanwhile, in a small saucepan over medium heat, melt butter. Using a whisk, stir in flour and cook, whisking vigorously, for 1 minute. Add milk all at once, whisking until well blended. Continue to cook, whisking constantly, for about 5 minutes or until sauce is thickened and smooth. Season with salt and pepper to taste and add nutmeg. Remove from heat.

3. Blend cheese into sauce, stirring until melted and very smooth. Pour sauce over pasta and mix well. Scrape mixture into prepared casserole dish.

4. *Topping:* In a small saucepan, melt butter. Stir in bread crumbs until coated. Spread over pasta mixture. Bake in preheated oven for 15 to 20 minutes or until topping is crisp and golden and cheese sauce is bubbly. Serve hot.

Gouda

Makes 4 lbs (2 kg)
12% yield

- 1 tomme mold, lined with cheese cloth
- Cheese press
- Cheese matting
- Ripening container

16 quarts	whole milk	16 L
½ tsp	mesophilic culture	2.5 mL
¾ tsp	calcium chloride	3.75 mL
¾ tsp	liquid rennet	3.75 mL
	Cool 18% saturated brine (see Tip, page 181)	
	Cheese wax	

Gouda is one of the simpler pressed cheeses and it ages fairly quickly, so you don't have to wait long to sample your handiwork! Originally made on farmsteads in Holland, Gouda is now well-known and enjoyed around the world. The process of washing the curd gives this cheese a sweet and elastic paste.

The development of pressed and waxed cheeses is attributed to the Dutch. Firm waxed cheeses could be stacked and transported around the world on their merchant ships for months at a time without spoiling.

1. Sterilize all equipment (see page 40). In a large stainless-steel pot set in a hot water bath over medium heat, warm milk to 85°F (29°C), stirring gently. Turn off heat.

2. Sprinkle culture over surface of milk and let stand for about 5 minutes to rehydrate. Using skimmer and an up-and-down motion, gently draw culture down into milk without breaking surface of milk.

3. Dilute calcium chloride in ¼ cup (50 mL) cool water. Add to milk using the same up-and-down motion.

4. Dilute rennet in ¼ cup (50 mL) cool water. Add to milk and, using the same up-and-down motion, draw rennet down into milk until well blended. Cover pot and let set for 30 minutes, maintaining temperature at 85°F (29°C).

5. Check for a clean break (see Tip, page 180). If necessary, let set for another 10 to 15 minutes or until you achieve a clean break. Using a long-bladed knife and skimmer, cut curd into ½-inch (1.25 cm) cubes (see Tip, page 191). Let stand for 5 minutes. Gently stir curds for 5 minutes. Let stand for 5 minutes again. The curds should sink to the bottom of the pot. If they do not sink, stir for another 5 minutes.

Tips: To remove one-third of the whey, simply measure one-third of the way down the pot. You are removing whey until the surface of the curds is just visible under the whey.

When washing the curd, increase or decrease the temperature of the added water as required to reach the goal temperature using the specified amount of water.

6. Using a measuring cup, remove 6 cups (1.5 L), or approximately 10%, of the whey from pot, taking care not to disturb the curds. Replace the whey with an equal amount of 140°F (60°C) water to bring the temperature to 92°F (33°C). Stir curds gently for 10 minutes. Let settle again.

7. Remove one-third of the whey this time (see Tips, left) until the surface of the curds is just visible under the whey and replace with an equal amount of 110°F (43°C) water to bring the temperature to about 98°F (37°C). Stir curds continuously for 20 minutes. The curds should shrink to the size of navy beans. Let curds settle and stand for another 10 minutes.

8. Drain off whey, pouring some through prepared mold to warm it. Curds will have knit together. Using your hands, break off large sections of the curd and place in the prepared mold, mounding it in a cone shape. It will drain fairly quickly, losing volume. Pull cloth up neatly around curds, easing out the wrinkles, and fold excess neatly over the top. Put on the lid.

9. Place mold in cheese press or place a weight on top. Press at light pressure for 30 minutes. Remove cheese from press and re-dress (see Tip, page 193). Continue pressing at medium pressure for 8 to 12 hours or overnight.

10. Remove cheese from press. Unwrap and place in brine solution for 12 hours, turning over after 6 hours.

11. Remove from brine and let dry on a cheese mat placed on a rack at room temperature for 2 to 3 days or until the rind is almost dry to the touch. Turn cheese daily to dry evenly. Place cheese on a clean cheese mat in a ripening container and ripen at 50° to 54°F (10° to 12°C) and 85% humidity for 1 week.

12. Coat cheese with 2 or 3 layers of cheese wax (see page 21). Return to ripening area and age for 6 weeks to several months, turning weekly.

Variations on next page…

Gouda continued...

Variations: *Hot Chile Gouda:* Boil 2 tbsp (30 mL) hot pepper flakes, or to taste (or 1 fresh jalapeño, roughly chopped) in 4 cups (1 L) water for 10 minutes. Be sure to protect your eyes from the steam of the cooking chiles. Let cool in the cooking liquid. Meanwhile, follow Gouda recipe (page 186) through Step 7. In Step 8, after draining off whey, pour the contents of the chile pot into the cheese pot and, wearing protective gloves, mix into curds by hand until evenly distributed. Continue with recipe.

Herbed Gouda: Follow Gouda recipe (page 186) through Step 7. In Step 8, after draining off whey, add 1 to 2 tbsp (15 to 30 mL) dried herb blend to the curds, mixing in with your hands until evenly distributed. Use a blend of your own garden herbs that have been washed, dried and crumbled, or substitute a store-bought blend (just make sure it contains no added salt, preservatives or flavor enhancers). A nice combination is parsley, celery leaves or lovage, chives and tarragon. If using your own harvested herbs, wash them, then microwave on High for 1 minute to kill any bacteria that may negatively affect the cheese during ripening. Then dry them until crisp. Begin with 1 tbsp (15 mL) and add more as you see fit. Too much can overwhelm the flavor. Continue with recipe.

Cheese and Apple Cake

Different than the usual sweet offering with a cup of coffee or tea, this cheese-laced coffee cake makes a nice accompaniment to a glass of white wine.

- Preheat oven to 350°F (180°C)
- 8-inch (2 L) square cake pan, buttered

1½ cups	all-purpose flour	375 mL
1 tsp	baking powder	5 mL
¼ tsp	salt	1.25 mL
½ cup	granulated sugar	125 mL
⅓ cup	butter, softened	75 mL
1	egg	1
½ cup	sour cream	125 mL
2	tart apples, cored, peeled and sliced into rings	2
6 oz	Gouda (page 186) or Edam (page 182), thinly sliced	175 g
½ cup	packed brown sugar	125 mL
½ cup	hazelnuts, chopped	125 mL

1. In a small bowl, sift together flour, baking powder and salt. Set aside.

2. In another bowl, using an electric mixer, cream together sugar and butter until light and fluffy. Add egg and beat well. Beat in sour cream.

3. Add dry ingredients and stir just until dry ingredients are moistened.

4. Spread half of the batter in prepared pan. Top with apple rings and cheese, reserving a few of each for the top of the cake. Spread remaining batter over apples and cheese, then arrange reserved cheese and apples on the top. Sprinkle with brown sugar and hazelnuts.

5. Bake in preheated oven for 30 to 40 minutes or until a toothpick inserted in the center comes out clean and topping is crisp. Serve warm or let cool in pan on a rack.

Leiden

Makes 4 lbs (2 kg)
12% yield

Cumin seeds add an exotic flavor to this cheese, which is especially well liked in Holland and Scandinavia.

Tip: To ascertain whether the curd is ready for the next step, check for a clean break: insert the long flat blade of a knife into the curd at a 30-degree angle and slowly lift the blade toward the surface of the curd. If the curd splits into a long clean break or crack, it is ready to cut. If the cut is wobbly or uneven, let the curd set for a few more minutes before trying again.

- 1 tomme mold, lined with cheese cloth
- Cheese press
- Cheese matting
- Ripening container

2 tbsp	cumin seeds	30 mL
16 quarts	whole milk	16 L
½ tsp	mesophilic culture	2.5 mL
¾ tsp	calcium chloride	3.75 mL
¾ tsp	liquid rennet	3.75 mL
	Cool 18% saturated brine (see Tip, page 181)	
	Cheese wax	

1. Sterilize all equipment (see page 40). In a small saucepan over medium heat, boil cumin seeds in 4 cups (1 L) water for 10 minutes. Let cool in the cooking liquid.

2. Meanwhile, in a large stainless-steel pot set in a hot water bath over medium heat, warm milk to 85°F (29°C), stirring gently. Turn off heat.

3. Sprinkle culture over surface of milk and let stand for about 5 minutes to rehydrate. Using skimmer and an up-and-down motion, gently draw culture down into milk without breaking surface of milk.

4. Dilute calcium chloride in ¼ cup (50 mL) cool water. Add to milk using the same up-and-down motion.

5. Dilute rennet in ¼ cup (50 mL) cool water. Add to milk and, using the same up-and-down motion, draw rennet down into milk until well blended. Cover and let set for 30 minutes, maintaining the temperature at 85°F (29°C).

6. Check for a clean break (see Tip, left). If necessary, let set for another 10 to 15 minutes or until you achieve a clean break. Using a long-bladed knife and skimmer, cut curd into ½-inch (1.25 cm) cubes (see Tip, opposite). Let stand for 5 minutes. Gently stir curds for 5 to 10 minutes. Let stand for 5 minutes again. The curds should sink to the bottom of the pot. If they do not sink, stir for another 5 minutes.

Tip: To cut curds: Holding a long-bladed stainless-steel knife straight up and down, draw knife through the curd, cutting it into strips. Proceed across the pot until you have reached the other side. Turn the pot and cut across the first strips to create squares. Using a skimmer, cut horizontally from side to side just under the surface of the curd to create cubes. Gradually move skimmer down through curd to cut layers of cubes. Using skimmer, gently stir curd cubes. Using a knife, cut any pieces that have been missed or are too large. For small-cut curds, you can use a large whisk for cutting.

7. Using a measuring cup, remove 6 cups (1.5 L), or approximately 10%, of the whey from pot, taking care not to disturb the curds. Replace the whey with an equal amount of 140°F (60°C) water to bring the temperature to 92°F (33°C). Stir curds gently for 10 minutes. Let settle again.

8. Remove one-third of the whey this time (see Tips, page 187), until the surface of the curds is just visible under the whey. Replace with an equal amount of 110°F (43°C) water to bring the temperature to 98°F (37°C). Stir curds continuously for 20 minutes. The curds should shrink to the size of navy beans. Let curds settle and stand for another 10 minutes.

9. Drain off whey, pouring some through prepared mold to warm it. Pour cumin seeds with cooking liquid over curds and mix in evenly with your hands. Fill prepared mold with curds. Pull cloth up neatly around curds, easing out wrinkles, and fold excess snugly over the top. Put on the lid.

10. Place mold in cheese press or place a weight on top. Press at light pressure for 30 minutes. Remove cheese from press and re-dress (see Tip, page 193). Continue pressing at medium pressure for 8 to 12 hours or overnight.

11. Remove cheese from press. Unwrap and place in brine solution for 12 hours, turning over after 6 hours.

12. Remove from brine and let dry on a cheese mat placed on a rack at room temperature for 2 to 3 days or until the rind is almost dry to the touch. Turn cheese daily to dry evenly. Place cheese on a clean cheese mat in a ripening container and ripen at 50° to 54°F (10° to 12°C) and 85% humidity for 1 week.

13. Coat cheese with 2 or 3 layers of cheese wax (see page 21). Return to ripening area and age for 6 weeks to several months, turning weekly

Goat's Milk Gouda

<table>
<tr><td>Makes 4 lbs (2 kg)
12% yield</td></tr>
</table>

Goat's milk makes a lovely Gouda cheese with a smooth flavorful paste. I recommend coating it with black cheese wax to enhance the look of the pure white cheese.

- 1 tomme mold, lined with cheese cloth
- Cheese press
- Cheese matting
- Ripening container

16 quarts	goat's milk	16 L
½ tsp	mesophilic culture	2.5 mL
¾ tsp	calcium chloride	3.75 mL
½ tsp	liquid rennet	2.5 mL
	Cool 18% saturated brine (see Tip, page 181)	
	Black cheese wax	

1. Sterilize all equipment (see page 40). In a large stainless-steel pot set in a hot water bath over medium heat, warm milk to 85°F (29°C), stirring gently. Turn off heat.

2. Sprinkle culture over surface of milk and let stand for about 5 minutes to rehydrate. Using skimmer and an up-and-down motion, gently draw culture down into milk without breaking surface of milk.

3. Dilute calcium chloride in ¼ cup (50 mL) cool water. Add to milk using the same up-and-down motion.

4. Dilute rennet in ¼ cup (50 mL) cool water. Add to milk and, using the same up-and-down motion, draw rennet down into milk until well blended. Cover pot and let set for 30 minutes, maintaining the temperature at 85°F (29°C).

5. Check for a clean break (see Tip, page 190). If necessary, let set for another 5 to 10 minutes or until you achieve a clean break. Using a long-bladed knife and skimmer, cut curd into ½-inch (1.25 cm) cubes (see Tip, page 191). Let stand for 5 minutes. Gently stir curds for 5 minutes. Let stand for 5 minutes again. The curds should sink to the bottom of the pot. If they do not sink, stir for another 5 minutes.

Tip: To re-dress the cheese, remove the mold from the press. Remove the cheese from the mold and unwrap. Place the cloth back in the mold; turn the cheese over and put back in the mold, then rewrap. Return mold to the press.

6. Using a measuring cup, remove 6 cups (1.5 L), or approximately 10%, of the whey from pot, taking care not to disturb the curds. Replace the whey with an equal amount of 140°F (60°C) water to bring the temperature to 92°F (33°C). Stir curds gently for 10 minutes. Let settle again.

7. Remove one-third of the whey this time (see Tips, page 187), until the surface of the curds is just visible under the whey. Replace with an equal amount of 110°F (43°C) water to bring the temperature to 98°F (37°C). Stir curds continuously for 20 minutes. The curds should shrink to the size of navy beans. Let curds settle and stand for another 10 minutes.

8. Drain off whey, pouring some through prepared mold to warm it. Curds will have knit together. Using your hands, break off large sections of the curd and place in the prepared mold, mounding it in a cone shape. It will drain fairly quickly, losing volume. Pull cloth up neatly around curds, easing out the wrinkles, and fold excess neatly over the top. Put on the lid.

9. Place mold in cheese press or place a weight on top. Press at light pressure for 30 minutes. Remove cheese from press and re-dress (see Tip, left). Continue pressing at medium pressure for 8 to 12 hours or overnight.

10. Remove cheese from press. Unwrap and place in brine solution for 12 hours, turning over after 6 hours.

11. Remove from brine and let dry on a cheese mat placed on a rack at room temperature for 2 to 3 days or until the rind is almost dry to the touch. Turn cheese daily to dry evenly. Place cheese on a clean cheese mat in a ripening container and ripen at 50° to 54°F (10° to 12°C) and 85% humidity for 1 week.

12. Coat cheese with 2 or 3 layers of cheese wax (see page 21). Return to ripening area and age for 6 weeks to several months, turning weekly.

Havarti

Makes 4 lbs (2 kg)

12% yield

This popular cheese of Danish origin has a mild paste and flexible texture, making it very approachable for people who have not developed a palate for strong-tasting cheeses.

- Cloth-lined colander
- 1 tomme mold, lined with cheese cloth
- Cheese press
- Cheese matting
- Ripening container

16 quarts	whole milk	16 L
½ tsp	mesophilic culture	2.5 mL
¾ tsp	calcium chloride	3.75 mL
¾ tsp	liquid rennet	3.75 mL
⅓ cup	pickling (canning) or kosher salt	75 mL
	Cheese wax	

1. Sterilize all equipment (see page 40). In a large stainless-steel pot set in a hot water bath over medium heat, warm milk to 90°F (32°C), stirring gently. Turn off heat.

2. Sprinkle culture over surface of milk and let stand for about 5 minutes to rehydrate. Using skimmer and an up-and-down motion, gently draw culture down into milk without breaking surface of milk. Cover and let ripen for 30 minutes, maintaining the temperature at 90°F (32°C).

3. Dilute calcium chloride in ¼ cup (50 mL) cool water. Add to milk using the same up-and-down motion.

4. Dilute rennet in ¼ cup (50 mL) cool water. Add to milk and, using the same up-and-down motion, draw rennet down into milk until well blended. Cover pot and let set for 45 minutes, maintaining the temperature.

5. Check for a clean break (see Tip, page 190). If necessary, let set for another 10 to 15 minutes or until you achieve a clean break. Using a long-bladed knife and skimmer, cut curd into ½-inch (1.25 cm) cubes (see Tip, page 191). Stir gently for 10 minutes; the curds will shrink slightly in size. Let curds settle.

Tip: When presenting waxed cheeses on a cheese board, remove the wax first and slice a few pieces from the cheese to indicate how guests should proceed when serving themselves.

6. Using a measuring cup, remove 5 quarts (5 L), or one-third, of the whey until you can just barely see the surface of the curds. Replace whey with an equal amount of 170°F (77°C) water to bring the temperature to 100°F (38°C) (see Tips, page 187). If necessary, raise the temperature by adding more hot water or, if you've overheated the curd, lower the temperature by adding cold water.

7. Add salt to pot, stirring thoroughly. Hold for 30 minutes at this temperature, stirring every 5 minutes or so to keep the curds from matting. After 30 minutes, let curds settle and mat on the bottom of the pot.

8. Pour contents of pot into a cloth-lined colander. Break up curds slightly to release as much whey as possible. Fill prepared mold with curds, making sure there are no empty spaces or air pockets between the curds. Pull cloth up neatly around curds, easing out wrinkles, and fold excess snugly over the top. Put on the lid.

9. Place mold in cheese press or place a weight on top. Press at light pressure for 20 minutes.

10. Remove cheese from press and re-dress (see Tip, page 193). Continue pressing at medium pressure for 6 to 8 hours.

11. Remove cheese from press. Unwrap and place on a cheese mat in a ripening container. Cover and ripen at 54°F (12°C) and 90% humidity for 4 weeks. Turn cheese daily for 1 week, removing any collected whey from the bottom of the container. Turn every second day thereafter.

12. Coat cheese with 2 or 3 layers of cheese wax (see page 21). Store in the refrigerator or continue ripening to taste.

Raclette

Makes 4 lbs (2 kg)
12% yield

Melted raclette cheese is the perfect meal after a day of skiing or a winter walk. Serve it with small boiled potatoes, and pickles and a glass of white wine. You will need about 7 oz (210 g) of cheese per person. There are special appliances that make it easy to melt the cheese at the table.

- Cloth-lined colander
- 1 tomme mold, lined with cheese cloth
- Cheese press
- Cheese matting
- Ripening container

16 quarts	whole milk	16 L
½ tsp	mesophilic culture	2.5 mL
Pinch	*Brevibacterium linens* ripening bacteria	Pinch
¾ tsp	calcium chloride	3.75 mL
¾ tsp	liquid rennet	3.75 mL
	Cool 18% saturated brine (see Tip, page 181)	
	Simple brine solution (see Tip, opposite)	

1. Sterilize all equipment (see page 40). In a large stainless-steel pot set in a hot water bath over medium heat, warm milk to 88°F (31°C), stirring gently. Turn off heat.

2. Sprinkle culture and *B. linens* over surface of milk and let stand for about 5 minutes to rehydrate. Using skimmer and an up-and-down motion, gently draw culture down into milk without breaking surface of milk. Cover and let ripen for 1 hour and 15 minutes, maintaining the temperature at 88°F (31°C).

3. Dilute calcium chloride in ¼ cup (50 mL) cool water. Add to milk using the same up-and-down motion.

4. Dilute rennet in ¼ cup (50 mL) cool water. Add to milk and, using the same up-and-down motion, draw rennet down into milk until well blended. Cover and let set for 40 to 50 minutes, maintaining the temperature.

5. Check for a clean break (see Tip, page 190). If necessary, let set for another 10 to 15 minutes or until you achieve a clean break. Using a long-bladed knife or whisk and skimmer, cut curd into pea-size pieces. Let stand for 5 minutes to firm up curds. Stir curds for 20 minutes. Let settle.

Tip: To make a simple brine solution for washing cheese rinds: Dissolve 1 tsp (5 mL) salt into ½ cup (125 mL) boiled water. Let cool. Do not reserve used brine for the next washing because there is danger of contamination from unwanted, even dangerous, bacteria.

6. Using a measuring cup, remove 4 quarts (4 L), or approximately 25%, of the whey from the pot, taking care not to disturb the curds. Replace the whey with an equal amount of 140°F (60°C) water to bring the temperature to 100°F (38°C), stirring gently (see Tips, page 187). Continue stirring for 10 minutes. Let settle.

7. Pour contents of pot into a cloth-lined colander. Fill prepared mold with curds. Pull cloth up neatly around curds, easing out wrinkles, and fold excess snugly over the top.

8. Place mold in cheese press or place a weight on top. Press at light pressure for 15 minutes. Remove cheese from press and re-dress (see Tip, page 193). Continue pressing at medium pressure for 8 to 12 hours or overnight.

9. Remove cheese from press. Unwrap and place in 18% saturated brine solution for 12 hours, turning over after 6 hours.

10. Remove cheese from brine and let dry on a cheese mat on a rack at room temperature for 24 hours. Turn after 12 hours to aid drying.

11. Place cheese on a clean cheese mat in a ripening container and ripen at 54° to 60°F (12° to 16°C) and 90% to 95% humidity.

12. After 3 days, wash cheese with a cloth dipped in simple brine solution and turn over. Wash cheese every second day thereafter for 1 month. A reddish smear will develop on the rind. Continue ripening, turning and washing the cheese twice weekly. A brownish-red rind will form and continue to develop for as long as you ripen the cheese. It will develop a pleasant smelliness. Ripen for 8 to 12 weeks, or to taste. Wrap in plastic wrap and store in the refrigerator once it is ripened to your liking.

Fontina

Makes 4 lbs (2 kg)

12% yield

A semifirm cheese from the mountains of northern Italy, Fontina is great sliced in a sandwich or melted over vegetables.

- Cloth-lined colander
- 1 tomme mold, lined with cheese cloth
- Cheese press
- Cheese matting
- Ripening container

16 quarts	whole milk	16 L
½ tsp	mesophilic culture	2.5 mL
¾ tsp	calcium chloride	3.75 mL
¾ tsp	liquid rennet	3.75 mL
	Cool 18% saturated brine (see Tip, page 181)	
	Simple brine solution (see Tip, page 197)	

1. Sterilize all equipment (see page 40). In a large stainless-steel pot set in a hot water bath over medium heat, warm milk to 88°F (31°C), stirring gently. Turn off heat.

2. Sprinkle culture over surface of milk and let stand for about 5 minutes to rehydrate. Using skimmer and an up-and-down motion, gently draw culture down into milk without breaking surface of milk. Cover and let ripen for 1 hour, maintaining the temperature at 88°F (31°C).

3. Dilute calcium chloride in ¼ cup (50 mL) cool water. Add to milk using the same up-and-down motion.

4. Dilute rennet in ¼ cup (50 mL) cool water. Add to milk and, using the same up-and-down motion, draw rennet down into milk until well blended. Cover pot and let set for 45 to 50 minutes, maintaining the temperature.

5. Check for a clean break (see Tip, page 190). If necessary, let set for another 5 to 10 minutes or until you achieve a clean break. Using a long-bladed knife or whisk and skimmer, cut curd into pea-size pieces. Let stand for 5 minutes to firm up curds. Stir gently for 10 minutes.

Tip: Whey is a very nutritious by-product of cheese making and contains lactose, protein, calcium, casein, phosphorus, sodium and fat. Since up to 90% of the original amount of milk is lost as whey, it is tempting to find a good use for it. Some suggestions include: make into ricotta, add to soups and sauces for enhanced flavor, use in place of milk or sour milk in baking, spread on your garden beds as fertilizer or add to your compost pile (the high amount of lactic bacteria makes it a wonderful catalyst). You can also feed whey to barnyard animals: mix with regular feed for chickens, cattle and pigs; do not exceed 10% of the daily ration of feed in whey.

6. Using a measuring cup, remove 4 quarts (4 L), or approximately 25%, of the whey from the pot, taking care not to disturb the curds. Replace the whey with an equal amount of 145°F (63°C) water to bring the temperature to 102°F (39°C), stirring gently (see Tips, page 187). Continue stirring for 10 minutes. Let settle.

7. Pour contents of pot into a cloth-lined colander. Let drain for 10 minutes.

8. Fill prepared mold with curds. Pull cloth up neatly around curds and fold excess snugly over the top. Put on the lid.

9. Place mold in cheese press or place a weight on top. Press at light pressure for 15 minutes. Remove cheese from press and re-dress (see Tip, page 193). Continue pressing at medium pressure for 8 to 12 hours or overnight.

10. Remove cheese from press. Unwrap and place in 18% saturated brine solution for 12 hours, turning over after 6 hours.

11. Remove cheese from brine and let dry on a cheese mat on a rack at room temperature for 24 hours. Turn after 12 hours to aid drying.

12. Place cheese on a clean cheese mat in a ripening container and ripen at 55° to 60°F (13° to 16°C) and 90% to 95% humidity.

13. After 3 days, wash cheese with a cloth dipped in simple brine solution and turn over. Wash cheese every second day thereafter for 1 month. Continue ripening, turning and washing the cheese twice weekly. The cheese will be ready after about 3 months. Wrap in plastic wrap and store in the refrigerator once it is ripened to your liking.

Bel Paese

Makes 2 lbs (1 kg)
12 to 15% yield

This Italian cheese, whose name means "beautiful country," is soft, fast-ripening, sweet and mild.

Tip: To ascertain whether the curd is ready for the next step, check for a clean break: insert the long flat blade of a knife into the curd at a 30-degree angle and slowly lift the blade toward the surface of the curd. If the curd splits into a long clean break or crack, it is ready to cut. If the cut is wobbly or uneven, let the curd set for a few more minutes before trying again.

- Draining container
- Cheese matting
- 1 tomme mold
- Ripening container

8 quarts	whole milk	8 L
¼ tsp	thermophilic culture	1.25 mL
½ tsp	calcium chloride	2.5 mL
½ tsp	liquid rennet	2.5 mL
	Cool 18% saturated brine (see Tip, page 181)	
	Simple brine solution (see Tip, page 197)	
	Cheese wax, optional	

1. Sterilize all equipment (see page 40). Prepare a draining container by placing a rack inside. Then place a cutting board on top, followed by a cheese mat, then the mold.

2. In a large stainless-steel pot over medium heat, warm milk to 108°F (42°C), stirring gently to avoid scorching. Remove from heat.

3. Sprinkle culture over surface of milk and let stand for about 5 minutes to rehydrate. Using skimmer and an up-and-down motion, gently draw culture down into milk without breaking surface of milk.

4. Dilute calcium chloride in ¼ cup (50 mL) cool water. Add to milk using the same up-and-down motion.

5. Dilute rennet in ¼ cup (50 mL) cool water. Add to milk and, using the same up-and-down motion, draw rennet down into milk until well blended. Cover and let set for 30 minutes, maintaining the temperature at 108°F (42°C).

6. Check for a clean break (see Tip, left). If necessary, let set for another 10 to 15 minutes or until you achieve a clean break. Using a long-bladed knife and skimmer, cut curd into ⅜-inch (0.9 cm) pieces (see Tip, page 191). Let stand for 5 minutes.

Tip: Always use the freshest possible milk for your cheeses. If you are purchasing packaged milk, look for the latest best-before date. If using your own milk, plan your cheese making for as soon after milking as possible. The older the milk, the more bacteria there are in it to compete with the lactic bacterial starter.

7. Using skimmer and maintaining temperature, stir curds for 20 to 30 minutes or until shrunken and beginning to mat. Let settle.

8. Using a measuring cup, dip off the whey from the top of the pot until you see the surface of the curds.

9. Gently ladle curds into mold. Place the lid on the mold. Place lid on draining container to keep the cheese warm. Let drain for 6 to 7 hours, flipping 6 or 7 times. The cheese should be firm enough to handle but still soft.

10. Remove cheese from mold. Place in 18% saturated brine solution for 6 hours, turning over after 3 hours.

11. Remove from brine and pat dry with a clean lint-free towel. Place cheese on a clean cheese mat in a ripening container and ripen at 40° to 42°F (4° to 6°C) and 80% to 90% humidity. Turn cheese every second day, removing any collected whey from bottom of container and wiping with paper towel. After about 10 days, a slimy coating will begin to form on the surface of cheese.

12. Wash cheese twice a week with a cloth dipped in simple brine solution to keep rind clean. After 3 weeks, remove cheese from draining container. Clean cheese by wiping with the brine-soaked cloth and dry it thoroughly. Wrap in foil and store in the refrigerator. Alternatively, coat with 2 or 3 layers of cheese wax and continue ripening for 2 to 6 weeks longer for more flavor development.

Butter Cheese

<table>
<tr><td>Makes 4 lbs (2 kg)
12% yield</td></tr>
</table>

This is not cheese made of butter but rather a soft, bland cheese with a smooth, buttery texture. It is popular in sandwiches or for snacking.

- Cloth-lined colander
- 1 brick-shaped mold or tomme mold, lined with cheese cloth
- Cheese press
- Cheese matting

16 quarts	whole milk	16 L
½ tsp	thermophilic culture	2.5 mL
¾ tsp	calcium chloride	3.75 mL
¾ tsp	liquid rennet	3.75 mL
	Cool 18% saturated brine (see Tip, page 181)	
	Cheese wax	

1. Sterilize all equipment (see page 40). In a large stainless-steel pot set in a hot water bath over medium heat, warm milk to 102°F (39°C), stirring gently. Turn off heat.

2. Sprinkle culture over surface of milk and let stand for about 5 minutes to rehydrate. Using skimmer and an up-and-down motion, gently draw culture down into milk without breaking surface of milk. Cover and let ripen for 40 minutes, maintaining temperature at 102°F (39°C).

3. Dilute calcium chloride in ¼ cup (50 mL) cool water. Add to milk using the same up-and-down motion.

4. Dilute rennet in ¼ cup (50 mL) cool water. Add to milk and, using the same up-and-down motion, draw rennet down into milk until well blended. Cover pot and let set for 30 minutes, maintaining temperature.

5. Check for a clean break (see Tip, page 190). If necessary, let set for another 10 to 15 minutes or until you achieve a clean break. Using a long-bladed knife and skimmer, cut curd into ½-inch (1.25 cm) cubes (see Tip, page 191). Let stand for 5 minutes. Stir the curds for 20 minutes. Let settle.

Tip: When presenting waxed cheeses on a cheese board, remove the wax first and slice a few pieces from the cheese to indicate how guests should proceed when serving themselves.

6. Using a measuring cup, remove half of the whey. Replace the whey with an equal amount of 140°F (60°C) water to bring the temperature to 108°F (42°C). Stir for 10 minutes (see Tips, page 187). Let curds settle. Let stand for 10 minutes.

7. Pour contents of pot into a cloth-lined colander. Fill prepared mold with curds. Pull cloth up neatly around curds, easing out wrinkles, and fold excess snugly over the top.

8. Place mold in cheese press or place a weight on top. Press at low to medium pressure for 30 minutes. Remove cheese from press and re-dress (see Tip, page 193). Continue pressing at medium pressure for 6 hours.

9. Remove cheese from press. Unwrap and place in brine solution for 12 hours, turning over after 6 hours.

10. Remove cheese from brine and let dry on a cheese mat on a rack at room temperature for 2 days, turning once or twice to aid drying, until surface is fairly dry.

11. Coat cheese with 2 or 3 layers of cheese wax (see page 21). Ripen at 54°F (12°C) and 85% humidity for 4 weeks. Store in the refrigerator.

Caciotta

Makes
3¼ lbs (1.6 kg)
20% yield

This soft sheep's milk cheese has a delicate buttery flavor. Its special yellow color is due to the infusion of saffron in the milk.

- Draining container
- Cheese matting
- 1 tomme mold, lined with cheese cloth
- Cloth-lined colander
- Cheese press
- Ripening container

8 quarts	sheep's milk	8 L
Pinch	saffron threads (see Tip, opposite)	Pinch
¼ tsp	mesophilic or aroma mesophilic culture	1.25 mL
¼ tsp	liquid rennet	1.25 mL
	Cool 18% saturated brine (see Tip, page 181)	
	Cheese wax, optional	

1. Sterilize all equipment (see page 40). Prepare a draining container by placing a rack inside. Then place a cutting board on top, followed by a cheese mat, then the mold.

2. In a large stainless-steel pot set in a hot water bath over low heat, warm milk and saffron to 90°F (32°C), stirring gently. Turn off heat.

3. Sprinkle culture over surface of milk and let stand for about 5 minutes to rehydrate. Using skimmer and an up-and-down motion, gently draw culture down into milk without breaking surface of milk. Remove saffron threads, if desired. Cover pot and let ripen for 30 minutes, maintaining the temperature at 90°F (32°C).

4. Dilute rennet in ¼ cup (50 mL) cool water. Add to milk and, using the same up-and-down motion, draw rennet down into milk until well blended. Cover and let set for 40 minutes, maintaining the temperature.

5. Check for a clean break (see Tip, page 190). If necessary, let set for another 5 to 10 minutes or until you achieve a clean break. Using a long-bladed knife and skimmer, cut curd into ½-inch (1.25 cm) cubes (see Tip, page 191). Let stand for 5 minutes.

Tip: Be sure to use pure, high-quality saffron threads, which are long and deep red. Saffron threads that are orange or yellow or broken into small pieces, though adequate, won't have the same wonderful flavor.

Variation: If you do not have sheep's milk, you can use whole cow's or goat's milk.

6. Return heat to low and slowly warm curds to 95°F (35°C), stirring slowly and gently, adjusting heat as necessary to make sure it takes 20 minutes to do so. Do not heat too quickly. Turn off heat and continue stirring for another 20 minutes. Let curds settle and stand for 10 minutes.

7. Pour contents of pot into a cloth-lined colander. Fill prepared mold with curds. Pull cloth up neatly around curds and fold excess snugly over the top. Put on the lid. Let drain on a rack in a draining container for 30 minutes, turning the mold over once after 15 minutes.

8. Place mold in cheese press or place a weight on top. Press at light pressure for 15 minutes. Remove cheese from press and re-dress (see Tip, page 193). Continue pressing at medium pressure for 6 hours.

9. Remove cheese from press. Unwrap and place in brine solution for 4 hours, turning over after 2 hours.

10. Remove from brine and pat dry with a clean lint-free towel. Place cheese on a clean cheese mat in a ripening container and ripen at 50° to 54°F (10° to 12°C) and 85% humidity for 4 weeks. Turn cheese daily for the first week, removing any collected whey from bottom of container and wiping with paper towel. This cheese can be ripened with a natural rind, rindless or waxed.

11. *For a natural rind:* After first week of ripening, turn twice weekly, removing any mold from rind with a cloth dipped in vinegar. Continue ripening for a total of 4 weeks.

12. *For waxed or rindless cheese:* After first week of ripening, coat cheese with 2 or 3 layers of cheese wax (see page 21) or wrap it tightly in foil and continue ripening for a total of 4 weeks.

Tomme

Makes 4 lbs (2 kg)
12% yield

Tomme is actually a generic name for any flat round cheese. It can be semisoft or semifirm, usually with a natural mixed-mold rind. It takes special care and extra work to develop the rind, but you will be rewarded with a special cheese. This recipe is made with cow's milk, but you can also make Goat's Milk Tomme (see Variation, opposite).

- Cloth-lined colander
- 1 tomme mold, lined with cheese cloth
- Cheese press
- Cheese matting
- Ripening container

16 quarts	whole milk	16 L
½ tsp	mesophilic culture	2.5 mL
Pinch	*Geotrichum candidum* 15 mold	Pinch
Pinch	Cylindrocarpon mold	Pinch
¾ tsp	calcium chloride	3.75 mL
¾ tsp	liquid rennet	3.75 mL
	Cool 18% saturated brine (see Tip, page 181)	

Bacteria for rind development

Pinch	*Brevibacterium linens* ripening bacteria	Pinch
Pinch	Cylindrocarpon mold	Pinch
Pinch	*Geotrichum candidum* 15 mold	Pinch

1. Sterilize all equipment (see page 40). In a large stainless-steel pot set in a hot water bath over medium heat, warm milk to 90°F (32°C), stirring gently. Turn off heat.

2. Sprinkle culture and mold powders over surface of milk and let stand for about 5 minutes to rehydrate. Using skimmer and an up-and-down motion, gently draw culture, mold and bacteria down into milk without breaking surface of milk. Cover and let ripen for 45 minutes, maintaining the temperature at 90°F (32°C).

3. Dilute calcium chloride in ¼ cup (50 mL) cool water. Add to milk using the same up-and-down motion.

4. Dilute rennet in ¼ cup (50 mL) cool water. Add to milk and, using the same up-and-down motion, draw rennet down into milk until well blended. Cover pot and let set for 40 minutes, maintaining the temperature.

5. Check for a clean break (see Tip, page 190). If necessary, let set for another 5 to 10 minutes or until you achieve a clean break. Using a long-bladed knife and skimmer, cut curd into ⅜-inch (0.9 cm) pieces (see Tip, page 191). Let stand for 10 minutes.

Variation: *Goat's Milk Tomme:* Use 16 quarts (16 L) goat's milk in place of cow's milk. Reduce calcium chloride and rennet to ½ tsp (2.5 mL) each. Follow ripening instructions right but ripen for only 3 to 4 months total.

6. Return heat to low and slowly warm curds to 99°F (37°C), adjusting heat as necessary to make sure it takes 40 minutes to do so. Do not heat too quickly. Turn off heat and cover pot. Cover and hold for 30 minutes, stirring once or twice to keep curds from matting.

7. Pour contents of pot into a cloth-lined colander and let curds drain for 5 minutes. Fill prepared mold with curds. Pull cloth up neatly around curds and fold excess snugly over the top. Put on the lid.

8. Place mold in cheese press or place a weight on top. Press at very light pressure. Re-dress the cheese once or twice during the next 12 hours to even out draining and pressing (see Tip, page 193). Press for 12 hours or overnight. Traditionally when several of these cheeses are made, they are stacked upon each other for pressing and no press is used, the weight of the cheeses being sufficient for pressing.

9. Remove cheese from press. Unwrap and place in brine solution for 12 hours, turning over after 6 hours.

10. Remove from brine and pat cheese dry with a clean lint-free towel. Place on a cheese mat in a ripening container and ripen at 54°F (12°C) and 90% humidity for 1 week, turning cheese daily.

11. *Rind development:* Start developing the rind after 1 week. Make a bacterial brine: Boil 1 cup (250 mL) water. Let cool. Stir in 1½ tsp (7.5 mL) salt until dissolved. Add *B. linens* bacteria, Cylindrocarpon and Geotrichum molds. Cover container, agitate gently and let rehydrate for 12 hours. Dip a clean cloth in the solution and rub it all over the rind of the cheese. Discard the solution after using. Repeat twice weekly for 1 month, making a new solution every time and discarding it after use. (The brine must be discarded, because dangerous *Listeria* bacteria can grow in the solution after using it to wash the cheese.) Continue developing the rind in this way until you have a good growth of blue, gray and brown color covering the cheese, from 1 month to 6 weeks. After the rind is well colored, discontinue washing and simply rub the rind with a dry cloth to help firm it up. Ripen for 4 to 6 months total.

Smoked Cheese

2 oz	wood chips (see Tip, left)	60 g
1 lb	cheese	500 g

Makes 1 lb (500 g)

Many people love the special flavor of smoked cheeses. Industrially, it is achieved using a flavor additive, but you can smoke cheese naturally if you have a smoker or small charcoal grill.

Tip: Choose wood, such as maple, cherry, apple or pear, that creates a relatively light smoked flavor so that it doesn't overwhelm the taste of the cheese. Avoid woods that offer intense, heavy flavors, such as mesquite and hickory.

1. Soak wood chips in water for 1 hour.

2. Light grill or smoker and allow the fire to burn down until just embers remain and no flames. Drain wood chips and evenly distribute them over the fire.

3. When wisps of smoke appear, place cheese on a piece of heavy-duty foil and place on the rack at the highest possible position away from the fire. Close the lid and open the air vents on the cover, or prop the lid slightly open, to allow smoke and heat to escape. For hot-smoked cheese, smoke at about 200°F (100°C) for 45 to 60 minutes. For cold- or light-smoked cheese, smoke at 60°F (16°C) for 75 minutes. To prevent the cheese from overheating during smoking, it may be necessary to vent the smoker even more by removing the lid entirely and placing it on props around the perimeter. You must monitor the temperature very carefully to avoid melting the cheese.

4. Remove cheese from smoker and let cool to room temperature. Wrap and refrigerate before serving.

Troubleshooting

The ripened cheese has light-colored spots in the paste.
Curd was not cut and stirred evenly, leaving large chunks of moist curd in the cheese when it was pressed; cut and stir evenly according to directions. Or cheese was pressed at too high a pressure too quickly; begin pressing lightly to knit the curd together and gradually increase pressure. Or curds were cooked too fast, making the outer skin of each curd too hard and trapping moisture within; cook slowly according to the recipe's recommendations.

The texture of the finished cheese is rubbery.
Too much rennet in the curd; reduce rennet. Or the lactic bacteria were too weak; next time use a fresh culture. Or washed-curd cheese was too diluted during washing; remove less whey when washing the curd or add less water after whey removal.

The cheese puffs up and splits soon after making.
There are yeasts or coliform bacteria in the milk; the cheese must be thrown out. Always use the highest-quality milk and maintain scrupulous hygiene standards.

The cheese puffs up and splits after 1 to 2 months of ripening.
There are bacteria in the milk that cause gas development; pasteurize correctly. Or there are legumes or silage in the animal feed; eliminate or increase quality of silage fed and remove legumes from fodder. The cheese is still safe to eat.

The rind on a natural-rind cheese, especially an older one, seems dusty and may rot and deteriorate.
Your ripening area could have cheese mites that bore into the rind; clean and sanitize the ripening area thoroughly. The cheese is still safe to eat.

The rind of an aging cheese is greasy.
Too much fat in the cheese (especially Cheddar); use lower-fat milk. Or the temperature in the ripening area is too high; reduce temperature.

continued on next page…

Waxed cheeses develop "bruised" spots, which then start to rot down into the cheese.

Moisture pockets under the wax contain bacteria that begin to destroy the cheese; be sure the cheese is dry before waxing. Or the wax has a small hole in it and bacteria have entered; be sure the wax coating is thick enough and remains intact throughout ripening. If you find rotting spots in your waxed cheese, cut open the wax and cut out the rot. Use right away or try re-waxing and continue ripening. Monitor the cheese closely.

Cheese puffs up when removed from the brine.

Moisture has soaked into the cheese; increase the salt content of the brine. Or bacteria are present and have caused gas production; keep brine at 54° to 60°F (12°C to 16°C) and salt content at approximately 20% to 25% salinity (18° to 20° Baumé: measure with brine meter; see Glossary, page 366).

Semifirm
and Hard Cheeses

These cheeses are made into large wheels, which are usually pressed firmly to remove as much moisture as possible. This lack of moisture allows the cheese to be ripened over long periods of time for superior flavor development and ensures that it will keep well under difficult conditions. From the Cheddars and Caerphillys of Britain to the Alpine cheeses, such as Gruyère, Emmental and Montasio, to the Mediterranean treasures of Sbrinz, Parmesan and Romano, there are cheeses for every palate and every purpose in this category.

continued on next page…

Semifirm and Hard Cheeses continued...

Cheddar

Makes
3¼ to 3½ lbs
(1.6 to 1.75 kg)
10 to 11% yield

A favorite with a long tradition, Cheddar is one versatile cheese. Its special texture and taste is due to the "cheddaring" process, which is unique to this cheese. Cheddar takes longer than most cheeses to produce, but the effort is worth it. It can be enjoyed at the curd stage before pressing, right after pressing as "farmer's cheese," and after several months of aging, when the flavor has had time to develop. The orange color normally associated with Cheddar cheese is created with a dye made from annatto seeds. You may add this color if you wish, but why not make a natural white Cheddar?

Variations: *Cheddar with Stout:* This is a novel, colorful variation on traditional Cheddar. The richness of the cheese and the smooth tanginess of the stout make for a tasty combination. Please note that Stirred-Curd

- Cloth-lined colander
- 1 tomme mold, lined with cheese cloth
- Cheese press
- Cheese matting

16 quarts	whole milk	16 L
½ tsp	mesophilic culture	2.5 mL
⅛ tsp	annatto, optional	0.65 mL
¾ tsp	calcium chloride	3.75 mL
¾ tsp	liquid rennet	3.75 mL
2½ tbsp	pickling (canning) or kosher salt	37.5 mL
	Cheese wax	

1. Sterilize all equipment (see page 40). In a large stainless-steel pot set in a hot water bath over medium heat, warm milk to 88°F (31°C), stirring gently. Turn off heat.

2. Sprinkle culture over surface of milk and let stand for about 5 minutes to rehydrate. Using skimmer and an up-and-down motion, gently draw culture down into milk without breaking surface of milk. Cover and let ripen for 40 minutes, maintaining the temperature at 88°F (31°C).

3. Dilute annatto, if using, in ¼ cup (50 mL) cool water and add to milk using the same up-and-down motion. Let stand for 15 minutes.

4. Dilute calcium chloride in ¼ cup (50 mL) cool water. Add to milk using the same up-and-down motion.

5. Dilute rennet in ¼ cup (50 mL) cool water. Add to milk and, using the same up-and-down motion, draw rennet down into milk until well blended. Cover pot and let set for 30 minutes, maintaining the temperature.

6. Check for a clean break (see Tip, page 215). If necessary, let set for another 5 to 10 minutes or until you achieve a clean break. Using a long-bladed knife and skimmer, cut curd into ½-inch (1.25 cm) cubes (see Tip, page 216). Let curds stand for 5 minutes to firm up.

7. Return heat to low and slowly warm curds to 102°F (39°C), stirring gently and continuously, adjusting the

continued on next page…

Cheddar continued...

Cheddar (page 215) will not work for this variation. Follow the recipe for Cheddar (page 213) through Step 10. In Step 11, cut curds but do not toss with salt. Instead, place curds in a bowl and pour 1 bottle or can (12 oz/341 mL) stout at room-temperature over curds, covering them entirely. Let soak for 30 minutes. Drain off stout and toss curds with salt. Fill prepared mold and continue with recipe.

Cheddar with Port: Try this variation for a splash of color and flavor on a holiday cheese board. Use a dark red port wine, or try one of the berry ports available, such as blueberry or blackberry. Again, the Stirred-Curd Cheddar recipe will not work for this cheese. Follow the recipe for Cheddar through to Step 10. In Step 11, cut curds but do not toss with the salt. Place them in a bowl and pour 2 cups (500 mL) room-temperature port wine over the curds and let soak for 30 minutes. Keep the curds immersed in the wine, if necessary turning them a few times to make sure all are well soaked. Drain off the wine and toss with the salt. Fill prepared mold and continue with the recipe.

heat as necessary to make sure it takes 45 minutes to do so. Do not heat too quickly. The curds will shrink to about the size of peas or beans.

8. Remove pot from heat, cover and hold for 30 to 40 minutes, maintaining the temperature at 102°F (39°C).

9. Drain whey and curds through a cloth-lined colander. (If you would like to make some ricotta, reserve the drained whey in a large pot. It must be used within 1 to 2 hours.)

10. Immediately return curds to the pot and place in a warm water bath to maintain temperature. Cover pot and let stand for 10 minutes. The curds will knit into a solid spongy mass. After 10 minutes, turn the mass over and cover the pot. Let stand for 10 minutes. Turn the mass on its side. Continue this process for 45 minutes or until all sides of the block of curds have been pressed. This is the "cheddaring" process, which continues the acidification of the curd and develops the unique texture of Cheddar cheese.

11. Remove block of cheese curds from pot and cut into 2- by ½-inch (5 by 1.25 cm) french fry–shape pieces. Place in a bowl and toss with salt.

12. Pack curds down into prepared mold, pressing down firmly as you fill. Pull cloth up neatly around curds and fold excess snugly over the top, with as few wrinkles as possible. Put on the lid.

13. Place mold in cheese press. Press at medium pressure for 1 hour. Remove cheese from press and re-dress (see Tip, page 228). Continue pressing at high pressure for 12 hours or overnight.

14. Remove cheese from press and unwrap. Dry on a cheese mat placed on a rack at room temperature for 1 to 2 days, turning once or twice, or until fairly dry to the touch (see Tip, page 218).

15. Coat cheese with 2 or 3 layers of cheese wax (see page 21). Ripen at 50°F (10°C) for 3 months for mild Cheddar, longer for sharper aged cheese. Cheddar can be aged for years to make a really sharp old cheese.

Stirred-Curd Cheddar

Makes
3¼ to 3½ lbs
(1.6 to 1.75 kg)
10 to 11% yield

This recipe is a shortcut version of the usual Cheddar recipe (page 213) but nevertheless offers a great-tasting traditional result.

Tip: To ascertain whether the curd is ready for the next step, check for a clean break: insert the long flat blade of a knife into the curd at a 30-degree angle and slowly lift the blade toward the surface of the curd. If the curd splits into a long clean break or crack, it is ready to cut. If the cut is wobbly or uneven, let the curd set for a few more minutes before trying again.

- Cloth-lined colander
- 1 tomme mold, lined with cheese cloth
- Cheese press
- Cheese matting

16 quarts	whole milk	16 L
½ tsp	mesophilic culture	2.5 mL
¾ tsp	calcium chloride	3.75 mL
¾ tsp	liquid rennet	3.75 mL
2 tbsp	pickling (canning) or kosher salt	30 mL
	Cheese wax	

1. Sterilize all equipment (see page 40). In a large stainless-steel pot set in a hot water bath over medium heat, warm milk to 88°F (31°C), stirring gently. Turn off heat.

2. Sprinkle culture over surface of milk and let stand for about 5 minutes to rehydrate. Using skimmer and an up-and-down motion, gently draw culture down into milk without breaking surface of milk. Cover and let ripen for 40 minutes, maintaining the temperature at 88°F (31°C).

3. Dilute calcium chloride in ¼ cup (50 mL) cool water. Add to milk using the same up-and-down motion.

4. Dilute rennet in ¼ cup (50 mL) cool water. Add to milk and, using the same up-and-down motion, draw rennet down into milk until well blended. Cover pot and let set for 30 minutes, maintaining the temperature.

5. Check for a clean break (see Tip, left). If necessary, let set for another 5 to 10 minutes or until you achieve a clean break. Using long-bladed knife and skimmer, cut curd into ½-inch (1.25 cm) cubes (see Tip, page 216). Let curds stand for 5 minutes to firm up.

6. Return heat to low and slowly warm curds to 102°F (39°C), stirring gently and continuously, adjusting the heat as necessary to make sure it takes 45 minutes to do so. Do not heat too quickly. The curds will shrink to about the size of peas or beans.

continued on next page…

Stirred-Curd Cheddar continued...

Tip: To cut curds: Holding a long-bladed stainless-steel knife straight up and down, draw knife through the curd, cutting it into strips. Proceed across the pot until you have reached the other side. Turn the pot and cut across the first strips to create squares. Using a skimmer, cut horizontally from side to side just under the surface of the curd to create cubes. Gradually move skimmer down through curd to cut layers of cubes. Using skimmer, gently stir curd cubes. Using a knife, cut any pieces that have been missed or are too large. For small-cut curds, you can use a large whisk for cutting.

7. Turn off heat, cover and hold for 30 to 40 minutes, maintaining the temperature at 102°F (39°C).

8. Using a measuring cup, dip off the whey until you see the surface of the curds. Stir curds continuously for about 20 minutes or until curds cling together when lightly squeezed in the hand. Let settle.

9. Drain curds in a cloth-lined colander and immediately return to the pot. Let stand for 5 minutes or until curds just begin to mat. Mix in salt with your hands, blending thoroughly.

10. Pack curds down into prepared mold. Pull cloth up neatly around curds and fold excess snugly over the top, with as few wrinkles as possible. Put on the lid.

11. Place mold in cheese press. Press at medium pressure for 1 hour. Remove from press and re-dress (see Tip, page 228). Continue pressing at high pressure for 12 hours or overnight.

12. Remove cheese from press. Unwrap and dry on a cheese mat placed on a rack at room temperature for 1 to 2 days, turning once or twice, or until fairly dry to the touch (see Tip, page 218).

13. Coat cheese with 2 or 3 layers of cheese wax (see page 21). Ripen at 50°F (10°C) for 3 months for mild Cheddar, longer for sharper aged cheese. Cheddar can be aged for years to make a really sharp old cheese.

Chihuahua

Makes about
3¼ lbs (1.6 kg)
10% yield

This cheese was first made by the Mennonites who immigrated to northern Mexico and takes its name from the state where it originated. It has a milky, slightly salty taste and, when aged, is similar to Cheddar. It is a great cooking and snacking cheese.

Tip: Non-homogenized milk, also known as cream line or standard milk, is always the best choice for successful cheese making. Non-homogenized milk is pasteurized milk that hasn't been homogenized and shouldn't be confused with raw milk. See Sources, page 372, for more information.

- Cloth-lined colander
- 1 tomme mold, lined with cheese cloth
- Cheese press
- Cheese matting

16 quarts	whole milk	16 L
½ tsp	mesophilic culture	2.5 mL
¾ tsp	calcium chloride	3.75 mL
¾ tsp	liquid rennet	3.75 mL
3 tbsp	pickling (canning) or kosher salt	45 mL
	Cheese wax	

1. Sterilize all equipment (see page 40). In a large stainless-steel pot set in a hot water bath over medium heat, warm milk to 90°F (32°C), stirring gently. Turn off heat.

2. Sprinkle culture over surface of milk and let stand for about 5 minutes to rehydrate. Using skimmer and an up-and-down motion, gently draw culture down into milk without breaking surface of milk. Cover and let ripen for 40 minutes, maintaining the temperature at 90°F (32°C).

3. Dilute calcium chloride in ¼ cup (50 mL) cool water. Add to milk using the same up-and-down motion.

4. Dilute rennet in ¼ cup (50 mL) cool water. Add to milk and, using the same up-and-down motion, draw rennet down into milk until well blended. Cover pot and let set for 30 to 40 minutes, maintaining the temperature.

5. Check for a clean break (see Tip, page 215). If necessary, let set for another 5 to 10 minutes or until you achieve a clean break. Using a long-bladed knife and skimmer, cut curd into ¼- to ½-inch (0.5 to 1.25 cm) cubes (see Tip, page 216). Let curds stand for 5 minutes to firm up.

6. Return heat to low and slowly warm curds to 102°F (39°C), stirring gently and continuously, adjusting the heat as necessary to make sure it takes 40 minutes to do so. Do not heat too quickly. The curds will shrink to about the size of peas or beans. Turn off heat. Let curds settle. Hold for 15 minutes.

continued on next page…

Chihuahua continued...

Chihuahua continued...

Tip: The rind should be fairly dry, or, as someone explained it to me, "like a clammy handshake." If completely dry, the closed rind could crack, allowing bacteria to enter the interior of the cheese.

7. Drain off the whey through a cloth-lined colander, either by tipping the pot or by dipping off the whey until you can safely tip the remaining whey out, leaving the curds in the bottom of the pot. Press down with your hand to create a cake of curd. Cover pot and let stand for 15 minutes.

8. Turn curd mass over in pot. Cover pot and hold for another 15 minutes.

9. Cut curd mass into 4 pieces and pile them one on top of the other in the pot. Cover and hold for another 15 minutes.

10. Remove curd from pot and place on a cutting board. Cut curd into 1- by $\frac{1}{2}$-inch (2.5 cm by 1.25 cm) pieces. Place in a bowl and toss with salt.

11. Fill prepared mold with curds. Pull cloth up neatly around curds and fold excess snugly over the top, with as few wrinkles as possible. Put on the lid.

12. Place mold in cheese press or place a weight on top. Press at medium pressure for 30 minutes. Increase pressure to firm and continue pressing for several hours or overnight.

13. Remove cheese from press and unwrap. Dry on a cheese mat placed on a rack at room temperature for 2 days, turning once or twice, or until fairly dry to the touch (see Tip, left).

14. Coat cheese with 2 or 3 layers of cheese wax (see page 21). Ripen at 50°F (10°C) for 6 weeks, turning the cheese daily to ensure even ripening. For a mild table cheese, you can eat it at 1 month. For more flavor, ripen for several months.

Cheshire

Makes about
3¼ lbs (1.6 kg)

10% yield

One of the oldest of
the English cheeses,
Cheshire is firm and
crumbly, with a silky
texture and rich flavor.
It is naturally white
but can be colored
with annatto to make
Red Cheshire (see
Variation, below).

Variation: *Red*
Cheshire Cheese:
Add ⅛ tsp (0.65 mL) .
annatto diluted in ¼ cup
(50 mL) cool water to
the ripened milk before
adding the calcium
chloride and rennet. Let
stand for 15 minutes.
Annatto must be
incorporated into the
milk at least 15 minutes
before the rennet is
added, as it can interfere
with the action of the
coagulant. Continue
with the recipe.

- Cloth-lined colander
- 1 tomme mold, lined with cheese cloth
- Cheese press
- Cheese matting
- Ripening container, optional

16 quarts	whole milk	16 L
½ tsp	mesophilic culture	2.5 mL
¾ tsp	calcium chloride	3.75 mL
¾ tsp	liquid rennet	3.75 mL
3½ tbsp	pickling (canning) or kosher salt	52.5 mL
	Cheese wax, optional	

1. Sterilize all equipment (see page 40). In a large stainless-steel pot set in a hot water bath over medium heat, warm milk to 86°F (30°C), stirring gently. Turn off heat.

2. Sprinkle culture over surface of milk and let stand for about 5 minutes to rehydrate. Using skimmer and an up-and-down motion, gently draw culture down into milk without breaking surface of milk. Cover and let ripen for 40 minutes, maintaining the temperature at 86°F (30°C).

3. Dilute calcium chloride in ¼ cup (50 mL) cool water. Add to milk using the same up-and-down motion.

4. Dilute rennet in ¼ cup (50 mL) cool water. Add to milk and, using the same up-and-down motion, draw rennet down into milk until well blended. Cover pot and let set for 40 minutes, maintaining the temperature.

5. Check for a clean break (see Tip, page 215). If necessary, let set for another 5 to 10 minutes or until you achieve a clean break. Using a long-handled whisk and skimmer, cut curd into ¼-inch (0.5 cm) pieces. Let curds stand for 5 minutes to firm up. Using a measuring cup, dip off one-third of the whey (see Tip, page 187).

6. Return heat to low and slowly warm curds to 88°F (31°C), stirring gently and continuously, adjusting the heat as necessary to make sure it takes 1 hour to do so. Do not heat too quickly. Turn off heat. Cover and hold for 40 minutes, maintaining the temperature at 88°F (31°C).

continued on next page…

Cheshire continued...

Tip: When pressed properly, the rind should be smooth and closed with no cracks or open spaces. If it is not, further pressing can help, but with cheeses such as Cheddar, where the curd is salted before pressing, it can be difficult to achieve, especially after the cheese has already been in the press several hours.

7. Tip pot and pour off whey through a cloth-lined colander. Pile curds on one side of the pot. Press curds down with your hand several times over the next 30 minutes to facilitate the release of the whey.

8. Remove the mass of curd from the pot. Cut curd mass into 4 or 5 large chunks. Drain any remaining whey from the pot and spread the chunks of curd over the bottom of the pot. Cover the pot and hold for 2 hours, turning occasionally, maintaining the temperature at 88°F (31°C).

9. Cut the chunks into cubes approximately ¾ inch (2 cm) in size. Place in a bowl and toss with salt.

10. Pack curds down into prepared mold. Pull cloth up neatly around curds and fold excess snugly over the top, with as few wrinkles as possible. Put on the lid.

11. Place mold in cheese press or place a weight on top. Press at medium to firm pressure for 30 minutes. Remove from press and re-dress (see Tip, page 228). Continue pressing at firm pressure overnight.

12. Remove cheese from press and unwrap. If it has not formed a closed rind (see Tip, left), rewrap and return to press and increase the pressure for another 2 to 3 hours. Remove from press and unwrap. If the rind is still not closed, dip cheese in scalding hot water. Dry on a cheese mat placed on a rack at room temperature for 2 to 3 days, turning once or twice, or until fairly dry to the touch (see Tip, page 218).

13. *For natural-rind cheese:* Wrap cheese tightly in cheese cloth. Place on a clean cheese mat in a ripening container. Ripen at 60°F (16°C) and 80% to 85% humidity for a minimum of 3 weeks, but preferably for 2 months to 1 year. Turn the cheese daily, then weekly after 1 month.

14. *For waxed cheese:* Coat cheese with 2 or 3 layers of cheese wax (see page 21). Ripen at 60°F (16°C) for a minimum of 3 weeks, but preferably for 2 months to 1 year. Turn the cheese daily, then weekly after 1 month.

Welsh Rarebit

Makes 4 servings

Not rabbit, as many believe, but rather a comfy cheese dish from the hills of Wales.

- Preheat broiler
- Baking sheet

2 tbsp	butter	30 mL
¼ cup	all-purpose flour	50 mL
½ cup	milk	125 mL
½ cup	beer	125 mL
1 cup	shredded Cheshire (page 219)	250 mL
1 tsp	dry mustard	5 mL
Pinch	cayenne pepper	Pinch
4	slices bread, toasted	4

1. In a saucepan over medium-low heat, melt butter. Using a whisk, stir in flour and cook, whisking, for 1 minute.

2. Add milk and beer, whisking until blended. Cook, whisking, for 6 to 7 minutes or until thickened. Remove from heat.

3. Add cheese, mustard and cayenne pepper, stirring just until blended.

4. Place toasted bread on a baking sheet. Divide cheese mixture evenly over toasts. Broil just until browned and beginning to bubble.

Caerphilly

Makes about
4 lbs (2 kg)
12% yield

Pronounced "CAR-filly," this cheese is named for a town in Wales that is also famous for its massive medieval castle. Though a member of the Cheddar family, Caerphilly does not go through the same texturing process and is aged for less time. It is an interesting cheese, because it is both creamy and sharp. If left to form a natural rind, the cheese will soften around the edges as it ages, but if it is waxed, it will remain firm throughout. It is a very nice table cheese and is said to have been a staple in the lunch boxes of Welsh miners in days gone by.

- 1 tomme mold, lined with cheese cloth
- Cloth-lined colander
- Cheese press
- Cheese matting
- Ripening container, optional

16 quarts	whole milk	16 L
1/4 tsp	mesophilic culture	1.25 mL
1/4 tsp	aroma mesophilic culture	1.25 mL
3/4 tsp	calcium chloride	3.75 mL
3/4 tsp	liquid rennet	3.75 mL
	Cool 18% saturated brine (see Tip, opposite)	
	Cheese wax, optional	

1. Sterilize all equipment (see page 40). In a large stainless-steel pot set in a hot water bath over medium heat, warm milk to 90°F (32°C), stirring gently. Turn off heat.

2. Sprinkle mesophilic and aroma mesophilic cultures over surface of milk and let stand for about 5 minutes to rehydrate. Using skimmer and an up-and-down motion, gently draw cultures down into milk without breaking surface of milk. Cover and let ripen for 30 minutes, maintaining the temperature at 90°F (32°C).

3. Dilute calcium chloride in 1/4 cup (50 mL) cool water. Add to milk using the same up-and-down motion.

4. Dilute rennet in 1/4 cup (50 mL) cool water. Add to milk and, using the same up-and-down motion, draw rennet down into milk until well blended. Cover pot and let set for 45 minutes, maintaining the temperature.

5. Check for a clean break (see Tip, page 215). If necessary, let set for another 5 to 10 minutes or until you achieve a clean break. Using a long-bladed knife and skimmer, cut curd into 1/2-inch (1.25 cm) cubes (see Tip, page 216). Let curds stand for 5 minutes to firm up.

Tip: To make an 18% saturated brine: Mix 1 part salt to 5 parts water. It may be necessary to warm the water to successfully dissolve the salt. If so, let the brine cool before immersing the cheese. The brine can be used over and over again for several batches of cheese (refrigerate between uses). The best temperature for brining cheese is 55°F (13°C). Replenish the salt after several uses and remove any floating bits of cheese with a strainer.

6. Return heat to low and slowly warm curds to 95°F (35°C), stirring gently and continuously, adjusting the heat as necessary to make sure it takes 30 minutes to do so. Do not heat too quickly. Turn off heat. Cover and hold for 45 minutes, maintaining the temperature at 95°F (35°C).

7. Place the prepared mold underneath a cloth-lined colander and drain off the whey, which will warm the mold.

8. Fill mold with curds, piling them higher in the center. Pull cloth up neatly around curds and fold excess snugly over the top, with as few wrinkles as possible. Put on the lid.

9. Place mold in cheese press or place a weight on top. Press at medium pressure for 30 minutes. Remove from press and re-dress (see Tip, page 228). Continue pressing at medium pressure for several hours or overnight.

10. Remove cheese from press. Unwrap and place in brine solution for 20 hours, turning over after 10 hours.

11. Remove from brine. Dry cheese on a cheese mat placed on a rack at room temperature for 2 to 3 days, turning once or twice, or until fairly dry to the touch (see Tip, page 218).

12. *For waxed cheese:* Coat cheese with 2 or 3 layers of cheese wax (see page 21). Ripen at 50° to 54°F (10° to 12°C) for 3 weeks, at which point the cheese will be ready to eat. You may age longer for sharper flavor.

13. *For natural-rind cheese:* Place cheese on a clean cheese mat in a ripening container. Ripen at 50° to 54°F (10° to 12°C) and 85% humidity, turning daily. Maintain the humidity by adjusting the lid of the container. After about 2 weeks, a whitish-gray mold will appear. Continue turning the cheese daily until a thicker crust forms. After about 4 weeks, the cheese will begin to soften just under the crust, possibly becoming runny. This cheese will not keep as long as the waxed version, as it will continue to soften. Use within 2 to 3 months.

Emmental

**Makes 8 to 9 lbs
(4 to 4.5 kg)**

10 to 11% yield

Originating in a valley in central Switzerland, this cheese is copied around the world. It is especially recognizable for its large holes, or "eyes," caused by propionic bacteria, which create gas during the ripening process. These bacteria are also responsible for the inherent sweetness of Emmental. This is one of the more difficult cheeses to make. It needs to be fairly large in order to allow for the proper development of the eyes — if there is not enough paste, the eyes will break through the surface of the cheese. In fact, the original Emmental cheeses weighed approximately 200 lbs (90 kg). While this recipe isn't anywhere near that big, it does require a lot of milk. Since most people don't have a cheese vat or pots large enough to hold all of it at one time, this recipe will be made twice, in two separate batches, and the curds combined in the mold.

- Cloth-lined colander
- One large 10- to 12-lb (5 to 6 kg) cheese mold, such as Kadova-style or other large mold, lined with cheese cloth (see Tips, opposite)
- Cheese press
- Cheese matting
- Ripening container

28 quarts	whole milk, divided	28 L
4 quarts	partly skimmed (1%) milk, divided	4 L
1 tsp	thermophilic culture, divided	5 mL
¾ tsp	propionic bacteria powder, divided	3.75 mL
1½ tsp	calcium chloride, divided	7.5 mL
1½ tsp	liquid rennet, divided	7.5 mL
	Cool 18% saturated brine (see Tip, page 223)	
	Pickling (canning) or kosher salt	
	Olive or vegetable oil, optional	

1. Sterilize all equipment (see page 40). In a large stainless-steel pot set in a hot water bath over medium heat, warm 14 quarts (14 L) milk and 2 quarts (2 L) partly skimmed milk to 90°F (32°C), stirring gently. Turn off heat.

2. Sprinkle ½ tsp (2.5 mL) culture and ⅜ tsp (1.95 mL) propionic bacteria over surface of milk and let stand for about 5 minutes to rehydrate. Using skimmer and an up-and-down motion, gently draw culture and bacteria down into milk without breaking surface of milk. Cover and let ripen for 10 minutes, maintaining the temperature at 90°F (32°C).

3. Dilute ¾ tsp (3.75 mL) calcium chloride in ¼ cup (50 mL) cool water. Add to milk using the same up-and-down motion.

4. Dilute ¾ tsp (3.75 mL) rennet in ¼ cup (50 mL) cool water. Add to milk and, using the same up-and-down motion, draw rennet down into milk until well blended. Cover pot and let set for 30 minutes, maintaining the temperature.

Make the second batch immediately after finishing the first, and keep the first batch covered and as warm as possible until the second is ready.

Tips: Kadova molds are made in Holland and come with an inner netting, which eliminates the need for cheese cloth. They are fairly expensive, but if you are planning to make a lot of large cheeses, the investment in convenience may be worth it. If you are using a different type of mold, you will need to line it with cheese cloth.

To make a vinegar-and-salt solution, dissolve 1 tbsp (15 mL) salt in ½ cup (125 mL) white vinegar.

5. Check for a clean break (see Tip, page 215). If necessary, let set for another 10 to 15 minutes or until you achieve a clean break. Using a long-handled whisk and skimmer, cut and stir curd to make pea-size pieces. This will take about 15 minutes.

6. Using skimmer, stir curds for 30 minutes, maintaining the temperature.

7. Return heat to low and slowly warm curds to 120°F (49°C), stirring slowly gently and continuously, adjusting the heat as necessary to make sure it takes 30 minutes to do so. Do not heat too quickly.

8. Turn off heat and continue stirring for another 30 minutes. Check curds by taking a handful and squeezing it. If the curds cling together but are easily broken apart again, they are ready to be put in the mold. If not, continue stirring and checking every 5 minutes.

9. Let curds settle. Drain off whey through a cloth-lined colander. Fill prepared mold with curds.

10. Cover mold with a clean towel to keep warm. Repeat entire process from Step 1 through Step 9, using remaining milk, culture, propionic bacteria, calcium chloride and rennet. Add curds to mold, mixing the two batches together well.

11. Pull cloth up neatly around curds and fold excess snugly over the top, with as few wrinkles as possible. Put on the lid. If using a Kadova-style mold, you will not need the cheese cloth; simply place the lid on the mold.

12. Place mold in cheese press. Press at light pressure for 10 minutes to release excess whey. Remove from press and re-dress (see Tip, page 228). Continue pressing at firm pressure for 12 to 18 hours or overnight.

13. Remove cheese from press. Unwrap and place in brine solution for 24 hours at 54°F (12°C). Turn cheese over in brine and leave for another 24 hours.

continued on next page…

14. Remove from brine. Dry cheese on a cheese mat placed on a rack at room temperature for 1 to 2 days, turning once or twice daily, until fairly dry to the touch (see Tip, page 218). Place in the ripening area. Ripen at 50° to 54°F (10° to 12°C) and 85% humidity for 2 weeks. Make a brine with 2 tbsp (30 mL) salt and 1 quart (1 L) water. Turn the cheese every day and wipe with a cloth soaked in a small amount of brine, removing any excess moisture from surface of the cheese. This will aid in firming up the rind.

15. Cheese must be further ripened at 65°F (18°C) and 85% humidity for 1 month. This period is when the eyes develop in the cheese. The cheese will begin to puff up and become round. Turn every 2 to 3 days for even development and wipe with the brine solution. Be careful not to allow the temperature in the room to exceed 65°F (18°C), as it can negatively affect the eye development.

16. After 1 month, return cheese to the 50° to 54°F (10° to 12°C) ripening area and continue ripening for at least 3 months. Watch the humidity carefully, keeping it at about 85% so that the rind does not dry out or become moldy. If mold appears, wipe with a brine and/or vinegar-and-salt solution (see Tips, 225). You can oil the cheese rind with olive or vegetable oil to help maintain its suppleness. Turn the cheese weekly and age for as long as desired, up to 1 year.

Leerdammer

Makes
3¼ lbs (1.6 kg)
10% yield

A Dutch cheese
with "eyes," or holes,
Leerdammer has a
sweet nutty flavor; this
recipe makes a baby
version of this usually
large cheese.

Tip: To remove 25%
of the whey, measure
down the side of the
pot and remove the top
quarter, basically until
you see the surface of
the settled curds. The
amount you remove
can be crucial, because
it has to be replaced
with an equal amount
of water. This step
will dictate how the
cheese turns out
(see Troubleshooting,
page 289).

- Cloth-lined colander
- 1 tomme mold, lined with cheese cloth
- Cheese press
- Cheese matting

14 quarts	whole milk	14 L
2 quarts	partly skimmed (1%) milk	2 L
½ tsp	thermophilic culture	2.5 mL
¼ tsp	propionic bacteria powder	1.25 mL
¾ tsp	calcium chloride	3.75 mL
¾ tsp	liquid rennet	3.75 mL
	Cool 18% saturated brine (see Tip, page 223)	
	Cheese wax	

1. Sterilize all equipment (see page 40). In a large stainless-steel pot set in a hot water bath over medium heat, warm milks to 88°F (31°C), stirring gently. Turn off heat.

2. Sprinkle culture and propionic bacteria over surface of milk and let stand for about 5 minutes to rehydrate. Using skimmer and an up-and-down motion, gently draw culture and bacteria down into milk without breaking surface of milk. Cover and let ripen for 30 minutes, maintaining the temperature at 88°F (31°C).

3. Dilute calcium chloride in ¼ cup (50 mL) cool water. Add to milk using the same up-and-down motion.

4. Dilute rennet in ¼ cup (50 mL) cool water. Add to milk and, using the same up-and-down motion, draw rennet down into milk until well blended. Cover pot and let set for 40 minutes, maintaining the temperature.

5. Check for a clean break (see Tip, page 215). If necessary, let set for another 5 to 10 minutes or until you achieve a clean break. Using a long-handled whisk and skimmer, cut curd into pea-size pieces. Let stand for 5 minutes to firm up. Stir curds for 20 minutes. Let settle.

6. Using a measuring cup, dip off 25% of the whey and replace with an equal amount of 88°F (31°C) water (see Tip, left).

continued on next page…

Leerdammer continued...

Tip: To re-dress the cheese, remove the mold from the press. Remove the cheese from the mold and unwrap. Place the cloth back in the mold; turn the cheese over and put back in the mold, then rewrap. Return mold to the press.

7. Return heat to low and slowly warm curds to 102°F (39°C), stirring gently and continuously, adjusting the heat as necessary to make sure it takes 30 minutes to do so. Do not heat too quickly. When the temperature has been reached, continue stirring for 30 more minutes.

8. Using a measuring cup, remove 3 cups (750 mL) of the whey. Add enough cool water to lower the temperature to 97°F (36°C). Let curds settle and hold for 10 minutes.

9. Pour contents of pot into a cloth-lined colander. Let curds drain for 10 minutes. Fill prepared mold with curds. Pull cloth up neatly around the curds and fold excess snugly over the top, with as few wrinkles as possible. Put on the lid.

10. Place mold in cheese press or place a weight on top. Press at medium pressure for 15 minutes. Remove from press and re-dress (see Tip, left). Continue pressing at medium pressure for 4 hours.

11. Remove cheese from press. Unwrap and place in brine solution for 20 hours at 54°F (12°C), turning over after 10 hours.

12. Remove from brine. Dry cheese on a cheese mat placed on a rack at room temperature for 2 days, turning to aid drying, or until fairly dry to the touch (see Tip, page 218).

13. Coat cheese with 2 or 3 layers of cheese wax (see page 21). Ripen at 40°F (4°C) for 2 weeks, turning daily.

14. After 2 weeks, return cheese to cool (65°F/18°C) room temperature and continue ripening for 4 more weeks. Continue turning daily to ensure even ripening

Jarlsberg

Makes
3¼ lbs (1.6 kg)
10% yield

A Norwegian version of Emmental, Jarlsberg has a sweet milky taste and slightly rubbery texture. The development of the large eye structure in the cheese is aided by ripening at cooler, then warmer temperatures.

- Cloth-lined colander
- 1 tomme mold, lined with cheese cloth
- Cheese press
- Cheese matting

14 quarts	whole milk	14 L
2 quarts	partly skimmed (1%) milk	2 L
½ tsp	thermophilic culture	2.5 mL
¼ tsp	propionic bacteria powder	1.25 mL
¾ tsp	calcium chloride	3.75 mL
¾ tsp	liquid rennet	3.75 mL
	Cool 18% saturated brine (see Tip, page 223)	
	Cheese wax	

1. Sterilize all equipment (see page 40). In a large stainless-steel pot set in a hot water bath over medium heat, warm milk to 92°F (33°C), stirring gently. Turn off heat.

2. Sprinkle culture and propionic bacteria over surface of milk and let stand for about 5 minutes to rehydrate. Using skimmer and an up-and-down motion, gently draw culture and bacteria down into milk without breaking surface of milk. Cover and let ripen for 45 minutes, maintaining the temperature at 92°F (33°C).

3. Dilute calcium chloride in ¼ cup (50 mL) cool water. Add to milk using the same up-and-down motion.

4. Dilute rennet in ¼ cup (50 mL) cool water. Add to milk and, using the same up-and-down motion, draw rennet down into milk until well blended. Cover pot and let set for 40 minutes, maintaining the temperature.

5. Check for a clean break (see Tip, page 215). If necessary, let set for another 5 to 10 minutes or until you achieve a clean break. Using a long-bladed knife and skimmer, cut curd into pieces the size of navy beans, stirring gently. When all the curd is cut, continue stirring for 20 minutes. Let curds settle and stand for 5 minutes.

continued on next page…

Jarlsberg continued...

Tip: Always use the freshest possible milk for your cheeses. If you are purchasing packaged milk, look for the latest best-before date. If using your own milk, plan your cheese making for as soon after milking as possible. The older the milk, the more bacteria there are in it to compete with the lactic bacterial starter.

6. Using a measuring cup, dip off about 30% of the whey or until you can just see the surface of the settled curds. Add slightly less 140°F (60°C) water than the amount of whey you have removed to bring the temperature to 100°F (38°C) (see Tips, page 187).

7. Return heat to low and slowly warm curds to 108°F (42°C), stirring gently and continuously, adjusting the heat as necessary to make sure it takes 30 minutes to do so. Do not heat too quickly. Let curds settle.

8. Pour contents of pot into a cloth-lined colander. Fill prepared mold with curds. Pull cloth up neatly around curds and fold excess snugly over the top, with as few wrinkles as possible. Put on the lid.

9. Place mold in cheese press or place a weight on top. Press at medium pressure for 30 minutes. Remove from press and re-dress (see Tip, page 228). Continue pressing at firm pressure for several hours or overnight.

10. Remove cheese from press. Unwrap and place in brine solution for 12 hours, turning over after 6 hours.

11. Remove cheese from brine. Dry cheese on a cheese mat placed on a rack at room temperature for 2 to 3 days, turning once or twice to aid drying, or until fairly dry to the touch (see Tip, page 218).

12. Coat cheese with 2 or 3 layers of cheese wax (see page 21). Ripen at 50°F (10°C) for 2 weeks, turning daily to ensure even ripening.

13. After 2 weeks, continue ripening cheese at 65°F (18°C) for 4 to 6 weeks, turning cheese twice weekly. After this step, the cheese is ready to eat.

Cheese Soufflé

Makes 4 servings

Nothing says "I can cook" like a perfect cheese soufflé served directly from the oven, and with your own handmade cheese, it is sure to impress.

- Preheat oven to 350°F (180°C)
- 1 quart (1 L) soufflé dish, buttered

¼ cup	butter	50 mL
¼ cup	all-purpose flour	50 mL
¼ tsp	salt	1.25 mL
¼ tsp	dry mustard	1.25 mL
	Freshly ground white pepper	
1 cup	whole milk	250 mL
1 cup	shredded cheese, such as Gruyère (page 232), Emmental (page 224) or Jarlsberg (page 229)	250 mL
3	eggs, separated	3
¼ tsp	cream of tartar	1.25 mL

1. In a small saucepan over low heat, melt butter. Whisk in flour, salt, mustard and pepper. Cook for 1 to 2 minutes, whisking constantly.

2. Add milk and cook, whisking, until smooth and mixture begins to bubble. Stir in shredded cheese until melted and smooth. Remove from heat and set aside.

3. In a large bowl, using an electric mixer, beat egg whites with cream of tartar until stiff peaks form.

4. In a small bowl, beat egg yolks until thick and light colored.

5. Using a wooden spoon, stir yolks into cheese mixture. Using a spatula, fold cheese mixture into egg whites. Spoon into prepared soufflé dish.

6. Bake in preheated oven for 50 to 60 minutes or until puffed and golden brown. Do not overbake.

7. Serve immediately, using two forks to split the soufflé apart and separate into portions.

Gruyère

Makes 4 lbs (2 kg)

12% yield

One of the most famous cheeses in the world, Gruyère is a beautiful nutty-flavored cheese that melts perfectly — it's indispensable on top of French onion soup. Without Gruyère, there can be no such thing as an authentic cheese fondue.

- 1 tomme mold, lined with cheese cloth
- Cloth-lined colander
- Cheese press
- Cheese matting
- Ripening container

16 quarts	whole milk	16 L
½ tsp	thermophilic culture	2.5 mL
¾ tsp	calcium chloride	3.75 mL
¾ tsp	liquid rennet	3.75 mL
	Cool 18% saturated brine (see Tip, page 223)	
	Simple brine solution (see Tip, opposite)	

1. Sterilize all equipment (see page 40). In a large stainless-steel pot set in a hot water bath over medium heat, warm milk to 90°F (32°C), stirring gently. Turn off heat.

2. Sprinkle culture over surface of milk and let stand for about 5 minutes to rehydrate. Using skimmer and an up-and-down motion, gently draw culture down into milk without breaking surface of milk. Cover and let ripen for 10 minutes, maintaining the temperature at 90°F (32°C).

3. Dilute calcium chloride in ¼ cup (50 mL) cool water. Add to milk using the same up-and-down motion.

4. Dilute rennet in ¼ cup (50 mL) cool water. Add to milk and, using the same up-and-down motion, draw rennet down into milk until well blended. Cover pot and let set for 40 minutes, maintaining the temperature.

5. Check for a clean break (see Tip, page 215). If necessary, let set for another 5 to 10 minutes or until you achieve a clean break. Using a long-handled whisk and skimmer, cut curd into very small bits, about the size of rice grains, using the skimmer to lift and move the curds gently to ensure that all are cut.

6. Return heat to low and slowly warm curds to 114°F (46°C), stirring gently and continuously, adjusting the heat as necessary to make sure it takes approximately 1 hour to do so. Do not heat too quickly. Let curds settle and stand for 5 minutes.

Tip: To make a simple brine solution for washing cheese rinds: Dissolve 1 tsp (5 mL) salt in ½ cup (125 mL) boiled water. Let cool. Do not reserve used brine for the next washing because there is danger of contamination by unwanted, even dangerous, bacteria.

7. Place the prepared mold underneath a cloth-lined colander and drain off the whey, which will warm the mold. Fill prepared mold with curds. Pull cloth up neatly around curds and fold excess snugly over top, with as few wrinkles as possible. Put on the lid.

8. Place mold in cheese press or place a weight on top. Press at medium pressure for 1 hour. Remove from press and re-dress (see Tip, page 228). Continue pressing at firm pressure for 12 hours or overnight.

9. Remove cheese from press. Unwrap and place in 18% saturated brine solution for 12 hours, turning over after 6 hours.

10. Remove from brine. Dry cheese on a cheese mat placed on a rack at room temperature for 2 to 3 days, turning once or twice daily, or until fairly dry to the touch (see Tip, page 218).

11. Place cheese on a clean cheese mat in a ripening container. Ripen at 50° to 54°F (10° to 12°C) at 85% humidity. With a soft cloth dipped in simple brine solution (see Tip, left), wash rind every second day for 1 month, turning cheese each time. Maintain the humidity by adjusting the lid of the container.

12. After 1 month, wash rind once a week. A rind displaying various molds and colors will begin to develop. After 2 months, discontinue washing the cheese; rub the rind with a cloth or a soft cheese brush to help to firm up the rind. Continue to turn the cheese weekly until it is at least 6 months old, preferably older. The cheese can be stored under these conditions for as long as you want to age it, up to 2 years. Once cut, wrap and store in the refrigerator.

Swiss Cheese Fritters

**Makes 6 to
8 servings**

*A specialty of western
Switzerland, these
beignets de Vinzell are a
good choice after a long
day outdoors. Serve hot
with a green salad and
a glass of dry white wine.*

1	loaf dense white bread	1
1 lb	Gruyère (page 232), shredded	500 g
2	eggs	2
¼ tsp	ground nutmeg	1.25 mL
¼ tsp	ground black pepper	1.25 mL
1	clove garlic, crushed	1
2 tbsp	all-purpose flour	30 mL
2 tbsp	Kirsch	30 mL
1 tsp	baking powder	5 mL
1	egg white	1
	Vegetable oil for deep-fryer	

1. Cut bread into ¼-inch (0.5 cm) thick slices and lay on a platter or waxed paper.

2. Place cheese in a bowl. Add eggs and mix well.

3. Mix in nutmeg, pepper, and garlic. Mix in flour, Kirsch and baking powder.

4. Stir egg white with a fork until blended but not frothy. Brush top side of bread slices with egg white.

5. Mound cheese mixture on bread slices, pressing the first spoonful well down onto the bread and creating a small mound.

6. Heat 3 inches (7.5 cm) vegetable oil in a deep-fryer or deep saucepan to 360°F (182°C). Place fritters in hot oil, cheese side up, one or more at a time depending on the size of the deep-fryer, and fry for 2 minutes or until lightly browned. Flip over and fry for about 1 minute or until center is hot and top is well browned. Remove from oil and drain briefly on paper towel–lined plate. Adjust temperature between batches as necessary. Serve hot.

Swiss Cheese Fondue

Makes 4 servings

Contrary to what most people believe, making real cheese fondue is not that difficult. The traditional Swiss fondue cheeses include Gruyère and Vacherin Fribourgeois. You can also try Gouda. A glass of chilled white wine is the perfect accompaniment. Alternatively, serve with hot mint tea. Both wine and tea will help you digest the cheese, as will a small glass of Kirsch to round out the meal.

- Fondue pot or flameproof casserole

1 cup	light dry white wine	250 mL
1 or 2	clove(s) garlic, peeled, or to taste	1 or 2
1 lb	cheese, 2 or 3 varieties, such as Gruyère (page 232), Vacherin Fribourgeois (page 239) or Emmental (page 224), coarsely shredded	500 g
3 tbsp	Kirsch	45 mL
1 tbsp	cornstarch	15 mL
	Freshly grated nutmeg and ground black pepper	
	Cubes of sturdy bread (day-old is preferable)	

1. Pour wine into a fondue pot over medium-low heat. Add whole garlic clove(s).

2. Add cheese and stir with a wooden spoon. Cook, stirring constantly, for 10 to 15 minutes or until cheese is melted and just begins to bubble.

3. Blend together Kirsch and cornstarch. Add to pot, stirring until blended and mixture is creamy and smooth. Season with nutmeg and pepper to taste. Place quickly over a chafing dish flame to keep the pot bubbling.

4. Serve with bread cubes. Spear cubes on the end of a long fondue fork. Dip bread into cheese mixture, stirring each time right to the bottom to keep cheese from sticking to the bottom of the pot.

Appenzeller

Makes
3¼ lbs (1.6 kg)
10% yield

Uniquely spicy and full of flavor, Appenzeller is made with pride and according to tradition in the mountain valleys of eastern Switzerland. The rind is developed by washing it with a brine made of wine and a special mix of herbs and spices, which is a trade secret. This is your chance to be creative and experiment with your own blend!

- Cloth-lined colander
- 1 tomme mold, lined with cheese cloth
- Cheese press
- Cheese matting
- Ripening container

16 quarts	whole milk	16 L
½ tsp	thermophilic culture	2.5 mL
¾ tsp	calcium chloride	3.75 mL
¾ tsp	liquid rennet	3.75 mL
	Cool 18% saturated brine (see Tip, page 223)	
	Pickling (canning) or kosher salt	

Wine-and-Herb Solution

2 tbsp	white wine	30 mL
Pinch	*Brevibacterium linens* ripening bacteria	Pinch
Pinch	pickling (canning) or kosher salt	Pinch
1 tbsp	herbs and spices, optional	15 mL

1. Sterilize all equipment (see page 40). In a large stainless-steel pot set in a hot water bath over medium heat, warm milk to 88°F (31°C), stirring gently. Turn off heat.

2. Sprinkle culture over surface of milk and let stand for about 5 minutes to rehydrate. Using skimmer and an up-and-down motion, gently draw culture down into milk without breaking surface of milk. Cover and let ripen for 45 minutes, maintaining the temperature at 88°F (31°C).

3. Dilute calcium chloride in ¼ cup (50 mL) cool water. Add to milk using the same up-and-down motion.

4. Dilute rennet in ¼ cup (50 mL) cool water. Add to milk and, using the same up-and-down motion, draw rennet down into milk until well blended. Cover pot and let set for 30 to 40 minutes, maintaining the temperature.

Tip: To re-dress the cheese, remove the mold from the press. Remove the cheese from the mold and unwrap. Place the cloth back in the mold; turn the cheese over and put back in the mold, then rewrap. Return mold to the press.

5. Check for a clean break (see Tip, page 215). If necessary, let set for another 5 to 10 minutes or until you achieve a clean break. Using a long-handled whisk and skimmer, cut curd into lentil-size pieces. Let curds settle and stand for 5 minutes.

6. Return heat to low and slowly warm curds to 118°F (48°C), stirring gently and continuously, adjusting the heat as necessary to make sure it takes 15 minutes to do so. Let stand for 5 minutes.

7. Using a measuring cup, remove 6 cups (1.5 L) of the whey and replace with an equal amount of 118°F (48°C) water. Stir for another 15 minutes. Let curds settle.

8. Pour contents of pot into a cloth-lined colander. Cover colander with pot lid to keep curds warm and let drain for 10 minutes.

9. Fill prepared mold with curds. Pull cloth up neatly around curds and fold excess snugly over the top, with as few wrinkles as possible. Put on the lid.

10. Place mold in cheese press or place a weight on top. Press at medium to firm pressure for 30 minutes. Remove from press and re-dress (see Tip, left). Continue pressing at firm pressure for several hours or overnight.

11. Remove cheese from press. Unwrap and place in brine solution for 12 hours, turning over after 6 hours.

12. Remove from brine. Dry cheese on a cheese mat placed on a rack at room temperature for 2 days, turning once or twice to aid drying, or until fairly dry to the touch (see Tip, page 218).

13. Place cheese on a clean cheese mat in a ripening container. Ripen at 57°F (14°C) and 80% humidity. Turn cheese daily for 1 week, sprinkling each side with about 1/2 tsp (2.5 mL) salt and rubbing it into the cheese.

continued on next page…

14. After 1 week, begin to wash the rind of the cheese. Make Wine-and-Herb Solution: combine wine, a minute amount (just a tiny bit on the point of a paring knife) of *B. linens* and a pinch of salt. Infuse herbs and spices in 1 cup (250 mL) hot water. Let cool. Strain out herbs. Blend 2 tbsp (30 mL) herb infusion into the wine mixture. (The remaining infused herb mixture can be covered, refrigerated and used for up to 1 week, as long as there is no *B. linens* in it.) Let wine-and-herb mixture stand for 2 to 3 hours to allow the ripening bacteria to rehydrate. Using a small soft brush or rough cloth, rub the solution on the rind of the cheese. Discard remaining solution after use.

15. Continue to make a new batch of wine mixture and wash and turn cheese daily for 3 to 6 months, or until desired ripeness has been reached. Once ripened to your taste, wrap and store in refrigerator.

A Special Inheritance

It is said that when an old Swiss cheese maker renowned for his superlative cheeses dies, his colleagues wait in line to be the first one to get into his cheese-making room. They are after his thermometer and his brine. In traditional Swiss cheese making, each thermometer is encased in a wooden frame, which is thrown into the vat and pulled back out with a cord. With time, the wooden frame becomes saturated with the lactic bacterial cultures that make the maker's cheese unique, and using his thermometer is a way to get his special recipe. The brine, too, becomes a unique brew filled with the flavors of the cheeses and can help guarantee a successful result.

Vacherin Fribourgeois

Makes 4 lbs (2 kg)
12% yield

This semifirm cheese is made from the milk of the black-and-white cows of the Fribourg area of Switzerland. It is one of the cheeses traditionally used for Swiss fondue.

Tip: Non-homogenized milk, also known as cream line or standard milk, is always the best choice for successful cheese making. Non-homogenized milk is pasteurized milk that hasn't been homogenized and shouldn't be confused with raw milk. See Sources, page 372, for more information.

- Cloth-lined colander
- 1 tomme mold, lined with cheese cloth
- Cheese press
- Cheese matting
- Ripening container

16 quarts	whole milk	16 L
½ tsp	mesophilic culture	2.5 mL
¾ tsp	calcium chloride	3.75 mL
¾ tsp	liquid rennet	3.75 mL
	Cool 18% saturated brine (see Tip, page 223)	
	Simple brine solution (see Tip, page 233)	

1. Sterilize all equipment (see page 40). In a large stainless-steel pot set in a hot water bath over medium heat, warm milk to 86°F (30°C), stirring gently. Turn off heat.

2. Sprinkle culture over surface of milk and let stand for about 5 minutes to rehydrate. Using skimmer and an up-and-down motion, gently draw culture down into milk without breaking surface of milk. Cover and let ripen for 15 minutes, maintaining temperature at 86°F (30°C).

3. Dilute calcium chloride in ¼ cup (50 mL) cool water. Add to milk using the same up-and-down motion.

4. Dilute rennet in ¼ cup (50 mL) cool water. Add to milk and, using the same up-and-down motion, draw rennet down into milk until well blended. Cover pot and let set for 50 minutes, maintaining the temperature.

5. Check for a clean break (see Tip, page 215). If necessary, let set for another 5 to 10 minutes or until you achieve a clean break. Using a long-handled whisk and skimmer, cut curd into pea-size pieces. Let stand for 10 minutes.

6. Return heat to low and slowly warm curds to 100°F (38°C), stirring gently and continuously, adjusting the heat as necessary to make sure it takes 35 minutes to do so. Do not heat too quickly. Let curds settle and hold for 10 minutes.

continued on next page…

Vacherin Fribourgeois continued...

Tip: The rind should be fairly dry, or, as someone explained it to me, "like a clammy handshake." If completely dry, the closed rind could crack, allowing bacteria to enter the interior of the cheese.

7. Pour contents of pot into a cloth-lined colander and let curds drain for 10 minutes.

8. Fill prepared mold with curds. Pull cloth up neatly around curds and fold excess snugly over the top, with as few wrinkles as possible. Put on the lid.

9. Place mold in cheese press or place a weight on top. Press at light to medium pressure for 30 minutes. Remove from press and re-dress (see Tip, page 237). Continue pressing at medium pressure for several hours or overnight.

10. Remove cheese from press. Unwrap and place in 18% saturated brine solution for 12 hours, turning over after 6 hours.

11. Remove from brine. Dry cheese on a cheese mat placed on a rack at room temperature for 24 hours, turning once to aid drying, or until fairly dry to the touch (see Tip, left).

12. Place cheese on a clean cheese mat in a ripening container. Ripen at 54°F (12°C) and 85% humidity. Turn cheese daily for the first week, removing any accumulated moisture from the container and wiping bottom with paper towel.

13. After 1 week, begin washing the cheese every second day with a cloth dipped in simple brine solution, turning the cheese over each time. Let cheese ripen for 3 to 4 months. Once ripened to your taste, wrap and store in the refrigerator.

Wensleydale

Makes 4 lbs (2 kg)
12% yield

Wensleydale is a magical valley in the Yorkshire Dales of northern England. Cheese-making history goes back a long way there, but, like many artisanal cheeses, Wensleydale cheese was in danger of being lost. However, the local village creamery has revived the tradition and makes wonderful cheese from local cow's and sheep's milk. Large viewing windows allow you to look in on the cheese making, and a small museum displays methods and tools from centuries past.

- Cloth-lined colander
- 1 tomme mold, lined with cheese cloth
- Cheese press
- Cheese matting

16 quarts	whole milk	16 L
½ tsp	mesophilic culture	2.5 mL
⅛ tsp	aroma mesophilic culture	0.65 mL
¾ tsp	calcium chloride	3.75 mL
¾ tsp	liquid rennet	3.75 mL
3 tbsp	pickling (canning) or kosher salt	45 mL
	Cheese wax	

1. Sterilize all equipment (see page 40). In a large stainless-steel pot set in a hot water bath over medium heat, warm milk to 86°F (30°C), stirring gently. Turn off heat.

2. Sprinkle mesophilic and aroma mesophilic cultures over surface of milk and let stand for about 5 minutes to rehydrate. Using skimmer and an up-and-down motion, gently draw cultures down into milk without breaking surface of milk. Cover and let ripen for 1½ hours, maintaining the temperature at 86°F (30°C).

3. Dilute calcium chloride in ¼ cup (50 mL) cool water. Add to milk using the same up-and-down motion.

4. Dilute rennet in ¼ cup (50 mL) cool water. Add to milk and, using the same up-and-down motion, draw rennet down into milk until well blended. Cover pot and let set for 30 minutes, maintaining the temperature.

5. Check for a clean break (see Tip, page 215). If necessary, let set for another 5 to 10 minutes or until you achieve a clean break. Using a long-bladed knife and skimmer, cut curd to ⅜-inch (0.9 cm) pieces. Let stand for 10 minutes to firm up.

6. Return heat to low and slowly warm curds to 95°F (35°C), stirring gently and continuously, adjusting the heat as necessary to make sure it takes 35 minutes to do so. Do not heat too quickly. Let curds settle.

continued on next page…

Wensleydale continued...

Wensleydale continued...

Tip: To re-dress the cheese, remove the mold from the press. Remove the cheese from the mold and unwrap. Place the cloth back in the mold; turn the cheese over and put back in the mold, then rewrap. Return mold to the press.

7. Drain off the whey through a cloth-lined colander, leaving the curds in the pot. Let curds mat and form a spongy mass on the bottom of the pot.

8. Cut curd mass into 4 blocks. Turn blocks on their sides in the bottom of the pot, turning every 10 minutes for 40 minutes. Keep lid on the pot to maintain warmth. Slice blocks into pieces approximately $\frac{1}{2}$ inch (1.25 cm) thick and 2 inches (5 cm) long. Place in a bowl and toss with salt.

9. Pack curds down into prepared mold, pressing down firmly as you fill. Pull cloth up neatly around curds and fold excess snugly over the top, with as few wrinkles as possible. Put on the lid.

10. Place mold in cheese press or place a weight on top. Press at medium pressure for 30 minutes. Remove from press and re-dress (see Tip, left). Continue pressing at firm pressure for several hours or overnight.

11. Remove cheese from press and unwrap. Dry cheese on a cheese mat placed on a rack at room temperature for 1 to 2 days, turning once or twice, or until fairly dry to the touch (see Tip, page 240).

12. Coat cheese with 2 or 3 layers of cheese wax (see page 21). Ripen at 50° to 54°F (10° to 12°C), turning once or twice weekly to ensure even ripening, for 3 weeks before eating. You may ripen longer for more-developed flavor. Once ripened to your taste, wrap and store in the refrigerator.

Sheep's Milk Wensleydale

Makes
3¼ lbs (1.6 kg)
20% yield

Sheep's milk contains more milk solids and fat than cow's milk, therefore the yield is much higher. This cheese is dense and delicious, creamy and tart at the same time.

- Cloth-lined colander
- 1 tomme mold, lined with cheese cloth
- Cheese press
- Cheese matting

8 quarts	sheep's milk	8 L
¼ tsp	mesophilic culture	1.25 mL
Pinch	aroma mesophilic culture	Pinch
¼ tsp	calcium chloride	1.25 mL
¼ tsp	liquid rennet	1.25 mL
2 tbsp	pickling (canning) or kosher salt	30 mL
	Cheese wax	

1. Sterilize all equipment (see page 40). In a large stainless-steel pot set in a hot water bath over medium heat, warm milk to 86°F (30°C), stirring gently. Turn off heat.

2. Sprinkle mesophilic and aroma mesophilic cultures over surface of milk and let stand for about 5 minutes to rehydrate. Using skimmer and an up-and-down motion, gently draw cultures down into milk without breaking surface of milk. Cover and let ripen for 1½ hours, maintaining the temperature at 86°F (30°C).

3. Dilute calcium chloride in ¼ cup (50 mL) cool water. Add to milk using the same up-and-down motion.

4. Dilute rennet in ¼ cup (50 mL) cool water. Add to milk and, using the same up-and-down motion, draw rennet down into milk until well blended. Cover pot and let set for 30 to 40 minutes, maintaining the temperature.

5. Check for a clean break (see Tip, page 215). If necessary, let set for another 5 to 10 minutes or until you achieve a clean break. Using a long-bladed knife and skimmer, cut curd into ⅜-inch (0.9 cm) cubes. Let stand for 10 minutes to firm up.

6. Return heat to low and slowly warm curds to 95°F (35°C), stirring gently and continuously, adjusting the heat as necessary to make sure it takes 35 minutes to do so. Do not heat too quickly. Let curds settle.

continued on next page…

7. Drain off the whey through a cloth-lined colander, leaving the curds in the pot. Let curds mat and form a spongy mass on the bottom of the pot. After 10 minutes, turn curd mass over and hold for another 10 minutes.

8. Cut curd into ¾-inch (2 cm) chunks. Place in a bowl and toss with salt.

9. Pack curds down into prepared mold, pressing down firmly as you fill. Pull cloth up neatly around curds and fold excess snugly over the top, with as few wrinkles as possible. Put on the lid.

10. Place mold in cheese press or place a weight on top. Press at light to medium pressure for 1 hour. Remove from press and re-dress (see Tip, page 242). Continue pressing at medium pressure for several hours or overnight.

11. Remove from press and unwrap. Dry cheese on a cheese mat placed on a rack at room temperature for 2 days, turning once or twice, or until fairly dry to the touch (see Tip, page 218).

12. Coat cheese with 2 or 3 layers of cheese wax (see page 21). Ripen at 50° to 54°F (10° to 12°C), turning once or twice weekly to ensure even ripening. The cheese will be ready 3 to 4 weeks after production but can be aged longer for more flavor. Once ripened to your taste, wrap and store in the refrigerator.

Cantal

Makes
3¼ lbs (1.6 kg)
10% yield

Cantal is a wonderful table and cooking cheese produced in the mountainous central region of France. It is often referred to as "the French Cheddar," because, of all the French cheeses, it is the only one made using a process that is similar to the one used to make Cheddar. Traditionally, it is a huge cheese, often weighing as much as 100 pounds (45 kg). The method here is a close approximation of the original, just in a smaller size. To make this cheese, you must have a good cheese press.

- Cloth-lined colander
- 1 tomme mold, lined with cheese cloth
- Cheese press
- Cheese matting
- Ripening container

16 quarts	whole milk	16 L
½ tsp	mesophilic culture	2.5 mL
¾ tsp	calcium chloride	3.75 mL
¾ tsp	liquid rennet	3.75 mL
3 tbsp	pickling (canning) or kosher salt	45 mL
	Simple brine solution (see Tip, page 233)	

1. Sterilize all equipment (see page 40). In a large stainless-steel pot set in a hot water bath over medium heat, warm milk to 86°F (30°C), stirring gently. Turn off heat.

2. Sprinkle culture over surface of milk and let stand for about 5 minutes to rehydrate. Using skimmer and an up-and-down motion, gently draw culture down into milk without breaking surface of milk. Cover and let ripen for 15 minutes, maintaining the temperature at 86°F (30°C).

3. Dilute calcium chloride in ¼ cup (50 mL) cool water. Add to milk using the same up-and-down motion.

4. Dilute rennet in ¼ cup (50 mL) cool water. Add to milk and, using the same up-and-down motion, draw rennet down into milk until well blended. Cover pot and let set for 1 hour, maintaining the temperature.

5. Check for a clean break (see Tip, page 215). If necessary, let set for another 5 to 10 minutes or until you achieve a clean break. Using a long-handled whisk and skimmer, cut curd into pea-size pieces. Let stand for 5 minutes to firm up.

6. Pour contents of pot into a cloth-lined colander. Let curds mat and form a spongy mass in the colander. Cut curd mass into several pieces.

continued on next page…

Cantal continued…

Tip: When making cooked pressed cheeses, it is important to choose the right moment to drain the cheese before filling the molds and pressing. If you do not own a pH meter, you can effectively judge the readiness of the curd by doing a texture test: reach to the bottom of the pot and scoop up a small handful of curds. Gently squeeze the curds in your hand and hold for a few seconds. If the curd is ready, it will mat together easily but still feel springy, and should break apart again when rubbed with your thumb. If the curds are squishy and do not stick together, they are not yet ready. Continue holding or stirring and try again a few minutes later.

7. Fill prepared mold with curds. Pull cloth up neatly around curds and fold excess snugly over the top, with as few wrinkles as possible. Put on the lid.

8. Place mold in cheese press and press at light pressure for 12 hours. Remove from press and re-dress (see Tip, page 242). Continue pressing at light pressure for another 12 hours. This time is important for developing the flavor of the cheese.

9. Remove from press and unwrap. Using your hands, break up cheese into 1-inch (2.5 cm) chunks. Place chunks in a large stainless-steel bowl and add salt, mixing and kneading well with your hands.

10. Wash and rinse cheese cloth and tomme mold. Line mold with cheese cloth. Refill prepared mold with salted curd. Pull cloth up neatly around curds and fold excess snugly over the top, with as few wrinkles as possible. Replace the lid and return mold to press. Press at firm pressure for 36 to 48 hours, re-dressing and turning in the press 2 or 3 times during the first 24 hours.

11. Remove from press and unwrap. Dry cheese on a cheese mat placed on a rack at room temperature for 2 days, turning once or twice, or until fairly dry to the touch (see Tip, page 240).

12. Place cheese on a clean cheese mat in a ripening container. Ripen at 50°F (10°C) and 85% humidity for 3 to 6 months. Twice a week, wash the rind with a cloth moistened in simple brine solution and turn the cheese. Once ripened to your taste, wrap and store in the refrigerator.

Sbrinz

**Makes about
2 1/2 lbs (1.25 kg)**
8% yield

*Pronounced "shbrints,"
this cheese is an AOC
treasure from the
mountainous region
of central Switzerland,
where the cows graze
on high Alpine pastures
to produce rich milk
for cheese making. The
name comes from the
Italian pronunciation of
the Swiss town of Brienz,
which is located beside a
deep lake surrounded by
snowy mountain peaks.
Here, the farmers would
bring their cheeses down
from the Alpine valleys
for transport via mule
train over the mountain
passes to Italy. It is
indeed a cheese with
a long history, as the
Italy-Brienz cheese trade
was first documented
in 1530. Patience is
required, however, as
Sbrinz needs at least
18 months to age.*

- Cloth-lined colander
- 1 tomme mold, lined with cheese cloth
- Cheese press
- Cheese matting
- Ripening container

16 quarts	whole milk	16 L
1/2 tsp	thermophilic culture	2.5 mL
3/4 tsp	calcium chloride	3.75 mL
3/4 tsp	liquid rennet	3.75 mL
	Cool 18% saturated brine (see Tip, page 223)	

1. Sterilize all equipment (see page 40). In a large stainless-steel pot set in a hot water bath over medium heat, warm milk to 90°F (32°C), stirring gently. Turn off heat.

2. Sprinkle culture over surface of milk and let stand for about 5 minutes to rehydrate. Using skimmer and an up-and-down motion, gently draw culture down into milk without breaking surface of milk. Cover and let ripen for 15 minutes, maintaining the temperature at 90°F (32°C).

3. Dilute calcium chloride in 1/4 cup (50 mL) cool water. Add to milk using the same up-and-down motion.

4. Dilute rennet in 1/4 cup (50 mL) cool water. Add to milk and, using the same up-and-down motion, draw rennet down into milk until well blended. Cover pot and let set for 30 minutes, maintaining the temperature.

5. Check for a clean break (see Tip, page 215). If necessary, let set for another 10 minutes or until you achieve a clean break. Using a long-handled whisk and skimmer, cut curd into very small bits, about the size of rice grains, using the skimmer to lift and move the curds gently to ensure all are cut. Let stand for 10 minutes to firm up.

6. Return heat to low and slowly warm curds to 131°F (55°C), stirring gently and continuously, adjusting the heat as necessary to make sure it takes 1 hour to do so. Do not heat too quickly. Turn off heat. Let curds settle.

continued on next page…

Sbrinz continued...

Serving suggestion:
A special way to serve this extra-hard cheese is the way the Swiss do: shave it into long, thin strips, roll them up and serve with a twist of freshly ground pepper and a glass of white wine. The thin flakes of cheese melt on the tongue with an extraordinary intensity of flavor. Sbrinz is also wonderful broken into pieces for an appetizer or grated for cooking.

7. Pour contents of pot into a cloth-lined colander. Fill prepared mold with curds. Pull cloth up neatly around curds and fold excess snugly over the top, with as few wrinkles as possible. Put on the lid.

8. Place mold in cheese press or place a weight on top. Press at firm pressure for 1 hour. Remove from press and re-dress (see Tip, page 242). Continue pressing at very firm pressure for 12 to 18 hours.

9. Remove cheese from press. Unwrap and place in brine solution for 18 hours, turning over after 9 hours.

10. Remove from brine. Rinse and dry cheese with a clean cloth. Place on a cheese mat in a ripening container, leaving the cover slightly ajar, and let stand at 65°F (18°C). This is called the "sweating" period. The cheese will lose moisture, and the rind will become greasy as fat from the cheese is released. Turn the cheese and wipe with a clean dry cloth every other day for 4 to 6 weeks. Remove any accumulated moisture from bottom of container and wipe dry with a paper towel as necessary.

11. Ripen cheese at 50°F (10°C) and 85% humidity for another 15 to 20 months, turning weekly. If desired, continue ripening the cheese for as long as you like. It will continue to harden and increase in flavor. Once aged to your taste, wrap and store in the refrigerator.

Savory Sbrinz Shortbread

<table>
<tr><td colspan="3">• Baking sheet, lined with parchment paper</td></tr>
<tr><td>1 tbsp</td><td>black peppercorns</td><td>15 mL</td></tr>
<tr><td>⅔ cup</td><td>butter, softened</td><td>150 mL</td></tr>
<tr><td>1 tsp</td><td>salt</td><td>5 mL</td></tr>
<tr><td>Pinch</td><td>ground nutmeg</td><td>Pinch</td></tr>
<tr><td>2 cups</td><td>grated Sbrinz (page 247)</td><td>500 mL</td></tr>
<tr><td>½ cup</td><td>water</td><td>125 mL</td></tr>
<tr><td>3⅓ cups</td><td>all-purpose flour</td><td>825 mL</td></tr>
<tr><td></td><td>Sea salt</td><td></td></tr>
<tr><td>1 cup</td><td>crème fraîche</td><td>250 mL</td></tr>
</table>

Makes about 50 pieces

Serve with a glass of red wine for an elegant evening appetizer. The rich shortbread is made especially piquant with the addition of ripe Sbrinz.

1. Place peppercorns in a small bowl and cover with water to soften them. Set aside.

2. In a large bowl, using an electric mixer or wooden spoon, beat butter until smooth. Stir in salt and nutmeg. Add Sbrinz and water; using a wooden spoon, mix thoroughly.

3. Stir in flour until blended, but do not knead. Cover bowl and let stand in the refrigerator for 1 hour.

4. Preheat oven to 350°F (180°C).

5. On a lightly floured surface, roll out dough into a ½-inch (1.25 cm) thick square. Place on prepared baking sheet and cut into diamond shapes. Do not separate the pieces; they will be broken apart once they are baked. Brush with water and sprinkle with sea salt.

6. Bake in preheated oven for 15 to 20 minutes or until lightly browned. Let cool on the baking sheet. Break into pieces.

7. Drain peppercorns. Mix them into crème fraîche and add sea salt to taste. Serve shortbread with a spoonful of the crème fraîche mixture on the side.

Manchego

**Makes 3²⁄₃ to
4 lbs (1.8 to 2 kg)**

18 to 20% yield

Manchego is another
cheese with a very old
tradition. Real Manchego
is made in the province
of La Mancha in central
Spain from milk of the
Manchega sheep. It has
Denominación de origen
controlada (DOC) status.
This recipe makes a
Manchego-style cheese
using sheep's milk.

- Cloth-lined colander
- 1 tomme mold, lined with cheese cloth
- Cheese press
- Cheese matting
- Ripening container

10 quarts	sheep's milk	10 L
1/2 tsp	mesophilic culture	2.5 mL
1/4 tsp	liquid rennet	1.25 mL
	Cool 18% saturated brine (see Tip, page 223)	
	Olive oil, optional	

1. Sterilize all equipment (see page 40). In a large stainless-steel pot set in a hot water bath over medium heat, warm milk to 86°F (30°C), stirring gently. Turn off heat.

2. Sprinkle culture over surface of milk and let stand for about 5 minutes to rehydrate. Using skimmer and an up-and-down motion, gently draw culture down into milk without breaking surface of milk. Cover and let ripen for 20 minutes, maintaining the temperature at 86°F (30°C).

3. Dilute rennet in 1/4 cup (50 mL) cool water. Add to milk and, using the same up-and-down motion, draw rennet down into milk until well blended. Cover pot and let set for 40 minutes, maintaining the temperature.

4. Check for a clean break (see Tip, page 215). If necessary, let set for another 5 to 10 minutes or until you achieve a clean break. Using a long-handled whisk and skimmer, cut curd into very small bits, about the size of rice grains, using the skimmer to lift and move the curds gently to ensure all are cut. Let curds stand for 5 minutes to firm up.

5. Return heat to low and slowly warm curds to 99°F (37°C), stirring gently and continuously, adjusting the heat as necessary to make sure it takes 30 minutes to do so. Do not heat too quickly. Let curds settle and hold for 10 minutes.

Tip: To make a vinegar-and-salt solution, dissolve 1 tbsp (15 mL) salt in ½ cup (125 mL) white vinegar.

6. Pour contents of pot into a cloth-lined colander. Fill prepared mold with curds. Pull cloth up neatly around curds and fold excess snugly over the top, with as few wrinkles as possible. Put on the lid.

7. Place mold in cheese press or place a weight on top. Press cheese at medium pressure for 30 minutes. Remove from press and re-dress (see Tip, page 242). Continue pressing at firm pressure for 12 hours or overnight.

8. Remove cheese from press. Unwrap and place in brine solution for 20 hours, turning over after 10 hours.

9. Remove cheese from brine. Dry cheese on a cheese mat placed on a rack at room temperature for 2 to 3 days, turning daily to aid drying, or until fairly dry to the touch (see Tip, page 240).

10. Place cheese on a cheese mat in a ripening container. Ripen at 54°F (12°C) and 85% humidity for 2 months for a young cheese or 1 year or more for an aged cheese. Turn the cheese daily for the first 2 weeks, then weekly thereafter. If mold appears on the rind, wipe with a cloth dipped in a vinegar-and-salt solution (see Tip, left). After 1 month of ripening, the cheese can be rubbed with olive oil to prevent the rind from drying; repeat once or twice during ripening period. Once ripened to your taste, wrap and store in the refrigerator.

Parmesan

**Makes about
2½ lbs (1.25 kg)**
8% yield

This is one of the
most-loved and copied
cheeses in the world,
and it has an amazing
flavor. Try to be patient
and age it for at least
a year for maximum
aroma development.
Though known mainly
as a topping on pasta,
Parmesan makes a
wonderful table cheese.
Shave or chip off fresh
pieces with a special
Parmesan knife and
serve with fresh figs and
crackers for a wonderful
treat. When grating for
a dish, prepare only the
amount needed — the
grated cheese loses flavor
quickly when stored.

- 1 tomme mold, lined with cheese cloth
- Cloth-lined colander
- Cheese press
- Cheese matting
- Ripening container

16 quarts	partly skimmed (2%) milk	16 L
½ tsp	thermophilic culture	2.5 mL
¾ tsp	calcium chloride	3.75 mL
¾ tsp	liquid rennet	3.75 mL
	Cool 18% saturated brine (see Tip, page 223)	
	Olive oil	

1. Sterilize all equipment (see page 40). In a large stainless-steel pot set in a hot water bath over medium heat, warm milk to 94°F (34°C), stirring gently. Turn off heat.

2. Sprinkle culture over surface of milk and let stand for about 5 minutes to rehydrate. Using skimmer and an up-and-down motion, gently draw culture down into milk without breaking surface of milk. Cover and let ripen for 45 minutes, maintaining the temperature at 94°F (34°C).

3. Dilute calcium chloride in ¼ cup (50 mL) cool water. Add to milk using the same up-and-down motion.

4. Dilute rennet in ¼ cup (50 mL) cool water. Add to milk and, using the same up-and-down motion, draw rennet down into milk until well blended. Cover pot and let set for 45 minutes, maintaining the temperature.

5. Check for a clean break (see Tip, page 215). If necessary, let set for another 5 to 10 minutes or until you achieve a clean break. Using a long-handled whisk and skimmer, cut curd into lentil-size pieces, using the skimmer to lift and move the curds gently to ensure all are cut. Let curds stand for 10 minutes to firm up.

Tip: To help inhibit mold growth on hard cheeses, such as Gruyère, Parmesan and Cheddar, while storing in the refrigerator, lightly dampen a paper towel with cider vinegar and fold around the cheese before wrapping. If a little mold does appear on your firm, semifirm or semisoft cheeses, just cut away the moldy portion and discard. Because of the denseness of the cheese and the relative lack of moisture, the mold will not penetrate the paste.

6. Return heat to low and slowly warm curds to 124°F (51°C), stirring gently and continuously, adjusting the heat as necessary to make sure it takes 1 hour to do so. Do not heat too quickly. Let curds settle. The curds should mat together. If they do not, stir for another 5 minutes and check again.

7. Place the prepared mold underneath a cloth-lined colander and drain off the whey, which will warm the mold. Fill prepared mold with curds. Pull cloth up neatly around curds and fold excess snugly over the top, with as few wrinkles as possible. Put on the lid.

8. Place mold in cheese press. Press at medium pressure for 30 minutes. Remove from press and re-dress (see Tip, page 242). Continue pressing at very firm pressure for 12 hours or overnight.

9. Remove cheese from press. Unwrap and place in brine solution for 20 hours, turning over after 10 hours.

10. Remove from brine. Dry cheese on a cheese mat placed on a rack at room temperature for 2 to 3 days, turning daily to aid drying, or until fairly dry to the touch (see Tip, page 240).

11. Place cheese on a clean cheese mat in a ripening container. Ripen at 50°F (10°C) and 85% to 90% humidity for 6 to 7 months, turning daily for the first 2 weeks, then weekly thereafter. If mold appears on the rind, wipe with a cloth dipped in a vinegar-and-salt solution (see Tip, page 251).

12. After 3 months, rub the rind with olive oil. Repeat every 2 or 3 months until ripening is complete.

Asiago

**Makes about
3½ lbs (1.75 kg)**
10% yield

Asiago is made in the
Veneto region of Italy and
comes in two versions:
Asiago pressato, a fresh
version made with whole
cow's milk that is eaten
after just 20 days of
ripening, and Asiago
d'allevo, which is usually
made with skimmed milk
and aged for up to 2 years.
This recipe makes an
aged version, though, as
with most cheeses, it is
good to eat at any stage
of ripening.

- 1 tomme mold, lined with cheese cloth
- Cloth-lined colander
- Cheese press
- Cheese matting
- Ripening container

14 quarts	whole milk	14 L
2 quarts	partly skimmed (2%) milk	2 L
½ tsp	thermophilic culture	2.5 mL
¾ tsp	calcium chloride	3.75 mL
¾ tsp	liquid rennet	3.75 mL
	Cool 18% saturated brine (see Tip, page 223)	
	Simple brine solution (see Tip, page 233)	

1. Sterilize all equipment (see page 40). In a large
   stainless-steel pot set in a hot water bath over medium
   heat, warm milks to 92°F (33°C), stirring gently. Turn
   off heat.

2. Sprinkle culture over surface of milk and let stand for
   about 5 minutes to rehydrate. Using skimmer and an
   up-and-down motion, gently draw culture down into
   milk without breaking surface of milk. Cover and let
   ripen for 40 minutes, maintaining the temperature at
   92°F (33°C).

3. Dilute calcium chloride in ¼ cup (50 mL) cool water.
   Add to milk using the same up-and-down motion.

4. Dilute rennet in ¼ cup (50 mL) cool water. Add to milk
   and, using the same up-and-down motion, draw rennet
   down into milk until well blended. Cover pot and let set
   for 45 minutes to 1 hour, maintaining the temperature.

5. Check for a clean break (see Tip, page 215). If necessary,
   let set for another 5 to 10 minutes or until you achieve a
   clean break. Using a long-handled whisk and skimmer,
   cut curd into pea-size pieces, using the skimmer to lift
   and move the curds gently to ensure all are cut. Let
   curds stand for 5 minutes to firm up.

Tips: To re-dress the cheese, remove the mold from the press. Remove the cheese from the mold and unwrap. Place the cloth back in the mold; turn the cheese over and put back in the mold, then rewrap. Return mold to the press.

The rind should be fairly dry, or, as someone explained it to me, "like a clammy handshake." If completely dry, the closed rind could crack, allowing bacteria to enter the interior of the cheese.

6. Return heat to low and slowly warm curds to 104°F (40°C), stirring gently and continuously, adjusting the heat as necessary to make sure it takes 20 minutes to do so. Do not heat too quickly. Turn off heat and stir for 20 minutes.

7. Return heat to low and warm curds to 118°F (48°C), stirring gently and continuously, adjusting the heat as necessary to make sure it takes 20 minutes to do so. Stir curds until firm but springy and a handful sticks lightly together when compressed. Let curds settle and hold at this temperature for 20 minutes.

8. Place the prepared mold underneath a cloth-lined colander and drain off the whey, which will warm the mold. Let curds drain in colander for 5 minutes.

9. Fill prepared mold with curds. Pull cloth up neatly around curds and fold excess snugly over the top, with as few wrinkles as possible. Put on the lid.

10. Place mold in cheese press or place a weight on top. Press cheese at medium pressure for 1 hour. Remove from press and re-dress (see Tips, left). Continue pressing at firm pressure for 1 hour. Re-dress and press at firm pressure for several hours or overnight.

11. Remove cheese from press. Unwrap and place in 18% saturated brine solution for 20 hours, turning over after 10 hours.

12. Remove cheese from brine. Dry cheese on a cheese mat placed on a rack at room temperature for 1 to 2 days, turning once or twice, or until fairly dry to the touch (see Tips, left).

13. Place cheese on a clean cheese mat in a ripening container. Ripen at 54°F (12°C) and 85% humidity, turning daily for the first week. Turn cheese and brush rind with a soft brush dipped in simple brine solution twice weekly for 2 months, then weekly thereafter.

14. Continue aging the cheese until desired ripeness is achieved. This cheese can be aged for up to 2 years for sharp flavor. Once ripened to your taste, wrap and store in the refrigerator.

Piora

Makes
3¼ lbs (1.6 kg)
10% yield

Piora is a hard cheese
with small "eyes," or
holes, made in the
Italian-speaking part
of the Swiss Alps. It is
normally made from
cow's milk, but sometimes
a mixture of cow's and
goat's milk is used, as in
the variation (opposite).

Tip: Non-homogenized
milk, also known as
cream line or standard
milk, is always the best
choice for successful
cheese making.
Non-homogenized
milk is pasteurized
milk that hasn't been
homogenized and
shouldn't be confused
with raw milk. See
Sources, page 372,
for more information.

- Cloth-lined colander
- 1 tomme mold, lined with cheese cloth
- Cheese press
- Cheese matting
- Ripening container

16 quarts	whole milk	16 L
½ tsp	thermophilic culture	2.5 mL
¾ tsp	calcium chloride	3.75 mL
¾ tsp	liquid rennet	3.75 mL
	Cool 18% saturated brine (see Tip, page 223)	
	Simple brine solution (see Tip, page 233)	

1. Sterilize all equipment (see page 40). In a large
   stainless-steel pot set in a hot water bath over medium
   heat, warm milk to 92°F (33°C), stirring gently. Turn
   off heat.

2. Sprinkle culture over surface of milk and let stand for
   about 5 minutes to rehydrate. Using skimmer and an
   up-and-down motion, gently draw culture down into
   milk without breaking surface of milk. Cover and let
   ripen for 15 minutes, maintaining the temperature at
   92°F (33°C).

3. Dilute calcium chloride in ¼ cup (50 mL) cool water.
   Add to milk using the same up-and-down motion.

4. Dilute rennet in ¼ cup (50 mL) cool water. Add to milk
   and, using the same up-and-down motion, draw rennet
   down into milk until well blended. Cover pot and let set
   for 40 minutes, maintaining the temperature.

5. Check for a clean break (see Tip, page 215). If necessary,
   let set for another 5 to 10 minutes or until you achieve a
   clean break. Using a long-handled whisk and skimmer,
   cut curd into very small bits, about the size of rice grains,
   using the skimmer to lift and move the curds gently to
   ensure all are cut. Let stand for 10 minutes. Stir gently
   for 10 minutes. Let stand again for 5 minutes. Stir again
   for 10 minutes.

continued on page 257…

Bel Paese (page 200)

Caerphilly (page 222)

Emmental (page 224)

Sage Derby (Variation, page 278)

Sheep's Milk Feta (page 292)

Halloumi (page 297)

Persian Sparkling Yogurt Drink (page 331)

Flavored Butters (clockwise from left): Lime and Coriander Butter (page 355),
Orange Honey Butter (page 346), Peppercorn Butter (page 350)

Variation: In place of all cow's milk, use 12¾ quarts (12.75 L) whole cow's milk and 3¼ quarts (3.25 L) goat's milk.

6. Return heat to low and slowly warm curds to 120°F (49°C), stirring gently and continuously, adjusting the heat as necessary to make sure it takes 40 to 45 minutes to do so. Do not heat too quickly. Once the temperature has been reached, continue stirring for another 30 minutes, maintaining the temperature. The curds should be quite firm and springy when squeezed in the hand.

7. Pour contents of pot into a cloth-lined colander. Fill prepared mold with curds. Pull cloth up neatly around curds and fold excess snugly over the top, with as few wrinkles as possible. Put on the lid.

8. Place mold in cheese press or place a weight on top. Press at medium pressure for 30 minutes. Remove from press and re-dress (see Tips, page 255). Continue pressing at very firm pressure for 12 hours or overnight.

9. Remove cheese from press. Unwrap and place in 18% saturated brine solution for 20 hours, turning over after 10 hours.

10. Remove from brine. Dry cheese on a cheese mat placed on a rack at room temperature for 2 to 3 days, turning once or twice, or until fairly dry to the touch (see Tips, page 255).

11. Place cheese on a clean cheese mat in a ripening container. Ripen at 50° to 54°F (10° to 12°C) and 85% to 90% humidity for 3 to 6 months. Turn cheese and wash with a cloth dipped in simple brine solution twice a week. Once the rind has firmed up and begins to develop, rub with a dry cloth to control mold but still allow it to grow on the cheese.

Kefalotyri

Makes 2½ to 3 lbs
(1.25 to 1.5 kg)
8 to 9% yield

A hard Greek cheese
with great personality,
kefalotyri (meaning
"hat-shaped cheese")
is usually grated over
pasta or vegetables and
used in savory dishes.
It is made of cow's milk
or a blend of cow's milk
and goat's or sheep's
milk. If using sheep's
milk, try to keep the fat
content at around 4% by
blending with skimmed
cow's milk.

- Cloth-lined colander
- 1 tomme mold, lined with cheese cloth
- Cheese press
- Cheese matting
- Ripening container

16 quarts	whole milk (see Intro, left)	16 L
½ tsp	thermophilic culture	2.5 mL
¾ tsp	calcium chloride	3.75 mL
¾ tsp	liquid rennet	3.75 mL
	Cool 18% saturated brine (see Tip, page 223)	
	White or cider vinegar	

1. Sterilize all equipment (see page 40). In a large stainless-steel pot set in a hot water bath over medium heat, warm milk to 92°F (33°C), stirring gently. Turn off heat.

2. Sprinkle culture over surface of milk and let stand for about 5 minutes to rehydrate. Using skimmer and an up-and-down motion, gently draw culture down into milk without breaking surface of milk. Cover and let ripen for 40 minutes, maintaining the temperature at 92°F (33°C).

3. Dilute calcium chloride in ¼ cup (50 mL) cool water. Add to milk using the same up-and-down motion.

4. Dilute rennet in ¼ cup (50 mL) cool water. Add to milk and, using the same up-and-down motion, draw rennet down into milk until well blended. Cover pot and let set for 45 minutes, maintaining the temperature.

5. Check for a clean break (see Tip, page 215). If necessary, let set for another 5 to 10 minutes or until you achieve a clean break. Using a long-handled whisk and skimmer, cut curd into very small bits, about the size of rice grains, using the skimmer to lift and move the curds gently to ensure all are cut. Let curds stand for 5 minutes to firm up.

Tip: When substituting sheep's or goat's milk for cow's milk in a recipe, remember to reduce the amount of rennet used by 20% to 25%; cook to 2°F (1°C) less than the temperature recommended in the cow's milk recipe.

6. Return heat to low and slowly warm curds to 113°F (45°C), stirring gently and continuously, adjusting the heat as necessary to make sure it takes 40 minutes to do so. Do not heat too quickly. Turn off heat and let stand for 15 minutes.

7. Pour contents of pot into a cloth-lined colander. Fill prepared mold with curds. Pull cloth up neatly around curds and fold excess snugly over the top, with as few wrinkles as possible. Put on the lid.

8. Place mold in cheese press or place a weight on top. Press at firm pressure for 30 minutes. Remove from press and re-dress (see Tips, page 255). Continue pressing at firm pressure for several hours or overnight.

9. Remove cheese from press. Unwrap and place in brine solution for 12 hours, turning over after 6 hours.

10. Remove from brine. Dry cheese on a cheese mat placed on a rack at room temperature for 2 to 3 days, turning once or twice, or until fairly dry to the touch (see Tips, page 255).

11. Place cheese on a clean cheese mat in a ripening container. Ripen at 54°F (12°C) and 90% humidity for 6 weeks. Turn cheese daily and remove any accumulated whey, wiping bottom of container with paper towel.

12. After 6 weeks, reduce the temperature to 48°F (9°C) and 90% humidity. Continue ripening cheese for another 4 to 8 weeks, turning weekly. If mold appears, wipe it away with a cloth dipped in vinegar. When ripened to your taste, wrap and store in the refrigerator. This cheese will keep for a very long time, becoming harder as it ages.

Romano

**Makes about
2¹⁄₂ to 3 lbs
(1.25 to 1.5 kg)**

8 to 10% yield

This hard grating cheese
is made in central Italy
near the city of Rome. It
must be aged for several
months for optimal flavor
development. This recipe
calls for cow's milk, but
you may blend equal
amounts of cow's and
goat's milk for a stronger-
tasting cheese.

- 1 tomme mold, lined with cheese cloth
- Cloth-lined colander
- Cheese press
- Cheese matting
- Ripening container

16 quarts	whole milk	16 L
¹⁄₂ tsp	thermophilic culture	2.5 mL
³⁄₄ tsp	calcium chloride	3.75 mL
³⁄₄ tsp	liquid rennet	3.75 mL
	Cool 18% saturated brine (see Tip, page 223)	
	Olive oil	

1. Sterilize all equipment (see page 40). In a large stainless-steel pot set in a hot water bath over medium heat, warm milk to 90°F (32°C), stirring gently. Turn off heat.

2. Sprinkle culture over surface of milk and let stand for about 5 minutes to rehydrate. Using skimmer and an up-and-down motion, gently draw culture down into milk without breaking surface of milk. Cover and let ripen for 15 minutes, maintaining the temperature at 90°F (32°C).

3. Dilute calcium chloride in ¹⁄₄ cup (50 mL) cool water. Add to milk using the same up-and-down motion.

4. Dilute rennet in ¹⁄₄ cup (50 mL) cool water. Add to milk and, using the same up-and-down motion, draw rennet down into milk until well blended. Cover pot and let set for 1 hour, maintaining the temperature.

5. Check for a clean break (see Tip, page 215). If necessary, let set for another 5 to 10 minutes or until you achieve a clean break. Using a long-handled whisk and skimmer, cut curd into ¹⁄₄-inch (0.5 cm) pieces, using the skimmer to lift and move the curds gently to ensure all are cut. Let curds stand for 5 minutes to firm up.

6. Return heat to low and slowly warm curds to 117°F (47°C), stirring gently and continuously, adjusting the heat as necessary to make sure it takes 45 to 50 minutes to do so. Do not heat too quickly or the curd will be brittle and dry. Turn off heat, cover pot and hold for 30 minutes.

7. Place the prepared mold underneath a cloth-lined colander and drain off the whey, which will warm the mold. Fill prepared mold with curds, piling them higher in the center. Pull cloth up neatly around curds and fold excess snugly over the top, with as few wrinkles as possible. Put on the lid.

8. Place mold in cheese press or place a weight on top. Press at medium pressure for 30 minutes. Remove from press and re-dress (see Tips, page 255). Continue pressing at medium pressure for 1 hour. Re-dress and press at firm pressure for 12 hours or overnight.

9. Remove cheese from press. Unwrap and place in brine solution for 20 hours, turning over after 10 hours.

10. Remove from brine. Dry cheese on a cheese mat placed on a rack at room temperature for 2 to 3 days, turning once a day to aid drying, or until fairly dry to the touch (see Tips, page 255).

11. Place cheese on a clean cheese mat in a ripening container. Ripen at 54°F (12°C) and 85% humidity for at least 5 months. Adjust the lid of the container periodically to maintain the humidity. Turn cheese daily for the first 2 weeks, then twice weekly for the next 6 weeks. After 2 months, turn cheese weekly. If mold appears, wipe rind with a cloth dipped in a vinegar-and-salt solution (see Tip, page 251).

12. After 3 months, rub the surface of the cheese with olive oil to prevent from drying out and to help develop a nice rind. Repeat as necessary, every month or two. Age cheese for up to 2 years for sharp flavor. Once ripened to your taste, wrap and store in the refrigerator.

Pecorino Romano

Makes 3½ to
4 lbs (1.75 to 2 kg)

18 to 20% yield

In Italian, the word
pecorino *denotes a*
sheep's milk cheese, just
as brebis *does in French.*
Because of the higher
amount of milk solids
in sheep's milk, you will
need less milk to make
the same amount of
cheese as you would for
traditional cow's milk
Romano.

- 1 tomme mold, lined with cheese cloth
- Cloth-lined colander
- Cheese press
- Cheese matting
- Ripening container

10 quarts	sheep's milk	10 L
½ tsp	thermophilic culture	2.5 mL
¼ tsp	liquid rennet	1.25 mL
	Cool 18% saturated brine (see Tip, page 223)	
	Olive oil	

1. Sterilize all equipment (see page 40). In a large stainless-steel pot set in a hot water bath over medium heat, warm milk to 90°F (32°C), stirring gently. Turn off heat.

2. Sprinkle culture over surface of milk and let stand for about 5 minutes to rehydrate. Using skimmer and an up-and-down motion, gently draw culture down into milk without breaking surface of milk. Cover and let ripen for 15 minutes, maintaining the temperature at 90°F (32°C).

3. Dilute rennet in ¼ cup (50 mL) cool water. Add to milk and, using the same up-and-down motion, draw rennet down into milk until well blended. Cover pot and let set for 1 hour, maintaining the temperature.

4. Check for a clean break (see Tip, page 215). If necessary, let set for another 5 to 10 minutes or until you achieve a clean break. Using a long-handled whisk and skimmer, cut curd into ¼-inch (0.5 cm) pieces, using the skimmer to lift and move the curds gently to ensure all are cut. Let curds stand for 5 minutes to firm up.

5. Return heat to low and slowly warm curds to 117°F (47°C), stirring gently and continuously, adjusting the heat as necessary to make sure it takes 45 to 50 minutes to do so. Do not heat too quickly or the curd will be brittle and dry. Turn off heat, cover pot and hold for 30 minutes.

Tip: To make a vinegar-and-salt solution, dissolve 1 tbsp (15 mL) salt in ½ cup (125 mL) white vinegar.

6. Place the prepared mold underneath a cloth-lined colander and drain off the whey, which will warm the mold. Fill prepared mold with curds, piling them higher in the center. Pull cloth up neatly around curds and fold excess snugly over the top, with as few wrinkles as possible. Put on the lid.

7. Place mold in cheese press or place a weight on top. Press at medium pressure for 30 minutes. Remove from press and re-dress (see Tips, page 255). Continue pressing for 1 hour at slightly increased pressure. Re-dress once more and press at firm pressure for 12 hours or overnight.

8. Remove cheese from press. Unwrap and place in brine solution for 20 hours, turning over after 10 hours.

9. Remove from brine. Dry cheese on a cheese mat placed on a rack at room temperature for 2 to 3 days, turning once a day to aid drying, or until fairly dry to the touch (see Tips, page 255).

10. Place cheese on a clean cheese mat in a ripening container. Ripen at 54°F (12°C) and 85% humidity for at least 5 months. Adjust the lid of the container periodically to maintain the humidity. Turn cheese daily for the first 2 weeks, then twice weekly for the next 6 weeks. After 2 months, turn cheese weekly. If mold appears, wipe rind with a cloth dipped in a vinegar-and-salt solution (see Tip, left).

11. After 3 months, rub the surface of the cheese with olive oil to prevent from drying out and to help develop a nice rind. Repeat as necessary, every month or two. Age cheese for up to 2 years for sharp flavor. Once ripened to your taste, wrap and store in the refrigerator.

Monterey Jack

Makes
3½ lbs (1.75 kg)
10% yield
(see Tip, opposite)

Very popular in the
U.S., Monterey Jack is
a Cheddar-style cheese
developed in California.
It is often spiced up with
the addition of chiles or
peppercorns. All kinds
of Jack are available,
including aged and
unaged.

Tip: The yield will be
approximately 8% if
you use skim or partly
skimmed milk.

- Cloth-lined colander
- 1 tomme mold, lined with cheese cloth
- Cheese press
- Cheese matting

16 quarts	whole milk	16 L
½ tsp	mesophilic culture	2.5 mL
¾ tsp	calcium chloride	3.75 mL
¾ tsp	liquid rennet	3.75 mL
	Cool 18% saturated brine (see Tip, page 223)	
	Cheese wax	

1. Sterilize all equipment (see page 40). In a large stainless-steel pot set in a hot water bath over medium heat, warm milk to 89°F (32°C), stirring gently. Turn off heat.

2. Sprinkle culture over surface of milk and let stand for about 5 minutes to rehydrate. Using skimmer and an up-and-down motion, gently draw culture down into milk without breaking surface of milk. Cover and let ripen for 45 minutes, maintaining the temperature at 89°F (32°C).

3. Dilute calcium chloride in ¼ cup (50 mL) cool water. Add to milk using the same up-and-down motion.

4. Dilute rennet in ¼ cup (50 mL) cool water. Add to milk and, using the same up-and-down motion, draw rennet down into milk until well blended. Cover pot and let set for 40 minutes, maintaining the temperature.

5. Check for a clean break (see Tip, page 215). If necessary, let set for another 5 to 10 minutes or until you achieve a clean break. Using a long-bladed knife and skimmer, cut curd into ½-inch (1.25 cm) cubes, using the skimmer to lift and move the curds gently to ensure all are cut. Let curds stand for 10 minutes to firm up.

Variation: *Jalapeño Jack:* In a small saucepan over medium-high heat, boil 3 tbsp (45 mL) crushed dried jalapeños in 2 cups (500 mL) water for 10 minutes. Let cool. Pour jalapeños and cooking water over the cheese curds just after draining in Step 7. Using fingertips, mix evenly into the curds without crushing them. Fill prepared mold with curds and continue with recipe.

6. Return heat to low and slowly warm curds to 100°F (38°C), stirring gently and continuously, adjusting the heat as necessary to make sure it takes 40 minutes to do so. Do not heat too quickly. Turn off heat and hold for 30 minutes, stirring occasionally to keep the curds from matting. Let curds settle and hold for another 30 minutes, maintaining the temperature at 100°F (38°C).

7. Pour contents of pot into a cloth-lined colander. Fill prepared mold with curds. Pull cloth up neatly around curds and fold excess snugly over the top, with as few wrinkles as possible. Put on the lid.

8. Place mold in cheese press or place a weight on top. Press at firm pressure for 1 hour. Remove from press and re-dress (see Tips, page 255). Continue pressing at firm pressure for 12 hours.

9. Remove cheese from press. Unwrap and place in brine solution for 12 hours, turning over after 6 hours.

10. Remove from brine. Dry cheese on a cheese mat placed on a rack at room temperature for 2 to 3 days, turning once or twice, or until fairly dry to the touch (see Tips, page 255).

11. Coat cheese with 2 or 3 layers of cheese wax (see page 21). Ripen at 50°F (10°C) for 2 to 3 months.

Goat's Milk Cheddar

<table>
<tr><td rowspan="2" align="center">Makes
3¼ to 3½ lbs
(1.6 to 1.75 kg)
10 to 11% yield</td></tr>
</table>

Makes
3¼ to 3½ lbs
(1.6 to 1.75 kg)
10 to 11% yield

You can make a lovely
Cheddar cheese with
goat's milk. Watch the
time carefully, as the
curds can acidify quickly,
resulting in a crumbly
cheese.

- Cloth-lined colander
- 1 tomme mold, lined with cheese cloth
- Cheese press
- Cheese matting

16 quarts	goat's milk	16 L
½ tsp	mesophilic culture	2.5 mL
½ tsp	calcium chloride	2.5 mL
½ tsp	liquid rennet	2.5 mL
2 tbsp	pickling (canning) or kosher salt	30 mL
	Cheese wax, preferably black	

1. Sterilize all equipment (see page 40). In a large stainless-steel pot set in a hot water bath over medium heat, warm milk to 88°F (31°C), stirring gently. Turn off heat.

2. Sprinkle culture over surface of milk and let stand for about 5 minutes to rehydrate. Using skimmer and an up-and-down motion, gently draw culture down into milk without breaking surface of milk. Cover and let ripen for 40 minutes, maintaining the temperature at 88°F (31°C).

3. Dilute calcium chloride in ¼ cup (50 mL) cool water. Add to milk using the same up-and-down motion.

4. Dilute rennet in ¼ cup (50 mL) cool water. Add to milk and, using the same up-and-down motion, draw rennet down into milk until well blended. Cover pot and let set for 30 minutes, maintaining the temperature.

5. Check for a clean break (see Tip, page 215). Using a long-bladed knife and skimmer, cut curds into ½-inch (1.25 cm) cubes, using the skimmer to lift and move the curds gently to ensure all are cut. Let curds stand for 5 minutes to firm up.

6. Return heat to low and slowly warm curds to 102°F (39°C), stirring gently and continuously, adjusting the heat as necessary to make sure it takes 45 minutes to do so. Do not heat too quickly. The curds will shrink to about the size of peas or beans.

7. Remove pot from heat, cover and hold for 30 to 40 minutes, maintaining the temperature at 102°F (39°C).

8. Using a measuring cup, dip off the whey down to the level of the curds until you see the surface of the curds. Stir the curds for 10 minutes. Let curds settle. With your hand, test that the curds are matting and sticking together. If not, stir for another 10 minutes and test again.

9. Drain off the remaining whey through a cloth-lined colander, leaving the curds in the bottom of the pot. Let curds settle. Using your hands, mix in the salt, blending thoroughly.

10. Pack curds down into prepared mold. Pull cloth up neatly around curds and fold excess snugly over the top, with as few wrinkles as possible. Put on the lid.

11. Place mold in cheese press or place a weight on top. Press at medium pressure for 1 hour. Remove from press and re-dress (see Tips, page 255). Continue pressing at firm pressure for 12 hours or overnight.

12. Remove cheese from press and unwrap. Dry cheese on a cheese mat placed on a rack at room temperature for 1 to 2 days, turning once or twice, or until fairly dry to the touch (see Tips, page 255).

13. Coat cheese with 2 or 3 layers of cheese wax (see page 21). Ripen at 50°F (10°C), turning weekly for even ripening, for at least 1 month for mild Cheddar, longer for a sharper aged cheese. When ripened to your taste, wrap and store in the refrigerator.

Goat's Milk Caerphilly

Makes 4 lbs (2 kg)
12% yield

This is a terrific cheese with a fine flavor and creamy texture. Because it doesn't need long ripening, it's a great choice for hard cheese if you don't want to wait for a long time to eat the results.

- 1 tomme mold, lined with cheese cloth
- Cloth-lined colander
- Cheese press
- Cheese matting

16 quarts	goat's milk	16 L
¼ tsp	mesophilic culture	1.25 mL
¼ tsp	aroma mesophilic culture	1.25 mL
½ tsp	calcium chloride	2.5 mL
½ tsp	liquid rennet	2.5 mL
	Cool 18% saturated brine (see Tip, page 223)	
	Cheese wax	

1. Sterilize all equipment (see page 40). In a large stainless-steel pot set in a hot water bath over medium heat, warm milk to 90°F (32°C), stirring gently. Turn off heat.

2. Sprinkle mesophilic and aroma mesophilic cultures over surface of milk and let stand for about 5 minutes to rehydrate. Using skimmer and an up-and-down motion, gently draw cultures down into milk without breaking surface of milk. Cover and let ripen for 30 minutes, maintaining the temperature at 90°F (32°C).

3. Dilute calcium chloride in ¼ cup (50 mL) cool water. Add to milk using the same up-and-down motion.

4. Dilute rennet in ¼ cup (50 mL) cool water. Add to milk and, using the same up-and-down motion, draw rennet down into milk until well blended. Cover pot and let set for 30 to 40 minutes, maintaining the temperature.

5. Check for a clean break (see Tip, opposite). Using a long-bladed knife and skimmer, cut curds into ½-inch (1.25 cm) cubes, using the skimmer to lift and move the curds gently to ensure all are cut. Let curds stand for 5 minutes to firm up.

Tip: To ascertain whether the curd is ready for the next step, check for a clean break: insert the long flat blade of a knife into the curd at a 30-degree angle and slowly lift the blade toward the surface of the curd. If the curd splits into a long clean break or crack, it is ready to cut. If the cut is wobbly or uneven, let the curd set for a few more minutes before trying again.

6. Return heat to low and slowly warm curds to 95°F (35°C), stirring gently and continuously, adjusting the heat as necessary to make sure it takes 30 minutes to do so. Do not heat too quickly. Cover pot and let stand for 45 minutes, maintaining the temperature at 95°F (35°C).

7. Place the prepared mold underneath a cloth-lined colander and drain off the whey, which will warm the mold.

8. Fill prepared mold with curds, piling them higher in the center. Pull cloth up neatly around curds and fold excess snugly over the top, with as few wrinkles as possible. Put on the lid.

9. Place mold in cheese press. Press at medium pressure for 30 minutes. Remove from press and re-dress (see Tips, page 255). Continue pressing at medium pressure for several hours or overnight.

10. Remove cheese from press. Unwrap and place in brine solution for 20 hours, turning over after 10 hours.

11. Remove cheese from brine. Dry cheese on a cheese mat placed on a rack at room temperature for 2 to 3 days, turning once or twice, or until fairly dry to the touch (see Tips, page 255).

12. Coat cheese with 2 or 3 layers of cheese wax (see page 21). Ripen at 50° to 54°F (10° to 12°C) for 3 weeks before eating. You may age the cheese longer for a sharper flavor. Once ripened to your taste, wrap and store in the refrigerator.

Lancashire

<table>
<tr><td rowspan="3">

Makes
3¹⁄₄ lbs (1.6 kg)
10% yield

</td></tr>
</table>

Makes
3¹⁄₄ lbs (1.6 kg)
10% yield

Similar to Cheddar but with more moisture and a stronger flavor, Lancashire is a very popular British cheese. In traditional cheese making, curds of different ages and acidity levels were often blended together, creating a cheese with a loose, friable texture.

- Cloth-lined colander
- 1 tomme mold, lined with cheese cloth
- Draining container
- Cheese press
- Cheese matting
- Ripening container

14 quarts	whole milk	14 L
2 quarts	partly skimmed (2%) milk	2 L
¹⁄₂ tsp	mesophilic culture	2.5 mL
¹⁄₂ tsp	calcium chloride	2.5 mL
¹⁄₂ tsp	liquid rennet	2.5 mL
3 tbsp	pickling (canning) or kosher salt	45 mL
	White or cider vinegar	

1. Sterilize all equipment (see page 40). In a large stainless-steel pot set in a hot water bath over medium heat, warm milks to 88°F (31°C), stirring gently. Turn off heat.

2. Sprinkle culture over surface of milk and let stand for about 5 minutes to rehydrate. Using skimmer and an up-and-down motion, gently draw culture down into milk without breaking surface of milk. Cover and let ripen for 45 minutes, maintaining the temperature at 88°F (31°C).

3. Dilute calcium chloride in ¹⁄₄ cup (50 mL) cool water. Add to milk using the same up-and-down motion.

4. Dilute rennet in ¹⁄₄ cup (50 mL) cool water. Add to milk and, using the same up-and-down motion, draw rennet down into milk until well blended. Cover pot and let set for 50 minutes, maintaining the temperature.

5. Check for a clean break (see Tip, page 215). If necessary, let set for another 5 to 10 minutes or until you achieve a clean break. Using a long-bladed knife and skimmer, cut curd into ³⁄₈-inch (0.9 cm) pieces, using the skimmer to lift and move the curds gently to ensure all are cut. Let curds stand for 5 minutes to firm up.

Tip: Always use the freshest possible milk for your cheeses. If you are purchasing packaged milk, look for the latest best-before date. If using your own milk, plan your cheese making for as soon after milking as possible. The older the milk, the more bacteria there are in it to compete with the lactic bacterial starter.

6. Stir curds for 10 minutes or until they release more whey, become firmer and float freely in the whey. Let settle.

7. Pour contents of pot into a cloth-lined colander. Return curds to pot and press down with your hand to knit them together. Put the lid back on the pot to keep the curds warm. Let stand for 15 minutes. Turn the cake of curd over and hold for 15 more minutes.

8. Cut cake of curd in half and pile one piece on top of the other in the pot. Cover and hold for another 15 minutes. The two halves will knit together into one piece.

9. Place curd on a cutting board and cut into 1-inch by $\frac{1}{2}$-inch (2.5 by 1.25 cm) pieces. Place in a bowl and toss with salt.

10. Fill prepared mold with curds. Pull cloth up neatly around curds and fold excess snugly over the top, with as few wrinkles as possible. Put on the lid. Place mold on a rack in a draining container and let drain overnight.

11. In the morning, place mold in cheese press or place a weight on top. Press at medium pressure for 1 hour. Remove from press and re-dress (see Tips, page 255). Continue pressing at medium to firm pressure for 6 hours.

12. Remove cheese from press. Unwrap and place on a cheese mat in a ripening container. Ripen at 54° to 60°F (12° to 16°C) and 85% to 90% humidity for 4 to 8 weeks, depending on your taste; 4 weeks for a milder cheese or 8 weeks for a sharper one. Turn cheese daily for the first week, then twice weekly thereafter. If mold appears, wipe rind with a cloth dipped in vinegar.

Montasio

Makes
3¼ lbs (1.6 kg)
10% yield

This hard Italian cheese is traditionally made from a blend of cow's and goat's milk. It is an Alpine cheese whose flavor reflects the sun-drenched meadows and fresh air of the mountains of northern Italy.

- Cloth-lined colander
- 1 tomme mold, lined with cheese cloth
- Cheese press
- Cheese matting
- Ripening container

8 quarts	goat's milk	8 L
8 quarts	whole cow's milk	8 L
½ tsp	thermophilic culture	2.5 mL
¾ tsp	calcium chloride	3.75 mL
¾ tsp	liquid rennet	3.75 mL
	Cool 18% saturated brine (see Tip, page 223)	
	Olive oil	

1. Sterilize all equipment (see page 40). In a large stainless-steel pot set in a hot water bath over medium heat, warm goat's and cow's milk to 95°F (35°C), stirring gently. Turn off heat.

2. Sprinkle culture over surface of milk and let stand for about 5 minutes to rehydrate. Using skimmer and an up-and-down motion, gently draw culture down into milk without breaking surface of milk. Cover and let ripen for 30 minutes, maintaining the temperature at 95°F (35°C).

3. Dilute calcium chloride in ¼ cup (50 mL) cool water. Add to milk using the same up-and-down motion.

4. Dilute rennet in ¼ cup (50 mL) cool water. Add to milk and, using the same up-and-down motion, draw rennet down into milk until well blended. Cover pot and let set for 30 to 40 minutes, maintaining the temperature.

5. Check for a clean break (see Tip, page 215). If necessary, let set for another 5 to 10 minutes or until you achieve a clean break. Using a long-handled whisk and skimmer, cut curd into pea-size pieces, using the skimmer to lift and move the curds gently to ensure all are cut. Let curds stand for 5 minutes to firm up.

6. Return heat to low and slowly warm curds to 110°F (43°C), stirring gently and continuously, adjusting the heat as necessary to make sure it takes 40 minutes to do so. Do not heat too quickly. Turn off heat and continue to stir curds for another 30 minutes. Let curds settle.

7. Pour contents of pot into a cloth-lined colander. Pack curds down into prepared mold. Pull cloth up neatly around curds and fold excess snugly over the top, with as few wrinkles as possible. Put on the lid.

8. Place mold in cheese press or place a weight on top. Press at firm pressure for 1 hour. Remove from press and re-dress (see Tips, page 255). Continue pressing for another 18 hours, re-dressing once or twice again during this time.

9. Remove cheese from press. Unwrap and place in saturated brine solution for 18 hours, turning over after 9 hours.

10. Remove cheese from brine. Dry cheese on a cheese mat placed on a rack at room temperature for 1 to 2 days, turning once or twice, or until fairly dry to the touch (see Tips, page 255).

11. Place on a clean cheese mat in a ripening container. Ripen at 54°F (12°C) and 85% humidity. Turn cheeses daily for 2 weeks, removing any collected whey and wiping bottom of container with paper towel. If mold appears, wipe rind with a cloth dipped in simple brine solution (see Tip, page 233).

12. After 2 weeks, turn the cheese weekly. When the rind is fairly dry and has begun to develop, after about 2 months, rub it with a cloth dipped in olive oil. Continue aging for up to 1 year for a piquant cheese. Once ripened to your taste, wrap and store in the refrigerator.

Cheese Crisps

**Makes 10 to
12 crisps**

*These rounds of fried
cheese taste wonderful.
For a quick, attractive
appetizer, top each crisp
with a spoonful of fresh
cream cheese blended
with crème fraîche
and add a caper or
an olive slice.*

2 cups	grated Montasio (page 272) or similar hard cheese	500 mL
1 tbsp	all-purpose flour	15 mL
1 tsp	olive oil	5 mL

1. In a bowl, combine cheese and flour until well mixed.

2. In a heavy-bottomed skillet, heat olive oil over medium heat until hot but not smoking.

3. For each crisp, place heaping tablespoonful (15 mL) cheese mixture in skillet and flatten slightly. Fry until cheese is melted, edges are golden brown and fat begins to release. Turn and fry for 1 minute more. Repeat with remaining cheese mixture, adjusting heat as necessary between batches.

4. Drain and let cool on paper towel–lined plate. Serve at room temperature.

Graviera

Makes 4 lbs (2 kg)
12% yield

Larger cow's milk cheeses are made in Greece using a recipe similar to a Swiss Gruyère. The addition of some goat's milk gives this cheese a spicy flavor.

- 1 tomme mold, lined with cheese cloth
- Cloth-lined colander
- Cheese press
- Cheese matting
- Ripening container

12 quarts	whole cow's milk	12 L
4 quarts	goat's milk	4 L
½ tsp	thermophilic culture	2.5 mL
¾ tsp	calcium chloride	3.75 mL
¾ tsp	liquid rennet	3.75 mL
	Cool 18% saturated brine (see Tip, page 223)	
	Simple brine solution (see Tip, page 233)	

1. Sterilize all equipment (see page 40). In a large stainless-steel pot set in a hot water bath over medium heat, warm cow's and goat's milk to 90°F (32°C), stirring gently. Turn off heat.

2. Sprinkle culture over surface of milk and let stand for about 5 minutes to rehydrate. Using skimmer and an up-and-down motion, gently draw culture down into milk without breaking surface of milk. Cover and let ripen for 10 minutes, maintaining the temperature at 90°F (32°C).

3. Dilute calcium chloride in ¼ cup (50 mL) cool water. Add to milk using the same up-and-down motion.

4. Dilute rennet in ¼ cup (50 mL) cool water. Add to milk and, using the same up-and-down motion, draw rennet down into milk until well blended. Cover pot and let set for 40 minutes, maintaining the temperature

5. Check for a clean break (see Tip, page 215). If necessary, let set for another 5 to 10 minutes or until you achieve a clean break. Using a long-handled whisk and skimmer, cut curd into very small bits, about the size of rice grains, using the skimmer to lift and move the curds gently to ensure all are cut. Let curds stand for 5 minutes to firm up.

continued on next page…

6. Return heat to low and slowly warm curds to 114°F (46°C), stirring gently and continuously, adjusting the heat as necessary to make sure it takes 1 hour to do so. Do not heat too quickly. Let stand for 5 minutes.

7. Place the prepared mold underneath a cloth-lined colander and drain off the whey, which will warm the mold.

8. Fill prepared mold with curds. Pull cloth up neatly around curds and fold excess snugly over the top, with as few wrinkles as possible. Put on the lid.

9. Place mold in cheese press or place a weight on top. Press at medium pressure for 1 hour. Remove from press and re-dress (see Tips, page 255). Continue pressing at firm pressure for 12 hours or overnight.

10. Remove cheese from press. Unwrap and place in 18% saturated brine solution for 12 hours, turning over after 6 hours.

11. Remove cheese from brine. Dry cheese on a cheese mat placed on a rack at room temperature for 2 to 3 days, turning once or twice, or until fairly dry to the touch (see Tips, page 255).

12. Place cheese on a clean cheese mat in a ripening container. Ripen at 50° to 54°F (10° to 12°C) and 85% humidity. Every second day for 1 month, wash the rind with a cloth dipped in simple brine solution, turning the cheese each time. After 1 month, wash once a week. A rind displaying various molds and colors will begin to develop.

13. After 2 months, discontinue washing the cheese; instead, rub the rind weekly with a soft brush or cloth and continue to turn the cheese weekly for 4 months. You can age this cheese longer if a stronger flavor is desired.

Derby

**Makes
3¼ lbs (1.6 kg)**
10% yield

A hard British cheese
in the Cheddar family,
Derby is moister than
Cheddar and ripens
more quickly. The sage
version of this cheese is
also well known, though
industrially produced
Sage Derby, rather than
being made with actual
sage leaves, is often
simply colored and
flavored with synthetic
ingredients.

- 1 tomme mold, lined with cheese cloth
- Cheese press
- Cheese matting

16 quarts	whole milk	16 L
½ tsp	mesophilic culture	2.5 mL
¾ tsp	calcium chloride	3.75 mL
¾ tsp	liquid rennet	3.75 mL
4 tbsp	pickling (canning) or kosher salt	60 mL
	Cheese wax	

1. Sterilize all equipment (see page 40). In a large stainless-steel pot set in a hot water bath over medium heat, warm milk to 85°F (29°C), stirring gently. Turn off heat.

2. Sprinkle culture over surface of milk and let stand for about 5 minutes to rehydrate. Using skimmer and an up-and-down motion, gently draw culture down into milk without breaking surface of milk. Cover and let ripen for 40 minutes, maintaining the temperature at 85°F (29°C).

3. Dilute calcium chloride in ¼ cup (50 mL) cool water. Add to milk using the same up-and-down motion.

4. Dilute rennet in ¼ cup (50 mL) cool water. Add to milk and, using the same up-and-down motion, draw rennet down into milk until well blended. Cover pot and let set for 1 hour, maintaining the temperature.

5. Check for a clean break (see Tip, page 215). If necessary, let set for another 5 to 10 minutes or until you achieve a clean break. The curd should be quite firm. Using a long-bladed knife and skimmer, cut curd into ⅜-inch (0.9 cm) pieces, using the skimmer to lift and move the curds gently to ensure all are cut. Let stand for 5 minutes to firm up.

6. Return heat to low and slowly warm curds to 96°F (36°C), stirring gently and continuously, adjusting the heat as necessary to make sure it takes 45 to 50 minutes to do so. Do not heat too quickly. Turn off heat and let the curds settle.

continued on next page…

Derby continued...

Variation: *Sage Derby:*
Wash 1 cup (250 mL)
fresh sage leaves. Chop
roughly and place in a
small bowl. Boil 2 cups
(500 mL) water and
pour over the leaves.
Let infuse for 30 minutes
or until cooled. Pour
sage and liquid over
the cut curds in Step 8
before adding salt. Mix
in thoroughly and let
soak for 15 minutes.
Drain off remaining
liquid. Add salt, tossing
well to blend. Continue
with recipe.

7. Carefully pour off the whey, leaving the curds in the bottom of the pot. Press the curds down lightly with your hand to help them knit together. Put the lid back on the pot to keep the curds warm. Let stand for 15 minutes. Turn the curd mass over in the pot, pressing again with your hands, more firmly this time, to expel more whey. Drain off any collected whey. Keeping warm, continue turning the curd mass in the pot, pressing each time, every 15 minutes for 1 hour.

8. Place the cheese on a cutting board and cut curd mass into 1-inch by ½-inch (2.5 by 1.25 cm) pieces. Place in a bowl and toss with salt.

9. Fill prepared mold with curds, pressing down firmly as you fill. Pull cloth up neatly around curds and fold excess snugly over the top, with as few wrinkles as possible. Put on the lid.

10. Place mold in cheese press or place a weight on top. Press at medium pressure for 30 minutes. Remove from press and re-dress (see Tips, page 255). Continue pressing at firm pressure for 12 hours or overnight.

11. Remove cheese from press unwrap. Dry on a cheese mat placed on a rack at room temperature for 3 days, turning daily to aid drying, or until fairly dry to the touch (see Tips, page 255).

12. Coat cheese with 2 or 3 layers of cheese wax (see page 21). Ripen at 54° to 60°F (12° to 16°C) for at least 1 month, preferably for 3 months. Turn cheese weekly to ensure even ripening. Once ripened to your taste, wrap and store in the refrigerator.

Double Gloucester

Makes
$3\frac{1}{4}$ lbs (1.6 kg)

10% yield

Double Gloucester is a hard cheese that originated in south central England. It has a smooth, firm and waxy texture and a mild, rich flavor. It is often tinted yellow with annatto, a natural colorant derived from the seeds of a South American plant.

- Cloth-lined colander
- 1 tomme mold, lined with cheese cloth
- Cheese press
- Cheese matting

16 quarts	whole milk	16 L
$\frac{1}{2}$ tsp	mesophilic culture	2.5 mL
$\frac{1}{8}$ tsp	annatto, optional	0.65 mL
$\frac{3}{4}$ tsp	calcium chloride	3.75 mL
$\frac{3}{4}$ tsp	liquid rennet	3.75 mL
3 tbsp	pickling (canning) or kosher salt	45 mL
	Cheese wax	

1. Sterilize all equipment (see page 40). In a large stainless-steel pot set in a hot water bath over medium heat, warm milk to 90°F (32°C), stirring gently. Turn off heat.

2. Sprinkle culture over surface of milk and let stand for about 5 minutes to rehydrate. Using skimmer and an up-and-down motion, gently draw culture down into milk without breaking surface of milk. Cover and let ripen for 1 hour, maintaining the temperature at 90°F (32°C).

3. Dilute annatto, if using, in $\frac{1}{4}$ cup (50 mL) cool water and stir into milk. Let stand for 15 minutes. Annatto must be incorporated into the milk at least 15 minutes before the rennet is added because it interferes with the coagulation.

4. Dilute calcium chloride in $\frac{1}{4}$ cup (50 mL) cool water. Add to milk using the same up-and-down motion:

5. Dilute rennet in $\frac{1}{4}$ cup (50 mL) cool water. Add to milk and, using the same up-and-down motion, draw rennet down into milk until well blended. Cover pot and let set for 45 minutes, maintaining the temperature.

6. Check for a clean break (see Tip, page 215). If necessary, let set for another 5 to 10 minutes or until you achieve a clean break. Using a long-bladed knife and skimmer, cut curd into $\frac{1}{4}$-inch (0.5 cm) pieces, using the skimmer to lift and move the curds gently to ensure all are cut. Stir gently for 15 minutes.

continued on next page…

Double Gloucester continued...

Tips: To re-dress the cheese, remove the mold from the press. Remove the cheese from the mold and unwrap. Place the cloth back in the mold; turn the cheese over and put back in the mold, then rewrap. Return mold to the press.

7. Return heat to low and slowly warm curds to 99°F (37°C), stirring gently and continuously, adjusting the heat as necessary to make sure it takes 45 minutes to do so. Do not heat too quickly. Let curds settle. Hold for 20 minutes.

8. Pour contents of pot into a cloth-lined colander. Return curds to pot. Press curds down with your hands into a flat cake to help them mat. Cover the pot and hold for 15 minutes. Turn cake of curd over in the pot. Cover and hold for another 15 minutes.

9. Cut curd mass into 4 pieces and pile them one on top of the other in the pot. Cover and hold for 15 minutes. Turn the whole stack of curd over. Cover and hold for another 15 minutes.

10. Place the curd on a cutting board and cut into 1-inch by 1/2-inch (2.5 by 1.25 cm) pieces. Place in a bowl and toss with salt. Fill prepared mold with curds, pressing down firmly as you fill. Pull cloth up neatly around curds and fold excess snugly over the top, with as few wrinkles as possible. Put on the lid.

11. Place mold in cheese press or place a weight on top. Press cheese at medium pressure for 1 hour. Remove from press and re-dress (see Tip, left). Continue pressing at firm pressure for several hours or overnight.

12. Remove cheese from press and unwrap. Dry cheese on a cheese mat placed on a rack at room temperature for 2 to 3 days, turning once or twice, until fairly dry to the touch (see Tips, page 255).

13. Coat cheese with 2 or 3 layers of cheese wax (see page 21). Ripen at 47°F (8°C) for at least 1 month or for up to 6 months for sharper flavor. Turn cheese weekly to ensure even ripening. Once ripened to your taste, wrap and store in the refrigerator.

Ossau-Iraty

**Makes about
3 lbs (1.5 kg)**

18% yield

Pronounced "OH-so
eer-ah-TEE," this is a
sheep's milk cheese from
the Pyrenees region of
southwestern France.
The dry hills and valleys
are home to large flocks
of sheep that are moved
in early summer from
the valley pastures to
the higher mountain
meadows and back down
again in the fall. This is
called "transhumance"
and was traditionally
carried out on foot, the
shepherds driving huge
flocks of sheep over a
period of several days
up to summer grazing
pastures. Nowadays,
it is more common for
stock trailers to do the
legwork, but the cheese
made from the summer
milk is just as good.

- Cloth-lined colander
- 1 tomme mold, lined with cheese cloth
- Cheese press
- Cheese matting
- Ripening container

8 quarts	sheep's milk	8 L
Generous 1/4 tsp	mesophilic culture	Generous 1.25 mL
Generous 1/4 tsp	calcium chloride	Generous 1.25 mL
1/4 tsp	liquid rennet	1.25 mL
3 tbsp	pickling (canning) or kosher salt	45 mL
	Cheese wax	

1. Sterilize all equipment (see page 40). In a large stainless-steel pot set in a hot water bath over medium heat, warm milk to 90°F (32°C), stirring gently. Turn off heat.

2. Sprinkle culture over surface of milk and let stand for about 5 minutes to rehydrate. Using skimmer and an up-and-down motion, gently draw culture down into milk without breaking surface of milk. Cover and let ripen for 45 minutes, maintaining the temperature at 90°F (32°C).

3. Dilute calcium chloride in 1/4 cup (50 mL) cool water. Add to milk using the same up-and-down motion.

4. Dilute rennet in 1/4 cup (50 mL) cool water. Add to milk and, using the same up-and-down motion, draw rennet down into milk until well blended. Cover pot and let set for 30 to 40 minutes, maintaining the temperature.

5. Check for a clean break (see Tip, page 215). If necessary, let set for another 5 to 10 minutes or until you achieve a clean break. Using a long-bladed knife and skimmer, cut curd into 1/2-inch (1.25 cm) cubes, using the skimmer to lift and move the curds gently to ensure all are cut. Let stand for 5 minutes to firm up.

continued on next page…

Ossau-Iraty continued...

Serving suggestion:
Ossau-Iraty is a firm cheese with an unctuous consistency. It can be enjoyed at any time alone or in a cheese dish. A delicious Basque custom is to serve Ossau-Iraty with black cherry jam or preserves. If you do not have black cherries, substitute a good-quality strawberry jam.

6. Return heat to low and slowly warm curds to 100°F (38°C), stirring gently and continuously, adjusting the heat as necessary to make sure it takes 30 minutes to do so. Do not heat too quickly. Cover and hold for 10 minutes.

7. Pour contents of pot into a cloth-lined colander. Cover curds in the colander with the pot lid to keep warm. Let drain for 1 hour. Break up the curds once or twice during this time to aid in draining, but do not squeeze them.

8. Place drained curd in a large bowl and break up with your hands, creating pieces about ¾ inch (2 cm) in size. Sprinkle salt over curds and toss together. Do not squeeze curds, handling them lightly.

9. Pack curds down into prepared mold, pressing down firmly as you fill. Pull cloth up neatly around curds and fold excess snugly over the top, with as few wrinkles as possible. Put on the lid.

10. Place mold in cheese press or place a weight on top. Press at light to medium pressure for 15 minutes. Increase to medium pressure and press for another 15 minutes. Remove from press and re-dress (see Tip, page 280). Continue pressing at firm pressure for several hours or overnight.

11. Remove cheese from press and unwrap. Dry cheese on a cheese mat placed on a rack at room temperature for 2 days, turning once or twice to aid drying, or until fairly dry to the touch (see Tips, page 255).

12. Place cheese on a clean cheese mat in a ripening container and ripen at 54°F (12°C) and 85% humidity for at least 10 weeks or for up to 6 months for sharper flavor. Turn cheese daily for the first week, wiping the rind with a simple brine solution, then twice weekly thereafter. After 2 months, turn the cheese and rub the rind with a dry cloth once a week. Once ripened to your taste, wrap and store in the refrigerator.

French Tomme

Makes
3¼ lbs (1.6 kg)
10% yield

In southern France, the local farmers' cows are kept on high summer pastures, where they produce an abundance of fresh milk. Hard pressed cheeses similar to this one are made to preserve this bounty for customers who eagerly await their arrival from the mountains in the fall. The cheeses are divided up among the farmers, who then continue aging them at home or sell them to consumers.

- Cloth-lined colander
- 1 tomme mold, lined with cheese cloth
- Cheese press
- Cheese matting
- Draining container
- Ripening container

16 quarts	whole milk	16 L
½ tsp	thermophilic culture	2.5 mL
½ tsp	calcium chloride	2.5 mL
½ tsp	liquid rennet	2.5 mL
	Pickling (canning) or kosher salt	

1. Sterilize all equipment (see page 40). In a large stainless-steel pot set in a hot water bath over medium heat, warm milk to 106°F (41°C), stirring gently. Turn off heat.

2. Sprinkle culture over surface of milk and let stand for about 5 minutes to rehydrate. Using skimmer and an up-and-down motion, gently draw culture down into milk without breaking surface of milk.

3. Dilute calcium chloride in ¼ cup (50 mL) cool water. Add to milk using the same up-and-down motion.

4. Dilute rennet in ¼ cup (50 mL) cool water. Add to milk and, using the same up-and-down motion, draw rennet down into milk until well blended. Cover pot and let set for 45 minutes, maintaining the temperature at 106°F (41°C).

5. Check for a clean break (see Tip, page 215). If necessary, let set for another 5 to 10 minutes or until you achieve a clean break. Using a long-bladed knife and skimmer, cut curds into ¾-inch (2 cm) cubes, using the skimmer to lift and move the curds gently to ensure all are cut. Let stand for 20 minutes. Gently stir curds for 30 minutes or until they begin to mat. Let curds settle.

6. Pour contents of pot into a cloth-lined colander. Let drain for 10 minutes.

continued on next page…

7. Fill prepared mold with curds. Pull cloth up neatly around curds and fold excess snugly over the top, with as few wrinkles as possible. Put the lid on.

8. Place mold in cheese press or place a weight on top. Press at light pressure for 1 to 2 hours. Remove from press and re-dress (see Tip, page 280). Continue pressing at medium pressure for 12 hours. Re-dress again and continue pressing at firm pressure for another 12 hours.

9. Remove cheese from press. Unwrap and place on a cheese mat on a rack in a draining container. Sprinkle top surface of cheese with 2 tsp (10 mL) salt. Rub in well. Let stand at room temperature for 24 hours. Turn cheese and salt the other side in same manner. Rub in well. Let stand at room temperature for another 24 hours.

10. Place cheese on a clean cheese mat in a ripening container. Ripen at 60°F (16°C) and 85% humidity for 6 weeks for a mild cheese or for up to 6 months for more-developed, stronger flavor. Turn cheese daily, rubbing the surface with a soft cheese brush. When cheese has reached desired ripeness, wrap and store in the refrigerator.

Raw Milk Tomme

Makes
3½ lbs (1.75 kg)
10% yield

If you are lucky enough to live on a farm or have access to raw milk, then here's a tomme recipe that makes the most of it. Remember that any time you are using raw milk, you must be absolutely sure of your source and use it as soon as possible after the cows are milked. Making this with evening milk is easiest because of the time required. Ripen this cheese for at least 5 months for authenticity; a minimum of 60 days is recommended to guarantee that your raw milk cheese is safe for consumption. This is great cheese to try if you have a natural cave for ripening.

- Cloth-lined colander
- 1 tomme mold, lined with cheese cloth
- Cheese press
- Cheese matting
- Ripening container

16 quarts	raw milk	16 L
¾ tsp	liquid rennet	3.75 mL
	Cool 18% saturated brine solution (see Tip, page 223)	

1. Sterilize a large stainless-steel pot (see page 40). In pot, ripen milk in a cool (50°F/10°C) room for 12 hours.

2. Sterilize all other equipment. Set pot of ripened milk in a hot water bath over low heat. Warm milk to 81°F (27°C), stirring gently. Turn off heat.

3. Dilute rennet in ¼ cup (50 mL) cool water. Using skimmer and an up-and-down motion, gently draw rennet down into milk, without breaking surface of milk, until well blended. Cover pot and let set for 1 hour, maintaining the temperature at 81°F (27°C).

4. Check for a clean break (see Tip, page 215). If necessary, let set for another 10 to 15 minutes or until you achieve a clean break. Using a long-handled whisk and skimmer, cut curd into very small bits, about the size of rice grains, using the skimmer to lift and move the curds gently to ensure all are cut. Let stand for 10 minutes to firm up.

5. Pour contents of pot into a cloth-lined colander. Cover curds in the colander with the pot lid to keep warm. Let drain for 2 hours, breaking curds up and mixing with your hands 3 times during this period to aid draining.

6. Fill prepared mold with curds. Pull cloth up neatly around curds and fold excess snugly over the top, with as few wrinkles as possible. Put on the lid.

continued on next page…

Tip: The rind should be fairly dry, or, as someone explained it to me, "like a clammy handshake." If completely dry, the closed rind could crack, allowing bacteria to enter the interior of the cheese.

7. Place mold in cheese press or place a weight on top. Press at low pressure for 30 minutes. Remove from press and re-dress (see Tip, page 280). Continue pressing at medium pressure for 30 minutes. Re-dress again and continue pressing at firm pressure for 12 hours.

8. Remove cheese from press. Unwrap and place in brine solution for 20 hours, turning over after 10 hours.

9. Remove cheese from brine. Dry cheese on a cheese mat placed on a rack at room temperature for 2 to 3 days, turning daily to aid drying, or until fairly dry to the touch (see Tip, left).

10. Place cheese on a clean cheese mat in a ripening container. Ripen at 54°F (12°C) and 85% humidity, turning every second day, for 5 to 15 months or until desired sharpness is attained. Remove any collected whey, wiping bottom of container with paper towel. The rind should harden and may develop one or more kinds of mold. Wipe weekly with a cloth or soft cheese brush to help develop the rind. Once ripened to your taste, wrap and store in the refrigerator.

Colonia

Makes
3¼ lbs (1.6 kg)
10% yield

Colonia is a semifirm cheese originally made in Uruguay by European settlers, namely the Swiss. Traditionally, it is made of raw milk and used as a grating or table cheese.

Tip: To remove one-third of the whey, simply measure one-third of the way down the pot. You are removing whey until the surface of the curds is just visible under the whey.

- Cloth-lined colander
- 1 tomme mold, lined with cheese cloth
- Cheese press
- Cheese matting
- Ripening container

16 quarts	whole milk	16 L
½ tsp	thermophilic culture	2.5 mL
¾ tsp	calcium chloride	3.75 mL
¾ tsp	liquid rennet	3.75 mL
	Cool 18% saturated brine (see Tip, page 223)	

1. Sterilize all equipment (see page 40). In a large stainless-steel pot set in a hot water bath over medium heat, warm milk to 93°F (34°C), stirring gently. Turn off heat.

2. Sprinkle culture over surface of milk and let stand for about 5 minutes to rehydrate. Using skimmer and an up-and-down motion, gently draw culture down into milk without breaking surface of milk. Cover and let ripen for 45 minutes, maintaining temperature at 93°F (34°C).

3. Dilute calcium chloride in ¼ cup (50 mL) cool water. Add to milk using the same up-and-down motion.

4. Dilute rennet in ¼ cup (50 mL) cool water. Add to milk and, using the same up-and-down motion, draw rennet down into milk until well blended. Cover pot and let set for 1 hour, maintaining the temperature.

5. Check for a clean break (see Tip, page 215). If necessary, let set for another 10 to 15 minutes or until you achieve a clean break. Using a long-handled whisk and skimmer, cut curds into pea-size pieces, using the skimmer to lift and move the curds gently to ensure all are cut. Let stand for 5 minutes to firm up. Stir gently for 25 minutes. Let curds settle.

6. Using a measuring cup, dip off about 30% (see Tip, left) of the whey, or until the curds are just barely visible under the whey. Stir for 5 minutes.

continued on next page…

7. Add enough 140° to 160°F (60° to 71°C) water to replace about half the amount of whey that was removed and to bring the temperature of the curds to 100°F (38°C) (see Tips, page 187).

8. Return heat to low and slowly continue to warm curds to 108°F (42°C), stirring gently and continuously, adjusting the heat as necessary to make sure it takes 35 minutes to do so. Do not heat too quickly. Turn off heat and let curds settle.

9. Pour contents of pot into a cloth-lined colander. Let curds drain for 5 minutes.

10. Fill prepared mold with curds. Pull cloth up neatly around curds and fold excess snugly over the top, with as few wrinkles as possible. Put on the lid.

11. Place mold in cheese press or place a weight on top. Press at medium pressure for 1 hour. Remove from press and re-dress (see Tip, page 280). Continue pressing at firm pressure for 12 hours or overnight.

12. Remove cheese from press. Unwrap and place in brine solution for 20 hours, turning over after 10 hours.

13. Remove cheese from brine. Dry cheese on a cheese mat placed on a rack at room temperature for 2 to 3 days, turning once or twice, or until fairly dry to the touch (see Tip, page 286).

14. Place cheese on a clean cheese mat in a ripening container. Ripen at 54°F (12°C) and 90% humidity for 2 weeks. Turn cheese daily and remove any collected whey, wiping bottom of container with paper towel. Keep covered and make sure the cheese doesn't dry out.

15. After 2 weeks, increase temperature to 72°F (22°C) for 1 week to aid in the formation of eyes, or holes, in the cheese. After 1 week, return cheese to the cooler ripening area and continue ripening for 4 to 6 months, or longer for more flavor. Once ripened to your taste, wrap and store in the refrigerator.

Troubleshooting

The cheese is difficult to press and, after pressing, shows cracks in the surface even though it has been pressed firmly. The finished cheese is dry and crumbly.
The curd was cooked to too high a temperature, making it too dry; watch cooking temperature carefully. Or the curd was stirred too long and lost too much whey; test the curd during cooking for correct texture.

The cheese has light-colored spots in the paste.
The curd was not cut and stirred evenly, leaving large chunks of moist curd in the cheese when pressed. Or the cheese was pressed too quickly at too high a pressure; begin pressing lightly to knit the curd and gradually increase the pressure. Or the curd was cooked too fast, making the outer skin of each curd too hard and trapping moisture within; cook slowly, according to the recipe's recommendations.

The texture of the finished cheese is rubbery.
Too much rennet in the curd; reduce rennet. Or the lactic bacteria was too weak; next time use a fresh culture. Or a washed-curd cheese was too diluted during washing; remove less whey when washing the curd or add less water after whey removal.

The cheese puffs up and splits soon after making.
There are yeasts or coliform bacteria in the milk; the cheese must be thrown out. Always use the highest-quality milk and maintain scrupulous hygiene standards.

The cheese puffs up and splits after 1 to 2 months of ripening.
There are bacteria in the milk that cause gas development; pasteurize correctly. Or there are legumes or silage in the animal feed; eliminate or increase quality of silage fed and remove legumes from fodder. The cheese is still safe to eat.

continued on next page…

The rind on a natural-rind cheese, especially an older one, seems dusty and may rot or deteriorate.
Your ripening area could have cheese mites that bore into the rind; clean and sanitize the ripening area thoroughly. Cheese whose rind is infested with cheese mites is still edible.

The rind of an aging cheese is greasy.
Too much fat in the cheese (especially Cheddar); use lower-fat milk. Or the temperature in the ripening area is too high; reduce temperature.

A waxed cheese develops "bruised" spots, which then start to rot down into the cheese.
Moisture pockets under the wax contain bacteria that begin to destroy the cheese; be sure the cheese is dry before waxing. Or the wax has a small hole in it and bacteria have entered; be sure the wax coating is thick enough and remains intact throughout ripening. If you find rotting spots in your waxed cheese, cut open the wax and cut out the rot. Use right away or try re-waxing and continue ripening. Monitor the cheese closely.

Cheese puffs up when removed from the brine.
Moisture has soaked into the cheese; increase the salt content of the brine. Or bacteria are present and have caused gas production; keep brine at 55° to 60°F (13° to 16°C) and salt content at approximately 20% to 25% salinity (18° to 20° Baumé; measure with brine meter).

Ethnic and Regional Cheeses

Throughout the centuries, simple cheeses have been made by most cultures and ethnic groups under varying, sometimes primitive, conditions. In this chapter, we will look at some of these original and often lesser-known cheeses. Sometimes you "had to have been there" to enjoy them, but one of the wonderful things about cheese is that there is something for every taste.

Feta

Makes
3½ to 4¼ lbs
(1.75 to 2.25 kg)

12 to 18% yield

Feta is a Greek word, meaning "slice." This cheese is beloved the world over and is especially popular on salads and in baked savories. Feta cheese originated with shepherds on the dry hillsides of the Balkans. It was made exclusively of goat's or sheep's milk, which is how it's still made today. It is stored in a brine solution, which allows it to be kept at warmer temperatures for long periods of time. If removed from the brine, the cheese will dry out quite quickly.

- Cloth-lined colander
- 1 tomme mold or 1-quart (1 L) plastic berry basket

12 quarts	goat's or sheep's milk	12 L
½ tsp	mesophilic culture	1.25 mL
½ tsp	liquid rennet	2.5 mL
	10% brine solution (see Tip, opposite)	

1. Sterilize all equipment (see page 40). In a large stainless-steel pot over medium-low heat, warm milk to 86°F (30°C), stirring gently to prevent scorching. Remove from heat.

2. Sprinkle culture over surface of milk and let stand for about 5 minutes to rehydrate. Using skimmer and an up-and-down motion, gently draw culture down into milk without breaking surface of milk. Cover and let ripen for 1 hour, maintaining temperature at 86°F (30°C).

3. Dilute rennet in ¼ cup (50 mL) cool water. Add to milk and, using the same up-and-down motion, draw rennet down into milk until well blended. Cover and let set for 30 minutes, maintaining the temperature.

4. Check for a clean break (see Tip, page 315). If necessary, let set for another 10 minutes or until you achieve a clean break. Using a long-bladed knife and skimmer, cut curd into ¾-inch (2 cm) cubes (see Tip, page 300). Let stand for 5 minutes to firm up.

5. Stir curds gently for 20 minutes for a softer cheese or for 30 minutes for a firmer cheese. The curds will firm up and shrink. Let stand for 5 minutes.

6. Ladle curds into a cloth-lined colander. Let drain for 5 minutes. Fill mold with curds. (The curd is quite soft to begin with but drains quite quickly, firming up enough to flip after 10 minutes.)

7. Let drain for 1 hour, flipping cheese in the mold every 15 minutes or so to aid draining. After 1 hour, let drain at room temperature, without flipping, for 18 to 24 hours or until cheese is quite firm.

Tip: To make a 10% brine solution: In a large plastic container with a lid, dissolve 1 lb (500 g) salt in 4 quarts (1 L) water.

Variation: *Cow's Milk Feta:* Follow the recipe, but in Step 2, when adding the culture, add ⅛ tsp (0.65 mL) lipase, an enzyme present in goat's and sheep's milk that gives them a stronger flavor.

8. Remove cheese from mold and place in brine solution. Cover container and let stand at room temperature for 3 or 4 days to aid in flavor development. After this time, you can refrigerate the cheese in the brine. If you will be using your feta soon (within 3 to 4 weeks after production), you do not need to worry about the brine pH. However, if you are making enough feta to store for long-term use, it is important to watch the pH or the cheese will not store well. Measure the pH of the brine once the cheese has been in it for about 4 days. It should be between 4.8 and 5.2; if the pH is higher than 5.2, add 1 tbsp (15 mL) white vinegar and test again in 24 hours.

Troubleshooting

Feta immersed in brine turns soft and mushy.
The brine is not acidic enough; measure with pH strips or a pH meter and lower the pH level to the optimum 4.8 to 5.2. To lower the pH, add acid in the form of white vinegar or whey from acidic cheeses, such as Cheddar.

Feta is very hard.
Curd was stirred too long; shorten stirring time.

Paneer

Makes 14 oz (400 g)
10% yield

Also spelled panir, *this cheese is a favorite in Indian cuisine. Essentially a simple acid-coagulated cheese, it can be made quickly and used in any number of dishes. Because it is not salted, it works in both savory and sweet recipes. It spoils quickly, so use it within 5 days.*

- **Cloth-lined colander**

4 quarts	whole milk	4 L
4 tbsp	freshly squeezed lemon juice, approx.	60 mL

1. Sterilize all equipment (see page 40). In a large stainless-steel pot over low heat, slowly bring milk to a boil, stirring gently to prevent scorching. Remove from heat.

2. Add lemon juice. Stir for 5 minutes or until milk begins to curdle and the solids rise to the top. If it does not curdle, add another 2 tbsp (30 mL) lemon juice and continue stirring.

3. Pour contents of pot into a cloth-lined colander. Let curds drain. Rinse curds with cold running water, then twist them in the cloth to remove as much of the water as possible.

4. Twist the cloth tightly around the cheese and place on a plate. Cover with another plate and place a 2-lb (1 kg) weight on top. Place in the refrigerator overnight.

5. Unwrap cheese and place in a small bowl. Cover and store in the refrigerator for up to 5 days.

Cumin Paneer

Makes 14 oz (400 g)

10% yield

This flavorful variation on fresh paneer keeps longer than the traditional one because of the added salt. The delicate aroma of cumin adds a whiff of the exotic to this cheese. Use it on vegetables, in curries or as a dip with flatbread.

- Cloth-lined colander

4 quarts	whole milk	4 L
½ tsp	cumin seeds	2.5 mL
2 tsp	salt	10 mL
4 tbsp	freshly squeezed lemon juice, approx.	60 mL

1. Sterilize all equipment (see page 40). In a large stainless-steel pot over low heat, combine milk, cumin seeds and salt. Slowly bring to a boil; boil for 2 to 3 minutes, stirring gently the whole time to prevent scorching. Remove from heat.

2. Add lemon juice. Continue to stir milk until milk curdles and the solids rise to the top. If it does not curdle, add another 2 tbsp (30 mL) lemon juice and continue stirring.

3. Pour contents of pot into a cloth-lined colander. Twist curds in the cloth to remove as much of the moisture as possible.

4. Twist the cloth tightly around the cheese and place on a plate. Cover with another plate and place a 2-lb (1 kg) weight on top. Place in the refrigerator overnight.

5. Unwrap cheese and place in a small bowl. Cover and store in the refrigerator for up to 2 weeks.

Queso Blanco

Makes 14 oz (400 g)

10% yield

This is the Latin American version of an acid-coagulated cheese, a very simple one that can be used with great variation in cooking. Stir-fry it with vegetables, toss with pasta or salad, or pan-fry slices and drizzle them with olive oil.

- Cloth-lined colander

| 4 quarts | whole milk | 4 L |
| 1/4 cup | white vinegar, approx. | 50 mL |

1. Sterilize all equipment (see page 40). In a large stainless-steel pot over medium heat, warm milk to 180°F (82°C), stirring gently to prevent scorching. Reduce heat to low and hold at this temperature for several minutes. The temperature may gain a few degrees, but make sure it doesn't go above 185°F (85°C). Remove from heat.

2. Add vinegar. Stir milk continuously for 10 minutes or until milk curdles and the solids rise to the top. If it does not curdle, add another 1 tbsp (15 mL) vinegar and continue stirring.

3. Pour contents of pot into a cloth-lined colander. Let curds drain for 15 to 30 minutes. Gather the corners of the cloth together and tie to form a bag. Hang the bag and let drain for 6 to 7 hours.

4. Unwrap cheese and place in a small bowl. Cover and store in the refrigerator for up to 1 week.

Halloumi

Makes 2 lbs (1 kg)
10% yield

A specialty of Cyprus, halloumi is made of goat's or sheep's milk, or a mixture of both. For authenticity, never use cow's milk for this cheese. The addition of fresh mint gives it a unique character and looks beautiful when sliced across the grain to expose the mint leaves sandwiched within the fold of the cheese. Grill or pan-fry halloumi and serve with other Mediterranean-style foods for a special meal or snack.

- 1 tomme mold, lined with cheese cloth
- Cheese press

10 quarts	goat's or sheep's milk, or a blend of both	10 L
¾ tsp	liquid rennet	3.75 mL
	Pickling (canning) or kosher salt	
	Fresh mint leaves	

1. Sterilize all equipment (see page 40). In a large stainless-steel pot over medium heat, warm milk to 90°F (32°C), stirring gently to prevent scorching. Remove from heat.

2. Dilute rennet in ¼ cup (50 mL) cool water. Using skimmer and an up-and-down motion, gently draw rennet down into milk, without breaking surface of milk, until well blended. Cover and let set for 45 minutes, maintaining the temperature at 90°F (32°C).

3. Check for a clean break (see Tip, page 315). Using a long-bladed knife and skimmer, cut curd into 1-inch (2.5 cm) cubes (see Tip, page 300). Let stand for 5 minutes.

4. Return heat to low and slowly warm curds to 104°F (40°C), stirring slowly, gently and continuously, adjusting heat as necessary to make sure it takes 40 minutes to do so. Do not heat too quickly. Once temperature is reached, continue to stir for another 20 minutes to firm up the curds. Let settle.

5. Using skimmer, ladle curds into prepared mold, reserving whey in the pot for Step 7. Pull cloth up neatly around curds and fold excess snugly over the top, with as few wrinkles as possible. Put on the lid.

6. Place mold in cheese press or place a weight on top. Press at medium pressure for 3 to 4 hours.

7. Remove cheese from press and unwrap. Place on a clean cutting board. Using a knife, cut into 4-inch (10 cm) squares that are about 1 inch (2.5 cm) thick. Heat the reserved whey in the pot to 190°F (88°C).

continued on next page…

Halloumi continued...

8. Place pieces of curd in the hot whey. At first, they will sink but they will rise to the top again when they are properly textured. Using a skimmer, lift pieces from the hot whey and place on a clean plate or cutting board to drain. Let cool for 15 minutes.

9. Sprinkle top surface of each cheese with ¼ tsp (1.25 mL) salt. Place a few mint leaves along one edge of each piece. Fold piece in half to enclose mint and create a "sandwich."

10. Turn cheeses over. Let drain and dry until completely cool.

11. Place cheese in a container and cover with brine made with 2 cups (500 mL) water and ¼ cup (50 mL) salt. Cover container and store in the refrigerator for up to 6 months.

Libyan Sheep's Milk Cheese

Makes
3¼ lbs (1.6 kg)
20% yield

This is a soft, milky cheese from northern Africa that's brushed with olive oil during curing. It can be eaten after 3 weeks of ripening or aged longer for a more piquant flavor.

- 2 tomme molds, or 5 to 6 smaller molds, such as St-Marcellin, or a combination
- Draining container
- Cheese matting
- Ripening container

8 quarts	sheep's milk	8 L
⅛ tsp	mesophilic culture	0.65 mL
¼ tsp	liquid rennet	1.25 mL
	Pickling (canning) or kosher salt	
	Olive oil	

1. Sterilize all equipment (see page 40). In a large stainless-steel pot over medium-low heat, warm milk to 88°F (31°C), stirring gently to prevent scorching. Remove from heat.

2. Sprinkle culture over surface of milk and let stand for about 5 minutes to rehydrate. Using skimmer and an up-and-down motion, gently draw culture down into milk without breaking surface of milk.

3. Dilute rennet in ¼ cup (50 mL) cool water. Add to milk and, using the same up-and-down motion, draw rennet down into milk until well blended. Cover and let set for 1 hour, maintaining the temperature at 88°F (31°C).

4. Check for a clean break (see Tip, page 315). If necessary, let set for another 10 to 30 minutes or until you achieve a clean break. A firm curd should form.

5. Using a long-bladed knife and skimmer, cut curd into ½-inch (1.25 cm) cubes (see Tip, page 300). Let stand for 5 minutes. Stir curds gently for 5 minutes. Let settle.

6. Using a measuring cup, dip off the whey until you can see the surface of the curds. Place molds on a rack in a draining container. Ladle curds into molds.

continued on next page…

Libyan Sheep's Milk Cheese continued...

Tip: To cut curds: Holding a long-bladed stainless-steel knife straight up and down, draw knife through the curd, cutting it into strips. Proceed across the pot until you have reached the other side. Turn the pot and cut across the first strips to create squares. Using a skimmer, cut horizontally from side to side just under the surface of the curd to create cubes. Gradually move skimmer down through curd to cut layers of cubes. Using skimmer, gently stir curd cubes. Using a knife, cut any pieces that have been missed or are too large. For small-cut curds, you can use a large whisk for cutting.

7. Let drain at room temperature for 3 to 4 hours, turning cheeses in the molds once or twice. Remove from molds. Sprinkle each side of each cheese with 1 tsp (5 mL) salt, or if you have used the 5 smaller molds, divide the salt up over 5 cheeses, and rub into the surface.

8. Place cheeses on a cheese mat in a ripening container. Ripen at 50°F (10°C) and 85% to 90% humidity. Turn cheeses daily, removing any collected whey from the bottom of the container and wiping with paper towel. Brush or rub rind with olive oil every 3 days. The cheeses are ready to eat 3 weeks after production, though you can continue aging the cheese for a stronger flavor.

Tomme d'Arles

Makes 16 cheeses, each 3 oz (90 g), or 8 cheeses, each 6 oz (175 g)

In days gone by, large flocks of sheep were tended in the Camargue region of southern France. Once the lambs were marketed in late spring, the sheep were milked to produce this small cheese. In the days of no refrigeration, the cheeses were salted then dried and stored in jute sacks. When needed, they were rehydrated by layering them with bay leaves in a terra-cotta jar and pouring in a glass of local brandy. The cheeses were then placed in a cool cellar for 2 to 3 weeks before they were ready for the table. This recipe is a modern rendition for artisanal cheese makers.

- 16 Crottin or 8 St-Marcellin molds
- Draining container
- Cheese matting

4 quarts	sheep's milk	4 L
⅛ tsp	mesophilic culture	0.65 mL
⅛ tsp	liquid rennet	0.65 mL
	Pickling (canning) or kosher salt	
	Ground black pepper	
	Dried thyme	
	Brandy or eau de vie of your choice, optional	
	Fresh or dried bay leaves, optional	

1. Sterilize all equipment (see page 40). In a large stainless-steel pot over low heat, warm milk to 90°F (32°C), stirring gently to prevent scorching. Remove from heat.

2. Sprinkle culture over surface of milk and let stand for about 5 minutes to rehydrate. Using skimmer and an up-and-down motion, gently draw culture down into milk without breaking surface of milk.

3. Dilute rennet in 2 tbsp (30 mL) cool water. Add to milk and, using the same up-and-down motion, draw rennet down into milk until well blended. Cover and let set for 1 hour at warm (77° to 86°F/25° to 30°C) room temperature. If the room is cool, cover pot with a towel or blanket to maintain temperature of milk at between 77° and 86°F (25° and 30°C).

4. Check for a clean break (see Tip, page 315). Using a long-bladed knife and skimmer, cut curd into 2-inch (5 cm) cubes. Let stand for 10 minutes.

5. Using a measuring cup, dip off any whey that has collected on the surface of the curds.

6. Place molds on a rack in a draining container. Ladle curd into molds, continuing to top off until all the curd is used. It will take time for the curds to drain down, but all the curd will fit into the molds. Do not be tempted to add more molds. Let drain for 2 hours.

continued on next page...

7. Flip cheeses in molds. Continue draining at room temperature for 24 hours, flipping in the molds several times.

8. Remove cheeses from molds. Dry cheeses on a cheese mat placed on a rack for 2 hours.

9. Sprinkle top surface of cheeses with a mixture of salt, pepper and dried thyme to taste. Let stand for 30 minutes. Turn cheeses over and season other side in same manner.

10. If desired, drizzle cheeses with brandy and top with a bay leaf.

11. Store in a covered container in the refrigerator for up to 2 weeks.

Fromage Fort

1 lb	leftover cheese, 3 or more varieties (see Tip, left)	500 g
2	cloves garlic, peeled	2
½ cup	dry white wine, approx.	125 mL
	Freshly ground black pepper	
	Chopped fresh herbs, such as parsley or tarragon, or spices, to taste, optional	
	Salt to taste	

Makes 1 lb (500 g)

This "strong cheese" is not so much a cheese as a cheese spread. Depending on the cheeses you include and the other ingredients you add, it can be creamy and savory, or very assertive indeed. This is an infinitely variable recipe, an opportunity to experiment with different cheeses and flavorings.

Tip: Use at least three kinds of cheese. The more types you use, the more interesting your fromage fort will be.

Variations: Try adding olive oil, olives, sun-dried tomatoes, shallots or brandy.

1. Remove any mold or dry edges from cheese and cut into equal-size pieces. Place in a food processor or blender.

2. Add garlic, wine, pepper, and herbs or spices, if using. Process for 1 to 2 minutes or until creamy. Do not overprocess. Add a little more wine if mixture seems dry.

3. Pack mixture into small jars. Cover and store in the refrigerator for up to 2 weeks. Many aficionados maintain that this mixture improves with aging in a dark cellar.

4. Let come to room temperature before using. Spread on sliced baguette, crackers or toast.

Chestnut Leaf–Wrapped Goat Cheese

<table>
<tr><td>

Makes 5 cheeses, each 4 oz (125 g)

15% yield

</td></tr>
</table>

- Cloth-lined colander
- 5 St-Marcellin molds
- Draining container
- Cheese matting
- Ripening container
- Strips of raffia or cord for tying

4 quarts	raw or pasteurized goat's milk (see Tip, opposite)	4 L
⅛ tsp	liquid rennet	0.65 mL
	Pickling (canning) or kosher salt	
	Large fresh chestnut leaves (30 to 35 depending on size)	
¼ cup	brandy or eau de vie of your choice, approx.	50 mL
	Freshly ground black pepper	

The Banon cheese of Provence in France has made famous the practice of wrapping goat cheese in chestnut leaves. Originally this was done to rehydrate cheeses that had been made in the summer then dried for long storage into the winter months when the goats produce little or no milk. When needed, the cheeses were soaked in water, wrapped in the leaves, then packed in ceramic jars where they ripened for 2 to 3 weeks before being consumed. In this way, the family could enjoy moist cheeses any time of the year. Because the chestnut leaves must be collected just before falling from the tree, you need to make these in the fall. Of course, you may wish to dry the cheeses in the traditional way and rehydrate them for consumption later (see Variations, opposite).

1. Sterilize all equipment (see page 40). In a large stainless-steel pot over low heat, warm milk to 95°F (35°C), stirring gently to prevent scorching. Remove from heat.

2. Dilute rennet in ¼ cup (50 mL) cool water. Using skimmer and an up-and-down motion, gently draw rennet down into milk, without breaking surface of milk, until well blended. Cover and let set for 8 to 9 hours or until a firm curd is achieved, maintaining the temperature at 95°F (35°C).

3. Check for a clean break (see Tip, page 315). Using a long-bladed knife and skimmer, cut curd into ¾-inch (2 cm) cubes (see Tip, page 300). Stir gently for 5 minutes. Let stand for 10 minutes.

4. Pour contents of pot into a cloth-lined colander. Let curds drain for 45 minutes.

5. Place molds on a rack in a draining container. Fill molds with curds. Let drain for 3 hours at room temperature. Flip cheeses in molds and let drain for another 10 hours. Keep container covered to keep cheeses warm.

6. Unmold cheeses onto a cheese mat and replace on the rack in the draining container.

Tips: To prepare chestnut leaves, collect the leaves just before they fall from the tree in the fall. Boil or steam them in water to which a small amount of vinegar or white wine has been added. Dry the leaves slightly on paper towels.

When using raw milk, remember that the milk from the morning milking contains more solids and will set more quickly than the evening milking.

7. Sprinkle top surface of each cheese with ¼ tsp (1.25 mL) salt. Let drain for 6 hours. Turn cheeses and salt the other side in same manner. Let drain for another 6 hours.

8. Places cheeses on a clean cheese mat in a ripening container. Dry for 4 or 5 days at cool room temperature (about 65°F/18°C). Turn cheeses daily, removing any collected whey from the container and wiping bottom with paper towel.

9. Prepare chestnut leaves (see Tips, left).

10. Moisten cheeses with brandy or eau-de-vie, pouring all over the surface of each cheese. Sprinkle sparingly with pepper.

11. For each cheese, lay out 6 or 7 chestnut leaves, overlapping to form a circle big enough to enclose the cheese. Place the cheese in the center and fold up the leaves to encase. Tie the package with raffia or cord. · Repeat with remaining cheeses.

12. To ripen the cheeses, pile them in a ceramic bowl or crock and cover with a cloth. Ripen at 54° to 59°F (12° to 15°C), turning cheeses once a week. They are ready to eat after 2 or 3 weeks.

Variations: *Dried Goat Cheeses:* To dry cheeses, follow recipe through Step 8. Continue to dry by allowing more air to move around them. To do this, leave lid of container ajar in ripening area. Continue to turn cheeses twice weekly to ensure even drying. Dry until hard. At this point, cheeses can be stored without fear of becoming moldy. Store in a cloth bag in a cool dry place.

To rehydrate the cheeses, soak in water for approximately 24 hours. The water may be salted or unsalted. Remove from water and let drain on a rack for 4 to 8 hours. Continue with recipe from Step 10. You may wish to salt the cheeses lightly when adding the pepper.

Grape Leaf–Wrapped Goat Cheese: Fresh or preserved grape vine leaves can be used instead of the chestnut leaves. You will need about a third more. For preserved leaves, rinse gently in cool water. Let dry slightly on paper towel then wrap (see Step 11). For fresh ones, see Tips, above.

Gjetost

25% yield

Gjetost, pronounced "YET-oast," is a very firm, caramelized whey cheese beloved by Norwegians. The name means "goat cheese." Because of the lactose in the whey, the cheese is quite sweet and is a rich, nutty brown color. Shave off slivers and try them on your morning toast. Save the whey from making goat cheese, but remember to process it shortly after cheese making. Any amount of whey can be used to make gjetost.

- Baking dish or cake pan, buttered

> Goat's milk whey reserved from cheese making
>
> Cinnamon or other spices, optional

1. Sterilize all equipment (see page 40). In a large stainless-steel pot over medium heat, bring goat's milk whey to a boil. Immediately reduce heat to low and continue to cook, stirring frequently, until reduced to a quarter of the original volume. (This will take 2 to 6 hours, depending on the amount of whey used.) Toward the end of the cooking, stir continuously and adjust the heat to prevent scorching. The mass will be thick and pasty and will turn a caramel brown color.

2. When sufficiently reduced, place pot in a sinkful of cold water and stir until cool. This prevents crystallization of the lactose while cooling.

3. Stir cinnamon into mass, if using. Pour the mass into prepared baking dish and let set at room temperature until firm.

4. Unmold cheese and store in the refrigerator for 6 to 7 weeks.

Variations: *Extra-Creamy Gjetost:* For a richer, creamier cheese, follow recipe through Step 2. Add cream at no more than 10% of the volume of the caramelized mass before pouring it into the pan in Step 3. Continue with recipe. The resulting cheese will be less firm than regular Gjetost.

Mysost: The name simply means "cow's cheese" in Norwegian. It is made just like Gjetost but with the whey leftover from cow's milk cheese production instead of goat's milk.

Handkäse

Makes
1⅓ lbs (650 g)
8% yield

Also called hand cheese, this skim milk cheese is usually German in origin. The name comes from the fact that the cheeses are shaped by hand. If you aren't using up all the skim milk after separating milk for butter making, try your hand at these.

Tip: To make a simple brine solution: Dissolve ½ tsp (2.5 mL) salt in ½ cup (125 mL) boiled water. Let cool. Do not reserve used brine for the next washing because there is a danger of contamination from unwanted, even dangerous, bacteria.

- Cloth-lined colander
- Cheese matting
- Ripening container

8 quarts	skim milk	8 L
¼ tsp	mesophilic culture	1.25 mL
Pinch	*Brevibacterium linens* ripening bacteria	Pinch
¼ tsp	liquid rennet	1.25 mL
2 tsp	pickling (canning) or kosher salt	10 mL
	Simple brine solution (see Tip, left)	

1. Sterilize all equipment (see page 40). In a large stainless-steel pot over low heat, warm milk to 77°F (25°C), stirring gently to prevent scorching. Remove from heat.

2. Sprinkle culture and *B. linens* over surface of milk and let stand for about 5 minutes to rehydrate. Using skimmer and an up-and-down motion, gently draw culture and bacteria down into milk without breaking surface of milk. Cover and let ripen for 30 minutes.

3. Dilute rennet in ¼ cup (50 mL) cool water. Add to milk and, using the same up-and-down motion, draw rennet down into milk until well blended. Cover and let set for 30 minutes.

4. Check for a clean break (see Tip, page 315). Using a long-handled knife and skimmer, cut curd into ½-inch (1.25 cm) cubes (see Tip, page 300). Let stand for 5 minutes.

5. Return heat to low and slowly warm curds to 120°F (49°C), adjusting the heat as necessary to make sure it takes 1 hour to do so. Do not heat too quickly. Turn off heat. Cover pot and hold for 1 hour.

6. Pour contents of pot into a cloth-lined colander. Transfer curds to a bowl and break up with your hands. Knead salt into curds.

7. Shape cheese by hand into 6 small cylinder shapes or round patties that fit in your palm. If desired, shape them by pressing into St-Marcellin molds. Dry cheeses

continued on next page…

Handkäse continued...

Tip: This is an authentic recipe usually made with raw or non-homogenized whole milk. If you are using homogenized cow's milk, it is strongly recommended that you add calcium chloride (see page 31) for best results. The addition of calcium chloride will stabilize the curd, hasten setting and increase yield. Use the same amount of calcium chloride as rennet called for in the recipe, dilute it with at least 10 times the amount of water and stir into the milk before adding the rennet.

on a cheese mat placed on a rack in a ripening container for 1 to 2 days, turning several times, or until dry. Remove any collected whey from the container, wiping bottom with paper towel.

8. Once cheeses are dry, place on a clean cheese mat in a ripening container. Ripen at 50°F (10°C) and 85% to 90% humidity. Wipe cheeses every second day with a cloth soaked in simple brine solution.

9. After about 2 weeks, a reddish smear will begin to develop on the rind of the cheese. Continue to wipe with brine every second day for another 4 to 6 weeks. The cheeses will become quite pungent and sharp. Once ripened to your taste, wrap and store in the refrigerator.

Cabra al Vino

Makes 4 lbs (2 kg)

12% yield

Cabra is a firm goat cheese made in Spain that can have many different types of rind, including herb-encrusted or oil-and-spice-rubbed. Soaking this cheese in red wine gives it wow factor. The stark white paste of the goat's milk cheese and the purple-red wine-soaked rind make a pretty picture on any cheese platter.

- Cloth-lined colander
- 1 tomme mold, lined with cheese cloth
- Cheese press
- Cheese matting
- Ripening container

16 quarts	goat's milk	16 L
½ tsp	mesophilic culture	2.5 mL
¾ tsp	calcium chloride	3.75 mL
¾ tsp	liquid rennet	3.75 mL
2 tbsp	pickling (canning) or kosher salt	30 mL
2	bottles (each 750 mL) red wine, Spanish if possible, approx.	2
	Simple brine solution (see Tip, page 310)	

1. Sterilize all equipment (see page 40). In a large stainless-steel pot set in a hot water bath over medium heat, warm milk to 90°F (32°C), stirring gently. Turn off heat.

2. Sprinkle culture over surface of milk and let stand for about 5 minutes to rehydrate. Using skimmer and an up-and-down motion, gently draw culture down into milk without breaking surface of milk. Cover and let ripen for 15 minutes, maintaining the temperature at 90°F (32°C).

3. Dilute calcium chloride in ¼ cup (50 mL) cool water. Add to milk using the same up-and-down motion.

4. Dilute rennet in ¼ cup (50 mL) cool water. Add to milk and, using the same up-and-down motion, draw rennet down into milk until well blended. Cover and let set for 1 hour, maintaining the temperature.

5. Check for a clean break (see Tip, page 315). Using a long-bladed knife and skimmer, cut curd into ½-inch (1.25 cm) cubes (see Tip, page 300). Let stand for 5 minutes.

6. Stir curds gently for 10 minutes. Let settle. Using a measuring cup, dip off whey until you just barely see the surface of the curds. Replace with an equal amount of warm water to bring the temperature up to 93°F (34°C).

continued on next page…

Cabra al Vino continued...

Tip: To make a simple brine solution: Dissolve ½ tsp (2.5 mL) salt in ½ cup (125 mL) boiled water. Let cool. Do not reserve used brine for the next washing because there is a danger of contamination from unwanted, even dangerous, bacteria.

7. Stir for 10 minutes. Let settle. Once again, remove whey just until you barely see the surface of the curds. Replace with an equal amount of hot water to bring the temperature up to 100°F (38°C) (see Tips, page 187). Stir for 10 minutes. Let curds settle. Cover and hold for 45 minutes. The curds should mat and form a slab.

8. Pour off whey through a cloth-lined colander, leaving the curd slab in the bottom of the pot. Let stand for 10 minutes, turning over once or twice. On a cutting board, cut slab into ¼-inch (0.5 cm) pieces. Place in a bowl and toss with salt.

9. Fill prepared mold with curds. Pull cloth up neatly around curds and fold excess snugly over the top, with as few wrinkles as possible. Put on the lid.

10. Place mold in cheese press or place a weight on top. Press at medium pressure for 12 hours. Remove from press and re-dress (see Tips, page 255). Continue pressing at medium pressure for 12 hours.

11. Pour red wine into a deep pot. Remove cheese from press. Unwrap and place in wine for 24 hours, turning frequently. Reserving wine, remove cheese from wine. Dry cheese on a rack at room temperature for 12 hours, turning once or twice to aid drying. Return to wine bath, topping up the wine if necessary, and soak for another 24 hours. Remove from wine and discard wine. Dry cheese on a rack at room temperature for 6 to 7 hours.

12. Place cheese on a cheese mat in a ripening container. Ripen at 50°F (10°C) and 85% humidity for 3 months. Turn cheese daily for the first 2 weeks, then twice weekly thereafter. If mold appears, wipe rind with a cloth soaked in simple brine solution. Once ripened, wrap and store in the refrigerator.

Domiati

Makes 2 lbs (1 kg)
25% yield

A popular cheese in Egypt and other North African countries, Domiati is "pickled," or stored in a brine, similar to feta. This cheese is unusual in that salt is added to the milk before setting. Usually it is made of cow's milk but can be made from goat's or even camel's milk.

Tip: This is an authentic recipe usually made with raw or non-homogenized whole milk. If you are using homogenized cow's milk, it is strongly recommended that you add calcium chloride (see page 31) for best results. The addition of calcium chloride will stabilize the curd, hasten setting and increase yield. Use the same amount of calcium chloride as rennet called for in the recipe, dilute it with at least 10 times the amount of water and stir into the milk before adding the rennet.

- 5 Camembert molds or 1 tomme mold
- Cheese matting
- Draining container

4 quarts	whole milk	4 L
⅔ cup	pickling (canning) or kosher salt	150 mL
¼ tsp	thermophilic culture	1.25 mL
⅛ tsp	liquid rennet	0.65 mL
	Brine solution made with reserved whey	

1. Sterilize all equipment (see page 40). In a large stainless-steel pot over medium heat, warm milk and salt to 100°F (38°C), stirring gently to prevent scorching. Remove from heat.

2. Sprinkle culture over surface of milk and let stand for about 5 minutes to rehydrate. Using skimmer and an up-and-down motion, gently draw culture down into milk without breaking surface of milk.

3. Dilute rennet in ¼ cup (50 mL) cool water. Add to milk and, using the same up-and-down motion, draw rennet down into milk until well blended. Cover and let set for 2 hours, maintaining the temperature at 100°F (38°C).

4. Check for a clean break (see Tip, page 315). Using a long-bladed knife and skimmer, cut curd into ½-inch (1.25 cm) cubes (see Tip, page 300). Let stand for 5 minutes. Stir for 15 minutes. Let settle.

5. Place mold(s) on a rack in a draining container. Ladle curd into prepared mold(s). It will drain quite quickly. Collect drained whey and add ⅓ cup (75 mL) salt per quart (1 L) of whey. Cover and reserve this whey brine at room temperature for storing the cheeses.

6. Let cheese(s) drain for 30 minutes. Flip cheese(s) in the mold(s). Cover to keep warm and let drain at room temperature for 12 hours or overnight, flipping frequently to aid in draining.

7. At this point, the cheese(s) may be eaten fresh. Or place cheese(s) in the whey brine and store in the refrigerator for 6 to 7 months. Turn cheeses in the brine at regular intervals to ensure that all sides are immersed. If slime develops on the exposed surface of the cheese, rinse it off and turn the cheese over in the brine.

Gammelost

Makes

1⅔ lbs (800 g)

5% yield

This traditional
Norwegian cheese is
made from very sour
skim milk. It can be
eaten after only 3 weeks
of ripening or, as many
Norwegians prefer it,
left to age for several
months to develop
various molds and
become quite pungent.
The mold found on
gammelost (which
means "old cheese")
is the Mucor mucedo
strain, usually extant in
the traditional ripening
cellars. It grows straight
up in long strands,
making the ripening
cheeses look like they
have hair. We will be
using Cylindrocarpon
spp. mold, which develops
a lovely complex rind on
this cheese.

- Cloth-lined colander
- 1 tomme mold, lined with cheese cloth (see Tip, opposite)
- Draining container
- Cheese press
- Cheese matting
- Ripening container
- Thin knitting needle or metal skewer

16 quarts	skim milk	16 L
½ tsp	thermophilic culture	2.5 mL
⅛ tsp	*Penicillium roquefortii* mold powder	0.65 mL
Pinch	*Cylindrocarpon* spp. mold powder	Pinch
1 tsp	pickling (canning) or kosher salt	5 mL

1. Sterilize all equipment (see page 40). Pour milk into a large stainless-steel pot and let come to room temperature.

2. Sprinkle culture over surface of milk and let stand for about 5 minutes to rehydrate. Using skimmer and an up-and-down motion, gently draw culture down into milk without breaking surface of milk. Cover and let stand at room temperature for 48 hours or until milk is very sour.

3. Set pot in a hot water bath over low heat and very slowly warm soured milk to 145°F (63°C). Turn off the heat and hold for 30 minutes. The solids will separate from the whey and form a stringy mass. Using the skimmer, dip curd mass from the pot and place in a cloth-lined colander. Fold some of the cloth over the curd and press curd through the cloth to expel as much excess whey as possible. Let drain for 6 to 7 hours.

4. Remove curd from cloth. Using your hands, break up into pieces and pack into prepared mold. Let drain on a rack in a draining container for 2 days at room temperature.

Tip: The tomme mold will make a round cheese about 1½ inches (4 cm) thick. If you want to make a thicker cheese in the traditional cylinder shape, use 2 molds with a smaller diameter, such as Camembert molds. Line each with a square of cheese cloth.

5. Remove cheese from mold and break up again into 1-inch (2.5 cm) pieces. Place in a bowl and sprinkle with *Penicillium roquefortii* and *Cylindrocarpon* spp. mold powders. Mix in salt. Pack cheese once again into the mold. Pull cloth up neatly around curds and fold excess snugly over the top, with as few wrinkles as possible. Put on the lid. Place mold in cheese press or place a weight on top. Press at light pressure for 12 hours or overnight.

6. Remove cheese from press and unwrap. Dry on a rack at room temperature for 2 or 3 days, turning daily. The cheese should start to turn yellowish and exude a pungent, yeasty smell.

7. Place cheese on a cheese mat in a ripening container. Ripen at 50°F (10°C) and 90% humidity for 3 weeks to 7 months. Mold will begin to grow on the surface. Turn cheese and rub mold down onto rind by hand three times weekly. After 2 weeks, pierce cheese with a knitting needle all the way through, vertically and horizontally, in several places to encourage blue veining in the interior.

Liptauer

Makes
1⅔ lbs (800 g)
10% yield

Liptauer is often defined as a cheese spread, but in Hungary, where it originated, it is an actual cheese, which is then used to make a spread. Real Liptauer is always made of sheep's milk.

- Cloth-lined colander
- 1 brick mold
- Draining container
- Cheese matting
- Ripening container

8 quarts	sheep's milk	8 L
¼ tsp	mesophilic culture	1.25 mL
¼ tsp	liquid rennet	1.25 mL
2 tbsp	pickling (canning) or kosher salt	30 mL

1. Sterilize all equipment (see page 40). In a large stainless-steel pot over low heat, warm milk to 80°F (27°C), stirring gently to prevent scorching. Remove from heat.

2. Sprinkle culture over surface of milk and let stand for about 5 minutes to rehydrate. Using skimmer and an up-and-down motion, gently draw culture down into milk without breaking surface of milk.

3. Dilute rennet in ¼ cup (50 mL) cool water. Add to milk and, using the same up-and-down motion, draw rennet down into milk until well blended. Cover and let set for 1 hour, maintaining the temperature at 80°F (27°C).

4. Check for a clean break (see Tip, opposite). Using a long-bladed knife and skimmer, cut curd into 1-inch (2.5 cm) cubes. Let stand for 10 minutes.

5. Using a measuring cup, carefully dip off any whey that has collected on the surface of the curd. Using skimmer, gently ladle curd into a cloth-lined colander. Let drain for 1 hour, moving the curd gently once or twice with the skimmer to aid draining. Gather the four corners of the cloth together and tie to form a bag. Hang the bag and let drain for 12 to 18 hours or until it no longer drips.

Tip: To ascertain whether the curd is ready for the next step, check for a clean break: insert the long flat blade of a knife into the curd at a 30-degree angle and slowly lift the blade toward the surface of the curd. If the curd splits into a long clean break or crack, it is ready to cut. If the cut is wobbly or uneven, let the curd set for a few more minutes before trying again.

6. Remove curd from bag. Using your hands, press curd into prepared mold, filling well. Place on a rack in a draining container and let drain at room temperature for 24 hours, turning once in the mold after 12 hours.

7. Remove cheese from mold. Place on a cheese mat in a ripening container. Ripen at 54°F (12°C) and 85% humidity for 10 days, turning daily.

8. After 10 days, remove cheese from container and trim off all the rind. Cut cheese into $\frac{1}{2}$-inch (1.25 cm) cubes. Place cubes in a bowl and toss with salt until well blended. Pack cheese down well. Cover bowl. Ripen at 54°F (12°C) for 6 to 7 days.

9. When ripened, the cheese should have a soft, buttery texture. Using a food mill or blender, grind the cheese into a smooth paste. Place in a bowl, cover and store in the refrigerator for up to 2 weeks. Use on its own or in traditional Hungarian Liptauer Cheese Spread (page 316).

Liptauer Cheese Spread

**Makes 2 cups
(500 mL)**

*Spread this on chunks of
crusty bread and serve
with fresh radishes and
green onions. Top with
a bit of caviar for a taste
of luxury and serve with
a cool, frothy beer.*

8 oz	Liptauer (page 314)	250 g
4 oz	butter, softened	125 g
1 tsp	paprika	5 mL
½ tsp	prepared mustard	2.5 mL
½ tsp	caraway seeds	2.5 mL
1	small onion, grated	1
½ tsp	anchovy paste	2.5 mL

1. In a bowl, using a fork or small whisk, blend together
   cheese and butter until smooth. Add paprika, mustard,
   caraway seeds, onion and anchovy paste and blend well
   until color is a uniform light red. Pack into a small bowl
   or jar and refrigerate for up to 2 weeks.

Yogurt and Kefir

Yogurt is a dairy food with an ancient history. It is believed to have originated thousands of years ago in the area encompassing modern-day eastern Europe through Central Asia, and its use and benefits have spread throughout the world. The word *yogurt* is Turkish in origin.

Strains of thermophilic, or "heat-loving," lactic bacteria are added to fresh pasteurized milk and allowed to ripen the milk, causing it to thicken and gel. It can be eaten as is or strained to make it thicker. Fruit or other flavorings can be added for variety, but natural unsweetened yogurt offers the most health benefits by far.

Making yogurt at home is one of the easiest ways to convert milk into dairy food, and it requires only simple equipment. Yogurt can be made from cow's, goat's or sheep's milk, or many other types milk, such as camel, horse and yak. Making yogurt from soy or rice milk requires special thickeners, as these "milks" lack the type of solids that respond to lactic bacteria acidification.

Yogurt Nutrition

- Yogurt is an excellent source of calcium, riboflavin and vitamin B_{12}.

- The live bacterial cultures present in yogurt aid digestion in the stomach and intestines. Yogurt can be used to settle an upset stomach, ease the pain and promote healing of stomach ulcers, and balance the intestinal flora. This balancing effect promotes fresh breath and clean, healthy teeth. Ancient Greek physicians even prescribed yogurt to clear the digestive system of poisons!

- Because the live lactic bacteria change the lactose in milk into lactic acid, yogurt is often tolerated by people who suffer from lactose intolerance.

- Yogurt can help balance the digestive systems of people taking pharmaceutical antibiotics.

- Eating yogurt can improve your ability to fight off disease and infection, because the lactic acid cultures prevent pathogenic bacteria from growing.

- Daily consumption of yogurt helps maintain healthy cholesterol levels.

- The calcium in cheese and yogurt is easily assimilated by the body and directed to bone growth, promoting strong, healthy bones.

- The consumption of yogurt is said to be responsible for the longevity of pastoral herding societies in Central Asia.

- Yogurt is often served as an accompaniment to spicy foods, as the casein in yogurt neutralizes capsaicin, the "hot" component in peppers.

- Not all yogurt contains live bacterial cultures. Some commercial yogurts are pasteurized after the addition of the culture, killing any live bacteria.

- Probiotic yogurt contains live active lactic bacteria, with all the benefits of traditionally made yogurt.

- There are many varieties of yogurt; however, varieties without added sugars or sweeteners are the best. Yogurt can be made with everything from low-fat milk to light cream, but all have similar health benefits.

- Yogurt made from goat's milk is more delicate and tends to be thinner than cow's milk yogurt. To thicken goat yogurt, drain in a cloth-lined colander or use a thickening agent, such as gelatin. If you would like to use gelatin, use at the ratio of $\frac{1}{8}$ tsp (0.65 mL) powdered gelatin to 1 quart (1 L) milk. Add to the milk along with the culture.

Making Yogurt

Once made, yogurt can be stored in the refrigerator for 2 to 3 weeks. There are several recipes in this chapter, each resulting in a slightly different product — choose according to your personal preference.. The basic technique remains the same.

Equipment Needed

- Heavy-bottomed stainless-steel pot or saucepan
- Spoon or skimmer
- Dairy thermometer — this tool is critical in yogurt making
- Sink or larger pot filled with cold or ice water
- Towels, tea cozies or a thermal blanket
- OPTIONAL: A yogurt maker or vacuum flask

Basic Technique

- Clean and sterilize the pot, spoon and thermometer using boiling water or a bleach solution made with 2 tbsp (30 mL) household bleach and 4 quarts (4 L) cool water. If using bleach, rinse twice to remove any trace of chlorine.

- In stainless-steel pot over medium-low heat, warm milk to 176°F (80°C), stirring or whisking gently. Milk used for yogurt needs to be heated to a higher temperature than it does for cheese making in order to remove any bacteria that would compete with the yogurt bacteria. Rule of thumb: Warm the milk slowly but cool it quickly. This gives the heat time to kill unwanted bacteria as the milk warms, and little time during the cooling period for new bacteria to gain a foothold.

- Turn off the heat and cover the pot. Hold for 5 minutes.

- Place the pot in a sinkful or larger pot of cold or ice water and whisk or stir milk until the temperature drops to 115°F (46°C).

- Remove pot from cold water. If using dry powdered culture, sprinkle on the surface of the milk and let stand for about 5 minutes to rehydrate, then stir or whisk into milk (alternatively, blend culture into a small amount of the milk from the pot before stirring or whisking into the remaining yogurt milk). If using fresh natural yogurt as a starter, let it come to room temperature before stirring it into the milk.

continued on next page…

Making Yogurt continued...

- Incubate for 4 to 6 hours. Longer incubation results in a yogurt with increased tartness and firmness. There are several methods that all work well.

  - To incubate the whole pot, cover with the lid, set it on a folded towel or hot pad, then cover with one or two tea cozies, or folded blanket or towels.

  - To incubate yogurt in a bowl or other container, transfer the inoculated milk to your chosen container, then wrap as for the whole pot, above.

  - If using a yogurt maker, transfer the yogurt to the jars provided and switch it on to incubation temperature according to manufacturer's directions.

  - To use a vacuum flask, pour in the inoculated milk and seal.

  - If you have a sunny window, set the pot in the warm sun.

  - Leave the pot near the stove while baking.

  - Place pot in an oven set at a temperature between 100°F (38°C) and 125°F (52°C).

  - Place pot in an insulated food chest, such as is used for camping, and pour 125°F (52°C) water around pot. Close the lid.

  - The incubation temperature should ideally not sink below 98°F (36.5°C) or exceed 130°F (54°C). Try to maintain the temperature at 122°F (50°C), which inhibits the growth of pathogenic bacteria but encourages the proliferation of thermophilic bacteria. Lower temperatures can retard the growth of the yogurt bacteria.

- Place in the refrigerator and chill overnight. The yogurt will firm up a bit more in the cold.

- You can strain the yogurt, if desired, for a thicker end result.

Ingredients

- **Milk:** You can make yogurt from any kind of milk or a blend of milks. Powdered skim milk is often added to whole milk to increase the amount of solids, resulting in a thicker product. In fact, you can successfully make yogurt from reconstituted powdered milk, either skim or whole.

  If using non-homogenized milk, the set yogurt will have a thin skin of cream on top. If you are using milk from your own animals, be sure that the quality is high — no mastitis, high bacteria count, antibiotics or colostrum. Again, fresh is best.

- **Lactic bacterial culture:** Yogurt requires a thermophilic culture because of the higher temperatures involved in production. There are many strains of culture available, each of which gives you a different result. Usually they consist of strains of *Streptococcus thermophilus* (ST) and *Lactobacillus delbrueckii* spp. *bulgaricus* (LB). These two strains work together to optimally acidify the milk, causing it to coagulate. Consult your supplier for cultures that suit your tastes. *Lactobacillus acidophilus* and *Bifidobacterium* spp. are lactic bacteria that are especially beneficial to the intestines, so they can be used to make a very healthful yogurt. Lactic bacterial cultures are available from your cheese making supply house or at health food stores.

  You can also make yogurt using an existing batch of natural (not flavored or sweetened) yogurt. Be sure that the yogurt you choose is fresh, contains live culture and does not contain stabilizers or additives, all of which should be noted on the label. Use approximately 10% fresh yogurt by volume. For instance, for 1 quart (1 L) milk, use approximately ½ cup (125 mL) fresh yogurt as a starter. You can use some of your own homemade yogurt to ripen the next batch. After 4 or 5 batches, start again with fresh culture, as the yogurt becomes more acidic with each use.

continued on next page…

Making Yogurt continued...

- **_Sweeteners or flavorings:_** Honey, jam or syrups can be added after ripening. Yogurt is either "set" style, in which the yogurt is allowed to thicken without stirring, or "stirred" style, which is thickened then stirred to create a creamy texture. Stirred yogurt usually requires a thickening agent, such as gelatin, pectin, cornstarch or carrageenan, a gelling agent found in a type of seaweed. Strained yogurt is set, then drained in a cloth-lined colander to remove some of the whey, resulting in a thick, creamy product.

Stirred Yogurt

Stirring yogurt breaks down the coagulum and results in a smooth spoonable product. It can become too runny, however, so the addition of a thickener, such as gelatin, pectin or cornstarch, is recommended. Add a spoonful of jam, syrup or fresh fruit purée to make a flavored yogurt.

Yogurt with Skim Milk Powder

Makes 1 quart (1 L)

The addition of dry milk powder increases the solids, which results in a thicker yogurt.

1 quart	cow's, goat's or sheep's milk	1 L
1/4 cup	skim milk powder	50 mL
1 tsp	dry yogurt culture	5 mL

1. In a large heavy-bottomed stainless-steel pot over medium heat, warm milk to 176°F (80°C), stirring gently to prevent scorching. Turn off heat. Cover and hold for 5 minutes.

2. Remove from heat and place in a cold water bath to cool milk as quickly as possible to 115°F (46°C), whisking or stirring to speed up cooling.

3. Sprinkle skim milk powder and yogurt culture over surface of milk and let stand for about 5 minutes to rehydrate. Using skimmer and an up-and-down motion, gently draw culture down into milk without breaking surface of milk.

4. Cover pot or use your preferred method of incubating (see page 320) and let set for 4 to 6 hours or until firm. Refrigerate for several hours or overnight before using.

Greek-Style Yogurt

Makes 1 quart (1 L)

This yogurt is rich, thick and not very acidic. It's entirely delicious and perfect for a healthy breakfast or light dessert (see Serving suggestions, below).

Serving suggestions: Serve the yogurt Greek-style by slicing fresh fruit and/or berries into a bowl and topping with Greek-Style Yogurt. Or drizzle with liquid Greek honey, or another dark honey, and sprinkle with chopped pistachios.

- Cloth-lined colander

1 quart	half-and-half (10%) cream	1 L
¼ cup	fresh plain live-bacteria yogurt	50 mL

1. In a large heavy-bottomed stainless-steel pot over medium heat, warm cream to 176°F (80°C), stirring gently to prevent scorching. Turn off heat. Cover and hold for 5 minutes.

2. Remove from heat and place in a cold water bath to cool milk as quickly as possible to 115°F (46°C), stirring or whisking to speed up cooling.

3. Stir or whisk yogurt into the milk. Cover pot or use your preferred method of incubating (see page 320), and let set for 4 to 6 hours or until firm.

4. Refrigerate for several hours or overnight. Drain yogurt through cloth-lined colander for 1 or 2 hours or until the desired thickness has been reached.

5. Place in a clean bowl, cover and refrigerate for up to 2 weeks.

Goat's Milk Yogurt with Gelatin

Makes 1 quart (1 L)

Goat's milk makes beautiful yogurt, but it is thinner than cow's milk yogurt. Straining through a cloth, as in Greek-Style Yogurt opposite, can help, as can the addition of a thickener, such as the gelatin used here.

1 quart	goat's milk	1 L
⅛ tsp	unflavored gelatin powder	0.65 mL
1 tsp	dry yogurt culture or ¼ cup (50 mL) fresh plain live-bacteria yogurt	5 mL

1. In a large heavy-bottomed stainless-steel pot over medium heat, warm milk to 176°F (80°C), stirring gently to prevent scorching. Turn off heat.

2. Sprinkle gelatin over ¼ cup (50 mL) of the warm milk and set aside to soften.

3. Remove from heat and immerse in a cold water bath to bring the temperature to 115°F (46°C), whisking or stirring to speed up cooling.

4. Add culture and gelatin mixture and whisk or stir in thoroughly. Cover pot or use your preferred method of incubating (see page 320) and let set for 4 to 6 hours, until firm.

5. Refrigerate for 6 to 7 hours or overnight for up to 2 weeks.

Bulgarian-Style Yogurt

1 quart	whole milk	1 L
1 tsp	Bulgarian yogurt culture	5 mL

Makes 1 quart (1 L)

Central Europe is said to be the birthplace of yogurt. Bulgarian-style yogurt tends to be thick and creamy.

1. In a large heavy-bottomed stainless-steel pot over medium heat, warm milk to 176°F (80°C), stirring gently to prevent scorching. Turn off heat. Cover pot and hold for 5 minutes.

2. Remove from heat and place in a cold water bath to cool milk as quickly as possible to 115°F (46°C), stirring or whisking to speed up cooling.

3. Dissolve dry yogurt culture in a small amount of the warm milk and stir back into the pot. Cover pot or use your preferred method of incubating (see page 320) and let set for 4 to 6 hours or until firm.

4. Refrigerate for several hours or overnight.

5. If a thicker yogurt is desired, strain through a cloth-lined colander for 1 to 2 hours.

6. Place in a bowl or container, cover and refrigerate for up to 2 weeks.

Chilled Blueberry Soup

Makes 4 servings

This pretty purple cold soup is a delicious and unique way to use yogurt as part of a meal.

2 cups	blueberries, fresh or frozen	500 mL
½ cup	water	125 mL
¼ cup	granulated sugar	50 mL
1 tsp	grated lemon zest	5 mL
2 tbsp	freshly squeezed lemon juice	30 mL
⅛ tsp	ground cinnamon	0.65 mL
1¾ cups	plain yogurt	425 mL
	Crème fraîche	
4	fresh mint leaves	4

1. In a saucepan, combine blueberries, water, sugar, lemon zest and juice and cinnamon. Cook over low heat, whisking, until berries burst and mixture is smooth. Let cool. Transfer to a bowl, cover and refrigerate for 2 hours or until cold.

2. Whisk yogurt into cold blueberry mixture until smooth and creamy. Ladle into bowls.

3. Top with a spoonful of crème fraîche and a mint leaf.

Chocolate Yogurt Cake

Makes 16 pieces

The tanginess of the yogurt and the richness of chocolate are a great pairing.

- Preheat oven to 350°F (180°C)
- 8-inch (2 L) square baking pan, lined with parchment paper

1½ cups	all-purpose flour	375 mL
½ cup	unsweetened cocoa powder	125 mL
1 tsp	baking soda	5 mL
¼ tsp	salt	1.25 mL
1 cup	granulated sugar	250 mL
⅓ cup	butter, softened	75 mL
2	eggs	2
1 cup	plain yogurt	250 mL
	Crème fraîche	

1. In a small bowl, sift together flour, cocoa, baking soda and salt. Set aside.

2. In a separate bowl, using an electric mixer, cream together sugar and butter until light and fluffy. Add eggs and beat until smooth.

3. Add half of the dry ingredients and stir well with a wooden spoon or spatula. Add yogurt and blend well. Add remaining dry ingredients and blend.

4. Pour into prepared baking pan, smoothing top. Bake in preheated oven for 30 minutes or until a toothpick inserted into the center comes out clean. Let cool in pan on a rack. Cut into 2-inch (5 cm) squares and serve with crème fraîche.

Yogurt Cheese

Yogurt cheese is the simplest cheese to make and can be substituted for cream cheese or sour cream except when making a cheesecake. Use fresh homemade yogurt.

- Draining bag or cloth-lined colander

  Fresh plain yogurt

1. Place yogurt in a soft cheese draining bag or cloth-lined colander and drain until a very thick, soft, spreadable consistency is reached.

2. Use immediately or transfer to a bowl, cover and refrigerate. Yogurt cheese will keep for 2 to 3 weeks.

Lebanese Yogurt Cheese

Makes 1 quart (1 L)

Also known as labneh, this soft cheese is a favorite meal accompaniment in Lebanese cuisine. Spread a spoonful of labneh on a small plate, drizzle with olive oil and serve with flatbread and olives.

- Draining bag or cloth-lined colander

| 1 quart | fresh plain yogurt | 1 L |
| 1 tsp | salt | 5 mL |

1. In a large bowl, combine yogurt with salt.

2. Pour into a draining bag or cloth-lined colander and drain until thick but still spreadable.

3. Use immediately or transfer to a bowl, cover and refrigerate. Yogurt cheese will keep for 2 to 3 weeks.

Labneh Cheese Balls

Here's a way to preserve fresh yogurt cheese almost indefinitely. Serve these balls with a bit of the olive oil as an appetizer, in a salad or spread on a slice of toasted baguette.

Fresh yogurt cheese
Olive oil

1. Roll generous tablespoonfuls of yogurt cheese into balls.

2. Place balls on a plate and dry at room temperature for several hours or overnight.

3. Place cheese balls in a jar with a lid and cover with olive oil. Seal and refrigerate.

Yogurt Drinks

Yogurt in drink form is especially popular in Eastern cultures, often with the addition of salt. Unless overly sweetened, yogurt drinks contain all the healthful benefits of plain yogurt and have even been used in hospitals to alleviate the side-effects of antibiotics. Some of the following recipes are quite unusual, but offer a unique way to enjoy yogurt.

Mango Lassi

Makes 4 to 6 servings

Lassi is an Indian drink made with yogurt. The acidity and sweetness perfectly balance the heat of a spicy curry.

3 cups	plain yogurt	750 mL
1 cup	sliced ripe mango	250 mL
1 cup	crushed ice	250 mL
	Sugar or other sweetener, such as honey, fruit juice or fruit pulp, to taste	
	Thick plain yogurt for topping	
	Chopped pistachios	

1. In a blender, purée yogurt, mango, ice and sugar until smooth.

2. Pour into glasses and top with a spoonful of thick plain yogurt. Sprinkle with chopped pistachios.

Persian Sparkling Yogurt Drink

Makes 4 servings

This favorite in the Middle East is definitely something unique.

1 cup	plain yogurt	250 mL
1 tsp	chopped fresh mint leaves	5 mL
½ tsp	salt	2.5 mL
¼ tsp	freshly ground black pepper	1.25 mL
1½ cups	sparkling mineral water or club soda	375 mL
4	fresh mint leaves	4

1. Whisk yogurt until smooth.

2. In a pitcher, combine yogurt, chopped mint, salt and pepper. Stir well.

3. Gradually add mineral water, stirring gently to blend.

4. Pour into glasses and top with a mint leaf.

Traditional Rose Water Lassi

Makes 4 servings

This delightfully refreshing drink is wonderful at the end of a spicy meal or as a quick healthy snack.

2	green cardamom pods	2
2 cups	cold water	500 mL
1 cup	plain yogurt	250 mL
1 tbsp	granulated sugar	15 mL
2 tsp	rose water	10 mL
4	fresh mint leaves	4

1. Crush cardamom pods and remove seeds, discarding pods.

2. In a blender, combine cardamom seeds, water, yogurt, sugar and rose water. Blend until smooth.

3. Pour into glasses and top with a mint leaf.

Troubleshooting

The yogurt will not set at all.
The milk was not pasteurized correctly and there are still bacteria in the milk; be sure to heat to 176°F (80°C) and hold at that temperature for at least 5 minutes before cooling. Or the temperature of the milk was too high or too low when yogurt culture was added; be sure to keep it between 110° and 118°F (43° and 48°C). Or the yogurt used as culture was inactive; if using purchased yogurt as starter, read the label to ensure it has live bacteria.

The yogurt has set but is stringy and slimy in texture, and it doesn't smell right.
The yogurt starter was contaminated with unwanted bacteria; use fresh culture or yogurt. Or the milk wasn't properly pasteurized. Do not eat the yogurt.

The yogurt is very firm and tastes quite sour.
You have incubated the yogurt too long, and the acidity has increased too much; incubate the yogurt just until firm. Test to see if it is set by tilting the pot slightly and observing the coagulum.

The yogurt has set for the required time but is still quite soft.
The culture was too weak; if re-culturing from previous batches, it is time to start with a fresh culture. Or the inoculation temperature was either too high or too low, inhibiting bacteria growth. Or the incubation temperature is too low, slowing down bacteria growth; insulate your container well for the duration of the time.

The yogurt is grainy.
The milk was heated too high (boiled) when pasteurizing; do not heat over 176°F (80°C).

Yogurt is gritty.
Milk was overheated; use a thermometer and stir gently when heating.

Yogurt tastes very sour.
It was set too long; next time, set for 4 to 6 hours as recommended. The longer yogurt is set, the more acidic it becomes.

Yogurt is very runny and did not set up adequately.
The culture is weak; use new culture or increase amount of starter yogurt. Or the setting temperature was too low or too high; keep milk at correct temperature and insulate well. Or the pot or container was disturbed during setting; be sure to set in a quiet, undisturbed place and do not move during incubation.

Kefir

Kefir is a fermented milk drink that offers huge health benefits. It can be made from any kind of milk, including whole or low-fat, and goat's or cow's. Some of the health benefits attributed to kefir are:

- Strengthens the immune system.
- Balances intestinal flora and the digestive system.
- Supports healthy internal-organ function.
- Reduces inflammation, due to its antibiotic properties.
- Promotes healthy skin and fights signs of aging.
- Helps maintain healthy cholesterol levels.
- Heals lactose intolerance.

Kefir differs from yogurt in that it is inoculated with yeast as well as lactic bacteria. The starter comes in a gelatinous, lumpy mass call "kefir grains," which are available at health food stores or online. These grains are composed of a complex blend of lactic bacteria and yeasts, which ripen and ferment the milk at the same time. Because of the yeast, kefir grains produce small amounts of alcohol, giving the finished product a carbonated effect.

Traditionally, kefir grains were shared by someone who had a live batch, and some people kept the same batch going for literally generations. If you are lucky enough to find fresh grains, you can begin using them right away. The grains will grow with each batch of kefir you make, so you, too, could have some to share with a fellow enthusiast. To keep your batch of kefir grains healthy:

- Never freeze them.
- Never let them come into contact with bleach.
- Never heat them above 104°F (40°C).
- Never let them dry out.
- When not using, always keep them moist with a bit of milk in a covered container in the fridge.
- Use only clean, dry utensils; non-metallic ones are best.

Basic Technique for Activating Kefir Grains

Use this technique to prepare and reactivate store-bought kefir grains.

- Dairy thermometer
- Wide-mouth glass jars or container with lid
- Nylon strainer

Milk, such as cow's, goat's or sheep's, pasteurized or raw (for information on using raw milk, see page 25)

Unrefined cane sugar, optional

Kefir grains

1. In a stainless-steel pot over low heat, warm 1 cup (250 mL) milk to 77°F (25°C) and place in a glass jar.

2. Add a pinch of unrefined cane sugar, if desired, and mix until dissolved.

3. Add ¼ tsp (1.25 mL) kefir grains and cover jar. Set aside in a warm place (room temperature or slightly warmer). Cover jar with a towel to hold the temperature and keep out light.

4. Every few hours, tilt and agitate the jar to move the milk around. Continue for 24 hours (agitate just before bed and then again first thing in the morning; the agitating helps keep it growing) or until the milk has coagulated throughout the jar and you can see some clear whey on the bottom. Shake the jar to remix the contents.

5. Strain the contents of the jar through a nylon strainer into a glass bowl, shaking the strainer slightly to separate the curds from the grains. The kefir grains will look like yellowish blobs in the strainer.

6. Reserve half of the coagulated milk, discarding the rest.

7. Transfer the reserved coagulated milk to a clean glass jar and fill with fresh 77°F (25°C) milk. Add the kefir grains and repeat the process as described above from Step 3 on. The second batch of kefir is drinkable, though it may take a few more repeats to get the final desired result and find the "rhythm" of fermenting the kefir to your taste and replacing the used kefir with fresh milk.

Making Kefir

To make subsequent batches of kefir, continue to remove some of the coagulated milk, replacing it with fresh warm milk. This way you can keep your batch going indefinitely.

- The grains will continue to increase in size and can be divided or left whole. If your grains are larger, you can make a larger batch of kefir, or a smaller batch in less time.

- The ratio of grains to milk ranges from about 1:20 to 1:60, depending on the activity level of the grains.

- The warmer the incubating temperature, the shorter the fermentation time. The cooler the temperature, the slower the process.

- A tight lid on the jar will keep the CO_2 produced during fermentation in the kefir. However, too much gas production can blow the lid off or break the container, so monitor it carefully, watching for frothing, releasing the lid if necessary. A loose lid allows the CO_2 to dissipate, so the resulting kefir will be flat rather than effervescent.

- The average time for fermentation is 24 hours. Longer fermentation results in a stronger, more acidic product.

- Continue to keep the grains active, even if you are not drinking all the kefir you produce. They will remain live for as long as you tend to them.

Kefir is often used for its specific health benefits. A small glass in the morning and another after the evening meal is recommended. Further research can help you choose a regimen that works for your personal health requirements.

Following are some ways to incorporate the probiotic benefits of kefir into your diet.

- Smoothies: Blend 1 cup (250 mL) kefir with a banana and some fresh blueberries for a powerful probiotic breakfast drink or snack.

- Blend half kefir and half fruit juice (orange, apple, etc.) for a lively drink.

- Stir a spoonful of kefir into a cream soup for a tangy variation.

- Replace sour cream with thick kefir on baked potatoes, vegetables or pierogies.

- Blend muesli with kefir and top with sliced fruit for a healthy breakfast.

- Replace the buttermilk in baking recipes with kefir.

- Mix kefir into your favorite salad dressing recipe.

Kefir Cheese

Makes 1 quart (1 L)

You can make a tasty fresh cheese from your homemade kefir. If your batches are getting ahead of you, this is a great way to make use of the excess.

- Cloth-lined colander

1 quart	kefir	1 L
	Salt, pepper and/or herbs	

1. Bring kefir to room temperature (the thicker the better).

2. Pour kefir into a cloth-lined colander. Bring up the corners of the cloth and tie together to form a bag. Suspend and let drain for 12 hours or until desired consistency has been reached.

3. Place the curd in a small bowl. Season with salt, pepper and/or herbs to taste.

Butter, Buttermilk and Crème Fraîche

continued on next page…

Butter, Buttermilk and Crème Fraîche
continued...

Making Butter

One of the finest treats of all, fresh churned butter is tops! You can make butter with purchased heavy cream as well as with your own cream from cows or goats. To make butter, the heavy cream is worked until the fat separates from the liquid.

1. Butter Making Facts

- Fresh whole (4% butterfat) cow's milk is about 10% cream.

- Whipping cream contains 30% to 40% butterfat and 60% to 70% other components.

- Traditional buttermilk is the liquid left over from butter making. Commercial buttermilk found at the market today is made from skim milk, to which lactic bacteria have been added (see page 358).

- You cannot use homogenized milk for butter making, because the cream can no longer be separated. If using purchased milk, you must use cream line, or non-homogenized, milk and separate the cream (see Sources, page 372).

- Butter made from cream separated from raw milk will have a shorter shelf life and a stronger flavor than butter made from pasteurized cream.

- Goat's milk has similar fat content to cow's milk; however, its fat particles are very fine and usually do not rise to the top of the milk. To collect cream from goat's milk, you must use a mechanical separator (centrifuge). If you don't have that option, you can try collecting the cream by letting the milk stand in the refrigerator for up to five days (see Preparing the Cream, page 341), but your yield will be quite small.

- The expected yield for butter is approximately 40% of the weight of the cream, or 4% of the milk. From 1 quart (1 L) whipping (35%) cream, you should have approximately 1 lb (500 g) butter.

- Cow's milk butter will be a creamy yellow color, whereas goat's milk butter will be pure white.

continued on next page...

2. Equipment Required

Butter can be churned using one of the following:

- **Butter Churn:** For home use, these typically consist of a large glass jar and lid, with beaters or paddles attached to the underside of the lid. The beaters are run by either a hand crank or a small electric motor affixed to the top of the lid. These are available from cheese making supply houses (see Sources, page 370).

- **Food Processor:** Butter can be quickly churned with a food processor. Pay close attention to avoid overprocessing.

- **Electric or Hand Mixer:** Small amounts of cream can be worked into butter using one of these common kitchen mixers.

- **Jar with Lid:** A simple way to make small amounts of butter is to shake the cream in a lidded jar until the butter forms.

Note: For optimal churning, do not fill the container more than one-third to one-half full of cream. If overfilled, the cream will not have room to expand in the container when churned. Under these conditions, the cream can also become too warm during churning, resulting in butter that is too soft and fluffy and that does not entirely release the buttermilk.

3. Separating the Cream

For butter making, you can buy regular pasteurized cream, or separate the cream from pasteurized cream line (non-homogenized) milk or your own or purchased raw milk (see Sources, page 372, for information on using raw milk). Homogenized milk cannot be used for butter making.

When selecting either cream or cream line (non-homogenized) milk for butter making, keep these factors in mind.

- Check the best-before date and get the freshest possible.

- Look for cream that has no additives or thickeners, such as agar, carrageenan or cellulose fiber.

- Choose cream or milk with the highest butterfat content available; for cream, at least 35%; for milk, as close to 4% as possible. If you have a local source of Jersey or Guernsey milk, buy that. Both are great choices, as they have a much higher than usual (often over 5%) butterfat content.

To separate the cream from cream line milk, you can use one of two methods.

1. Pour the fresh whole milk into a wide shallow bowl. Cover with a lid to prevent bacteria from entering and culturing. Let stand undisturbed for 24 hours at room temperature to allow the cream to rise to the top of the milk. Place the bowl in the refrigerator for 12 hours. Remove bowl from refrigerator and, using a large shallow serving spoon, skim the cream from the top of the milk.

2. Use a mechanical cream separator. If you plan to do a lot of this, it may be a useful investment. Separators are available from some cheese making or dairy supply houses, and from companies that specialize in homesteading equipment. Sometimes they can be found at farm sales or advertised in farm-related publications, but make sure all the parts are included, as they can sometimes be difficult to replace. Separators work on a centrifuge system, run either by an electric motor or a hand crank, spinning the milk at a very high speed. The lighter cream rises to the top and flows out an upper spout, and the skim milk flows out a lower spout. You just pour the milk into the bowl of the separator, turn it on and collect the thick cream.

4. Preparing the Cream

There are three basic types of butter to be made from cream:

1. Sweet cream butter made from fresh uncultured cream.

2. Cultured butter made from cream ripened with lactic bacterial culture.

3. Cultured butter made from raw milk cream ripened naturally with no added bacterial culture (see Sources, page 372, for information on using raw milk).

continued on next page…

Making Butter continued...

Tip: To pasteurize cream, warm it in a stainless-steel pot over medium heat to 145°F (63°C), stirring gently. Turn off the heat. Cover the pot and·leave on the burner. Let stand for 30 minutes. Cool quickly by placing the pot in a sink or pan full of ice water, stirring to aid in cooling.

Sweet Cream Butter: Made directly from thick cream, with no ripening or souring. Use cream with a minimum of 35% butterfat or separate the cream from cream line (non-homogenized) milk (see Step 3, page 341).

To prepare for churning, remove cream from refrigerator and let come to 54°F (12°C). Proceed to Step 5 (opposite).

Bacterially Ripened Cream Butter: Made from pasteurized cream that has been inoculated with mesophilic bacterial culture or starter. Use purchased cream or separate the cream from cream line milk (see Step 3, page 341). If you are using raw milk or cream, pasteurize it before inoculating (see Tip, left).

1. In a stainless-steel pot over medium heat, warm the cream to 68°F (20°C), stirring gently. Remove from heat.

2. For every 3 quarts (3 L) cream, sprinkle 1/4 tsp (1.25 mL) mesophilic culture or aroma mesophilic culture over surface of cream and let stand for about 5 minutes to rehydrate. Using skimmer and an up-and-down motion, gently draw culture down into cream without breaking surface of cream until well blended. Alternatively, omit culture and blend 1/4 cup (50 mL) buttermilk into cream.

3. Cover and set aside to ripen at room temperature for 12 hours.

4. Place container in the refrigerator and chill for 12 hours.

5. Remove from refrigerator and let come to 54°F (12°C).

6. Proceed to Step 5 (opposite).

Naturally Ripened Cream Butter: Made from raw milk (see Sources, page 372) that has been left to stand at room temperature for 24 hours. This allows the naturally present lactic bacteria in the milk to multiply and "sour" it; it is not inoculated with additional bacteria.

1. Pour milk into a large shallow bowl or pot. Cover with a clean cloth and let stand for 24 hours at room temperature.

2. Place in the refrigerator for 12 hours. This will firm up the butterfat. Separate by skimming as outlined in Step 3, page 341.

3. Bring cream to 54°F (12°C) for churning.

4. Proceed to Step 5, below.

5. Churning the Cream

Fill the churn container, or a deep narrow bowl if using a mixer, one-third to one-half full. Attach the lid of the churn, or cover if using a food processor, and begin churning. If you are using the old-fashioned method of shaking the cream in a jar, fill as above, tighten the lid and start shaking! This is a good time to watch TV or read a book.
The cream will go through several stages in the process:

1. The cream will thicken and become whipped cream.

2. The whipped cream will become very stiff, until you think nothing more is going to happen.

3. Gradually the whipped cream will begin to collapse and lose volume. The color will change from white to yellowish, and the texture will be grainy.

4. The contents of the churn will become more liquid and you will hear a sloshing sound.

5. Flecks of butter will begin to separate from the buttermilk. Do not overchurn at this point or the butter will become greasy. You will hear a difference in the sound of the motor — it will become quieter, and there will be a splashing sound from the buttermilk. Stop churning.

6. Rinse a mesh strainer in cold water and strain the butter and buttermilk through the strainer. Catch the buttermilk in a bowl and use for cooking or cheese making.

continued on next page…

Making Butter continued...

7. Rinse the butter under cold running water, shaking the strainer to rinse well. The water should run clear, with no residual milkiness. Collect the butter into a ball and place in a chilled bowl.

8. Using a spatula, a spoon or your hands (they must be cold!) press and knead the butter to remove the water. Traditionally, the water was worked out of the butter using grooved wooden paddles, or "Scotch hands." These helpful tools are still available from cheese making and dairy supply companies.

9. Knead and press the butter into a firm ball or other desired shape or proceed with one of the flavored butter recipes starting on page 346. Wrap in parchment paper or foil, or place in a container, and refrigerate. Butter should be protected from light, which can fade the color and deteriorate quality.

To Make Salted Butter

Regular Salted Butter: Add 1 tsp (5 mL) salt per pound (500 g) butter. Work into butter before shaping.

Demi-Sel (Low-Salt) Butter: Add ½ tsp (2.5 mL) salt per pound (500 g) butter. Work into butter before shaping.

Troubleshooting

The butter is too greasy.
The butter was overchurned; stop churning just when the flecks of butter have separated from the buttermilk and the buttermilk begins to splash.

The cream is too foamy during churning.
The cream was too old; use fresh cream or add 1 tsp (5 mL) baking soda to the cream before churning. Or the temperature at the time of churning is too high or too low; adjust the temperature. If too cold, let stand at room temperature for a short time; if too warm, add some ice water to the cream (the water will churn out).

The butter is light-colored, has a whipped texture and will not separate from the buttermilk.
The temperature is too warm; chill the cream by adding some ice water to the churn. Or the churn is overfilled; fill only one-third to one-half full. If you are using milk from your own production, the quality of the cream could possibly have been compromised, such as by mastitis; check milk quality before making butter.

Flavored Butters

Flavored butters add a special flair to a snack or a meal and can give a simple dish that unforgettable touch. The butter can be stored in a container but is very convenient and attractive when piped into rosettes. Freeze and use as needed. Or shape it into a log and roll in waxed or parchment paper, so it can conveniently be sliced into pieces of a desired thickness.

Garlic and Pepper Butter

1 cup	unsalted butter, at room temperature (see Tip, left)	250 mL
2	cloves garlic, crushed or finely chopped	2
¼ tsp	freshly ground black pepper	1.25 mL
Pinch	salt	Pinch

Makes 1 cup (250 mL)

Try this on grilled meats.

Tip: If you wish to use salted butter, omit the salt.

1. In a small bowl, combine butter, garlic, pepper and salt. Blend until smooth and creamy.

2. Serve immediately or refrigerate, tightly covered, for up to 1 week.

Orange Honey Butter

½ cup	unsalted butter, at room temperature	125 mL
4 tsp	grated orange zest	20 mL
2 tsp	freshly squeezed orange juice	10 mL
2 tsp	liquid honey	10 mL

Makes ½ cup (125 mL)

Very tasty on a breakfast muffin or croissant.

1. In a small bowl, combine butter, orange zest and juice, and honey. Blend until smooth and creamy.

2. Serve immediately or refrigerate, tightly covered, for up to 1 week.

Provençal Herb Butter

Makes 1 cup (250 mL)

This is wonderful on a baguette with a slice of hard or semisoft goat cheese. Try melting a chilled nugget of this butter on a grilled steak.

Tip: If you wish to use salted butter, omit the salt.

1 cup	unsalted butter, at room temperature (see Tip, left)	250 mL
1½ tsp	finely chopped fresh rosemary	7.5 mL
2 tbsp	finely sliced black olives	30 mL
1 tsp	finely chopped garlic	5 mL
1 tsp	freshly ground black pepper	5 mL
Pinch	salt	Pinch

1. In a small saucepan over low heat, melt 1 tbsp (15 mL) of the butter. Add rosemary and heat until butter just begins to brown. Remove from heat. Let cool.

2. In a small bowl, mix together olives, garlic, pepper, salt and remaining butter. Add butter-rosemary mixture and blend together well.

3. Serve immediately or refrigerate, tightly covered, for up to 1 week.

Roasted Hazelnut Butter

Makes 1 cup (250 mL)

Melt this on freshly grilled trout for a special occasion meal.

- **Preheat oven to 400°F (200°C)**

½ cup	fresh hazelnuts or filberts	125 mL
½ cup	unsalted butter, softened	125 mL
½ tsp	freshly grated lemon zest	2.5 mL

1. Spread hazelnuts on a baking pan or sheet and roast in preheated oven for 10 minutes. Let cool for 10 minutes. Rub nuts between your hands to remove the papery skins. Let cool completely.

2. In a food processor or mini chopper, coarsely grind nuts.

3. Place butter in a small bowl. Add nuts and lemon zest and blend into butter until smooth and creamy.

4. Serve immediately or refrigerate, tightly covered, for up to 1 week.

Strawberry and Rose Petal Butter

¼ cup	fresh unsprayed scented rose petals	50 mL
½ cup	unsalted butter, softened	125 mL
¼ cup	small strawberries, chopped into small pieces	50 mL

Makes ¾ cup (175 mL)

Fresh baked scones spread with this butter will make you wonder why the Queen hasn't been invited!

Tip: The fat in the butter helps preserve the fresh fruit.

1. Strip rose petals from flower stems and rinse in a colander under cool running water. Pat dry on paper towel, then slice petals finely, discarding the thickened part at the base.

2. Rinse and dry strawberries and finely chop. Let drain on paper towel to remove excess moisture.

3. Place butter in a small bowl. Add strawberries and rose petals and blend until smooth and creamy.

4. Serve immediately or refrigerate, tightly covered, for up to 1 week.

Cinnamon Honey Butter

½ cup	creamed honey	125 mL
1 cup	unsalted butter, softened	250 mL
1 tsp	ground cinnamon	5 mL

Makes 1½ cups (375 mL)

This wonderful spread is addictive on hot toast!

1. In a small saucepan over medium-low heat or in microwave at Medium-Low, warm honey until liquefied. Do not boil. Let cool to room temperature.

2. Place butter in a small bowl. Sprinkle cinnamon over butter and blend. Add honey and blend until smooth and creamy.

3. Store in a bowl or container and use as desired. This will keep quite well even if not refrigerated for up to 10 days at room temperature.

Horseradish and Mustard Butter

**Makes ¹⁄₂ cup
(125 mL)**

Glaze a beef prime rib roast or grilled steak or rub a freshly roasted piece of beef with this butter to create a photo-perfect glazed effect.

¹⁄₂ cup	salted butter, softened	125 mL
1 tbsp	ground horseradish root or drained prepared horseradish	15 mL
1 tbsp	grainy Dijon mustard	15 mL

1. Place butter in a small bowl. Add horseradish and mustard and blend until smooth and creamy.

2. Chill for 1 hour or until butter is firm enough to shape but not too hard. Place in a piping bag fitted with a star tip. Pipe into small rosettes onto waxed paper. Chill until firm.

3. When serving grilled beef, place 1 rosette on each serving. Refrigerate any leftover rosettes in a small container, tightly covered, for up to 1 week.

Dill and Lemon Butter

**Makes ¹⁄₂ cup
(125 mL)**

Dress fresh steamed garden vegetables with a dollop of this butter.

¹⁄₂ cup	salted butter, softened	125 mL
1 tbsp	freshly grated lemon zest	15 mL
1 tbsp	finely chopped fresh dill	15 mL

1. Place butter in a small bowl. Add lemon zest and dill and blend until smooth and creamy.

2. Serve immediately or refrigerate, tightly covered, for up to 1 week.

Peppercorn Butter

**Makes ½ cup
(125 mL)**

Sauté some finely chopped shallots in this butter, and deglaze with a small glass of red wine. Drizzle over grilled meat. There are many varieties of peppercorns available: try pink, green and any others you can find for this butter.

| ½ cup | salted butter, softened | 125 mL |
| 1 tbsp | mixed whole peppercorns | 15 mL |

1. Place butter in a small bowl.

2. With the flat side of a large chef's knife, crush peppercorns. Do not grind.

3. Add crushed peppercorns to butter and blend until creamy and smooth. Let infuse at room temperature for 2 hours before refrigerating. Refrigerate, tightly covered, for up to 1 month.

Chocolate Butter

**Makes ½ cup
(125 mL)**

Truly decadent! Try on waffles and pancakes.

½ cup	unsalted butter, softened	125 mL
1 tbsp	unsweetened cocoa powder	15 mL
1 tbsp	confectioner's (icing) sugar	15 mL
1 tbsp	finely chopped pecans	15 mL

1. Place butter in a small glass or stainless-steel bowl. Sift cocoa powder and sugar over top and blend in thoroughly with a spoon.

2. Stir in pecans and mix to distribute evenly.

3. Serve immediately or refrigerate, tightly covered, for up to 1 week.

Blue Cheese Butter

Makes ½ cup (125 mL)		
½ cup	unsalted butter, softened	125 mL
2 tbsp	blue cheese, softened	30 mL

Rich and flavorful, this makes a classy topping for a good steak.

1. Place butter in a small bowl. Add blue cheese and mash with a fork to blend into butter.

2. Serve immediately or refrigerate, tightly covered, for up to 1 week.

Apple Maple Butter

Makes ½ cup (125 mL)		
2 tbsp	apple jelly	30 mL
½ cup	unsalted butter, softened	125 mL
2 tbsp	pure maple syrup	30 mL
¼ tsp	ground cinnamon	1.25 mL

This is what has been missing from your morning pancakes! Serve with a side dish of apple slices sautéed in butter with a squeeze of lemon juice.

1. In a small saucepan or in a bowl in the microwave, melt apple jelly. Set aside and let cool slightly.

2. Place butter in a small bowl. Add apple jelly and maple syrup and blend with a fork. Add cinnamon and mix well.

3. Cover and chill for 1 hour or until butter is firm enough to shape but not too hard. Place butter on a piece of waxed paper and, using paper, roll and shape into a 1-inch (2.5 cm) square stick, about 6 inches (15 cm) long. Return to refrigerator and chill until firm.

4. To serve, slice squares of butter and serve on hot pancakes or waffles. The square shape looks interesting on round pancakes. Refrigerate, tightly covered, for up to 1 week.

Flower Petal Butter

Makes 1 cup (250 mL)

Serve a delightful bouquet of edible flowers in a spoonful of sweet butter. Use a variety of petal colors to make it truly decorative. Serve on fresh baked scones with a dollop of crème fraîche.

1 cup	unsalted butter, softened	250 mL
2 tbsp	confectioner's (icing) sugar	30 mL
3 tbsp	edible flower petals, such as bachelor's buttons, marigolds, nasturtiums or roses	45 mL
½ tsp	grated lemon zest	2.5 mL

1. Place butter in a small bowl. Beat with a fork until creamy.

2. Sift icing sugar over butter and stir in well with fork. Add flower petals and lemon zest, stirring until evenly blended.

3. Let stand at room temperature for 1 hour to develop flavors, then serve or refrigerate, tightly covered, for up to 5 days.

4. If you wish to make rosettes, refrigerate for 1 hour or until firm enough to shape but not too hard. Place in a piping bag fitted with a star tip. Pipe rosette shapes onto waxed paper and chill until firm.

Paprika Butter

Makes ½ cup (125 mL)

This is great on chicken.

1 tbsp	liquid honey	15 mL
½ cup	salted butter, softened	125 mL
1	clove garlic, crushed	1
½ tsp	sweet paprika	2.5 mL

1. In microwave or small saucepan, warm honey. Set aside.

2. Place butter in a small bowl. Using a fork, beat until creamy. Blend in honey. Add garlic and paprika and blend well. Let stand for 15 minutes to develop the flavor.

3. Serve immediately or refrigerate, tightly covered, for up to 1 week.

Lemon Poppy Seed Butter

½ cup	salted butter, softened	125 mL
1 tbsp	poppy seeds	15 mL
½ tsp	finely grated lemon zest	2.5 mL
1 tbsp	freshly squeezed lemon juice	15 mL

> **Makes ½ cup (125 mL)**

Poppy seeds are a favorite addition to breads and sauces for their crunchy texture and unique flavor. Use this butter on steamed vegetables or to dress up a side dish of noodles.

1. Place butter in a small bowl. Beat with a fork until creamy. Add poppy seeds and stir well to distribute evenly. Add lemon zest and juice.

2. Serve immediately or refrigerate, tightly covered, for up to 1 week.

Cranberry Orange Butter

1 tbsp	dried cranberries, finely chopped	15 mL
2 tbsp	freshly squeezed orange juice	30 mL
1 tbsp	liquid honey	15 mL
½ cup	unsalted butter, softened	125 mL
1 tsp	finely grated orange zest	5 mL

> **Makes ½ cup (125 mL)**

Your breakfast muffin will thank you for this!

1. In a small bowl, combine cranberries and orange juice. Let soak for 1 hour.

2. In microwave or small saucepan, warm honey. Set aside.

3. Place butter in a small bowl. Beat with a fork until creamy. Add cranberries with juice, honey and orange zest and mix vigorously to blend well.

4. Serve immediately or refrigerate, tightly covered, for up to 5 days.

Morel Mushroom Butter

<table>
<tr><td>**Makes 1½ cups
(375 mL)**</td></tr>
</table>

½ cup	fresh morels or ¼ cup (50 mL) dried morels	125 mL
1 cup	salted butter, softened	250 mL
1 tbsp	finely grated shallots	15 mL
¼ tsp	freshly ground pepper	1.25 mL

If you are lucky enough to find wild morels, here is a recipe you can try. If not, check with your local shops when morels are in season, or use dried ones. Place this on top of a fresh omelet or on grilled meat.

1. If using dried morels, rinse and soak in lukewarm water for 1 hour or until softened, to rehydrate. Drain and pat dry with paper towel.

2. Slice morels into thin strips. Set aside.

3. Place butter in a bowl. Beat with a fork until creamy. Add morels, shallots and pepper and mix well to blend evenly. Let stand for 15 minutes at room temperature to develop the flavors.

4. Serve immediately or refrigerate, tightly covered, for up to 5 days.

Jalapeño Butter

<table>
<tr><td>**Makes ½ cup
(125 mL)**</td></tr>
</table>

½ cup	salted butter, softened	125 mL
1 tsp	finely chopped fresh parsley	5 mL
¼ tsp	dried jalapeño pepper or ½ tsp (2.5 mL) finely chopped fresh jalapeño pepper	1.25 mL

Dab a bit of this spicy treat on corn on the cob or steamed vegetables.

1. Place butter in a small bowl. Beat lightly with a fork until creamy. Add parsley and jalapeño and mix well. Let stand for 15 minutes at room temperature to develop the flavors.

2. Serve immediately or refrigerate, tightly covered, for up to 1 week.

Lime and Coriander Butter

Makes ½ cup (125 mL)

Grilled fish takes on an exotic taste when paired with this butter.

½ cup	salted butter, softened	125 mL
1 tbsp	finely chopped fresh coriander	15 mL
1 tsp	finely grated lime zest	5 mL
1 tbsp	freshly squeezed lime juice	15 mL

1. Place butter in a small bowl. Beat lightly with a fork until creamy. Add coriander, lime zest and juice to butter and blend well.

2. Place butter on a piece of waxed paper. Roll and shape into a log about 1 inch (2.5 cm) in diameter. Refrigerate until firm.

3. Slice butter into rounds to place on the top of each serving. Refrigerate any remaining butter, tightly covered, for up to 5 days.

Clarified Butter

Clarified, or drawn, butter is the choice of fine chefs and discerning home cooks, because it has the frying capabilities of oil with some of the wonderful flavor of butter. The milk solids in butter burn at temperatures over 250°F (120°C), so foods that require high cooking temperatures usually need to be fried in oil. But by removing these solids, you leave just the buttery-tasting oil, which is excellent for frying and many other purposes.

Tip: When making clarified butter, consider that you will lose approximately 25% of the original amount, so plan accordingly.

- Small sieve, lined with cheesecloth

  Unsalted butter

1. In a saucepan over low heat, melt unsalted butter. It will separate into three layers: the whey proteins will rise to the top in the form of a white foam; the pure butter oil will form the middle layer; and the milk solids will form a layer of sediment on the bottom of the pan.

2. While the pan is still on the heat, use a spoon to skim off the foamy layer of whey protein as it forms. You can discard this or add it to a soup or sauce.

3. Once you have skimmed off all the white foam and the butter has stopped bubbling, remove the pan from the heat.

4. Set aside for several minutes to allow the milk solids to collect on the bottom of the pot.

5. Strain the melted butter through the prepared sieve. Discard the milk solids.

6. Cover and refrigerate. The clarified butter will keep for many weeks, even up to several months. It will become grainy when chilled but will perk back up when reheated.

Beurre Noisette

Called simply "brown butter" in English, beurre noisette is used in French-style cooking when a more intense flavor is desired.

- Small sieve, lined with cheesecloth

  Unsalted butter

1. Proceed as for Clarified Butter (above); when you have skimmed off the whey solids, continue to cook the butter over low heat until the milk solids begin to brown. Watch the pot very carefully, as the milk solids can burn very easily, causing the butter to become bitter. Strain as directed above.

Ghee

Ghee is the key fat used in Indian cuisine and can be kept for a very long time without refrigeration. Extra cooking removes all water, leaving you with pure butter oil.

Tip: Not sure if all the water has been cooked out of the ghee? Try this test: Over the sink, pour a small amount of ghee onto a piece of paper and light on fire. If the paper crackles or splutters as it burns, that means there is still water in the ghee. Cook a bit longer.

- Small sieve, lined with cheesecloth
- Glass jar with tight-fitting lid

Unsalted butter

1. In a heavy-bottomed saucepan over medium-low heat, melt unsalted butter. Once all the butter has melted, reduce the heat to low and continue to cook.

2. The butter will bubble and splutter as the water evaporates out. The whey solids will rise to the top in the form of white foam. Skim off the foam with a clean, dry spoon (be sure the spoon is dry, as you do not want to introduce any more water into the butter).

3. Continue to cook, removing any foam as it rises. The butter will turn a clear golden color, and the milk solids will collect on the bottom of the pot. Do not allow solids to blacken or burn.

4. When the spluttering has stopped, remove the pot from the heat and let cool until just slightly warm.

5. Strain the ghee through the prepared sieve. Discard the milk solids.

6. Store the ghee in a glass jar with a tight-fitting lid. It can be kept at room temperature, because all the water has been removed, making it impossible for bacteria to grow in the oil. Do not allow any water to be introduced into the ghee, such as using a wet spoon to dip out the contents.

Buttermilk

Buttermilk is a beautiful by-product of butter making that can be used in baking or cooking or made into cheese. Buttermilk has a long shelf life due to the action of the lactic bacteria, which inhibit the growth of spoilage-causing and pathogenic bacteria.

Traditional buttermilk is the liquid left over after churning butter. In "old-fashioned" butter making, the raw milk was left out to sour slightly before the cream was removed and churned into butter. The lactic bacteria in the milk ripened the cream, creating acidity and giving the buttermilk its thick texture.

Cultured Buttermilk

The buttermilk found at the market today is made from skim milk to which lactic bacteria has been added. This is called "cultured buttermilk." Here's how to make your own.

- **Glass jar with tight-fitting lid**

>   Whole, partly skimmed (2%) or skim milk
>   Aroma mesophilic culture

1. Sterilize a clean glass jar with a tight-fitting lid by rinsing with boiling water. Drain well. Fill with milk.

2. Sprinkle aroma mesophilic culture over the surface of the milk, using $1/8$ tsp (0.65 mL) per quart (1 L). Let stand for several minutes to allow culture to rehydrate. Put the lid on the jar and shake until blended.

3. Let ripen at room temperature for 24 hours.

4. Refrigerate for up to 3 weeks. You can make new batches of buttermilk from the old one: blend 1 part buttermilk with 4 parts fresh milk. Let ripen at room temperature for 24 hours or until thick.

Jane's Irish Soda Bread

**Makes 1 loaf,
about 20 slices**

*My daughter has
recently discovered the
joys of baking and has
produced this tasty
version of a classic Irish
soda bread to everyone's
delight. Enjoy fresh and
warm from the oven.*

- Preheat oven to 375°F (190°C)
- Large baking sheet, greased

4 cups	all-purpose flour	1 L
4 tbsp	granulated sugar	60 mL
1 tbsp	baking powder	15 mL
1 tsp	baking soda	5 mL
½ tsp	salt	2.5 mL
¾ cup	butter, softened, divided	175 mL
1¼ cups	buttermilk, divided	300 mL
1	egg	1

1. In a large bowl, combine flour, sugar, baking powder, baking soda, salt and ½ cup (125 mL) butter.

2. Stir in 1 cup (250 mL) of the buttermilk and egg until a soft dough is formed.

3. On a lightly floured surface, knead dough 10 to 12 times or until it just holds together. Form into a tight round ball and place on prepared baking sheet.

4. Melt remaining ¼ cup (50 mL) butter and combine with remaining ¼ cup (50 mL) buttermilk in a small bowl. Brush over the surface of the loaf; set remainder aside. Using a serrated knife, score a ½-inch (1.25 cm) deep cross into the top of the loaf.

5. Bake in preheated oven for 50 minutes, brushing loaf with remaining buttermilk mixture once or twice during baking, until a toothpick inserted into the center comes out clean. Let cool on a wire rack.

Buttermilk Soup

Makes 4 servings

Whip up this quick, light soup with a special "something."

1	onion, chopped	1
1 cup	chopped bell peppers, such as red, green, yellow or orange	250 mL
1 tbsp	all-purpose flour	15 mL
4 cups	buttermilk	1 L
	Salt and freshly ground black pepper	

1. In a large saucepan over medium-low heat, cook onion and peppers, stirring, until softened. Reduce heat to low. Cover and let vegetables sweat for 6 to 7 minutes until soft. Do not brown.

2. Add flour and cook, stirring, until blended. Pour in buttermilk and whisk together. Season with salt and pepper to taste. Serve hot.

Buttermilk Cheese

Makes ³⁄₄ cup (175 mL)

A fresh tangy cheese can be made from the buttermilk left over from churning butter. It can be used like cottage cheese or ricotta. Since the curds in buttermilk cheese are very fine, use a clean lint-free kitchen towel or linen cloth for draining.

- Cloth-lined colander

4 quarts	fresh buttermilk from butter making	4 L
	Salt	

1. Pour buttermilk into a bowl and cover with a clean cloth. Let ripen at room temperature for 24 hours to further develop the acidity.

2. In a large stainless-steel pot over medium heat, warm buttermilk to 162°F (72°C), stirring gently to prevent scorching. The solids will separate from the whey. Remove from heat. Let stand for 6 to 7 minutes.

3. Pour contents of pot through a cloth-lined colander. Tie four corners of cloth together to form a bag. Hang from a wooden spoon laid over the cooking pot. Drain for 6 to 7 hours or until desired thickness is reached. Remove curds from cloth. Add salt to taste. Store in a covered container in the refrigerator for up to 2 weeks.

Buttermilk Hand Cheese

<table>
<tr><td style="border:1px solid">Makes ³⁄₄ cup
(175 mL)</td></tr>
</table>

The name of this cheese comes from the fact that the cheeses are formed by hand into small rounds or log shapes. German in origin, they develop a pungent flavor, often with a smear-ripened rind. See page 307 for fresh cow's milk version.

Tips: Since the curds in buttermilk cheese are very fine, use a clean lint-free kitchen towel or linen cloth for draining.

To make a simple brine solution: Dissolve ½ tsp (2.5 mL) salt in ½ cup (125 mL) boiled water. Let cool. Do not reserve used brine for the next washing because there is danger of contamination from unwanted, even dangerous, bacteria.

- Cloth-lined colander (see Tips, left)
- Cheese matting
- Ripening container

4 quarts	buttermilk	4 L
	Salt	
¼ tsp	caraway seeds, optional	1.25 mL
	Simple brine solution (see Tips, left)	

1. Pour buttermilk into a bowl and cover with a clean cloth. Let ripen at room temperature for 24 hours.

2. In a large stainless-steel pot set in a hot water bath over medium heat, warm buttermilk to 125°F (52°C), stirring gently. Turn off heat. Continue stirring for 20 minutes, maintaining heat. Cover and let set for another 2 hours.

3. Pour contents of pot through a cloth-lined colander. Tie four corners of cloth together to form a bag. Hang from a wooden spoon laid over the cooking pot. Drain for 6 to 7 hours.

4. Remove curds from cloth. Add salt to taste. Add caraway seeds, if using. Mix well and shape curd into small patties or logs.

5. Dry cheeses on a cheese mat placed on a rack at room temperature for 2 to 3 days, turning twice a day, until dry to the touch.

6. Place on a clean cheese mat in a ripening container. Cover and ripen at 50°F (10°C) and 90% humidity. Keep lid on container to create a humid environment. Turn daily.

7. Wash surface of cheese twice weekly with a cloth dipped in simple brine solution (see Tips, left) to encourage the rind to develop and to remove any mold growth. Ripen for 6 to 8 weeks. Wrap in plastic wrap and store in the refrigerator.

Sour Cream

Makes 1 quart (1 L)		
1 quart	table (20%) cream	1 L
¼ tsp	aroma mesophilic culture	1.25 mL

Making sour cream at home is so easy, and it is simply delicious.

1. In a large stainless-steel pot over low heat, warm cream to 75°F (24°C), stirring gently to prevent scorching. Remove from heat.

2. Sprinkle culture over surface of cream and let stand for about 5 minutes to rehydrate. Using skimmer and an up-and-down motion, gently draw culture down into cream without breaking surface of cream. Cover and let ripen at room temperature for 24 to 36 hours.

3. Place the thickened cream in a covered container and refrigerate. It will keep for up to 10 days.

Crème Fraîche

Makes 1 quart (1 L)		
1 quart	whipping (35%) cream	1 L
¼ tsp	aroma mesophilic culture	1.25 mL

This whole rich dairy cream, ripened to a thick spoonable consistency, is sour cream taken to another level. Use it in great dollops on cake or pie, float it on soup or add to a sauce. Fresh berries become the seasonal dessert of choice when dressed with a spoonful of crème fraîche.

1. In a large stainless-steel pot over low heat, warm cream to 75°F (24°C), stirring gently to prevent scorching. Remove from heat.

2. Sprinkle culture over surface of cream and let stand for about 5 minutes to rehydrate. Using skimmer and an up-and-down motion, gently draw culture down into cream without breaking surface of cream. Cover and let ripen at room temperature for 48 hours. The cream should be very thick.

3. Place in the refrigerator for 12 hours or overnight; it should thicken even more.

4. Spoon into an airtight container, cover and refrigerate. It will keep for up to 10 days.

Quick Berry Cream Cakes

Serves 4

This is a simply fabulous and fabulously simple dessert, almost like an instant miniature cheesecake.

1 cup	fresh or frozen berries (such as blueberries, raspberries, blackberries, or a mixture)	250 mL
2 tbsp	liqueur or vodka, approx.	30 mL
	Granulated sugar	
½ cup	Crème Fraîche (opposite)	125 mL
½ cup	Fromage Frais (page 43)	125 mL
8 or 12	ladyfinger biscuits	8 or 12

1. In a bowl, combine berries and liqueur. Add sugar to taste, especially if using vodka. Let stand for 30 minutes or until berries start to release their juices.

2. In a small bowl, using a whisk or an electric mixer on low speed, beat crème fraîche and fromage frais with 2 tbsp (30 mL) sugar or to taste until light and fluffy. Do not overbeat or the cheese and cream can become buttery.

3. On each serving plate, make a base of 2 or 3 ladyfingers. Drizzle with a little of the juice from the macerated berries. Spoon a portion of the crème fraîche mixture over top and surround with berries. Drizzle the top of the cream mixture with a little more berry juice or liqueur.

Clotted Cream

10% yield

This is the delectable thick, rich cream served with afternoon scones and tea. Here is the traditional recipe for those who have access to whole non-homogenized milk, preferably high-fat.

Whole non-homogenized milk

1. Pour milk into a large wide stainless-steel pot and cover with a clean cloth. Let stand for 12 hours if the room is quite warm or up to 24 hours in a cooler environment. This allows the lactic bacteria in the milk to develop and ripen the milk for greater flavor and yield.

2. Place pot over low heat and slowly warm milk until very hot. It is very important not to boil it. You will see the surface of the milk barely quivering. Control the heat so that it continues to quiver but not boil. As the cream thickens, the "waves" on the surface of the cream will seem thicker. Hold the cream at this temperature for 1 hour, if possible, by adjusting or turning off heat as necessary.

3. Turn off heat and let cool.

4. When cool, move pot very carefully into the refrigerator to chill. When completely chilled, skim off the thick cream and store in jars in the refrigerator. Use the remaining skim milk for cooking.

Library and Archives Canada Cataloguing in Publication

Amrein-Boyes, Debra, 1953–
    200 easy homemade cheese recipes : from cheddar to brie to butter and yogurt /
    Debra Amrein-Boyes.

Includes index.
ISBN 978-0-7788-0218-1

    1. Cheesemaking. I. Title. II. Title: Two hundred easy homemade cheese recipes.

SF271.A47 2009   637'.3   C2008-907679-6

Glossary

Acid-coagulated curd: the semisolid gel created when lactic bacteria change lactose into lactic acid.

Acidity: the measurement of sourness, usually determined using a pH meter or by titration.

Aging: holding a cheese for a period of time under specific conditions to allow the flavor to develop.

Annatto: a coloring derived from the seeds of a South American plant; used especially in certain hard cheeses.

Aroma mesophilic culture: a blend of mesophilic bacteria with an added strain of lactic bacteria.

Bacteria: single-cell organisms. In cheese making, milk is inoculated with strains of lactic bacteria to create flavor and raise acidity.

Baumé: the measurement of salt content in a solution, expressed in degrees.

Brevibacterium linens: a ripening bacteria that imparts a distinct flavor to the cheese and creates a reddish-orange smear on the rind.

Brine: a solution of salt and water. Cheese is washed in brine to assist in surface ripening or immersed in brine to add salt to the cheese.

Brine meter: an instrument that measures specific gravity to determine the salinity of a brine.

Butterfat: the fat in milk, measured in percentage.

Buttermilk: the liquid that remains after churning the fat (butter) out of cream. Commercial buttermilk is made by ripening skim milk with lactic bacteria.

Butter muslin: a loosely woven but firm cloth made for draining curd or butter. It can be used to press the buttermilk out of butter, as it will soak up the moisture but will not stick to the butter.

Calcium chloride: a calcium salt solution added in small amounts to the cheese milk before the rennet, which offers a source of free calcium ions to replace some that are lost during pasteurization or homogenization.

Cheddaring: a step in making Cheddar and related cheeses that involves turning blocks of finished curd to release whey and lower the pH, thereby texturing the curd and causing it to become more acidic and rubbery.

Cheese cloth: a woven cloth used for draining soft cheeses and lining molds for pressing firm cheeses. It is a loosely woven muslin, available in cotton or plastic, that is washable and reusable indefinitely. If using plastic cheese cloth, do not boil it (it will melt); wash in warm soapy water, rinse in clean water mixed with a small amount of bleach and hang to dry. The cheesecloth sold in grocery stores in plastic packages is not acceptable. It is what was once used to bandage natural-rind, or cloth-bound, Cheddar cheeses.

Cheese matting: plastic mesh used for draining soft-ripened cheeses, such as Brie and Camembert.

Cheese wax: a special wax made for coating cheese, which seals in moisture and seals out unwanted mold and bacteria. Paraffin or other waxes are not suitable.

Clean break: the test to ascertain whether the curd is ready to be cut (see page 16).

Coagulation: the process of thickening milk through the addition of lactic bacteria or enzymes (rennet).

Cooking: heating the cut curds so that they shrink in size and expel whey.

Culture: a blend of lactic bacteria added to milk to acidify it and flavor the resulting cheese.

Cutting the curd: using a long-bladed knife or special multi-blade tool (called a curd knife or harp) to cut the curd into small pieces, which allows the whey to be released.

Dairy thermometer: thermometer with a stainless-steel casing and sealed dial that can be clipped onto the side of the cheese pot. The range should be from 39° to 212°F (4° to 100°C).

Direct-set culture: lactic bacteria in dry powder form that is added as is to the cheese milk. It is used throughout the book for ease of handling and consistent results.

Draining: the act of releasing the whey from finished cheese curd.

Enzyme: a naturally occurring protein that, when added to milk, acts on milk protein, causing the solids to precipitate out. In cheese making, the source of enzymes is usually rennet, which contains the enzymes chymosin and pepsin.

Fresh lactic cheese: cheese coagulated by the action of lactic bacteria (acid-coagulated), usually at low temperature and over 18 to 36 hours, then drained in a cloth or bag. Very little, if any, rennet is used.

Geotrichum candidum: a fast-growing mold used in surface-ripened cheeses, often in combination with *P. candidum*.

Homogenization: the process whereby milk is forced through a very fine nozzle, shattering the fat globules so finely that they remain suspended in the milk.

Hooping: filling a mold with finished cheese curd for pressing.

Hygrometer: an instrument that measures humidity. It often has an integrated thermometer.

Inoculating: adding bacteria and mold to the cheese milk.

Lactic acid: an acid produced in cheese making when lactic bacteria feed on the lactose in milk.

Lactic bacteria: single-cell organisms naturally found in milk but also added in cheese making, which increase acidity and add flavor.

Lactose: the naturally occurring sugar in milk. Lactose is changed into lactic acid through the action of lactic bacteria.

Matting: the knitting together of the curd into a spongy mass.

Mesophilic bacteria: lactic bacteria used to flavor and acidify cheeses that are not cooked above 102°F (39°C).

Milling: cutting the curd for hard cheese into small pieces before salting.

Mold: a form used for shaping cheese.

Mold-ripened cheese: a soft cheese, such as Camembert or Brie, which is ripened by surface mold.

Natural-rind cheese: a cheese that is ripened without the protective coating of cheese wax, using various techniques to develop the rind.

Pasta filata cheese: a cheese that is heated and stretched in hot water, resulting in a fibrous, chewy paste.

Paste: the body of a cheese.

Pasteurization: the process of destroying pathogenic bacteria by heating milk to 145°F (63°C) and holding that temperature for 30 minutes.

Penicillium candidum: a white mold that grows on the surface of cheeses such as Brie and Camembert, causing the paste to soften during ripening.

Penicillium roquefortii: a blue mold that lends flavor and acidity to cheeses such as Roquefort, Stilton and Gorgonzola.

pH: a measurement of acidity or alkalinity. Fresh milk has a pH of 6.7; the addition of lactic bacteria helps to lower it to cheese-making levels. pH can be measured with a meter or using strips available from cheese making supply houses or pharmacies.

pH meter: an instrument used to measure acidity.

Pressing: placing a weight on a cheese in order to expel whey and knit the curd together.

Raw milk: milk that has not been pasteurized.

Re-dressing: the process of removing a cheese from the press and its mold, rearranging the cheese cloth, turning the cheese, putting it back into the mold and replacing the mold in the press before pressing further.

Rennet: a blend of acid-loving enzymes found naturally in the stomachs of calves, kids or lambs, which causes the protein in milk to solidify and precipitate out. It is available in liquid or tablet form. Vegetable rennet is derived from plants, and microbial rennet is formulated by fermentation of a specific type of mold.

Rind: the firm outer surface of a pressed cheese.

Ripening: the acidification of milk through the addition of lactic bacteria.

Ripening bacteria: strains of bacteria that lend a unique flavor and color to the rinds of certain cheeses.

Salting: adding salt to a cheese, either by immersing it in brine or sprinkling and rubbing the surface with dry salt. Salting is required to stabilize the pH of the cheese, thereby preserving it from spoilage.

Scalding: the technical term for heating the cheese curd after cutting; also called *cooking*.

Setting: allowing the milk to gel after the addition of the coagulant.

Skimmer: a spoon-like utensil with a large flat perforated bowl and a long handle, used to stir and ladle cheese.

Stirring: the slow agitation of the curd to increase expulsion of whey and prevent curds from matting during cooking, thereby allowing even heating and shrinking of all the curds.

Straw matting: natural rye straw stitched into long mats, used for ripening soft French-style cheeses in traditional farmstead production. Used now mostly for decoration. Plastic straw is now available for commercial use.

Stretched-curd cheese: see Pasta filata.

Sweet curd cheese: curd that has been coagulated without previous acidification.

Texture: the feel of the cheese at a certain stage of development. When checking the texture of the cheese curd after cooking, grip a small handful of curds in your hand. The curds should stick lightly together to form a ball but should then be easily crumbled apart.

Thermophilic culture: lactic bacteria that can withstand cooking temperatures over 102°F (39°C).

Tomme: the French term for a flat, round cheese of any size or weight. In this book, the tomme mold used is approximately 4 inches (10 cm) high and 8 inches (20 cm) in diameter and has a lid. It will make a cheese of 2 to 5 lbs (1 to 2.5 kg).

Up-and-down motion: a stirring method in which a skimmer is held underneath the surface of the cheese milk and slowly lifted up and down without breaking the surface of the milk, used to incorporate a culture and/or other ingredients into the milk without stirring in excess air.

Washed-curd cheese: a cheese that has been cooked by draining off a percentage of the whey and adding hot water to increase the temperature.

Washed-rind cheese: a natural-rind cheese that is regularly wiped with a cloth moistened in a solution of salt and ripening bacteria in order to develop a flavorful rind.

Water bath: a large outer pot fitted with the smaller cheese pot and filled with water, which creates a thermal layer for heating and holding the cheese milk at specified temperatures.

Whey: the liquid in milk that is expelled during cheese making. Whey contains protein and lactose and can be further processed to precipitate solids left over from cheese making to make other types of cheese.

Sources

FOR MANY YEARS, cheese-making ingredients were available in industrial format only. The few home cheese makers were left to improvise with old-fashioned Junket tablets and industrially produced buttermilk as sources of cheese cultures. But today, with the increased interest in artisanal and home cheese making, there are more and more small companies catering to the needs of the smaller-scale cheese maker. Here are some that offer a wide range of cultures, molds and other ingredients.

Note: When sourcing your ingredients, be aware that there are some restrictions governing the shipment of animal products (such as rennet) over international borders.

Canada

Danlac Canada Inc.
466 Summerwood Place
Airdrie, Alta. T4B 1W5
Tel: (403) 948-4644
Web: www.danlac.com
E-mail: egon@danlac.com

Cultures, ripening bacteria, coagulants and recipes (for a small fee); can source large equipment. Also offers a newsletter and troubleshooting.

Fromagex
62, rue des Ateliers
Rimouski, Que. G5M 1B2
Tel: (418) 722-0193 or 1-866-437-6624
Web: www.fromagex.com
E-mail: info@fromagex.com

Cultures, ripening bacteria, coagulants, small and large equipment, accessories, supplies and books.

Glengarry Cheesemaking and Dairy Supply Ltd.
5926 Hwy #34, RR#1
Lancaster, Ont. K0C 1N0
Tel: 1-888-816-0903
Web: www.glengarrycheesemaking.on.ca
E-mail: info@glengarrycheesemaking.on.ca
Also serves U.S. customers at P.O. Box 92, Massena, NY 13662 U.S.A.

Cultures, ripening bacteria, coagulants, small and large equipment, accessories, supplies and books. Staff offer good advice and troubleshooting for clients. Workshops and consulting are also available.

United States

The CheeseMaker
c/o Cedarburg Homebrew and Wine
W62 N590 Washington Ave.
Cedarburg, WI 53012
Tel: (262) 377-1838
Web: www.thecheesemaker.com
E-mail: steve@thecheesemaker.com

Specializes in ingredients for Brie, Camembert and Stilton-style blue cheeses. Kits, cultures, ripening bacteria, coagulants, supplies and presses. Also offers workshops.

Dairy Connection Inc.
501 Tasman St.
Suite B
Madison, WI 53714
Tel: (608) 242-9030
Web: www.dairyconnection.com
E-mail: getculture@ameritech.net

Cultures, ripening bacteria, coagulants, supplies, equipment and books.

Leeners
9293 Olde Eight Rd.
Northfield, OH 44067
Tel: 1-800-543-3697
Web:
www.leeners.com/cheesemaking.html

Kits, molds, cultures, ripening bacteria, coagulants, accessories, equipment and supplies.

Lehman's
P.O. Box 270
Kidron, OH 44636
Tel: 1-877-438-5346
Web: www.lehmans.com

Cultures, ripening bacteria, coagulants, supplies, equipment, kits and presses. The store and mail-order catalog carry lots of old-fashioned wares.

New England Cheesemaking Supply Company
P.O. Box 85
Ashfield, MA 01330
Tel: (413) 628-3808
Web: www.cheesemaking.com
E-mail: info@cheesemaking.com

Cultures, ripening bacteria, coagulants, supplies, small equipment and recipes. Also offers a newsletter and workshops.

United Kingdom

Ascott Smallholding Supplies Ltd.
Units 9/10 The Old Creamery
Four Crosses, Llanymynech SY22 6LP
Web: www.ascott.biz
E-mail: sales@ascott.biz
Tel: (44) 0845 130 6285

Equipment, supplies, cultures, ripening bacteria, coagulants and presses.

Moorlands Cheesemakers
Brewhamfield Farm
North Brewham, Bruton, Somerset
BA10 0QQ
Tel: (44) 01749 850 108
Web: www.cheesemaking.co.uk
E-mail: info@cheesemaking.co.uk

Cultures, ripening bacteria, coagulants, supplies, equipment and kits. Also offers courses.

Smallholder Supplies
The Old Post Office
6 Main St.
Branston, Nr. Grantham, Lincolnshire
NG 32 1RU
Tel/Fax: (44) 01476 870 070
Web: www.smallholdersupplies.co.uk
E-mail: info@smallholdersupplies.co.uk

Cultures, ripening bacteria, coagulants, equipment, supplies, presses and vats. Mail order only.

Australia

Cheeselinks
15 Minns Rd.
P.O. Box 146
Little River, Victoria 3211
Tel: (61) (0)3 52831396
Web: www.cheeselinks.com.au
E-mail: info@cheeselinks.com.au

Cultures, ripening bacteria, coagulants, equipment, supplies and kits. Also offers workshops.

Milk Sources

Non-Homogenized Milk

When choosing milk for cheese making, non-homogenized milk, also called standard or cream line milk, is always a better choice than homogenized. During the process of homogenization, the fat is shattered into such fine particles that they remain suspended in the milk rather than rising to the top in the form of cream. In cheese making this breaking up of the fat reduces the ability of the milk components to bind together and form curd.

To find a local source of non-homogenized milk, check farmer's markets for small producers who sell milk products; contact local artisanal or small-scale cheese makers, who source milk locally for their products; or look around at supermarkets or health food stores that offer organic milk and milk products. Organic milk processors are more likely to offer non-homogenized milk than conventional processors. You can also try contacting your state or provincial dairy organization — while their mandate does not necessarily include providing lists of processors to consumers, they will be familiar with the local dairy industry and may be able to point you in the right direction. If you have access to the Internet, a search including the words non-homogenized milk, cream line milk or standard milk plus your local area name can help get you started.

Raw Milk

The sale of raw milk is controlled almost everywhere in the developed world. If you really want an unlimited source of raw milk for drinking and cheese making, the best way is to get your own cow or goat! In some places, schemes such as "cow sharing," which make raw milk available for consumption, are becoming popular. But be careful: These are often designed to make use of loopholes in the law and can be controversial. It is recommended that you do lots of research before taking steps to procure raw milk.

AUSTRALIA: The sale of raw milk, whether fresh or for cheese making, is illegal at this time across the country, though studies are underway to look at options.

CANADA: The sale of raw milk is illegal across the country.

UNITED KINGDOM: Raw milk from certified producers is available in some farm shops and farmer's markets. Pasteurized, non-homogenized milk is also available, though not widely.

UNITED STATES: Raw milk laws are a matter of state jurisdiction, so consult your local health department for the legislation in your area. The sale of raw milk is completely prohibited in 15 states. Twenty-nine states permit the sale of raw milk for human consumption or will support stewardship programs. Two states permit the sale of raw goat milk with a medical prescription. Four states prohibit the sale of raw milk for human consumption but permit the sale of raw milk with no added food dye for animal consumption, implying that human consumption is feasible.

Going Pro

If you are thinking of selling your cheese on any kind of commercial level, you must first contact the ruling authority in your area. There is legislation in place in most countries that strictly governs all sales of cheese and milk products off the farm. This can even include small amounts of fresh milk given to a neighbor. For up-to-date information and regulations governing milk and milk product sales and re-sales, contact your local health authority, dairy board or center for disease control.

Index

Note: The notation (v) beside a recipe name indicates a variation.

Chocolate Butter, 350
Cranberry Almond Baked Brie, 98
Fresh Goat Cheeses (v), 67
Roasted Hazelnut Butter, 347

O

olives
  Bite-Size Cheese Canapés, 153
  Provençal Herb Butter, 347
orange
  Cranberry Orange Butter, 353
  Orange Honey Butter, 346
Ossau-Iraty, 281

P

Paneer, 294, 295
Paprika Butter, 352
Parmesan, 252
  Bite-Size Cheese Canapés, 153
pasta
  Baked Macaroni and Cheese, 185
  Pasta with Broccoli and Brie, 99
pasta filata cheese, 14-15, 73-94.
  See also specific cheeses
pasteurization, 26
Pecorino Romano, 262
Peppercorn Butter, 350
peppers
  Baked Red Peppers, 105
  Buttermilk Soup, 360
  Gouda (v), 186
  Jalapeño Butter, 354
  Monterey Jack (v), 264
Persian Sparkling Yogurt Drink, 331
Piora, 256
pizza, 67
Port Salut, 156
  Port Salut Potatoes, 158
Pouligny-St-Pierre, 120
Provençal Chèvre, Traditional, 56
Provençal Herb Butter, 347
Provolone, 82

Q

Quark, 42
Queso Blanco, 296
Quick Berry Cream Cakes, 363

R

Raclette, 196
raw milk, 25-26, 57
  butter from, 339, 342-43
  cream from, 339
  Raw Milk Tomme, 285
Reblochon, 159
  Reblochon and Apple Sandwich,
  159
Red Cheshire Cheese, 220 (v)
rennet, 13, 24, 31
ricotta, 53-54
Roasted Hazelnut Butter, 347
Romano, 260, 262
Roquefort, 138-41
  Bite-Size Cheese Canapés, 153
  Roquefort and Mushroom Salad,
  141
rose petals
  Flower Petal Butter, 352
  Fresh Goat Cheeses (v), 67
  Strawberry and Rose Petal Butter,
  348
Rose Water Lassi, Traditional, 331

S

Saganaki, 93
Sage Derby, 278 (v)
St-Marcellin, 112
Ste-Maure, 116
salt, 19, 32
sanitation, 12, 25, 40
Savory Brousse Omelet, 61
Sbrinz, 247-49
  Bite-Size Cheese Canapés, 153
  Savory Sbrinz Shortbread, 249
Scamorza, 86

More Great Books
from Robert Rose

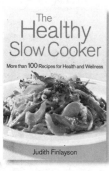

Appliance Cooking

- The Dehydrator Bible
  *by Jennifer MacKenzie,
  Jay Nutt & Don Mercer*
- The Mixer Bible
  Second Edition
  *by Meredith Deeds and
  Carla Snyder*
- The Juicing Bible
  Second Edition
  by Pat Crocker
- 200 Best Panini Recipes
  by Tiffany Collins
- 200 Best Pressure
  Cooker Recipes
  by Cinda Chavich
- 300 Slow Cooker
  Favorites
  by Donna-Marie Pye
- The 150 Best Slow
  Cooker Recipes
  by Judith Finlayson
- Delicious &
  Dependable Slow
  Cooker Recipes
  by Judith Finlayson
- 125 Best Vegetarian
  Slow Cooker Recipes
  by Judith Finlayson
- The Healthy Slow
  Cooker
  by Judith Finlayson
- The Best Convection
  Oven Cookbook
  by Linda Stephen
- 250 Best American
  Bread Machine
  Baking Recipes
  *by Donna Washburn
  and Heather Butt*
- 250 Best Canadian
  Bread Machine
  Baking Recipes
  *by Donna Washburn
  and Heather Butt*

Baking

- The Cheesecake Bible
  by George Geary
- 1500 Best Bars, Cookies,
  Muffins, Cakes & More
  by Esther Brody
- The Complete Book
  of Baking
  by George Geary
- The Complete Book
  of Bars & Squares
  by Jill Snider
- The Complete Book
  of Pies
  by Julie Hasson
- 125 Best Chocolate
  Recipes
  by Julie Hasson
- 125 Best Cupcake
  Recipes
  by Julie Hasson
- Complete Cake
  Mix Magic
  by Jill Snider

Healthy Cooking

- The Vegetarian Cook's
  Bible
  by Pat Crocker
- The Vegan Cook's
  Bible
  by Pat Crocker
- 125 Best Vegetarian
  Recipes
  *by Byron Ayanoglu
  with contributions from
  Algis Kemezys*
- The Smoothies Bible
  by Pat Crocker
- 125 Best Vegan
  Recipes
  *by Maxine Effenson Chuck
  and Beth Gurney*

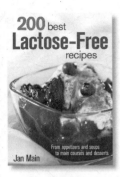

- 200 Best Lactose-Free Recipes
  by Jan Main
- 500 Best Healthy Recipes
  Edited by Lynn Roblin, RD
- Complete Gluten-Free Cookbook
  by Donna Washburn and Heather Butt
- 125 Best Gluten-Free Recipes
  by Donna Washburn and Heather Butt
- The Best Gluten-Free Family Cookbook
  by Donna Washburn and Heather Butt
- Diabetes Meals for Good Health
  Karen Graham, RD
- Canada's Diabetes Meals for Good Health
  Karen Graham, RD
- America's Complete Diabetes Cookbook
  Edited by Katherine E. Younker, MBA, RD
- Canada's Complete Diabetes Cookbook
  Edited by Katherine E. Younker, MBA, RD

Recent Bestsellers

- 125 Best Soup Recipes
  by Marylin Crowley and Joan Mackie
- The Convenience Cook
  by Judith Finlayson
- 125 Best Ice Cream Recipes
  by Marilyn Linton and Tanya Linton

- Easy Indian Cooking
  by Suneeta Vaswani
- Baby Blender Food
  by Nicole Young
- Simply Thai Cooking
  by Wandee Young and Byron Ayanoglu

Health

- 55 Most Common Medicinal Herbs Second Edition
  by Dr. Heather Boon, B.Sc.Phm., Ph.D. and Michael Smith, B.Pharm, M.R.Pharm.S., ND
- Canada's Baby Care Book
  by Dr. Jeremy Friedman MBChB, FRCP(C), FAAP, and Dr. Norman Saunders MD, FRCP(C)
- The Baby Care Book
  by Dr. Jeremy Friedman MBChB, FRCP(C), FAAP, and Dr. Norman Saunders MD, FRCP(C)
- Better Baby Food Second Edition
  by Daina Kalnins, MSc, RD, and Joanne Saab, RD
- Better Food for Pregnancy
  by Daina Kalnins, MSc, RD, and Joanne Saab, RD
- Crohn's & Colitis
  by Dr. A. Hillary Steinhart, MD, MSc, FRCP(C)
- Crohn's & Colitis Diet Guide
  by Dr. A. Hillary Steinhart, MD, MSc, FRCP(C), and Julie Cepo, BSc, BASc, RD

Wherever books are sold

Robert ROSE

Also Available
from Robert Rose

The Complete Book of

Pickling

250 recipes from pickles &
relishes to chutneys & salsas

Jennifer MacKenzie

ISBN 978-0-7788-0216-7 $24.95 Canada / $24.95 U.S.

For more great books, see previous pages

Robert
ROSE